Canal Dreamers

JESSICA M. LEPLER

Canal Dreamers

The Epic Quest to Connect the Atlantic and Pacific in the Age of Revolutions

The University of North Carolina Press *Chapel Hill*

Set in Arno Pro by Westchester Publishing Services
Manufactured in the United States of America

Complete Cataloging-in-Publication Data for this title is available from the Library of Congress at https://lccn.loc.gov/2025013869.

ISBN 9781469690544 (cloth: alk. paper)
ISBN 9781469690551 (pbk.: alk. paper)
ISBN 9781469679518 (epub)
ISBN 9781469691596 (pdf)

Cover design by Chris Tobias.

For product safety concerns under the European Union's General Product Safety Regulation (EU GPSR), please contact gpsr@mare-nostrum.co.uk or write to the University of North Carolina Press and Mare Nostrum Group B.V., Mauritskade 21D, 1091 GC Amsterdam, The Netherlands.

To Michael and Eggy Dube

Contents

Illustrations

FIGURES

MAPS

Canal Dreamers

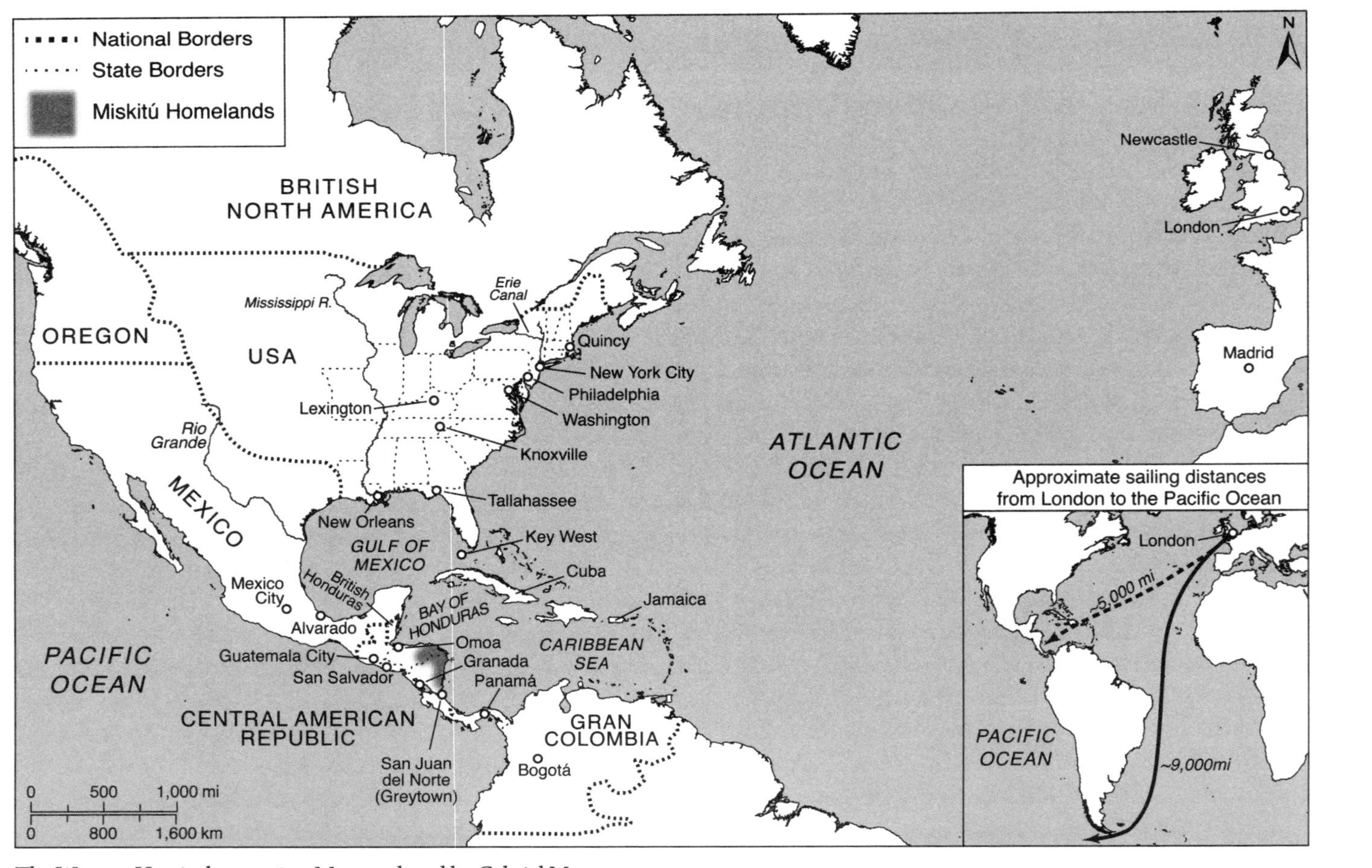

The Western Hemisphere c. 1825. Map produced by Gabriel Moss.

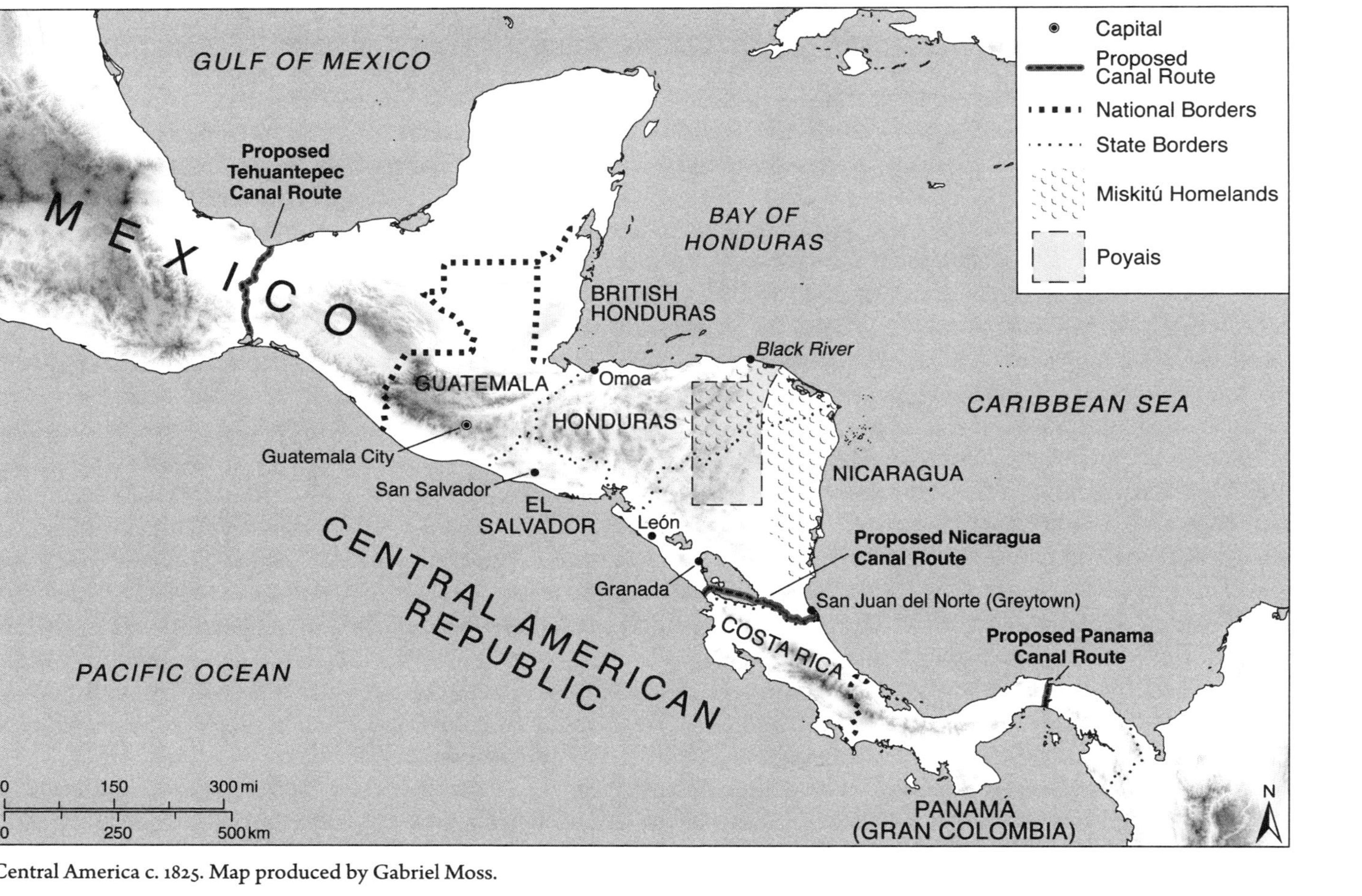

Central America c. 1825. Map produced by Gabriel Moss.

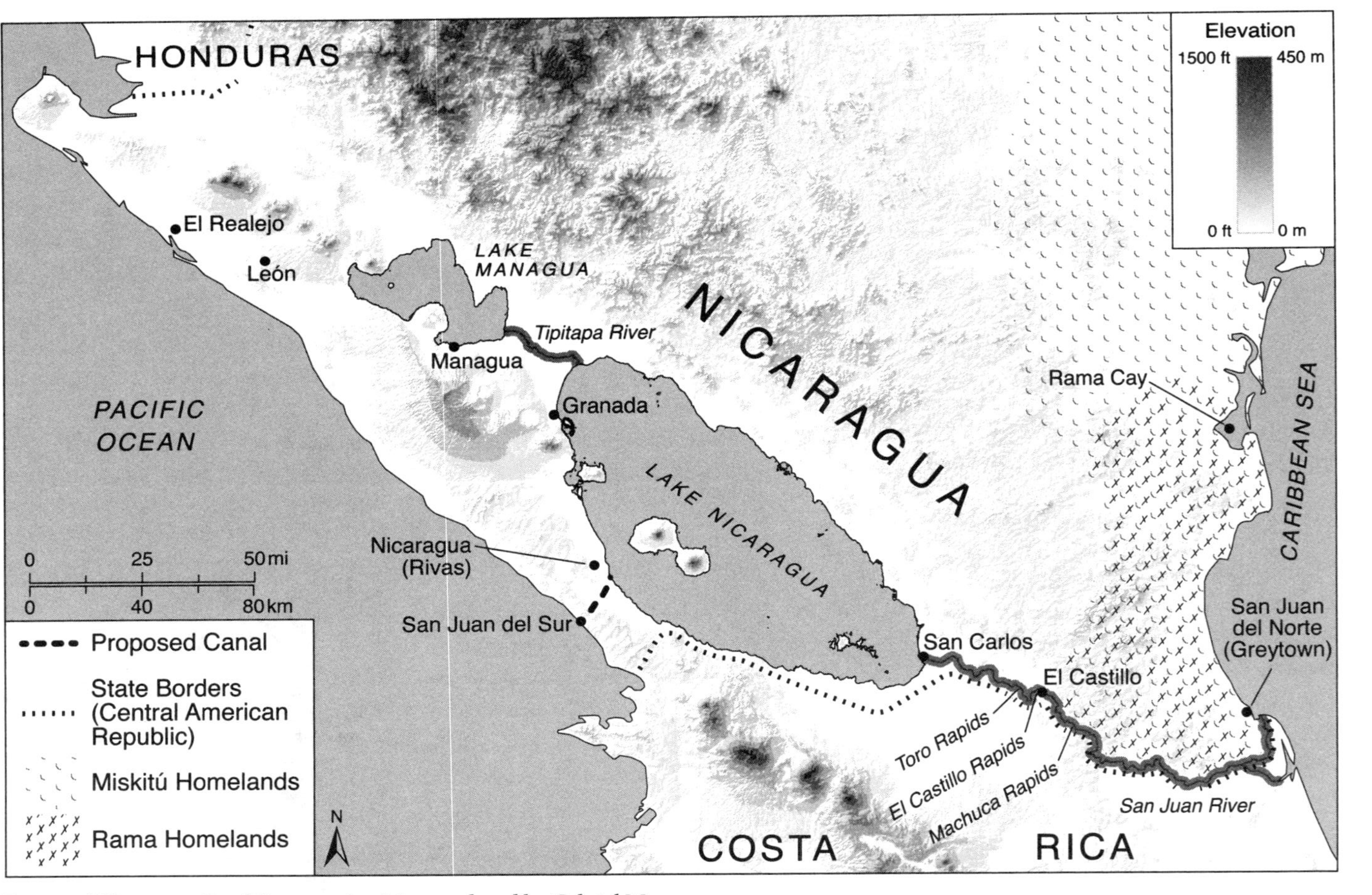

Proposed Nicaragua Canal Route c. 1825. Map produced by Gabriel Moss.

Introduction
Treasure Isthmus

The blue caught my eye, a turquoise jewel buried in an oversized archival folder. Even under the harsh fluorescent lights, the hand-colored ocean, lake, river, and sea glistened. From the National Archives reading room southwest of London, the tint transported me much farther south and west to the center of the Americas, to a place with more water than land, where the land might become water, and the water could change the world.

The bright blue captured my imagination. In contrast, the land blended into the background, a visual hint that it might as well not exist. That was the point. In a time before cars, planes, or trains, eliminating the land could create the world's most anticipated shortcut: a waterway from the Atlantic Ocean to the Pacific Ocean through the center of the Americas.

A vision of what might be, large letters proclaimed the map to be a "*Plano Ídeal*."[1] An English translation of the map's Spanish text described the document as a "plan" by which "a communication can be effected between the Pacific, and the Atlantic."[2] For those seeking a fast water route between Europe and Asia, it was a treasure map.[3]

The treasure, the map suggested, was mostly unburied. Little digging would be required to turn isthmian land into interoceanic water because so much water already existed. Indeed, from the lower right-hand corner's cyan shore of the "*Mar de las Antillas*"—an Atlantic Sea—a serpentine line representing the San Juan River wound its way up to Lake Nicaragua at the center of the page. Between the turquoise lake and the nearby cerulean shore of the Pacific Ocean, tiny print labeled thin parallel lines "*canal proyectada*" or projected canal.[4] The "ground" beneath the lines, the map's text advised, would be "easy to open"—an artificial waterway so short and narrow that it nearly vanished between the brilliant blues.[5] The map argued through words and images that the work of digging up the land would be minuscule compared with its enormous consequence. Drafted almost fifty years after the Declaration of Independence launched the "Age of Revolutions" with the assertion that individuals possessed inalienable rights and that colonies could be independent nations, the map proposed the tumultuous era's most extreme change: a human-created revolution of the earth itself.[6]

In 1825, George Alexander Thompson submitted this colorful copy of Manuel Antonio de la Cerda's *Plano Ídeal* to the British government. MPK 153/3(3), The National Archives of the UK.

Well before the creation of the map, the quest for a fast water route between Europe and Asia had proven enormously consequential. In the late fifteenth century, Christopher Columbus's voyages had been motivated by this desire. For the next three centuries, Spanish colonizers considered but never constructed the shortcut.[7] When the Spanish American empire collapsed in the first quarter of the nineteenth century, interoceanic canal dreams had already spread well beyond Spain.[8]

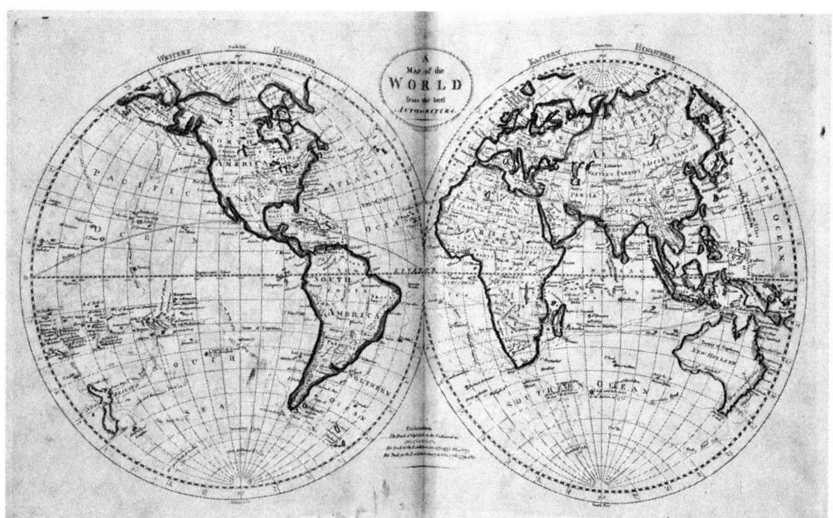

The narrow isthmus of Central America appears toward the center of this 1815 world map. Mathew Carey, "A Map of the World," *Carey's General Atlas, Improved and Enlarged: Being a Collection of Maps of the World and Quarters, Their Principal Empires, Kingdoms, &c.* (Philadelphia: M. Carey, 1815). Courtesy American Antiquarian Society.

As the Age of Revolutions created new Spanish American nations, a canal boom spread on both sides of the Atlantic Ocean. Great Britain reconfigured its rivers for industrialization and opened a waterway that allowed ships to sail through Scotland.[9] In the United States, the Erie Canal's rerouting of the North American continent's produce from the Mississippi Valley to the Atlantic Ocean ratcheted up the intensity with which Easterners coveted Indigenous Westerners' lands.[10] No longer believing themselves constrained by natural waterways, US citizens and British subjects, as well as Central Americans, Mexicans, and others, clamored for an interoceanic route. Visions of a waterway accelerating trade with China, speeding access to Pacific fisheries, and connecting continental and oceanic empires attracted the attention of public servants and private investors.

The big picture was obvious to these canal dreamers. Like a giant X marking the spot, world maps centered the former Kingdom of Guatemala—the territory currently governed by the Mexican state of Chiapas and the modern nations of Guatemala, Honduras, El Salvador, Nicaragua, and Costa Rica.

On many hemispheric maps of the era, the land linking the American continents tapered so severely that the isthmus almost vanished. Squint, and the land disappeared. It seemed that easy. In the early 1820s, the

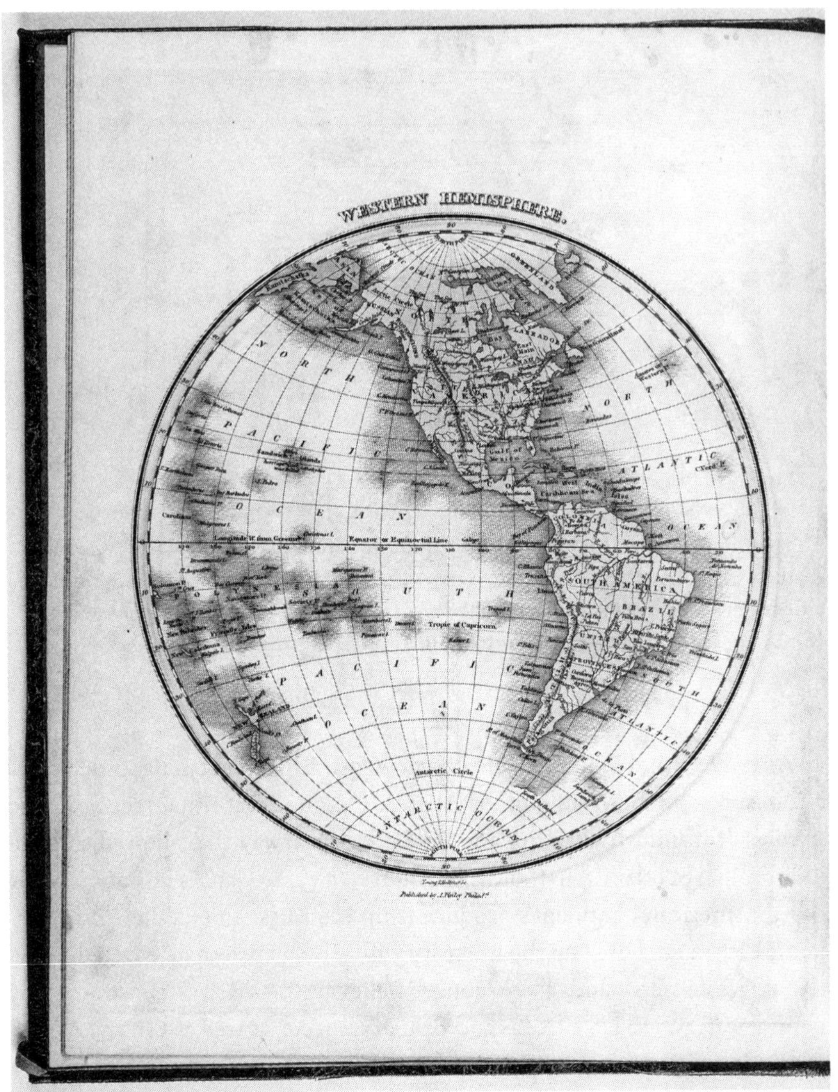

The Central American isthmus narrows dramatically on this 1820s hemispheric map. Anthony Finley, "The Western Hemisphere," *A New General Atlas* (Philadelphia, 1827). Courtesy American Antiquarian Society.

prevailing question was not whether a Central American waterway would be opened, but by whom.

THE *PLANO ÍDEAL* tried to answer this question. In February 1823, Don Manuel Antonio de la Cerda, the first person to govern the Nicaraguan lakeside city of Granada after the end of Spanish rule, created the map to persuade his political superiors to construct the canal.[11] Maps were scarce in colonial Central America, and most scientific knowledge was designed for local use, not for larger purposes.[12] Lacking accurate surveys of the land and water, the *Plano Ídeal* was cartographically imprecise.

Its political geography also reflected its creator's ideals and not on-the-ground reality. The European-descended rulers of the cities on the western side of the isthmus claimed all the unbounded land depicted on the page. But much of the map's empty space stretched over the territory of unconquered Indigenous nations. The only hint of their sovereignty was a small label near the mouth of the San Juan River that read "*Costa de los Mosquitoes*," a reference not to the abundant insect vectors of deadly viruses but to the powerful Miskitú nation.[13]

Yet the Indigenous Rama nation really ruled the river. Living along the tributaries of the San Juan and paying tribute to Miskitú leaders, Rama people knew every bend and sandbar. Living in one of the wettest territories on earth, they adapted their lives to the water's seasonal rhythms and guarded their knowledge from those who sought to turn their riverine world into a waterway to connect the globe.[14]

De la Cerda's ignorance of the river made the *Plano Ídeal* even more imprecise. Depicted as an undifferentiated teal ribbon winding across the page, the map ignored the river's rapids, currents, and seasonal sedimentation that would present unsurmountable obstacles to sailing vessels.[15] Even Lake Nicaragua, one of the world's largest bodies of fresh water, experienced deadly windstorms. Absent any shade of gray, the plan did not consider the unknown geology of the land and riverbed. Lacking the greens and browns that might indicate the lush plant and animal life along the route, de la Cerda's map turned one of the most biologically diverse places on earth into a barren canvas.[16]

Meanwhile, it papered over political problems on the western half of the isthmus, where sovereignty was as fluid as the landscape. Still under Spanish control in 1820, Central America was late to the Age of Revolutions. Nearly a half century after 1776, the provinces of Central America declared independence in 1821, only to be quickly annexed by the newly formed Mexican Empire. In February 1823, de la Cerda sent his map to a member of the Mexican government.[17]

Within a month, the Mexican emperor abdicated, and five Central American provinces—including Nicaragua—seceded to form a new country. The Mexican politician lost power but kept the map.[18]

The same month that Central America declared independence from Mexico, de la Cerda sent a second copy of his map to the new nation's capital in Guatemala City. "Kindly propose the project to Congress and let me know its result," he requested of a representative in the provisional legislature.[19] "The canal for the union of the two seas is undoubtedly an object worthy of all the attention of the united provinces of Central America," the congress decreed, but beyond praising de la Cerda's "patriotic zeal," it ignored his plan.[20] More concerned with constructing a country than a canal, the legislature likely loaned out its copy of the map.[21]

The two "original" versions of the *Plano Ídeal*—one in Mexico and one in Guatemala City—moved into private hands and out of the public record. Before their archival disappearance, both maps were copied by foreign agents.

The maps multiplied. In July 1825, a British special agent copied the version in Guatemala City.[22] Embellishing the bodies of water with a palette of blue, he expected to capture the imaginations of imperial officials and British capitalists, but the map arrived too late to be enticing. By early 1826, London's interest in investing in the new Spanish American nations had evaporated. The British government shelved the plan, eventually housing it in the oversized folder where I found it two centuries later.[23]

Across the ocean, copies of the Mexican map fueled the plans of US politicians and investors.[24] One copy did not survive a disastrous surveying expedition through war-torn Nicaragua. Another made its way to President John Quincy Adams. Black ink on ragged tan paper, the version deposited in the US National Archives was less colorful but more consequential.[25] The map launched a cutthroat race to turn a contract into a canal. As various would-be canal contractors competed for presidential patronage and private capital, nationwide debates about the waterway's likely environmental effects spread a wave of support for the project. The crest came too soon. By the time the contract arrived, changing political tides drained its support. The US copy of the *Plano Ídeal* also found its way to a folder.

After the archiving of de la Cerda's map, generations of canal dreamers created more precise means to depict the region's potential as an interoceanic waterway.[26] In the early twenty-first century, more than a hundred years after the opening of the Panama Canal, interest in constructing a waterway through Nicaragua persisted. Reversing the direction but not the dream, the most re-

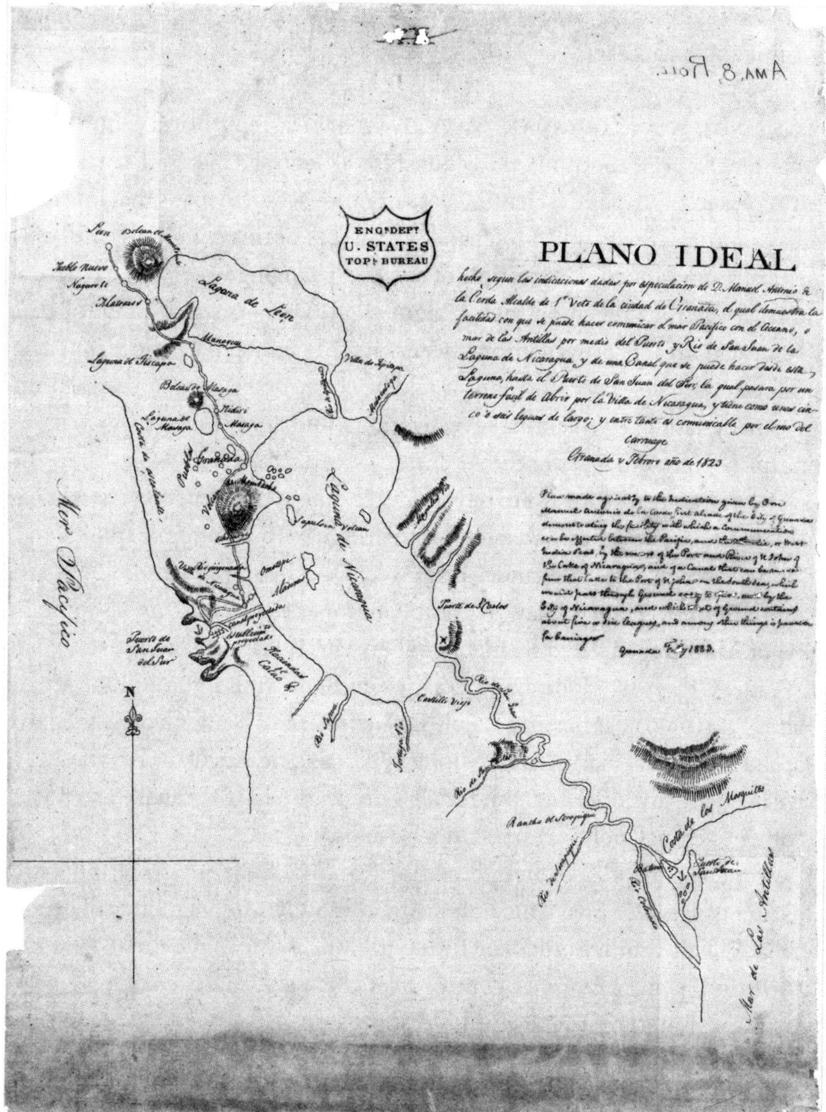

By early 1825, this version of Manuel Antonio de la Cerda's *Plano Ídeal* made its way to Washington, DC. Less colorful than the British copy, the US government's version includes English translations of the map's Spanish text. *Plano Ídeal—Proposed communication between Pacific Ocean, Lake Nicaragua, Central America, by canal*, RG77-CWMF-AMA-8, NAID: 16905096, Cartographic Research Room, National Archives, College Park, MD.

cent canal contractor sought a waterway to link his nation, China, with its Atlantic trade partners.[27]

PLANS FOR A NICARAGUAN WATERWAY have a long history, but there's something special about the 1820s quest for a Central American canal. Without access to the types of scientific data or more accurate maps that informed later proposals, the would-be canal constructors of this era blindly and optimistically envisioned the creation of a world-changing waterway. In place of information, they relied on their imaginations. Dreams substituted for data. Their canal dreams proved impractical, but quite influential. The idea that an interoceanic waterway could and should be constructed shaped international diplomacy, launched scientific investigations, and contributed to speculative enterprises on both sides of the Atlantic.

And yet, canal dreams were never entirely about constructing a waterway. Some canal dreamers earned fame for their Age of Revolutions exploits, such as John Quincy Adams, Manuel José Arce, David Barclay, Jeremy Bentham, Simón Bolívar, Henry Clay, DeWitt Clinton, Alexander von Humboldt, Gregor MacGregor, Jared Sparks, Stephen Van Rensselaer, and José Cecilio del Valle. Others like John Baily, Charles de Beneski, Edmund Blunt, Curtis Bolton, Antonio José Cañas, Isaiah Doane, Miskitú King George Frederic, Aaron H. Palmer, Charles Savage, John Williams, and Augustus B. Woodward have been mostly forgotten. But for all these dreamers, the canal was a means to other personal, political, or economic ends.

Ultimately, the idea of an interoceanic canal proved too revolutionary for the Age of Revolutions. This politically, culturally, and economically transformative half-century produced the conditions that inspired canal dreams. It ended the Spanish Empire's control over the canal route, enabling foreign pursuits of waterway rights and unleashing new nations and citizens to reimagine the planet. With a project dependent on the diplomatic recognition of new nations, expansion of individual property rights, and application of enlightenment science, canal dreamers aimed to unite the oceans and thereby revolutionize the land and water of the earth itself. Dreaming of a revolution more globe-altering than any nation-creating constitution, they saw their quest as the climactic fulfillment of the Age of Revolutions.

Instead, it evinced the era's conclusion. The timing was the trouble. Canal dreams arrived too late to be fulfilled. From our twenty-first century perspective, digging a tropical canal without mosquito nets or steam shovels might suggest that these visions arrived too early, but a civil war in Central America, a financial crisis in Britain, and the rise of partisanship in the United States prevented any construction crew from testing the limits of 1820s ingenuity. Canal dreams never had the chance to be technologically impossible because the political and financial context changed between idea and implementation. Too late, canal dreamers demanded capital from saturated markets that were already turning to coal and cotton. They sought cosmopolitan fluidity from solidifying nation-states and depended on personal patronage as new political parties formed. And they imagined an investment in water when empires craved land. Even the water itself ebbed and flowed with an untamed seasonality ignored by would-be investors who did not conceptualize the reengineering of the landscape as environmentally destructive. Plagued by timing troubles as granular as the water cycle and as grand as political revolution, the canal proved eminently dreamable but entirely undoable even for some of the world's most powerful people.

Although the canal remained unbuilt, the 1820s quest itself connected some of the era's most famous events: the drafting of the Monroe Doctrine, the Erie Canal's opening, the Corrupt Bargain that allegedly decided the US election of 1824 and ended the Era of Good Feelings in US politics, the bursting of London's first Spanish American financial bubble in the Panic of 1825, Simón Bolívar's Pan-American congress, Indigenous dispossession, slavery's expansion, the turn to fossil fuels, the Perry Mission to Japan, and the rise and fall of both the First Mexican Empire and the Republic of Central America. The unbuilt waterway's capacity to link these seemingly disconnected events has not previously been unearthed because isthmian transit histories often leap over the 1820s to the California gold rush, William Walker's filibustering, and the rivalry with Panamá.[28] Most existing narratives have rested on the assumption that the Nicaraguan quest resulted only in failure.[29] It is hard for historians to see the significance of something unbuilt. We tend to truck less in undoable dreams and more in the definitively done. The Panama Canal incontestably made history, but could history also be made of imagined waterways? I think so.

If we escape the false binary of success and failure, and instead take our cue from Columbus's unfulfilled quest, we need not squint to see the historical power of unrealized dreams. By transforming the journey into the destination, the pages that follow tell a tale of global history in a uniquely fluid moment as political sovereignty and the structures of finance rested on shifting ground.

When the British agent applied blue ink to his beige paper, the construction of an interoceanic waterway built along the Nicaragua route appeared to its visionaries as predestined. Believers on both sides of the Atlantic Ocean attempted to reengineer political, economic, and environmental systems to turn their dreams into reality. In the process, they promoted the recognition of countries, the incorporation of companies, and the publication of information about a place that was largely terra incognita to those outside Central America. Full of adventure, corruption, and unintended consequences, the story of these canal dreamers was until now a buried treasure, hidden in the absence of firm historical ground.

To unearth this tale, I have dug through multilingual sources from more than fifty archives located in ten countries on three continents. Like the *Plano Ídeal,* this world of evidence directs us toward our starting point: an alluring watery land teeming with possibility.

CHAPTER ONE

Fluid Sovereignty

In the brackish waters at the mouth of the San Juan River, where the American continents narrow into a slender neck separating the Atlantic from the Pacific Ocean, newborn bull sharks enter the murky warm water tail first, already swimming.[1] Some never leave the salt water of the isthmian coast, but more intrepid sharks move inland.

Bull sharks' ability to adjust their internal salinity allows them to survive in the salty waters of the world's oceans as well as inland fresh water, including the Central American isthmus's largest lake. In English, this body of water is often called Lake Nicaragua, but its Nahuatl and Spanish names—Lago Cocibolca and Mar Dulce—describe its lush wildlife and potable water. Long thought to be an exclusively freshwater species, the sharks living in Lake Nicaragua must travel from their coastal birthplaces more than a hundred miles over rocky rapids and shifting sandbars against the current of the San Juan River. Able to hunt but not to breed in the lake's fresh water, mature sharks recalibrate their body chemistry as they reverse their trek to their saltier nursery.[2]

As recently as three million years ago, when sharks could swim from the Atlantic to the Pacific in tropical salty water between North and South America, such adaptations may not have been necessary. But over the next few hundred thousand years, tectonic shifts, volcanic eruptions, and sedimentation formed the Central American isthmus. This "great American schism" severed the seas and trapped marine animals in two isolated oceans.[3] With their adaptable bodies, the sharks could swim inland, but the new land bridge put limits on their domain. By the time humans arrived in Central America, sometime in the last 40,000 years, less than twenty miles of dry land separated the Pacific Ocean from the lake and river waters that drained to the Atlantic Ocean.[4] The sharks might be the most powerful predators in the water, but people controlled the surrounding land.

Seeking to undo millions of years of geological work, the Spanish conquistadores and their descendants imagined reconnecting the Atlantic and Pacific by digging through the isthmus and turning the sharks' route into an interoceanic waterway. Although artificial rivers designed to irrigate fields and transport goods had been constructed for millennia, this would be the most audacious canal ever imagined, a direct passage between two oceans. Despite centuries of transporting Pacific treasures to Europe, the Spanish Empire never cut through the continents, nor did it allow others to explore this option.

By the early 1820s, the construction of a world-changing waterway seemed more doable than ever. As five decades of the Age of Revolutions' intense global warfare calmed into a new peace, new possibilities opened. Spain lost control over the Central American isthmus just as massive canal projects in Britain and the United States inspired interest in creating an oceanic shortcut. But in London and New York publications and the conversations that this print provoked, the isthmus received relatively little attention compared to the more dramatic stories of revolution from elsewhere in Spain's collapsing empire.

Based on the little information about Central America that appeared in English, the engineering of the canal seemed easy, but obtaining the construction rights posed a problem. To finance the waterway, supreme political authority over the route—its sovereignty—needed to be recognized abroad.

Who controlled this watery land? Although this might seem like a simple question, our story of the 1820s quest for an interoceanic waterway begins with its complex answer. From New York and London, isthmian sovereignty seemed as murky as the sharks' nursery.

THE IDEA OF A NICARAGUAN CANAL had a history that stretched back centuries, but as the 1820s dawned, British readers most recently learned about it from the celebrated pen of Baron Alexander von Humboldt, who traveled through much of Spain's American empire during its twilight. Written in French and translated into English in 1811, Humboldt's *Political Essay on the Kingdom of New Spain* inspired merchants, investors, and mercenaries looking to profit from the disintegration of Spanish power in the Western Hemisphere. Humboldt suggested "nine points" as routes for "the communication between the two seas."[5]

Although he did not visit the Nicaraguan route, Humboldt researched it "in the archives of Madrid," where he consulted previously sequestered Spanish sources as well as "several French and English memoirs."[6] He found conflicting accounts of whether a natural interoceanic waterway already existed and whether there was a break in the mountain chain that linked "the Andes of Peru to the mountains of Mexico." The lack of reliable topographical information posed, as Humboldt exclaimed, "problems whose solution is equally interesting to the statesman and the geographical naturalist!"[7] Contemplating construction of a canal demanded solving puzzles of science and sovereignty.

Writing before the region's independence, Humboldt recognized that Spain controlled the Pacific coast and lake but had never completely conquered the isthmus. He knew that British subjects had been trading with

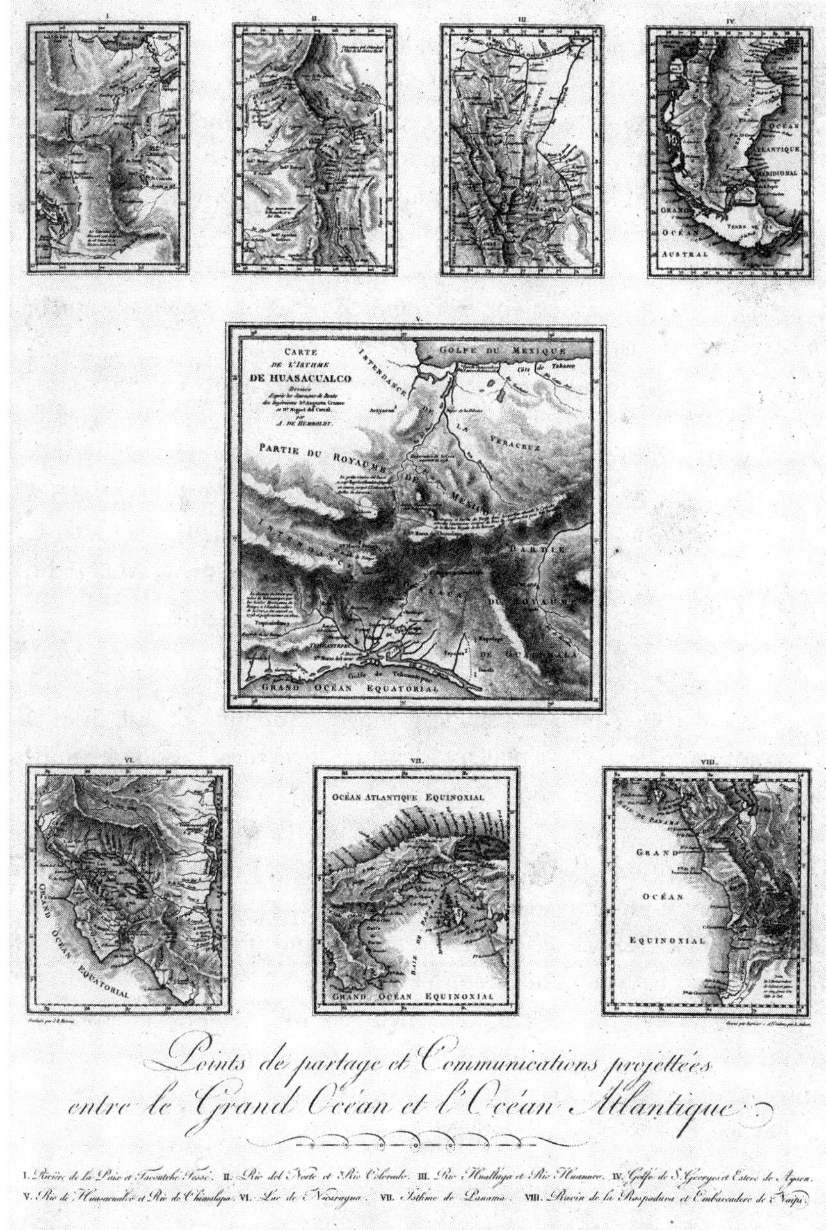

In an atlas designed to accompany the original French edition of his *Political Essay on the Kingdom of New Spain,* Alexander von Humboldt included this illustration of the "nine points" he suggested for "the communication between the two seas." The route through Lake Nicaragua is on the bottom left. J. B. Poirson, "Points de portage et Communications projetteés entre le Grand Océan et l'Océan Atlantique," in Alexander von Humboldt, *Atlas géographique et physique du royaume de la Nouvelle-Espagne* (Paris: F. Schoell, 1811), map 4. Courtesy of David Rumsey Map Collection, David Rumsey Map Center, Stanford Libraries.

unconquered Indigenous nations on the Caribbean shore for centuries. Humboldt credited the "celebrity" of the "project of the communication between the two seas" to the "commerce carried on by the English on the coast of *Mosquitos*."[8] Although insects abounded in these watery lands, the "Mosquito Coast" referred to the Indigenous Miskitú people, who derived their name from the British muskets that ensured their power.[9] The Spanish had never conquered the San Juan River's watershed or the Miskitú nation's larger homelands that stretched along five hundred miles of Caribbean shoreline and deep into the isthmus's inland rainforests.

For centuries, Miskitú leaders had been operating outside Spanish monopoly laws and trading mahogany, silver, turtle shells, guns, and enslaved people with British subjects. What began as barter turned into coastal logging camps that eventually developed into sugar plantations along the Black River (now known as Río Sico). These operations depended on the labor and expertise of enslaved Indigenous and African-descended people sold to British settlers by the Miskitú.[10]

Seventeenth-century British governors of Jamaica had developed a "crowning" ritual suggesting Miskitú society was monarchical, but the political structure was not unified behind a singular "king."[11] Adopting English titles like "governor" and "general," hereditary Miskitú leaders ruled specific territories, including the riverine portion of the canal route.[12] The British government held no authority over Miskitú lands. Neither did the Spanish, but this did not stop Europeans from claiming control. The Treaty of Paris of 1763 guaranteed British mahogany logging rights, but its language was vague about whether the British could create permanent settlements in lands that were, according to European dictates, within the Spanish Empire.[13]

European claims to sovereignty carried little weight on the ground. After centuries of failed conquest, the Spanish generally ignored the Miskitú; the British unofficially allied with them. By the 1770s, British settlement stretched far beyond the Black River with Miskitú protection, which was necessary because many of the newer settlements occupied the homelands of neighboring Indigenous nations.[14]

At the dawn of the Age of Revolutions, shortly after colonists in North America protested British rule by tossing tea into Boston harbor, the young man who would become the Miskitú's most powerful king sailed to London. Sent to protest imperious colonists in the region's British settlements, "Musquito Prince George" lingered in London for more than a year as he honed his spoken English fluency and confirmed his people's authority.[15] During the voyage home, a fellow passenger—the recently emancipated writer Olaudah Equiano—taught the eighteen-year-old to read with hopes of converting the "attentive" prince into a Christian. But by the time the ship reached the Central American shore, the savvy teenager rejected Equiano's evangelization. He wanted the words without the worship. Upon his father's imminent death, the shrewd prince became "King George II" or "Young George."[16]

Equiano kept sailing south beyond the king's lands into a lagoon in what would now be considered Nicaragua.[17] Here, "some of the native Indians" boarded the vessel; perhaps these were Rama men and women who called the San Juan River home.[18] Equiano differentiated these "Indian" locals from Young George's people who blended Indigenous and African heritage.[19] Recognizing Miskitú power over the coast's other Indigenous communities, Equiano observed how the regional leader and "his gang" dominated "our good neighbouring Indians" through plunder, violence, and tribute.[20]

Shortly after Equiano's observations, as Spain allied with the North American revolutionaries, officials in London and Jamaica planned to seize the San Juan River with the goal of creating a British interoceanic transit route across the isthmus.[21] In 1780, a twenty-year-old captain in the Royal Navy, whose later victories would immortalize him as Admiral Nelson, joined other officers in leading 1,000 men up the river.[22] About a third of these troops were Miskitú and their Indigenous neighbors, including knowledgeable Rama men in their shallow dugout vessels.[23]

Although they succeeded in occupying and destroying the river's only significant Spanish fort, Nelson and other soldiers fell ill with fever and dysentery.[24] As many British troops died, the Miskitú leaders grew frustrated and "deserted."[25] Defeated by disease and abandoned by its local allies, the British military gave up on its effort to control the interoceanic route. The soldiers withdrew after only nine months and without reaching Lake Nicaragua, let alone the Pacific Ocean.[26] Only the Rama remained on the river.

Meanwhile, the Miskitú had committed so many men to the campaign that they could not defend the settlers in their midst. Spanish forces raided Black River.[27] In 1786, the kings of Britain and Spain agreed to evacuate all British subjects from "the Country of the MOSQUITOS."[28] In total, 1,677 enslaved Black and Indigenous people and their 537 white enslavers moved north to the unofficial colony of British Honduras (now Belize). At Black River, Spanish soldiers and a few settlers moved into the "neat English village."[29] Not a party to the negotiation in Europe, the Miskitú king asserted his sovereignty on the ground. In 1800, Young George's men captured the town and expelled all the Spanish from the Mosquito Coast.[30]

With the Spanish gone, Miskitú people eagerly rekindled their relationship with the colonists of British Honduras. The British government never opened diplomatic negotiations with the Miskitú as a sovereign nation, but the Miskitú people embraced British culture. In 1805, witnesses reported that Miskitú leaders "dressed in British regimentals, with epaulettes, sword, [and] sash."[31]

As Young George expelled the Spanish from Miskitú territory, Humboldt traveled through Spain's American empire. Although the European explorer had not visited the Central American isthmus, he recognized that the Spanish did not control the river portion of the proposed canal route. Without detailing the region's complex history, he referenced the cultural and commercial ties between the Miskitú and their British trade partners. Flagging opportunity for English-speaking canal dreamers, Humboldt hinted that sovereignty over this interoceanic route was more fluid than other "points" in the Spanish Empire.

But soon Spain would lose control over most of its American colonies; sovereignty throughout South and Central America became swampy. Focusing on the fall of Spain, the next decade's anglophone canal dreamers mostly dismissed the real rulers of the river. As English speakers sought to wring profits from the collapse of the Spanish Empire, Miskitú power on the ground was ignored overseas.

PUBLISHED IN LONDON IN 1821, William Davis Robinson's *Memoirs of the Mexican Revolution* fed interest in "a navigable or rapid communication between the Pacific and Atlantic oceans."[32] Acknowledging Humboldt's proposal of "*Nine* different routes" for the canal, Robinson focused on the three most likely candidates: Colombia (including what is now Panamá), Nicaragua, and Mexico.[33]

About the route through Lake Nicaragua, Robinson praised the "section of the American continent, where the magnificent scheme of cutting a navigable canal, between the two oceans, appears unincumbered with any natural obstacles." The word "appears" did a lot of work for Robinson. Like Humboldt, he had not seen the route for himself and complained, "no accurate description of the country has ever been published."[34] Indeed, Robinson's description of the "country" verged on imaginary. Claiming to have been informed by "several traders," he presented as "fact" a complete fiction: "at present large brigs and schooners sail up the river into the lake."[35] Although at the very height of the rainy season, water might flood the rapids to ease the passage of a shallow Rama canoe or lake-bound bull shark, deep-hulled seaworthy vessels could not ascend the river.[36]

Such optimism characterized Robinson's description of the entire route. He turned the western canal construction—where land would need to become water—into a project of enlarging "small rivers" and perhaps digging through "dead level" ground.[37] Minimizing the region's seasonal windstorms, or "*Papagayos*," Robinson reported that experienced sailors thought them "trifling" compared to "the dreadful hurricanes" of the Caribbean. As for human obstacles, Robinson turned descriptions of the "finely formed and robust race of Indians" who inhabited the route into evidence that their land was "the most salubrious of all the tropical regions" and would therefore be safe for Europeans. Robinson ignored the strength of Miskitú sovereignty, seeing only their strong immune systems.[38]

Even Robinson's backup plan was glowing. If unanticipated "obstructions" were discovered, he argued that a canal could easily be cut through "the entire Isthmus." Instead of serving as the waterway, the river and lake would provide "an abundant supply of water" for a manmade river, which would be "at most *two hundred miles*." Alluding to the longer Erie Canal then under construction in New York, he assured, "the magnitude of such an undertaking would not be a material objection, in the present age of enterprise and improvement."[39]

Satisfied that he had dismissed any "difficulty" that might prevent the canal's physical construction, he considered the political and financial obstacles. Ignoring the Miskitú and imagining Spanish rule replaced by "a liberal government," Robinson prophesied, "capital in abundance would speedily be forthcoming, either from Great Britain or from the United States." Such quick capitalization would require the formation of "Enterprising companies." He confidently predicted "*canal stock* of such an association would yield a profit far greater than that of any other company in the world."[40] Such profitability, in part, depended on his expectation that Indigenous people from throughout the isthmus would flock to work on the canal for "moderate compensation."[41] Arguing that "Every Indian" would view the canal's "obvious advantages to his country," Robinson failed to see that some people might not want their homelands turned into "the greatest commercial thoroughfare in the world."[42]

It was entirely beyond Robinson's imagination to conceive of the Miskitú nation as a sovereign power that might have the right to decide whether the world's waterway would be constructed through its territory. But as conditions on the Mosquito Coast changed between Humboldt's publication and Robinson's, a new king dreamed of just such diplomatic recognition.

In 1800, Young George, Equiano's old shipmate who had consolidated Miskitú power under his crown, died under mysterious circumstances.[43] His

GEORGE AUGUSTUS FREDERICK, KING OF MOSQUITO.

It is unclear whether this late nineteenth-century portrait depicts King George Frederic Augustus (c. 1798–1824) or his nephew King George Augustus Frederic II (c. 1833–64). "George Augustus Frederick, King of Mosquito," C. Napier Bell, *Tangweera: Life and Adventures among Gentle Savages* (London: E. Arnold, 1899), plate facing 274.

heir possessed nowhere near his stature; George Frederic Augustus was only about seven years old. A "plain puny looking child" studying in Jamaica, the boy wore a "silver gilt" crown "ornamented with mock stones." Despite what a Jamaican colonist described as his "very high and determined spirit," the boy was not ready to wield the heavy-handed control that had consolidated his father's power.[44] For more than a decade, as George Frederic continued his education in Jamaica and became a passionate reader of British literature, regional Miskitú leaders exploited the regency to claw back their power.[45]

In 1816, King George Frederic Augustus I assumed his father's crown. Now in his mid-twenties, the "handsome" and agile young man, whose "long curly hair" framed his "bright copper" face, would have to deal with dissension within the Miskitú ranks.[46] Rejecting his authority, two of the regional leaders refused to attend his coronation.[47] Moreover, British Honduras was roiled by attempts to end Indigenous slavery; the Miskitú might lose their long-time trade partners.[48] And so, King George Frederic, who believed he held the same power as his father over all the Miskitú people and territories, began to formulate a plan that would cultivate new commercial relationships, replace the insubordinate regional leaders, and obtain overseas recognition of his sovereignty.[49]

The new king contemplated how to realize his dream. Meanwhile, no one knew his plans for proclaiming his sovereignty to the world. This included William Davis Robinson, who allowed his prejudices to guide his perceptions of the potential interoceanic canal route. Encouraging a presumably male reader to "cast his eye upon the map," Robinson turned European cartographic traditions into the canal's most compelling evidence. With the isthmus centrally located on nearly every global map, he enthused, "it appears to be the favoured spot destined by nature to be the heart of the commerce of the world."[50] Like a giant X at the middle of the map, the river, lake, and land that could become water appeared to be a natural treasure.

Sovereignty over such aqueous land also seemed naturally fluid to Robinson. He did not want "any one kingdom or state" to control the canal. Instead, it should be "like the ocean, a highway of nations." In fact, he expected the region's rulers—whomever they might be—not to "hesitate in the relinquishment of a few leagues of territory on the American continent, for the general benefit of mankind."[51]

THE IDEA OF A WATERWAY that benefited as many people as possible appealed to philosopher Jeremy Bentham. Citing Robinson's book as the "most recent" and "most determinate" source, Bentham detailed his own canal plan, which he entitled "Proposals for the Junction of the Two Seas,—the Atlantic and Pacific, by Means of a Joint-Stock Company, to be Styled The Junctiana Company."[52] Bentham believed Robinson's consideration of potential "net profit" narrowed down Humboldt's nine potential interoceanic canal routes "to *one*": Nicaragua.[53]

But given Miskitú control over the river, was the route really in Nicaragua? Bentham could not even conceive of this question. Like Humboldt and Robinson, the philosopher had never been to the isthmus. By 1822, the seventy-four-year-old Bentham's health was declining; he employed secretaries to read to him and write for him.[54] He described the Westminster home he inherited from his father as his "Hermitage," suggesting monastic isolation, but the wealthy Bentham relished entertaining, especially Spanish American visitors.[55] As he dreamed up his Junctiana proposal, he met with Venezuelans, Colombians, Chileans, and Mexicans. He wrote to British-born men in South America and to the leaders of each new state.[56] To these interlocutors, he evangelized his "fundamental principle" of judging systems by whether they elicited the "*greatest happiness of the greatest number.*"[57] From these conversations and to serve this utilitarian ideal, he imagined reengineering political power halfway around the world.

In June of 1822, as he dictated his Junctiana proposal, a Mexican Empire was forming that would claim sovereignty over the entire Central American isthmus including both the Spanish-descended people to the west and the unconquered Indigenous people to the east.[58] To Bentham, this was unacceptable. Mexico was "in utter darkness," Bentham argued, "to the eye of an English capitalist."[59]

Bentham also looked askance at the new republic south of the route. He thought that the English fluency of many of Colombia's leaders—who had either spent time in London or emigrated from Britain—provided some comforting "circumstantial evidence of English ideas and affections." But even this "first-born and best known of the two infant states" would leave British potential investors uneasy.[60] If English language and a long history of governance were his only criteria, Bentham might have found King George Frederic an acceptable ruler over the route, but Bentham considered only governments controlled by European-descended people. He believed neither of the neighboring Spanish American nations offered a "sufficient ground for confidence" to his targeted "prudent set of capitalists."[61] To Bentham, the views of investors—not conditions on the ground—should determine sovereignty over the route.

In this capitalist utopia, the philosopher envisioned the creation of a new state he called the "Republic of *Junctiana.*" Ignoring the existence of Spanish-descended Nicaraguans as well as the Miskitú and Rama, he claimed that along the route a "mass of wealth and population" would be created "out of nothing."[62] A joint-stock company incorporated in London would have to pay not only to construct the canal but also to buy the "matchless jewel" of sovereignty over the route from the Mexican government.[63] A believer in the sanctity of private property, Bentham expected the company to secure title from all landowners, "original inhabitants styled *Indians* included."[64] Denying Indigenous peoples' existence in one section of his proposal, Bentham deployed an old colonization strategy and recognized the salability of their land in another.[65]

But his reverence for property was not absolute; Bentham distinguished between property in land and property in people. "No *slavery*, in any shape, to be allowed," emphasized the proposal, making clear that transit through the canal would legally emancipate any enslaved person aboard any vessel.[66] He mentioned nothing about the company compensating either the emancipated or their enslavers. Nor did he consider the Indigenous slave trade that sustained Miskitú power. Human property was simply not part of Bentham's dream.

British capital, however, was at its core. As decades of war concluded and the British government lowered its interest rates, investors flocked to higher yielding opportunities in Spanish America. Bentham wanted the Junctiana company to absorb some of this capital "which as yet is in an overflowing state, not yet settled, in channels from which it cannot be diverted."[67]

To direct this flow of money in the near term, would-be shareholders would need to believe in the security of their capital for the long term. Eventually, stockholders could expect to see significant dividends from land sales and the "price of transit" paid by vessels traversing the canal.[68] But to allow these revenue streams to develop, the route needed to be protected by a stable and trustworthy government. Bentham believed Junctiana's government should be entrusted only to the "old established Republic of the Anglo-American United States."[69] Surviving nearly fifty years of independence, the US government should "nurse" Junctiana to prepare it to be "admitted on the same footing" as other new states like Missouri.[70]

Bentham's confidence that the United States—a country he called "Washingtonia"—would eagerly annex these Central American lands reflected his idealism, but it had some basis in reason.[71] Ratified in 1821, the Adams-Onís or Transcontinental Treaty ceded Spain's claim to Florida and the Oregon Territory to the United States, but British claims to land in the Pacific Northwest persisted. Bentham insisted that the canal would ease the movement of US settlers to Oregon and enable US merchants to dominate global trade. Washingtonia's embrace of the plan, in Bentham's estimation, seemed "hardly to be doubted."[72]

But if the US government even considered Bentham's plan, domestic politics would challenge annexation of a Central American state. With its location well to the south of the 1820 Missouri Compromise line, Bentham's determination to turn the canal into a freedom passage might not be acceptable to proslavery politicians. While Bentham might ignore the Catholic, Spanish-speaking, and Indigenous inhabitants of the canal route, the incorporation of these people into the US republic might not appeal to the nation's predominantly white, mostly Protestant, mainly English-speaking, and entirely male electorate. Although Nicaragua was closer to Washington than Oregon, tropical diseases and Caribbean pirates could make the 2,000-mile trip deadly. The US's slave-based property regime, the voters' prejudices, and the physical difficulties of tropical travel should have given Bentham reason to doubt.

But doubt he did not. In early June of 1822, he wrote about the plan to the South American liberator Simón Bolívar, the first minister of Buenos Ayres, and others.[73] The idea of Junctiana circulated through Spanish America.

MEANWHILE, ON LAND SPAIN HAD NEVER CONQUERED but nonetheless claimed, Miskitú King George Frederic planned to solidify his control over the isthmus's Caribbean coast, including the San Juan River. The youthful ruler began granting land—especially in his rivals' territories—to British adventurers who might cultivate new markets without abolitionist agendas, replace insubordinate regional rulers, and generate overseas recognition of his sovereignty.[74]

On April 29, 1820, at his home along the Caribbean coast, as newborn shark pups entered the region's estuaries, the king offered a British-born mercenary named Gregor MacGregor around 8 million acres of land that included the long abandoned Black River settlement.[75] This offer ignored the treaty between Britain and Spain that had required British subjects to flee decades earlier.[76] The Miskitú king asserted his own—and not Spanish—sovereignty over the land. In the previous decade and a half, MacGregor had quit the British army, married Bolívar's cousin, and created two short-lived independent countries carved out of the Spanish Empire.[77] A British treaty might not apply to either man.

Nonetheless, King George Frederic's deed followed British formalities.[78] Although Spanish-speaking Central Americans generally avoided describing land in terms of latitude and longitude, the Miskitú king adopted English scientific standards.[79] As boundaries, the document detailed coordinates based on "the Meridian of London."[80] It even cited as its source an old British chart in a British atlas by the British cartographer to the British king.[81]

The atlas's several maps of the isthmus suggested that the deed encompassed much of the interior of the "Mosquito Shore," including land labeled "Honduras," "Nicaragua," and "English Settlements."[82] This was not just any land. Since Young George had evicted the Spanish two decades earlier, the village, mills, and farms of the Black River settlement had been overtaken by the forest. The "sugar-cane, plantains, bananas, pineapples, coffee bushes, &c." cultivated by former British settlers thrived "in a state of wild luxuriance."[83] The canopy of cedar and mahogany trees inhabited by snakes, sloths, and toucans had grown since King George Frederic was a boy in Jamaica where he learned the profitability of producing cash crops through forced labor. At Black River, the Miskitú king saw an untapped engine for his nation's economic development awaiting excavation from the jungle.

More than land, the king's deed granted MacGregor judicial, military, and economic authority over a region that had been governed by one of the Miskitú leaders who had refused to attend the king's coronation. Grown powerful during King George Frederic's childhood, this recently deceased man had forced the neighboring Poyais people to harvest sarsaparilla, a medicinal herb used in the treatment of syphilis. He then sold this thorny vine—along with some of its human harvesters—to merchants in British Honduras.[84] The king's deed formalized these predations defining the territory of "Poyais" within MacGregor's land.[85] An act of imperialism, the deed expanded the Miskitú king's reach deeper into the isthmus.

The king defended his power even over MacGregor, who might replace a rival but could not make himself a king. In the same paragraph that granted the adventurer legal, military, and economic power, the deed made a large exception. Beginning with three letters measuring at least a third taller than the letters that followed, it read: "But let it be clearly understood, that there is nothing contained in this Deed, which shall be construed into a Cession of the Sovereignty of the Country as now held by His Mosquito Majesty."[86] With his big "But," King George Frederic proclaimed in beautiful swirls of English penmanship his sovereign rule over much of the Central American isthmus, which included not only MacGregor's tract but also the eastern half of the potential canal route.

To his new neighbors, MacGregor issued a "MANIFESTO, addressed to the AUTHORITIES and INHABITANTS of the adjoining SPANISH AMERICAN PROVINCES of HONDURAS and NICARAGUA."[87] Although it was one of the few words in lower-case letters, "adjoining" was the most important word in this sentence. It raised the central question of Central American sovereignty: Was the Mosquito Coast next to or part of Honduras and Nicaragua? The answer would shape political history and determine who controlled the rights to the canal route.

Just a few months later in 1821, as Hondurans and Nicaraguans declared independence from Spain, the new authorities would consider Miskitú, Poyais, Rama, and other Indigenous lands to be within their new states. In Guatemala City and Mexico City—new capitals of new countries clamoring for international recognition as sovereign nations—maps would absorb the "Country" of the Miskitú king into the provinces of Central America. To these new leaders, the land deeded to MacGregor was primarily in Honduras and the canal route was entirely in Nicaragua. But when MacGregor brought the Miskitú king's deed to Britain, would the financiers of London agree?

WHEN HE ARRIVED IN LONDON with the worn and stained deed in his pocket, MacGregor waged a publicity campaign. His chief military officer Captain Thomas Strangeways wrote a more than 300-page *Sketch of the Mosquito Shore*. Printed in Scotland in late 1822, this propagandistic guidebook taught would-be settlers how to refine sugar and make sandpaper from sharkskin. Ruing the association with "disagreeable insects," it renamed the sovereign power of the Central American Caribbean coast "Mosquitia."[88] Like Washingtonia and Junctiana, Mosquitia served as a new name for a distant place that conjured illusions of control in British imaginations.

Unlike most other English-language authors writing about Central America in the early 1820s, Strangeways's goal of legitimizing MacGregor's deed demanded that his book acknowledge the "native tribes" who ruled Mosquitia.[89] Providing Europeans with a sense of the approximately "70,000 square miles" under Miskitú control, he described the area as "one-third larger than the Kingdom of Portugal."[90] Although "geographers" considered the San Juan River "as the southern extremity of the Mosquito Shore," Strangeways explained that "the king of the Mosquito nation" claimed more: "all the eastern part of the province of Nicaragua" through Costa Rica into Panamá.[91] The Miskitú exacted "an annual tribute" from their Indigenous neighbors in this southern territory, including along the San Juan River where "Ramas occupy the country."[92]

Like all the other authors of books on Central America appearing in London's bookstores in the early 1820s, Strangeways did not visit the riverine homeland of the Rama people. Although he shared the same sources as Humboldt and Robinson, Strangeways acknowledged more of the route's challenges. He discussed the river's strong current, sedimentation, and rapids, which "render its navigation difficult." He confessed, "the Indians are the only ones who know how to get over these obstacles."[93]

When Strangeways published this description, the Miskitú king had not yet given away his southernmost rival's land, which included this obstacle-filled river. But because this insubordinate local ruler also refused to attend King George Frederic's coronation, his lands—and more importantly, water—might be ripe for the king's deeding.[94] By describing the route's challenges and confirming Miskitú sovereignty, Strangeways angled both to frighten competitors and to help MacGregor acquire a second Miskitú land grant—this time including the potential canal route.

Even without title to the San Juan River, MacGregor benefited from British interest in the waterway because the construction of "the long wished for passage from the Atlantic into the Pacific" might increase his land's value.[95] Toward the end of his book, Strangeways back-paddled from his description of a river navigable only by Rama people. Considering the potential for "incalculable benefit" from an interoceanic waterway, the book embraced the "prevalent opinion" that "the practicability" of a canal "has never been doubted." He assured, "it will ultimately take place through a part of the Mosquito Territory, or its immediate neighbourhood, under its control."[96]

STRANGEWAYS'S ASSERTION OF Miskitú control over the eastern half of the proposed canal route did not attract the notice of Jeremy Bentham, whose Junctiana plan had been circulating for more than a year. Instead, the arrival in London of a self-described member of "the first families in Guatemala" brought Junctiana back to the philosopher's mind.[97] "I have read with the greatest pleasure your plan to realise the junction of the Atlantic and Pacific Seas," wrote the Guatemalan. "I am quite convinced," he continued, "you have found the only means of putting in execution a project from which all the humankind will derive every kind of advantage."[98]

Bentham's plan, however, required modification. As his eyesight failed, the elderly utilitarian re-envisioned the region's sovereignty not because he wanted to recognize the Miskitú but because the Mexican Empire had collapsed. The Central American agent informed Bentham that "the Lake of Nicaragua belongs to the Kingdom of Guatemala." He offered to send Bentham's plan to the new government forming in Guatemala City, "to which the Province of Nicaragua will be joined." Implying that the philosopher ought to write the Mexicans and Colombians out of the proposal while continuing to ignore the Indigenous nations along the Caribbean coast, the Guatemalan explained that only his "Government" would "make the cessions of Land to the contractors."[99]

As the Guatemalan traveled to Paris, where the "first person" he wanted to see was Humboldt, Bentham decided to share his plan with Washington.[100] He invited the US minister in London to dinner. Bentham wanted to ask the diplomat to copy "a paper"—probably his Junctiana proposal—and send it to Secretary of State John Quincy Adams.[101] The minister responded that he was overwhelmed with work, including secretarial tasks. "My government allows to this Legation neither clerk nor private secretary," he complained, explaining to Bentham that he even served as his own "copiest."[102] But finding an unexpected break in his schedule, the diplomat expressed his intention "to jump into my gig tomorrow, Sunday as it is, at two o clock and drive down to the Hermitage."[103]

In the month after this Sunday meeting, the minister reported in his official dispatches to Adams on British claims to Oregon, proposals for Caribbean lighthouses, and rumors of European recognition of new American countries.[104] He omitted Junctiana. The US government and many of its citizens would soon share Bentham's interest in an interoceanic canal. But at this moment, perhaps the plan seemed too utopian to be worth the hand cramps of copying its many sections outlining an outdated scheme of Central American fluid sovereignty.

STRANGEWAYS'S ASSERTION OF indigenous sovereignty over the Mosquito Coast also quickly grew outdated. Distancing himself from the king's deed, MacGregor established a diplomatic "Legation." Already employing the title of "Cazique," MacGregor began referring to himself as "Gregor the First, Sovereign Prince of the State of Poyais."[105] Here MacGregor literally used the word "Sovereign"—a term explicitly denied to him by King George Frederic's big "But."

MacGregor defied the deed to go into debt. In 1822, London investors craved high yielding bonds of new American countries. Not authorized to negotiate a Miskitú loan, MacGregor turned Poyais into its own polity. Signing elaborately printed documents, MacGregor's "Poyais Loan" beat Mexico and Central America to the London capital market.[106] For all these new countries, sovereignty was—at least in part—a cultural construction claimed to market credit instruments.

Equated with Italian and German states in newspapers' lists of "Foreign Securities," Poyaisian bond prices were buoyed by reports that "the Mosquito Country" was a potential location for the construction of "a water communication between the two oceans."[107] The price of Poyais bonds was inextricably linked to a future canal.

Poyais's value was also linked to its past. Describing the man from whom "Sir Gregor McGregor obtained the grant of that large tract of country called Poyais," one newspaper argued, "Mosquito is under the Government of an absolute Sovereign whom the Spaniards have never been able to conquer." An Indigenous king whose "habits are quite English," King George Frederic was described as contemplating ceding his sovereignty for "British protection."[108] A new version of the same old strategy deployed by countless would-be colonizers, these statements recognized Indigenous sovereignty only enough to steal it.

ON MARCH 28, 1823, as pregnant bull sharks swam in the brackish waters of the Caribbean coast, the curly-haired king who loved to read British novels and dress in English clothes responded to the news from London by decreeing, "the grant of land given to Sir Gregor Macgregor is null and void." King George Frederic condemned MacGregor's "having contracted a debt upon a part of my territory without my consent, assuming to himself the title of Cazique of Poyais, and declaring the aforesaid grant to be an independent state."[109] As much as he had wanted to repopulate Black River with new trade partners and replace a rival, the Miskitú king could not abide MacGregor's claims to ruling an independent country. He wanted recognition of his sovereignty above all.

When British Hondurans rescued MacGregor's sickly settlers whom they found near the overgrown plantations, they interviewed the king. He confirmed feeling "greatly deceived" because he never wanted "the establishment of a separate Government in his country."[110] He had insisted on his big "But" because he wanted to confirm his power both at home and abroad. He got the opposite: a diminishment of his sovereignty everywhere.

Despite MacGregor eventually being remembered as the "king of conmen" and Poyais as an "imaginary Central American country" in a "Land that Never Was," the cazique's propaganda respected Indigenous knowledge and power.[111] Unusual for his time, Strangeways made one of the strongest cases in the early nineteenth-century English-language press for Miskitú sovereignty over the Central American coast, including the canal route.

Nonetheless, despite its careful construction according to British science and law, MacGregor's deed had been disastrous for the Miskitú king both at home and abroad. Unlike the bull sharks who reigned at the top of the food webs along his salty coast as well as up his freshwater rivers, King George Frederic's claims to sovereignty could not survive in both worlds.

By the end of 1823, the Miskitú king's quest to assert his sovereignty over all his lands—including the potential interoceanic canal route—proved unachievable but consequential. Because would-be canal contractors ignored the region's Indigenous people, they lost the opportunity to learn from those who most intimately knew the river's considerable quirks. Dismissing the disgraced Strangeways, canal dreamers based their plans for the route on the optimistic claims of Humboldt and Robinson.

In sending MacGregor to London, the Miskitú king inadvertently enabled this rogue agent to provide a model for representatives of other countries lacking official diplomatic recognition. With some of the same strategies as MacGregor, agents of newly forming Spanish American states claimed sovereignty, sponsored publications, established legations, and sold bonds guaranteed by dreams of future prosperity. As suggested by Humboldt, Robinson, and Bentham, joint-stock companies sold shares in promising Spanish American mines, roads, and canals.

For the remainder of the 1820s, neither the countries nor the companies seeking canal rights would consult with the Rama communities along the river or negotiate with the Miskitú king. Mosquitia's existence would be ignored; the region's fluid sovereignty would be channeled only toward new nations established by Spanish descendants. For rights to the Nicaragua route, British and US agents would exclusively negotiate canal contracts with the government forming in Guatemala City.

With King George Frederic and his descendants written out of diplomacy, London loan sharks preyed on other not-quite-sovereign American states. Meanwhile, adaptable apex predators continued navigating the salt and fresh waters that canal dreamers wanted to transform into the world's waterway.

CHAPTER TWO

The Race to Guatemala

In 1823, five years after the British Royal Marines halved his pay and removed him from active duty as part of a larger peacetime retrenchment, Lieutenant John A. Baily translated a Guatemalan author's history of the relatively unknown isthmus at the center of the American continents. Although Baily had likely never set foot on isthmian soil, his translation of the decade-old work represented the cutting edge of British knowledge about the region.[1]

Ready to trade his post-war armchair for new adventures in the field, Baily's publication served as a calling card, announcing his expertise to potential employers interested in sending a commercial agent to the country forming between the not-yet-recognized nations of Mexico and Colombia. The book worked. Within a year of its publication, Baily left London headed south and west across the Atlantic and then up from the Caribbean coast to Guatemala City, 5,000 feet above but only fifty miles away from the Pacific Ocean. Baily settled into the remote city nestled at the foot of several active volcanoes.

The men who sent Baily on his errand into the isthmus had been commissioning similarly tasked men to the Western Hemisphere for years. Transforming deals negotiated by these agents into securities sold to British investors, Baily's new employers wrung enormous profits out of Spain's dissolving American empire. Although the British government did not recognize the sovereignty of these new Spanish American countries, eager capitalists clamored for the yields promised by their bonds. With Baily as bait, the London loan sharks sought to make another killing by contracting for the debt and resource rights of Central America.

But Baily arrived early. In 1824, Central American sovereignty was still in flux. After three centuries of Spanish control and a short spell of Mexican imperialism, Guatemala City's government buildings hosted a provisional congress tasked with crafting what many hoped would be a more permanent national constitution. This limited Baily's initial negotiations, but it gave him time to earn the trust of locals before an influx of other foreign agents overwhelmed the capital.

If Baily was early, Central America was late. A half-century before independence reached the isthmus, Britain's rebelling North American colonies launched the Age of Revolutions. During the next five decades, revolutions in favor of individual rights and national self-governance spread through Europe and beyond. By the 1820s, almost all Spain's South American provinces fought costly wars that transformed the peripheries of a centrally controlled empire into independent and indebted nation states, which were themselves imperialist in their aims to control lands and peoples both within and beyond their hazy borders. Central America shed Spanish and Mexican imperial domination only as these other new countries firmed up their borders and financed their debts in London.

The centuries of Spanish imperial history that Baily translated had not yet resolved the question of isthmian independence. This did not stop capitalists and countries from sending agents to the city that had historically been the capital of the narrow region between the oceans. Dreaming of cutting through Rama, Miskitú, and Nicaraguan land, Baily and many other men raced not to the would-be waterway but hundreds of miles north to negotiate in the repurposed government structures of Guatemala City. They did not stop to consider the chicken-or-the-egg quandary of which comes first: the recognition of the country or its ability to contract.

"SPANISH AMERICA WILL PROBABLY, in a short time, open a most extensive field for the employment of British capital and British industry," Baily predicted in his book's preface.[2] By 1823, when these words reached readers, Britons were indisputably invested in Spanish America. Between 1822 and 1826, loans with a total paid-in capital of £17,500,000 would be contracted with Chile, Peru, Poyais, Mexico, Buenos Ayres, Brazil, and Central America.[3] Even more money would be poured into stocks to develop Spanish American resources like mineral mines and world-changing canals.

Baily further predicted that these British investments would "ultimately prove an inexhaustible source of advantage."[4] This remained to be seen. Last to independence, the Kingdom of Guatemala's liberation from Spanish rule in 1821 freed foreigners to dream of turning a slice of this land into an interoceanic waterway. But with markets already overflowing with Spanish American securities, Central American investments were a gamble.

From his post-war home across the Thames and about a mile from Parliament, Baily bet that this distant isthmus, half a world away, would become desirable.[5] He justified his "humble" book about the region as an "addition to the very slender stock of information we already possess, of any portion of that interesting Country."[6] Market forces mingled with military interests in motivating Baily's translation. He dedicated the book to his former boss, the viscount who headed Britain's navy. This "patronage," Baily confessed, "calls forth my anxiety as well as my gratitude."[7]

The anxious lieutenant had his own and Britain's interests in mind. Based on a work originally published in Guatemala City and written in Spanish by "Don Domingo Juarros, a Native of New Guatemala," Baily consolidated two volumes into a 500-page English-language tome, which sold for sixteen shillings, about a week's pay for an unskilled laborer.[8] Reading about Guatemala was reserved for the rich, which made sense because the book's goal was to entice investors' interest in Central America.

But when it came to the country's most valuable asset—its potential as the site for an interoceanic canal—the book fell silent. The Guatemalan Juarros probably opposed earlier Nicaraguan attempts to improve the San Juan River, so Baily's translation referenced only the conquistadores' "ambition to find out the channel by which the South Sea [Pacific Ocean] and the Atlantic were connected."[9] His readers might connect the dots between this sixteenth-century desire for a natural channel and the present potential for constructing what nature had not.

Other recent publications had introduced the concept of a Nicaraguan canal to the British reading public. Like disgraced Poyaisian propagandist Thomas Strangeways—and unlike adventurer William Davis Robinson or theorist Jeremy Bentham—Baily's book would recognize the existence and power of Indigenous nations along Central America's Caribbean coast. Describing the isthmus's southeastern coast as "the territories of the uncivilized Indians," Baily employed the present tense.[10] The book described these "unconverted Indians" as "of various nations."[11] It explained, "all these nations speak different languages, have distinct governments, manners, and customs; and they are also distinguished by variety of colour."[12] Juarros defined these unconquered and unconverted people as divided into distinct communities that could not be controlled by Guatemala City, but existed, nonetheless, within Spanish territory.

These descriptions carried different valences when Baily published them. In London in the early 1820s, the word "nation" was being applied to the new countries developing out of Spain's former colonies.[13] Baily's use of "nation" might suggest more Indigenous sovereignty over the region than Juarros meant to imply. Spanish-speaking elites in Guatemala City and those in the leading Nicaraguan cities of León and Granada argued that Indigenous territories fell within their national and provincial sovereignties. British investors agreed, including the men who hired John Baily and sent him to

Guatemala City to negotiate with Spanish-descended Central Americans for the right to build a waterway through Indigenous nations' homelands.

BARCLAY, HERRING, RICHARDSON & COMPANY (BHRC)—the partnership that hired Baily—consisted of six men who had come together to capitalize on Spanish American independence. No centuries-old bank or chartered corporation, the partnership was formed to broker not-quite-sovereign bonds, but was even less solid than the sovereignty of the new countries in which it invested.

Individually liable for the company's risks, the partners of BHRC each brought experience, capital, and connections to the business. The first named and most prominent was David Barclay. Barclay's father owned the world's largest brewery, which annually produced upward of 260,000 barrels of beer.[14] The brewer's sons turned beer money into banking capital. In 1823, just shy of forty years old and preparing to run for political office, David Barclay not only headed his own banking house but also served as an insurance company auditor and a director of the Bank of England, the most powerful financial institution in the British Empire and perhaps the world.[15]

The second named partner of BHRC was Charles Herring, who was one of the original British investors in Spanish America. Herring and two partners negotiated an 1822 loan to Colombia, which became the model for all subsequent loans to not-quite-sovereign countries. The loan consolidated wartime debts and made it more likely that Herring and his fellow merchants-turned-bond-brokers would be repaid. Paying these debts, the partners argued, would bolster the nation's case for British diplomatic recognition.[16] Countries could claim sovereignty, but only recognition by other countries could solidify it.[17]

And sovereign countries could raise funds by selling debt in the form of bonds. Since the end of the Napoleonic Wars, the British government had been reducing the interest it paid on its debt instruments; wealthy Britons chased higher yields by investing in loans to other countries. The Colombia loan was modeled on successful London bond issues by France, Denmark, Russia, and Prussia.[18] Regarded as riskier than these European securities, Colombia's loan enticed investors by promising yields so high that the contract had to be signed in Paris to circumvent British usury laws.[19]

A large part of the proceeds of the bond sales, however, did not go to the struggling new nation. Colombia could expect access to only about three-quarters of its £2,000,000 loan; most of the remaining funds would be divided among the loan contractors.[20] At a time when a skilled male laborer earned about £50 per year, Herring and his partners each stood to pocket around £100,000.[21] Herring plowed some of the capital generated from the Colombia loan into other investments, including BHRC.[22]

Herring brought his family and friends into the business. His namesake son, a long-time business partner, the son of another Colombian loan contractor, and a former British government agent to Colombia completed the BHRC partnership.[23] Once formed, BHRC cast its nets north of South America searching for new opportunities for profit.

BEFORE BHRC HIRED JOHN BAILY, the company focused its attention on Mexico, Central America's northern neighbor. Mexico's sovereignty shape-shifted in the early 1820s. During the short-lived Mexican Empire that followed the end of Spanish rule, a London-based merchant advised that "any nation which lends money to another nation acquires an interest in the continuance of the latter's independence."[24] The emperor abdicated before he could learn whether bonds might be the best path to diplomatic recognition. In the spring of 1823, the interim Mexican government that replaced the emperor empowered the merchant to negotiate a loan in London. The timing was less than ideal.

1823 was a tough year for Spanish American bond sales because disgruntled bondholders challenged a Peruvian loan's legality in London's Chancery Court. Trying to get their money back by invalidating the bonds, the plaintiffs' case focused on whether the Peruvian agents who negotiated the loan could do so on behalf of a "Government" that was not recognized by the British government.[25] If the court ruled in favor of the plaintiffs, all Spanish American not-quite-sovereign bonds might be invalidated.[26]

New loan negotiations paused as investors waited to learn the outcome of the case. After several tense months, the bewigged judge punted: "What right have I, as the King's Judge, to interfere upon the subject of a contract with a country which he does not recognize?"[27] Any ruling about the legality of the loan might be interpreted as establishing a precedent of "tacit recognition."[28] The judge refused to do what the king had not.

Indeed, during the first half of the 1820s, the British government refused to officially recognize the sovereignty of any of the new Spanish American countries. Eager to join the bonanza in Spanish American debt, prominent financiers—including the venerable banking house of Baring Brothers—petitioned the British government to recognize the new nations. Concerned about the implications of Spanish American recognition for Britain's peaceful relationship with Spain, the foreign secretary refused.[29] A year later, he decided that he would send "Consular Agents" to the "provinces of Spanish America."[30] Consuls lacked formal diplomatic power. Instead of negotiating with governments, the consuls would serve the more than eighty British mercantile offices that had sprouted in Spanish American soil. The sending of an army of consuls was recognition by the British government of British subjects' substantial investments in these diplomatically ambiguous places. Like the judge's decision that the legality of loans to not-quite-sovereign countries could not be decided in British courts, the sending of consuls was a win for the bond brokers.

The market rebounded. In early 1824, this was doubly true for Mexico, where the combination of a communication lag and unstable sovereignty resulted in two separate Mexican loans competing for London investors.[31] One loan had its origins in the end of the Mexican Empire. The other had been negotiated by BHRC's agent with the rising Mexican republic. Royalists supported the first; republicans supported the second.[32] Aiming to preserve its profits, BHRC negotiated a consolidation of the loans and sought a more multifaceted approach to making money from Mexico. BHRC's agents pitched the creation of a new Mexican bank. They obtained the rights to extract minerals from abandoned silver mines.[33] They pursued the rights to build Mexican infrastructure—especially roads and canals.[34] And they sold shares in companies devoted to these ventures in London. Silver mines joined not-quite-sovereign bonds as part of a plan to market the products of British industrialization to millions of new Spanish American consumers. The circuit of bonds, stocks, mines, canals, and manufactured goods aimed to channel Aztec silver to British pockets.[35]

BHRC's pivot from bonds to stocks joined a tsunami of new publicly traded companies that flooded London in 1824 and 1825. In just these two years, British capitalists proposed more than 600 joint-stock companies with a total projected value of more than £370 million devoted to mining, gas lighting, docks, tunnels, railroads, steamships, distilleries, pearl fisheries, canals, and more.[36]

With so much money on the line, the directors of joint-stock companies generally sought incorporation by Parliament through "Private Bills" that would grant companies the right to sue and be sued. This eliminated the liability of individual partners for the company's risks and enabled the anonymous trading of thousands of shares. Designed to capitalize projects promoting the public good, the creation of joint-stock companies was intended to be limited, but in the flush days of 1824 and 1825, the number of private bills exceeded the legislature's capacity for thorough consideration.[37]

Members of Parliament—all wealthy men in this era of limited British franchise—were also investors.[38] Debating the conflict between private interests and public duties in February 1825, Alexander Baring—a partner in the banking house of Baring Brothers—argued, "any Hon. [Honorable] Member who had a direct interest in a Private Bill before them should, as a man of honour, avoid voting upon it." But he acknowledged that few abstained. He condemned: "Every body knew that the success of a private Bill depended, not on its merits, but on the interest by which it was supported or opposed."[39]

The same day that Baring decried public officeholders' self-interest, a private bill was introduced to enable the "Atlantic and Pacific Canal Company to sue and be sued in the name of their secretary."[40] The name changed as the bill recruited votes. On Saturday, March 5, 1825, the "new Atlantic and Pacific Junction Company" offered its stock for sale to the public for the first time. With a down payment of only £10 per share, investors subscribed to all 10,000 shares. The "chief attraction" in the day's financial markets, the stocks were soon selling at a premium.[41] Hardly limited to theorists like Bentham or Central American experts like Baily, canal dreams inspired the purchase of stocks by hundreds if not thousands of Britons.

Whereas Bentham's Junctiana proposal argued that a joint-stock company should be formed only *after* a reorganization and recognition of the sovereignty over the canal route, the Atlantic and Pacific Junction Company's stock sales suggested this political work was unnecessary. Its stock sold at a premium *before* the company acquired a canal contract from a recognized government. By 1825, the new republic forming in Central America claimed the right to negotiate any such contract, but it had not yet authorized any canal plan. The company sold stock anyway.

It was not alone. A newspaper reported, "no less than three Companies formed for the same purpose." The report elaborated, "an eminent South American merchant and a loan contractor expect every day a grant from the Government of Guatimala for the exclusive privilege." They were not the only competitors: "In the United States the project is also in contemplation." Even if the Guatemalan government made an "exclusive" grant to one of these British or US companies, Humboldt had suggested other potential routes. "A similar plan," the newspaper confirmed, "is under consideration of the Government of Mexico."[42] Reports circulated that "the illustrious Humboldt" had personally entered the race as "President" of a French company that "proposes to cut a ship canal by the Isthmus of Tehuantepec, in the state of Mexico."[43] Interoceanic canal competition was intense and international.

In 1825, agents representing companies from several countries pursued waterway contracts in at least three new nations. In Colombia, various contractors negotiated with Simón Bolívar's government for a canal through Panamá. In Mexico, Humboldt's association competed with BHRC and others for the rights to the Tehuantepec route. And in Central America, the competition was a free-for-all. Agents representing at least four British and two US companies, as well as French and Dutch companies, made their way to the capital deep in the interior of the isthmus, high above the oceans that lapped at both shores.

IN EARLY 1824, Baily may have been the first British agent to appear in the tropical yet temperate capital of the new country lying just to the south of Mexico. Baily's arrival preceded the drafting of the new Central American constitution.[44] An interim government composed of an executive triumvirate and a national congress ruled between the end of Mexican annexation in 1823 and the inauguration of the new constitutional government in 1825.

On September 18, 1824, before the new constitution had even been announced, Baily submitted a canal proposal to the interim government.[45] We do not know the terms of Baily's proposal. But a letter sent to BHRC's Mexican agents by lawyers for "Mr. Barclay" and some associates suggests a rough outline of what Baily's employers might have desired. The "Instructions" for a Mexican canal stipulated that the "British Capitalists" should control construction of the canal, but the new country should pay for it. Because of the lack of scientific surveys, the cost of the project was "impossible" to estimate, but the country's payment should be facilitated through its London loan. In addition to fees and commissions, the British capitalists wanted a significant share of the "net profits" of the canal for at least a quarter of the nineteenth century. Thus, for the honor of completing "so stupendous and magnificent a work" of turning American land into a global waterway, the new nation would bear the burdens of decades of debt and receive only a portion of the canal profits.[46]

Although it shared the joint-stock investment structure with Bentham's Junctiana plan, this was no utilitarian dream of providing the greatest happiness to the greatest number. Like the bonds originally masterminded by Herring and his associates, Barclay's interoceanic canal scheme was designed primarily to channel profit to London pockets.

But in Central America, Baily was too early to negotiate. He had to wait for the new government to form before it would consider his proposal. Meanwhile, he made friends. Baily's credentials as Juarros's translator gained him access to "families of influence and distinction."[47] Within a year, Lieutenant John Baily had transformed into "Mr. Juan Baily" in the government press.[48]

A British official traveling through the new nation's capital the next year described Baily as "long resident here."[49] A year seemed "long" in the frenzied atmosphere of the moment. One contemporary suggested, "more European strangers (not Spaniards) visited Guatemala in 1825, than had been there from the conquest of Mexico."[50] John Baily may have been the first to arrive, but before long, he was surrounded by competitors.

A PARTNER IN THE "HOUSE OF ANGAS AND CO." based in the northern English city of Newcastle, R. J. Andrew joined the throngs.[51] Longtime traders with the colonists of British Honduras, Angas and Company supported antislavery and evangelical causes. The Angas and Barclay families mingled in partnerships, but in Guatemala, Andrew was exclusively the agent of George Fife Angas.[52]

In April 1823, Angas's thoughts drifted to the American tropics, pondering "the approaching crisis of opening a regular communication between the Atlantic and Pacific Oceans." He wrote a letter arguing, "there is not on the globe a point which may involve more consequences to British commerce than what nation is to have control of the Isthmus of Darien, or rather, perhaps the Channel between the seas through the Mosquito Land and Lake Nicaragua, &c., to the Pacific." Concerned by the political challenges of Colombian-controlled Darien (now Panamá), Angas believed that the British government needed to negotiate control over the Nicaragua route with several parties: the Miskitú king, "old Spain," and the new "Government of Guatemala." This diplomatic work ought to precede the private work of "raising a Company of British Merchants who would undertake the measure of opening out the communication." He believed the English possessed the "capital and ability" to construct the canal, especially "upon the principle of shareholders."[53] Angas's canal dream—similar to Bentham's Junctiana plan—downplayed the engineering challenges and hinged private profits for thousands of investors on government negotiations with multiple polities.

By 1825, Angas's dream simplified. No longer convinced he needed Miskitú, Spanish, or British participation, Angas sent Andrew to obtain a canal contract directly and exclusively from the government in Guatemala City. In May 1825, Andrew and his Scottish partner James Wilson travelled "to Guatemala on the business of their house." The two men spent four months in the new nation's capital.[54] Wilson knew almost nothing about the geography. Six weeks into his stay in Guatemala City, he learned the names of the bodies of water that would form the proposed waterway. He harrumphed in his diary, "the maps intended to delineate the interior of the country are merely guess work."[55]

Andrew and Wilson's lack of knowledge about the route would not hinder their contract negotiations. Andrew "consulted the authorities there with regard to the scheme, and found there was a willingness on their part to grant the necessary concessions."[56] But unbeknownst to Andrew and Wilson, back in Newcastle, the tide had turned.

By the time his agents arrived in Guatemala City, Angas had already decided against investing in the canal. The future founder of South Australia confided to his diary in early 1825, "I recommended a cut into the Pacific through Lake Nicaragua, but I cannot see my way clear to attend to such a work."[57] As his vision for an interoceanic waterway receded, Angas could not stop the mission of his agents. Suffering from the same communication lag that contributed to the conflicting Mexican loans, Andrew pursued a deal that would be dead on arrival.[58]

MAYBE BAILY SENSED that Andrew's offer was inconsequential. Despite the arrival of Andrew and other agents, Baily's confidence grew. In early June of 1825, Baily told a visiting British government agent "that there was every probability" that his employers "would get the privilege of opening a water communication between the two seas at the lake of Nicaragua."[59] He had a $7 million reason for this confidence. At the end of 1824, before the first Central American presidential election, the country's interim government had "sanctioned the loan of Messrs. Barclay and Co. for 7,142,047 dollars."[60] Worth nearly £1.5 million, the bonds would follow the Colombian model.[61] Baily immediately issued a significant advance to the new government to enable the country to send a minister to London with the goal of negotiating recognition.[62] Baily could only imagine that this advance would make his canal proposal especially appealing. Once an anxious translator, the agent's confidence about the canal overflowed.

It may even have rippled out from Guatemala City. In early April 1825, while Andrew, Wilson, Baily, and other agents awaited the formation of the new Central American government, "Advices" from Peru reached London asserting that the "Atlantic and Pacific Junction Company have concluded a contract with the Government of Guatimala, for cutting a navigable ship canal between the two oceans."[63] The rumored contract's terms echoed those that Barclay's lawyers had sent to Mexico. The Central American government had allegedly agreed to repay "the capital laid out in the work" and provide the company with "two thirds of all tolls." The newspaper also reported that the company "obtained, for a term of forty years, the exclusive right of carrying on a steam navigation in the River San Juan, and on the Lake Nicaragua."[64] It would be hard to imagine more ideal terms—shifting the cost to the country, earning the lion's share of the tolls, and securing a transit monopoly. The report sounded almost too good to be true.

And it was. The reports had more to do with desired future events in London stock markets than deals done in Guatemala City. Two days later, the rumor accomplished its goal when newspapers reported that "Shares are rather higher."[65] With such fantastic terms, one might expect British investors to recognize the rumor as a manipulation of the company's stock prices. Nevertheless, hundreds if not thousands of canal dreamers believed.

British investors owned no exclusive right to canal dreams. Across the Atlantic, other competitors representing countries and capitalists also raced to Guatemala City to secure the right to bring the Age of Revolutions to its fulfillment—a reordering of the world's oceans that would revolutionize the land and waters of the earth itself.

CHAPTER THREE

Consul Savage and Secret Agent Mann

On March 24, 1824, between the publication of Baily's book and his arrival in Guatemala City, Charles Savage visited the US State Department in Washington, DC, begging to be appointed "Consul in the new Republic of Guatimala, with a Salary for a year or two."[1] Secretary of State John Quincy Adams was annoyed. Pushing the president for a consular appointment to Guatemala hardly seemed pressing when the commercial potential and political independence of this barely known region remained uncertain. Why was Savage so wild about going to Central America, a not-yet-formed country in a notoriously hard-to-reach region that enjoyed no significant trade with the United States? Was he desperate for a government job?

If so, Savage was not alone. Office seekers flocked to Adams's office, to his residence in Washington, even to his family's home in Massachusetts. He was besieged by men in search of jobs. The aftermath of the Panic of 1819, the first nationwide economic catastrophe in US history, motivated some men to seek out stable government employment. For others, a need to cultivate overseas trade partners or desire for adventure drove them to Adams's office. But regardless of their motivation, all the men who solicited the secretary wanted to personally profit from a public post. Politicians also wanted to profit from the men they recommended. Especially in the "Era of Good Feelings," a period without organized political parties, reciprocal promises of personal and political gain were the unspoken give and take that dominated local, state, and federal government.[2]

For roughly forty years, since the ratification of the US Constitution, the federal government had controlled the United States's foreign policy. Washington needed citizens to serve in a variety of capacities overseas: sailors, soldiers, special agents, diplomats, consuls, and more. For some posts, the applications poured in. Other positions required wrangling to rustle up recruits. All posts demanded allegiance to national interests, which could clash with personal interests. Sometimes the opportunities for private profit overwhelmed the responsibility to represent the government. At other times, national duty destroyed an agent's life.

Such was the case for the men who sought appointments to Central American posts. The men sent from the United States to Guatemala City interacted with the people, weather, land, plants, animals, and even microbes that made Central America one of the federal government's deadliest appointments. Whether they came to the job by begging or were begged to take it, few men stayed in office long. The physical perils often overwhelmed the potential for profit.

MARCH 24, 1824, WAS NOT THE FIRST TIME Charles Savage appeared in Adams's office. Savage's campaign for a federal post began ten months earlier when the US quartermaster general introduced the merchant to the secretary. Savage explained to Adams the geography of his life. The third son of a doctor from Barnstable in Adams's home state of Massachusetts, Savage had spent nearly a decade as a western merchant. Now, he intended "to quit" Lexington, Kentucky.[3] Although Adams did not record it in his diary and Savage probably did not mention it, the merchant was struggling. His commission business was half of an unofficial partnership with an older brother who lived in St. Louis, Missouri. A victim of the "great hard times" of the early 1820s, the brothers corresponded regularly about the challenges of obtaining money and goods.[4] In 1822, the older brother recommended that Charles take a trip to Washington to acquire the rights to extract lead from Sauk and Meskwaki lands along the northern Mississippi River.[5] Sometime during Charles's eastward journey his goal transformed from gaining title to an Indigenous lead mine to securing a government post that might prove a commercial gold mine.

Savage wanted "to quit" Kentucky, but he was uncertain where he would move next. Initially he "intended to apply for the Consulate of Cadiz," but when he learned this post was unavailable, he told Adams he would "apply for something else."[6] "He would be glad to have that of Liverpool, or that of Havre," chuckled Adams in his diary after another visit from Savage nearly two months later.[7] The consulates in England and France were among the most coveted posts in the world, and they were not vacant. Even if one was available, Adams would advise the president, James Monroe, to award the lucrative office to a more politically valuable man. A sixty-five-year-old revolutionary war veteran from Virginia, Monroe understood the power to be derived from conveying coveted appointments.[8]

Not all consular posts paid well. The profitability of a consulate was determined by the volume of US trade in the port; this was one difference between consuls and diplomats. One diplomatic legation resided in each country's capital city. In contrast, multiple US consuls often served in any given foreign nation, each assigned to a different port, city, or region. Diplomats dealt with foreign governments; consuls facilitated the trade of US citizens abroad.

Emblematic of the financial differences between the offices, Congress allowed the president to outfit legations at a cost of up to one year of the diplomat's salary.[9] In contrast, consuls literally had to "outfit" themselves; they were provided with a description of the gold embroidered "consular uniform" so that they could pay to have one made.[10] US ministers earned a salary of up to $9,000 per year. Outside of five ports in North Africa, consuls worked for fees.[11]

In foreign posts, consuls got their hands dirty and their pockets lined dealing with legal disputes, authenticating documents, and defending the rights of US citizens. In most ports, consuls supplemented these meager fees by operating their own commercial businesses. Such private enterprise by public officeholders was not seen as corrupt; it was required.

Consuls learned on the job. They were provided with printed "Consular Instructions," which offered some obvious recommendations like "not to fatigue the government in which you reside" and communicate "in the most temperate and friendly terms." With no requirement for good handwriting, foreign languages, bookkeeping abilities, legal training, or experience abroad, consuls were typically qualified only on the basis of their patronage.[12]

Much closer to the people than diplomats, most consuls proved to be invaluable eyes, ears, and pens reporting back to Washington. They were required to submit to the State Department semi-annual reports tabulating the US vessels passing through their ports. They were also instructed to relay "information of all military preparations" by their host nation, publications about "epidemical disorders," and "such political and commercial intelligence as you may think interesting to the United States." Consuls needed to be selective; the government limited postage reimbursements "to ten dollars annually."[13]

Since they cost the government almost nothing, the number of consuls grew tremendously over the nineteenth century. In 1826, nineteen men served overseas as salaried diplomats; five times that number served as unpaid consuls.[14] By the end of the century, the number of diplomats stationed overseas doubled to forty, but the number of consuls octupled to nearly 800.[15] Armed with a stamp, a flag, and some stationary, consuls were the State Department's unpaid infantry.

This army congregated in the Western Hemisphere. By 1830, a third of all consuls were assigned to Spanish America.[16] Some of the consular posts in the Americas were plum gigs with established trade networks; most were gambles.

Even the riskiest required political dealmaking. To get the necessary presidential nomination and Senate confirmation, Savage would have to start by impressing the secretary of state. One of five candidates in the race to become the next US president, Adams judged Savage by his recommenders. After appearing in person with the quartermaster general, Savage furnished a letter from Henry Clay—fellow Kentuckian, Speaker of the House, and one of Adams's presidential rivals.[17] Savage next returned with a US senator from Kentucky who supported Clay's candidacy. Harnessing the reputations of these men did nothing to help Savage's cause with Adams because they were among the secretary's political opponents. As Adams reflected in his diary, "His recommendations are his Misfortunes." When the secretary looked at Savage on his many visits, he saw only a political dolt, the stooge of his rivals, trying to wring money from a "profitable Office."[18]

When the recommendations failed, Savage's strategy, counter to the Consular Instructions, was to "fatigue" his way into office. He met with Adams at least fifteen times in pursuit of a consular post. As if that was not enough, he also sent his recommenders to pester Adams. When a senator visited Adams on March 19, 1824, he named the Pacific port of Guayaquil in Ecuador as a potential consulate for Savage; Adams "advised him rather to think of the Island of St. Bartholomew."[19] The senator did not like this suggestion of a volcanic island of ten square miles on the outskirts of the Caribbean, and parted suggesting that Adams would lose the presidential election. As this retort implied, Savage was a pawn in a bigger political fight between more powerful men.

When finally on March 24, 1824, Savage solicited the appointment to Guatemala, Adams listened. Savage suspected the post would be unprofitable in the beginning and demanded a few years of federal salary.[20] Congress prohibited the payment of consuls outside of North Africa. There could be no salary, and because there was no known trade with the region, the income from fees would be minuscule. Both the secretary and Savage recognized Guatemala as a gamble.

Savage persisted. Two days later, he left Adams with "a written application" including "several Letters of recommendation to be laid before the President."[21] It is unclear whether Adams presented the packet to Monroe before Savage's next visit. The secretary was blunt: "the President did not think such an appointment expedient." Savage would not take Monroe's supposed "no" for an answer. As Adams recalled, "Savage thought he could convince him by an Argument."[22]

Two days later, Savage returned to Adams's office armed with a letter that lambasted the United States for failing to pay "the least attention" to this promising place with "convenient and safe harbors."[23] Savage recognized the potential for "much commerce between the ports on both seas." He imagined

This 1826 engraving by Asher B. Durand enabled the mass production of a portrait of John Quincy Adams (1767–1848) originally painted by Thomas Sully in late 1824 when the sixth president still served as secretary of state. A map of a proposed canal is partially visible on the floor to the left of the chair. "John Quincy Adams, President of the United States / painted by T. Sully; eng. by A.B. Durand" (Philadelphia: W. H. Morgan, 1826), LCCN 96523718, LC-DIG-ppmsca-15717, Prints and Photographs Division, Library of Congress.

even more in the future: "It is anticipated that a canal will be formed in Guatimala, which shall unite the Pacific & Western waters thro' the Lake of Nicaragua." Expressing his canal dreams in the passive voice, Savage deemphasized the greatest possible personal payout of the post. Instead, he focused attention on competition with the "British Government." He closed his letter by offering to serve "as an agent of these States to Guatimala."[24]

Despite Savage's arguments, when the would-be consul returned to see Adams, the secretary "again dissuaded him from expecting" the nomination.[25] At the White House the next day, something—perhaps Savage's letter—convinced Monroe that Central America deserved more attention. The president decided to appoint a "special agent" who could serve as a quasi-diplomat to the as-yet-unrecognized country.[26] Focusing on the diplomatic appointment, Monroe did not immediately give Adams an answer about creating a consular post for Savage.[27] Finally, on Saturday, April 10, 1824, Monroe offered to "nominate Savage, as Consul at any Port in Guatimala."[28] The president may have been convinced by Savage's arguments, but more likely, Savage's signature got him the job. In 1819, Savage had entertained Monroe when the president had visited Louisville.[29] Hospitality in Kentucky translated to patronage in Washington. To Adams, most of Savage's recommendations might be "his Misfortunes," but his relationship with the president put him in his post.

On Monday, Adams informed Savage that "the President would nominate him as Consul at the City of Guatimala." Instead of thanking the secretary, Savage launched into a description of his plans. An exasperated Adams interrupted "telling him that his personal affairs were his own, and the Government had nothing to do with them." Adams elaborated, "The appointments of the Government were made upon public considerations, and it was for every individual to consider whether the appointment offered him would suit him or not." Chastened, Savage shrunk back, saying "he would take time to determine whether to accept the appointment or not."[30] Adams was furious. So many meetings, such political frustration, and Savage was not even certain he would accept the post. Adams could no longer chuckle; he could only stew. He confessed to his diary, "This man has worn down my Patience, till I had none left."[31] The fatiguing strategy worked, and now Savage had to decide whether he really wanted to move to a place few US citizens had ever seen and where few if any US vessels dared to dock.

It did not take him long to decide. Within twenty-four hours, Savage "consented to be nominated as Consul for the City of Guatemala and the adjoining country."[32] Things moved quickly after this point. On April 14, Monroe officially nominated "Charles Savage, of Kentucky, to be Consul at Guatimala and the adjacent places under the same allegiance." Within a week and without any recorded debate, the Senate consented to the appointment.[33] Monroe signed Savage's commission the same day.[34]

In late June of 1824, Adams sent Savage a letter stating, "I have the honor herewith of enclosing your commission, accompanied with printed Consular Instructions and a blank Consular Bond."[35] Savage's copies of these documents have not survived, but this hint of their existence tells us much about Savage's assignment. First, the commission documented that Savage was officially appointed a consul; he had the paper to prove it. Second, consular instructions were so standardized as to be printed; Adams provided no directions particular to Central America or to being posted to a not-yet-recognized nation. Third, the US government offloaded the financial risk of a consular post to the consul. Savage would have to return to the secretary a completed bond with an attached "certificate" from a district attorney confirming that moneyed men backed the mission.[36] Together these evidentiary ghosts suggest that the US government approved of an official on the ground in Guatemala but did not want to spend time or money ensuring his success.

A month after Adams sent these documents to Savage, the consul acknowledged receipt from his parents' Barnstable home. Savage informed the secretary that he would be departing "for the western country in one month and to leave New Orleans for Guatemala in October."[37] He would not be traveling alone. Some consuls moved their entire families to their posts but Savage's wife Susan, who had already moved from Maine to Kentucky, stayed with his parents in Massachusetts. Traveling west to go south, Savage collected his nephew Henry in St. Louis, recruited a few other men, and cut the Atlantic Ocean out of his voyage.

On February 22, 1825, after nearly five months of travel, Charles Savage arrived in Guatemala City. Savage had turned forty during the trip, and it had been a terrible voyage.[38] Twice he was "partially shipwrecked" off the coasts of Belize and Honduras.[39] It had taken him a month to get from the coastal port of Omoa, Honduras to the national capital in Guatemala.[40] Sickness quickly descended on all the "Gentlemen" with whom he traveled. Savage explained, "Fevers, agues, and other illness have attended them all for two months." Savage left one sick member of his team in the port of Omoa "as head of my commercial branch there." The rest of the party continued to the capital despite their infirmities. To improve his Spanish fluency, Henry took up residence "in a private genteel Spanish family where not but the Spanish language is spoken." Feverish, the young man could only communicate when "his hours of relief from illness permit."[41]

The healthy consul immediately got to work. Savage informed the provisional government—"the Supreme Executive power of the United Provinces of Central America"—of his arrival. In his response, the Secretary of State and of Foreign Relations Marcial Zebadúa welcomed Savage and expressed his government's "hopes that the bonds of friendship which it wishes may unite your nation and mine will be drawn close."[42] On February 28, 1825, Savage officially presented his credentials. Before the end of the day Secretary Zebadúa had confirmed that Savage would be recognized as consul of the United States by the government in Guatemala City. In returning Savage's commission, Zebadúa sought to assure the consul, "my government desires to draw closer the mercantile relations of this nation with yours."[43] And with these "most temperate and friendly terms," Charles Savage became the first US government agent to be recognized by the government in Guatemala City.[44]

THE HONOR WAS NOT SUPPOSED to be Savage's. Before he agreed to the consul's appointment, President Monroe proposed nominating Thomas N. Mann of North Carolina to represent the United States as a "special agent" in Guatemala City.[45] Like Savage, Mann did not initially seek an appointment to Central America. In 1823, his powerful recommenders asked for Mann to be appointed to a diplomatic post in "the South of Europe"—some suggested France, others Portugal. The recommenders soon expanded their search "to South America or some Southern Court." The letters described Mann as a "young man of great promise" and "great moral worth" who "is surpassed by few, if any, of his age, in talents and acquirements." Mann's potential, the recommenders explained, required a change in geography. He had been forced to abandon a promising law career and his seat in the state legislature because of a "pulmonary complaint." "His object, I am persuaded," assured a letter writer, "is not emolument from the appointment—he asks but to get in some climate calculated to ameliorate his health."[46] The profit Mann sought from office holding was physical, not financial.

Although Mann had not specifically sought the Guatemalan post, Monroe decided he was the man for the job. On April 21, 1824, Adams explained to Mann that Monroe had "determined to employ an informal agent to view the Country situated in South America between the Republic of Colombia, Mexico, and Peru, which appears to have established the separate government of Guatemala." The secretary offered Mann the job of basically serving as a spy. This became clearer as Adams continued, "The object will principally be the collection and transmission of information relating to the State and prospects of the Country." For this work, Adams offered Mann a salary of "three thousand dollars a year." Adams cautioned, "It is desirable that this agency which is of a confidential character, may for the present remain unknown, and that you will keep it undisclosed."[47] His Guatemalan mission, if he chose to accept it, would transform the wealthy but wheezy young lawyer, two-term state legislator, landowner, and enslaver into secret agent Mann.[48]

Within a month, Mann traveled to Washington. He met with the president and "made many enquiries, concerning the character of his agency; the objects to which it would be devoted, and its probable duration." Afterward, he met with Adams to discuss logistics. When would he leave? How would he get to Central America? And, most irksome to Adams, what property could he bring? In his diary, Adams recalled, "He spoke of his baggage and library, as being desirous of taking them with him." Considering such requests more broadly, Adams continued, "These private economics of our Public Ministers and Agents, are among the most disagreeable appendages to my public duties."[49] The frugal Yankee secretary wanted to separate private costs from public posts, especially for a man earning a considerable government salary. But the agent wanted his library, and the president wanted Agent Mann.

Eager for Mann's acceptance, Adams informally explained the "principal objects" of the mission: "the first of them was to obtain and transmit information, respecting the Country to which he was going—A new central South-American, and as it would seem confederated Republic—Situated at and including the Isthmus of Panama, a position of the highest Geographical importance." With this statement Adams conveyed three significant pieces of information. First, the form of government of the new country mattered; the United States welcomed another "confederated Republic." Second, Adams did not know the geography. Panamá was part of Colombia; it was not included in the new nation. And third, the region's "position of highest Geographical importance" implied its potential for an interoceanic canal.

But the country might have other significance. Like Savage, Adams considered the new Central American republic in terms of the United States's greatest diplomatic concern: competition with Great Britain. By acting quickly, Mann could provide the United States with an isthmian foothold. The British already had "commercial connections and lodgments on the soil" at the nearby "Bay of Honduras and Mosquito shore."[50] But Adams had good reason to believe that the new republic might prefer alliance with the United States over any European power.

He relayed an important and generally unknown history to Mann. In early 1822, when leaders in Guatemala City approved the Mexican Empire's annexation of the region, San Salvador's leaders refused to replace Spain's monarchical empire with that of Mexico. Attempting to force the Salvadorans into submission, the imperial Mexican army invaded the small but densely populated province on the isthmus's Pacific coast. The Salvadorans fought back, but Guatemala's army joined the Mexicans' siege.[51] Near the end of 1822, the Salvadoran provincial congress tried to halt the dual invasion by passing a law threatening to unite the province "in federation with the United States of America with the condition of forming a State."[52] Although some have labeled the Salvadoran attempt at annexation a "pathetic effort," the Salvadorans were serious about becoming what one US newspaper described as "The New State."[53] In a manifesto issued in December 1822, the Salvadoran president referred to his province's statehood not as a question of "if" but of "when." He praised the United States: its federal structure, its "heroic lessons" and "virtues" worthy of "imitation," its potential protection, and its declaration of the right to pursue happiness. "People of St. Salvador," he ordered in his manifesto declaring US annexation, "prepare yourselves to be happy."[54]

To turn the president's proclamations into reality and facilitate the details of US annexation, five Salvadoran "Commissioners" secretly set off for Washington in early 1823.[55] General Manuel José Arce, who had commanded the Salvadoran troops against the dual invaders, led the Washington-bound delegation. Death, disease, and delay defined the mission. One of the men died en route. After arriving in Boston, the surviving four Salvadorans' travel abruptly halted in Philadelphia where Arce sought medical care for a relapse of a disease that he had contracted during an earlier fight for Salvadoran self-rule.[56]

Arce's delay proved convenient. While the commissioners crept toward the US capital, the short-lived Mexican Empire tottered and fell. Central America declared itself a separate country. US newspapers reported that the Guatemalans "will make common cause with the republic of St. Salvador."[57] Future leaders of a new regional republic, the delegation no longer desired US annexation. The commissioners wanted to return to the isthmus to ensure the establishment of a republican structure for their new country's government.

Before they left the United States, they sought a meeting with Secretary Adams, but he had not yet returned to Washington from his summer in Massachusetts.[58] Unable to meet in person, the Salvadorans expressed in writing their "sentiments of friendship" and their "sympathy in Principles" with the US government.[59] They enclosed copies of the evidence of San Salvador's pursuit of US statehood. The Salvadorans argued that their province was the only portion of Spanish America, "which after her Independence has not humbled herself before the Throne of a Tyrant, and who alone . . . has adhered to a Sister Nation the greatest and the most admirable for its institutions in the known world."[60] The Salvadorans offered Adams evidence that US annexation might be desirable. In the months that followed the Salvadorans' mission, Adams drafted the hemispheric policy that became known as the Monroe Doctrine, which opposed European colonization but did not preclude US annexation in the Americas.[61]

While Adams drafted this fundamental foreign policy, Arce returned to Central America, where he had been selected to serve as one of three members of what became known as the Supremo Poder Ejecutivo (SPE), which would lead the new country.[62] When Adams relayed this history to Mann, including the news that "one of the deputies who came here on that occasion was now or recently had been at the head of the new Guatemalan Government," Arce had not yet sworn the oath of office to serve in the SPE. But his future colleagues had already taken steps to turn Arce's Salvadoran overtures into Central American recognition. If the newspapers were to be believed, the new nation had already appointed "a public agent or Minister to come to the United States." Before this agent started negotiating, Adams wanted to know more about the new republic because "our information concerning it was scanty."[63]

When Mann inquired about logistical instructions, Adams referred him to the secretary of the navy to determine which ship would bring the special agent to Central America.[64] His plans in motion, Mann sent his official acceptance of the post. "After mature consideration of the duties and responsibility I am about to enter upon and undertake," wrote the twenty-six-year-old, "I have resolved to accept this agency."[65]

Within a week, however, Mann returned to Adams's office to renegotiate his compensation. He was accompanied by a powerful senator from North Carolina. The recommenders again proved the agent's misfortune. With one of Adams's opponents as his patron, Mann would not find a sympathetic secretary of state. Advocating for his proxy, the senator noted a disparity between the secretary's $3,000 offer and one made by the president of "at least 3000. and from that up to 4500. dollars, with contingencies generally." Moreover, the senator explained, "Mr. Mann would take a Servant, and wished to take a Secretary—and seemed to enquire if these and their travelling expenses would be allowed as contingencies." "I said no," recalled the frustrated Adams, who had already lamented Mann's negotiations of private needs imposing on public expenditures.[66] In terms of Mann's request for a secretary, Adams had the law on his side. Only ministers plenipotentiary, the United States's highest ranking overseas diplomatic officers, were granted a salaried secretary. The North Carolinian's servant, perhaps an enslaved person, was another story. Not yet the firebrand of antislavery he would become later in life, Adams had enough trouble paying to ship Mann's library; Mann's human property should be his own problem.

And it would be a problem. Whether his reasons stemmed from concern for money or morals, Adams's stance regarding Mann's enslaved servant was prescient. The news had not yet arrived in the United States, but less than one month earlier, the government in Central America issued a decree abolishing slavery, compensating slave owners, and outlawing the slave trade. The law also prohibited foreigners from bringing enslaved people to the country; enslaved people who entered Central America would be liberated.[67] Mann would likely be denied entry into Central America when his traffic in human property was discovered.

The US government would not directly pay to send the spy's secretary and servant to Central America. But Adams would consider increasing Mann's salary, which would have the effect of paying for both. Adams promised, "I would speak to the President, who would I had no doubt adopt the allowance."[68] No free consul, Special Agent Mann would be expensive.

Or at least he would be, if he ever departed for Central America. Without getting very far, the agent spent a lot of time thinking about his trip. In June, Adams arranged for Mann to travel to Central America on the U.S.S. *Hornet* out of Norfolk, Virginia. Mann "set out, without hesitation," from his home in North Carolina.[69] On July 4, 1824, Mann wrote to Adams from Norfolk to describe his "serious anxiety" about the journey, especially about the route between the Caribbean and Guatemala City. After reviewing "jejune and imperfect accounts" of how to get to Guatemala, Mann discussed the journey with the captain of the *Hornet* and his experienced crew. He reported two alternative routes to Adams. If the ship landed at the head of the "unsafe" Bay of Honduras, it would be approximately 180 miles, he estimated, from the coast to the capital. "The country is rude and mountainous; the road scarcely worthy the title, and, being the track of some merchandize, is much infested by bandits, as well as without the accommodation of inns," relayed Mann. Rough terrain, nowhere to sleep, and thieves; all sounded terrible. Worse yet, he would have to ride on a mule. "Travelling by a peasant on a mule might be safe," but Mann suspected that a "stranger of tolerable aspect is almost certain to invite the fatal attention of these licentious mountaineers." Fearing for his life, Mann rejected this route.[70]

Instead, he advocated for a second option, a longer but presumably safer route from Vera Cruz in Mexico. The land voyage, Mann estimated, would be 330 miles "but under circumstances wholly variant from that other route.

Here will be presented a good road, and a travelled one; furnished with inns and which, in fact, is a great post road from Guatimala to the sea-coast." Mann glowed, "an escort might be procured, if thought advisable." He imagined Guatemala would send one "without hesitation." To take this more "circuitous" route, Mann requested six months advance on his salary and reimbursement of travel expenses. And he informed the secretary that he was traveling with his "body servant . . . as a part of my family, a young gentleman." Perhaps because he had heard the news from Central America of that nation's abolition of slavery, Mann's servant would not be enslaved, and he would do the work of two men. He explained to Adams, "He is a relation, whose kindness in my present situation, I know not to dispense with; moreover, his assistance as a private secretary is invaluable." With his servant/secretary, library, and now an escort, Mann could hardly be planning a secret mission; despite the confidentiality demanded in the letter offering him the job, he was turning himself into a minister in all but title.[71]

And perhaps this made sense; he was being treated like an official diplomat. On July 17, 1824, Adams composed lengthy official diplomatic instructions to the special agent. He began by explaining that the instructions were delayed because the secretary was waiting for the impending arrival of Central America's diplomat, another Salvadoran military and political leader named Antonio José Cañas. Adams was "constantly expecting to see him," but he had not arrived. And now, as Adams explained to Mann, "the vessel in which you are to embark cannot without inconvenience be detained." Adams would have to write the instructions "without the advantage of a previous interview with Mr. Cañaz [*sic*]."

Mann's official instructions launched into a history of the United States and "the Republic of Guatimala." Adams cited "circumstances in the history of its origin which give it a claim to the interest and regard of the United States perhaps even superior to that which they have felt in any other of the Southern Republics." Adams relayed the story of the rise and fall of the Mexican Empire, the foundation of a separate republic in Central America, and the Salvadoran annexation mission. Adams explained that the Salvadorans "declared that the people, their constituents, were animated with the sincerest sentiments of attachment to the Government of the United States." Laying the groundwork for a future international alliance, Adams recalled that the Salvadorans explained "that there was a great similitude of principles between them and the people of this Union." Even though the mission for annexation was ultimately abandoned, Adams assured "it cannot be doubted that the proposal itself, and the spirit in which it was made, were adapted to inspire the warmest sentiments of regard and attachment on our part towards a people who thus confided in our honor and justice." Not prone to exaggeration, Adams concluded that the Central Americans "thus gain in the face of all mankind the most glorious of testimonials to the wisdom of our Institutions and to their sense of their tendency to promote the happiness of those who live under them."

From history, Adams turned to "Other considerations." Here he explained the practical value of Central America to Washington: its geography. He instructed, "Situated precisely at the Isthmus which forms the connexion between the two American Continents, and at the seat of commerce carried on by the bay of Honduras, the Mosquito Shore; between the Gulph of Mexico and the Southern Ocean [Pacific], here drawn in their closest proximity to each other." Although US trade with Central America was basically nonexistent, this narrow land between important waters promised to grow in commercial and political significance. He did not mention a canal, but he did not need to. The narrowness of the land implied the value. The secretary directed the spy to investigate the "geographical boundaries of the Republic," its relationship with its neighbors and with European nations, "the present state of its government," its constitutional prospects, and "its future capabilities of a commerce mutually advantageous with the United States."

Finalizing the negotiations over Mann's salary, Adams instructed, "Your compensation will be at the rate of three thousand five hundred dollars a year." The salary would begin when Mann left home and end three months after Washington recalled him. Adams underlined, "The expenses of your voyage out and home and <u>necessary</u> travelling expenses may be added as the only admissible extra charges."[72]

So much time spent planning, instructing, and arguing over money, and Mann never got paid. Thomas N. Mann died the same day that Adams penned his instructions. He never left Norfolk.

On July 21, 1824, Adams's chief clerk wrote to one of Mann's would-be companions on the *Hornet* expressing the secretary's "utmost concern" and surprise at Mann's death. As the clerk explained, Mann's last two letters did not let on that he was dying: "from neither of which could this disturbing event have been anticipated by any information or indication whatever that the fatal malady of which he died had gained ground upon him."[73] But Adams had missed a clue. In pleading for the necessity of his servant/secretary, Mann described in code befitting a would-be spy the relation's "kindness in my present situation."[74] Mann's tuberculosis, it turned out, was beyond the help of kindness or climate.

Expressing Adams's "full and sincere sympathy" to Mann's relatives, the clerk asked that Mann's official instructions be returned to the State Department.[75] The State Department would have to start all over again in getting a diplomat to Guatemala City, but at least the instructions were drafted. And, as Adams knew all too well, the United States would soon have a man on the ground in Central America; he was an unpaid consul who was not opposed to riding on mules.

BUT CHARLES SAVAGE was not yet in Guatemala City when Mann died, and when he arrived, he would not stay for long. The Central American government recognized Savage on March 1, 1825. Three weeks later, he requested permission to take "a tour to Realejo, Leon, and Managua," the principal cities of the canal route. Citing his "spirit of inquiry," Savage made the case for his "personal investigation." With apologies "for thus troubling the Executive," the consul planned to evaluate the nation's most valuable resource: its potential for an interoceanic canal.[76]

He was not the only man in Guatemala with a canal on his mind. As he prepared for his trip, Savage wrote a lengthy letter to his mother. Writing on April 2, 1825, he told her that he planned to leave the "day after tomorrow to proceed on a journey to the Southern extremity of this Republic." He provided her with a rough itinerary of his 1,000-mile trip. By a combination of land and sea, he would visit all the cities near "the great Lakes of Leon & Nicaragua. I shall proceed from here to the Pacific." Presuming Guatemalan sovereignty, he did not mention traversing the San Juan River to negotiate with the Miskitú and Rama about waterway rights in their territory.

Following this announcement of his itinerary, he wrote several pages in very small hand describing the wardrobes of "Indians and mixed race" residents of Guatemala City, complaining about the food, providing detailed recipes for hot chocolate and bread, and assuring that this diet led to nearly universal toothlessness. After composing six dense pages, Savage stopped for the evening.

Continuing the next night, his pen turned from culture to capitalism: "I have just returned from dining with Mr. Hayne an English gent. who is endeavoring to contract with Gov^{t} for a loan to make a canal thru the state—and is competitor of Mr. Baily who will probably get the loan." As this suggests, two agents of private British companies were already on the ground in Guatemala City lobbying for a canal contract. Other attendees included an unnamed traveling Frenchman, a Central American legislator, and a New Orleanian merchant named Mr. Miller. To Savage, the dinner party was a multilingual farce: "The

Frenchmen could not speak English. The MP could not speak French or English. I could not speak Spanish or French but we got along tolerably well through our interpreters—and ate our soup of turkey just as well as tho' we could converse as freely as we could wish." To Savage, the dinner was hilarious. To the other men, this was no laughing matter; it was a sizing up of the competition.

As Savage explained to his mother, Mr. Miller had become the consul's friend and housemate. "Conversant in French and Spanish," a former deputy customs collector, and a "very sensible man" who was only three years older than the consul, Miller was a valuable companion. He was also good fun; Savage described him as "esteemed in N. Orleans as a man of character and worth, but, as crass as I am at any time." The consul's trip to the canal route had become Miller's trip as well. Already invested in trade in Guatemala, Miller saw opportunity in Nicaragua, and he hitched his mule to his nation's agent.

Unfortunately for us, and for Savage's mother, the waxy red seal on the consul's letter resulted in a large tear in the text. From the words left intact, we can just barely make out Savage's pride in enjoying the confidence of two nations and his regret that the lack of trade stifled his commission business. As this suggests, only one half of Savage's double duty as a consul was successful; he was a trusted government agent but an unsuccessful businessman. But even in his public role, Savage was not particularly adept. No spy or master of subtlety, he failed to see the information he acquired at the dinner party as worthy of communicating to the State Department. Reported only as a humorous anecdote in a letter to his mother, the consul had nonetheless identified several competitors for the most important (and yet unspoken) object of Mann's mission: gathering information about a potential canal.[77]

On April 5, 1825, Zebadúa responded to Savage's request to travel to Nicaragua. The minister reported, "The Supreme Executive power constant in its desire to extend and draw closer the relations of this nation with yours has ordered me to make known to you that you may at any time commence the voyage or journey which you propose." Moreover, the central government would send notices to provincial leaders alerting them to treat the consul "with the consideration due to your character." Zebadúa recognized the journey as "advantageous to both Republics."[78]

Meanwhile, another man born in Massachusetts—this time representing private investors—beat Savage to Nicaragua. Not every canal dreamer raced to the mountainous Central American capital seeking permission to explore the river, lake, and Pacific coast. Some set their sights more directly on the wet lowlands of the canal route, putting the practicalities of constructing a waterway ahead of politics.

CHAPTER FOUR

The Rain

Warmed by the sun shining on the tropical waves of the Caribbean Sea, a tiny water molecule, imperceptible to the human eye, vaporized. As a gas, it rose until the atmosphere's cooler air condensed it back into liquid. Around a dust particle, the molecule and its neighbors formed a cloud.[1] Tropical trade winds pushed the cloud west until it hovered over one of the wettest lands on earth.[2]

Here high above the massive Lake Nicaragua watershed, the cloud's water molecules bumped into each other, forming droplets. Accompanied by thunder and lightning, the heaviest fell to the earth as a tropical rainstorm. But the lighter moisture lingered, slowly succumbing to gravity in prolonged *temporales*, a persistent rain that soaks this region from May through October.[3] Like a river in the sky, this slow and steady precipitation drenched the soil, filled the lake, and gushed down the *desaguadero*, or drain, an old Spanish term for the San Juan River.[4] Rushing over the river's rapids and avoiding evaporation or absorption, the well-traveled water molecule reentered the salty Caribbean Sea, its cycle completed.

Upward of 27 trillion gallons of water fill the Lake Nicaragua and San Juan River watershed, which stretches over 16,000 square miles, an area bigger than Switzerland. On just the lake, an average of more than 100,000 gallons of rain falls each second.[5] But not all seconds are equal.

Predictably seasonal and yet full of variable microclimates, the water cycle shaped life along the would-be canal route. The Rama-speaking inhabitants of some of the wettest of these lands migrated with the rain.[6] The Spanish descendants, who lived along the western and northern reaches of the watershed, built Granada's sidewalks two feet higher than the seasonally flooded streets.[7] Even Nicaraguans' politics followed the rhythm of the rains. In 1824, a bloody civil war ebbed and flowed, resolving just before the rainy season of 1825.

Canal dreamers, who wanted to turn this watershed into a waterway, might cut through the land or circumvent the rapids, but they could not change the cycle's timing. Too much rain in the summer, too little in the winter, and furious winds in between turned the task of surveying the route into a race against the rain. Such was the case for the only surveyor to reach the canal route in the 1820s. Hired by an international network of canal dreamers, he tried to chart a means to connect the oceans, but the water falling from the skies proved a formidable foe.

IN FEBRUARY 1823, ABOUT A MILE from the shore of Lake Nicaragua, Manuel Antonio de la Cerda dreamed of turning Granada into the center of world trade. Briefly in the sixteenth century, gold and silver from the Pacific-facing Spanish colonies traveled to the Atlantic treasure fleet via the proposed canal route. Predatory pirates and a seventeenth-century earthquake ended this transit.[8] Ever since, Granada's leaders had been vying for its reestablishment, but their efforts were stymied by colonial elites in the capital of Guatemala City and nearby rivals in the city of León.[9] With independence from Spain and annexation by the Mexican Empire, de la Cerda sought to convince his new government to reopen the transit by building a waterway.

A lawyer embroiled in the Age of Revolutions' conflicts, de la Cerda spent much of the previous decade imprisoned in Guatemala and Spain where he worked as a shoemaker. As the first *alcalde,* or mayor, to lead the largest city on the lake after the end of Spanish control, de la Cerda instructed an artist to depict his *Plano Ídeal.* More of a sketch than a study, the simple map reflected neither an accurate depiction of the river's seasonally shifting course nor a clear scale of the canal to be cut. It entirely ignored the Rama people, who lived along the river, and assumed Miskitú territory ended north of the river's mouth. The alcalde sent a copy of his idealized plan to Nicaragua's first representative in the Mexican Congress.[10]

The choice to send the map to Mexico reflected de la Cerda's conservative politics. He believed in authoritarian rule, especially by American-born elites of Spanish descent. Many did not agree. As he proposed his *Plano Ídeal,* a rebellion against Mexican annexation overtook Granada. His office was seized by an independence fighter whose mixed African and Spanish heritage reflected the racial egalitarianism embodied in the rebels' republicanism.[11] By sending his canal plan to Mexico City, the deposed alcalde cobbled together canal dreams and political resurgence. He sought to channel trade to his city, revert power to the colonial elite, and reassert his authority.

But by the time the *Plano Ídeal* reached Mexico, the empire had been dissolved. De la Cerda fled north to the city of Managua, which overlooked a smaller lake that connected to Lake Nicaragua by a vast stretch of wetlands. By July 1823, when de la Cerda realized that Mexico's new republican leadership would not respond to his request, months of rain had turned the swamps between the lakes into a navigable river. Despite his dislike for republicanism, he sent his plan to the new Central American government convening in

Guatemala City. Preoccupied with forming a government, the congress thanked the Nicaraguan for his "patriotism" but passed on immediately pursuing the canal project.[12]

When de la Cerda received this news, in the dry months late in 1823, he had moved again, this time to his rural *hacienda*, or plantation, situated between the cities of León and Granada.[13] Both the monarchists in León and the republicans in Granada wanted to rule the roughly defined province of Nicaragua, which encompassed the western land between the Pacific Ocean and the lakes and sometimes included parts of what is now Costa Rica to the south but never controlled the Indigenous population of the east. Neither city wanted to yield power to the new government forming in Guatemala City.

Under the bright sun of January 1824, Nicaraguan troops fought each other. Soon they also fought Guatemalan and Salvadoran soldiers sent to force Nicaragua's participation in the still-forming Central American nation. A powder keg of ideological, local, and regional rivals, Nicaragua's western rim of formerly Spanish colonial settlements exploded in a multisided war. Even the rains of 1824 could not cool the conflict.

MEANWHILE, THE MAP DE LA CERDA sent to Mexico found new life. The Mexican politician showed the *Plano Ídeal* to his brother and a friend who had represented Nicaragua in the Mexican Empire's legislature.[14] All three had ties to elite monarchists in León who, they imagined, would rule the province and authorize a canal. No longer able to depend on Mexican government financing, they pitched de la Cerda's dream to agents of foreign capitalists.[15]

In the spring of 1824, some of the Mexicans met with two such men.[16] Described as the "most elegant man in Boston," the first was George Lyman, a US merchant.[17] Like John Baily and Gregor MacGregor, the second was a footloose British veteran named Col. Charles Bourke.[18] The dandy and the mercenary agreed to recruit US investors to finance de la Cerda's canal.[19] The Mexican politicians provided extracts from old topographical documents, but were waiting on "the map." Promising to send a copy of the *Plano Ídeal* "by hand, or by mail, as soon as it reaches us," the politicians assured they had "officially reported your proposal to the Nicaraguan Government." Touting their connections with Mexican imperialists and leaders in Nicaragua, they promised assistance "to enable you to inspect the river and lake with safety, & to obtain land concessions on the banks of the river, & such privileges for steam navigation, construction & importation of any kind of machinery as you may desire to ask."

They devised a plan as idealistic as de la Cerda's map. While the men in Mexico would acquire the rights "within three months, more or less" from their friends in León's government, Bourke and Lyman would travel to convince their "partners in the United States" of the "great advantages" of the project. The group would reconvene in Mexico City in late June 1824. From the Mexican capital, most of them would travel together to Nicaragua "to inspect with safety those regions, and to finish your contract with the parties of the Province."[20] The entourage would arrive at the mouth of the San Juan River in the early fall, as a season's worth of rain swelled its flow. This would ease their ascent and hide the river's sedimentation. Such good timing would also enable the men to explore the western coast of Nicaragua as the rains diminished. They could return down the San Juan before the springtime when its driest bends became impassable. Following this schedule, the foreign investors would never learn the reality of the rain.

THE PLAN FELL BEHIND IMMEDIATELY. Lyman and Bourke arrived in New York around the time they were supposed to return to Mexico. They found merchants awed by the profitability of the recently opened Erie Canal and especially primed to invest in an interoceanic waterway.[21] But in the early summer of 1824, after the United States had extended diplomatic recognition to Mexico but before it recognized an independent Central America, a Mexican route seemed more promising. As Bourke later recounted, "the attention of the principal Merchants of the States was fixed on the Isthmus of Tehuantepec."[22]

Nonetheless, the Boston dandy and British mercenary found three New York City merchants interested in Nicaragua. Two were brothers, John and Curtis Bolton, who had moved to New York City from Savannah, Georgia.[23] They were joined by a New England Quaker captain turned New York City merchant, banker, and insurance company director.[24] The three merchants bought a two-masted vessel to send to Central America. They probably got a good deal on the *Mary Livingston* because it had recently been repaired from having "unshipped" its rudder on a Mexican sandbar.[25] To finance the canal mission, the merchants filled the hold with goods to sell in Central America.

They also hired a crew, including mariners to work the ship and a captain to command the vessel. As their agent, the merchants chose Robert Clossey, a multilingual translator.[26] Drawing on his Spanish skills, Clossey would oversee the sale of the cargo, represent the New York investors in negotiations, and supervise the most valuable member of the mission's team, Edmund Blunt.[27]

Born in Newburyport, Massachusetts, Blunt was a twenty-five-year-old hydrography prodigy. Reared in the family business of publishing nautical guides, a teenage Blunt charted New York City's booming harbor.[28] Eager to survey the world's first interoceanic canal and leave behind publishing office work, Blunt agreed to join the mission for "Sixty Dollars per Month" along with "reasonable personal expenses" and his "passage and stores" to and from Central America.[29] Per the orders of the merchants, Clossey would not reveal the specific details of the surveyor's instructions until they reached Mexico.[30] To Blunt's later regret, the partners utilized neither his surveying experience nor his scientific training in their plan for the mission.[31] Instead, they treated Blunt solely as an instrument for the collection of proprietary data on one of the world's most valuable and uncharted places.

DEPARTING NEW YORK CITY in early September 1824, three months behind schedule, the *Mary Livingston* traveled south with its motley canal crew: the captain, the dandy, the mercenary, the translator, and the surveyor. The ship set sail for Mexico. Headwinds, abundant rain, and pirates threatened the voyage in its first three weeks. On October 11, 1824, Blunt sighted the volcano Orizaba "rising majestically above the clouds in the west," and that evening, the brig laid anchor in the Gulf of Mexico outside the harbor of Alvarado, Mexico. While they waited for the wind and water to enable entry into the port, the men gambled. Blunt "very foolishly" lost his beaver hat. He resolved "never to bet again"—an ironic vow for a man sent to assess a gamble of global proportions.[32]

The next afternoon, as the tides turned, the *Mary Livingston* attempted to enter the harbor, but a sandbar threatened the ship. Although the brig passed the bar, it tipped so steeply that Blunt's boat, attached to its side, "swamped" with water. To save the brig, the crew released the surveying vessel, which drifted out to sea. The frustrated surveyor realized his relatively good fortune when another ship got stuck on the bar and "went to pieces."[33]

Upon their arrival in Alvarado, Blunt accepted his instructions from Clossey. The narrow avoidance of a shipwreck barely tempered his frustrations with the instructions' series of conditional statements that he described as "unintelligible language."[34] He had to determine *if* the San Juan River was navigable or could be made navigable for large ships or steamboats. *If* this proved positive, *then* he was to make his way across Lake Nicaragua. *If* the lake was sufficiently deep, *then* he was to search for an existing waterway to the Pacific Ocean. *If* he could not find one, *then* he was to look for and document through "scientific measures" a level, short path for engineering a canal or a road between the lake and "a tolerable port on the Pacific side."[35] *If* all of this proved feasible, *then* he would return to the United States and report to his employers. *If* they agreed with his assessment, *then* he would return to Nicaragua to take more precise measurements and conduct a full survey. But none of this could happen without an earlier conditional statement proving true. Clossey was to provide the instructions only *if* he thought the mission would proceed past Alvarado. By giving the instructions to Blunt, Clossey clearly had faith in the mission, but getting beyond Alvarado was far from a certainty.

At first, Blunt was confined to the port. He wanted to explore more of Mexico, but Clossey interpreted the instructions as not permitting the surveyor to do anything beyond his scientific task. Blunt described Alvarado as a "most miserable place."[36] It was "unhealthy," too. Within a week, Clossey fell ill. Having fatally "fatigued himself," he would never leave Alvarado.[37] After a Catholic funeral held on October 26, 1824, Blunt reported Clossey's death to his New York employers and noted that the translator was the first US citizen buried in the churchyard.[38]

With Clossey dead, the surveyor seized the opportunity to get out of Alvarado. Learning that the veteran Bourke was ill in Mexico City, Blunt and the stylish Lyman headed toward the capital with hopes of saving the mission. With an eye for "Spanish romances," Blunt appreciated the "very fine" music of "two Spaniards with guitars."[39] He enjoyed the "very sociable" company of "some Spanish ladies."[40] At a ball celebrating the new republican Mexican constitution, he praised the "Spanish contra-dances."[41] As he romanticized the region's Spanish past, Blunt perceived a promising Mexican future, noting that "the country is improving under the new order of things."[42]

Although Blunt aimed to see the capital of the new nation, the trip's continued troubles prevented him from doing so. Delayed in selling the ship's cargo, Lyman ran "out of funds." To get the documents promised by the Mexican politicians and move on with their mission, Lyman borrowed Blunt's horse to get to the capital.[43] The surveyor was stranded two hundred miles short of Mexico City.

In early December 1824, nearly three months after arriving in Mexico and six months behind the initial plan's schedule, Lyman hastily wrote Blunt from Mexico City, "I take with me all documents that are necessary to insure our good success and happy reception."[44] The crew would divide. Bourke would trek overland to Guatemala City to pursue a canal contract; he traveled without the Mexicans who did not fulfill their promise to join the mission.[45] Lyman, Blunt, and a British merchant with Spanish language skills named

Robert H. Parker would head to the San Juan River on the brig. Lyman encouraged Blunt, "be ready!"[46]

Stuck in Alvarado weeks later, Blunt penned a Christmas Eve letter to his employers expressing his concern that the delay in Mexico had been so long that "the time has nearly expired which we calculated to be absent." He complained, "We are now only waiting for the wind to leave this place."[47] When they finally lifted anchor three days later, the *Mary Livingston*—a magnet for sand—struck the bar "several times."[48] Fortunately, it survived, and the team continued south to find the San Juan River.

This proved harder than expected. The brig got lost and overshot its destination. They had to ask for directions. Blunt frustratingly noted in his journal: "charts incorrect."[49] Finally, on January 11, 1825, the *Mary Livingston* dropped anchor at the mouth, or *boca*, of the San Juan River, the anticipated Caribbean terminus of the canal route. Reminding the surveyor of Cape Cod's Provincetown, the bay at the boca seemed wide enough "to contain the largest navy in the world."[50] At the old Spanish coastal fort, six soldiers wearing "ludicrous" uniforms "were very much alarmed at the appearance of the Brig, and fired several shots at us."[51] Hardly a "happy reception," their arrival was treated more like an invasion than an authorized surveying mission.[52]

AS THE *MARY LIVINGSTON* headed south, Blunt's letters about Clossey's death and the Mexican delays travelled north to New York. Upon learning that his agent was dead and yet the others continued, Curtis Bolton, the youngest of the three merchants, set out to regain control of the mission.[53]

He would need help. On Friday, January 28, 1825, he called on Secretary of State John Quincy Adams. Armed with a letter of introduction from Blunt's brother, Bolton used the surveyor's New England ties to gain Adams's attention for his "project for opening a passage, from the Atlantic to the Pacific Ocean." Determined to lead the mission, Bolton asked for "passage in a public vessel to Guatemala, and armed men to ascend the river San Juan." The secretary promised to consult the president.[54] Monroe told Adams to "examine further" into Bolton's plan.[55]

Obligingly, Adams found time in his very busy schedule to meet several more times with the would-be canal contractor.[56] Bolton accompanied a group of powerful men including Secretary of the Navy Samuel Southard to discuss the plan with Adams. They brought with them what Adams described as "a map of the Isthmus of Panama, shewing the projected communication between the two Seas."[57] Although the secretary described the map as documenting the "Isthmus of Panama," this was probably the *Plano Ídeal*. Bolton was not interested in Panamá; he was invested in Nicaragua. But reflecting the general lack of US knowledge about Central America, Adams misconstrued the isthmus's geography. In early 1825, before Congress determined the outcome of the contentious presidential election, Adams did not have time to differentiate the competing canal routes; the secretary spent his days mapping his path to the White House.

One of the few cabinet members not running for president, Southard found time to help Bolton. He arranged for the would-be canal contractor to travel on a naval vessel, which according to newspaper reports was about to depart "on a *secret* cruize [*sic*]" to the Caribbean.[58]

Far from secret, Bolton's trip to Nicaragua soon garnered coverage in the press. About a month after his departure, rumor spread that the ship "landed" Curtis Bolton at the "St. John's River" with the "purpose of surveying the line for a canal."[59] Other reports asserted Bolton had "gone out for the purpose of surveying a route for a Canal across the *Isthmus of Darien*," a contemporary term for Panamá.[60] More than mangling the geography, this scuttlebutt turned the mission's backer into its surveyor. Circulating rumors also swelled the significance of the voyage. Some suggested Bolton was "sent out by our government, it is said, at the solicitation of the government of Guatimala, which proposes to open the communication jointly with the U. States."[61] Others diminished his role, depicting him as merely an agent of "a company of New-York merchants."[62] Far from a capitalist protecting his investment, Bolton seemed a servant of higher powers.[63]

The government may have paid for Bolton's passage, but the merchant paid Blunt's salary. And as the surveyor's letters suggested, the mission's delays augmented this bill. The merchant was determined to redirect the mission's course and rein in costs. But as Bolton would soon see, the mission had spiraled out of anyone's control.[64]

WHEN THEY DISEMBARKED from the *Mary Livingston* in the middle of the dry season in January 1825, Blunt, Lyman, and their new translator Parker sought passage up the river and across the lake on two "bongies"—shallow-draft vessels—they found at the river's mouth.[65] The small boats had been hired by a Colombian merchant; they were already full, each with a captain, crew, cargo, and Colombian. The three men divided up and squeezed aboard. There was no room for Blunt's scientific equipment or the dry goods. Delaying the brig's return to New York, they stored these things in the ship's hold, made their way to Granada to hire their own bongies, and planned to return to collect the cargo.[66]

The ascent was challenging, even for the experienced rowers. The vast watershed had been drying out for three months. Along the river, downpours from tropical storms kept the foliage lush. Long-nosed anteaters dined on the insects inside mangroves, palms, and hard wood trees. Betrunked tapirs, a large mammal sacred to the Rama and related to the rhinoceros, nibbled on leaves.[67] At its wide mouth, the river's bed was so full of small stones that the water could support only the shallowest of vessels. Fishing and hunting birds along the way, the crew and passengers dined and slept on pebble islands—evidence of seasonal sedimentation.

Further upstream where the river narrowed, water levels increased, which meant that the men rowing the heavily laden bongies up the river had to navigate several rushing rapids. When they reached the "Falls," no amount of muscle could counter the current. "The goods are landed," Blunt recorded. Walking barefoot on an unpaved footpath "covered with sharp stones," the crew carried the cargo to "the landing above." Blunt watched thirteen of these men draw each "empty canoe of about thirty feet in length" past the raging water. Blunt was not awed by the bongie men's strength and footing; he condemned the lack of improvement by the river's "inhabitants."[68]

Who were the "inhabitants"? For all his skill as a surveyor, Blunt struggled to see social nuance. Like his comments praising "Spanish" culture in a Mexico reconstructing itself as an independent republic, Blunt did not distinguish between his bongie's crew and its captain. Given their knowledge of how to navigate the river, the former may have been Rama men, perhaps forced to labor.[69] The overseeing "patrons" from Granada, in contrast, likely traced their lineage to Spain, ignoring any Indigenous heritage. Unlike the unconquered communities of the eastern Caribbean, to claim indigeneity on the Pacific coast incurred restrictions and taxes created during the conquest.[70] When Nicaraguans from the Pacific coast did identify with their Indigenous heritage, they claimed Aztec ancestry with no connection to the Miskitú, Rama, and Afro-Caribbean peoples of the Atlantic.[71] As such, they could not improve the land around the river; it was not theirs to pave. And the Rama, who were the "inhabitants" of the river, saw little reason to invite additional traffic by easing the river's ascent.[72]

Blunt missed the human context; he assessed only the river's physical features. The dry bends of the river continued to be treacherous with rocks that grounded the vessel several times. In Blunt's mind, the river's obstacles all pointed to one key fact: "a canal might be made around them with the *greatest ease.*"[73]

A little over a week after starting from the boca, the bongies reached the fort which "stands on an eminence at the entrance of the Lake." Although Blunt considered the fort's current condition to be "in bad order," he interpreted its past glory as demonstrating "what the Spanish power once was—indeed, every work of the kind we see shows the greatness of their undertakings."[74] However much he romanticized the Spanish, Blunt would soon learn that their power paled in comparison to the ecosystem he had been sent to assess.

In the middle of the dry season, neither rain nor drought proved dangerous, but the January wind was another story. "Papagayos," which Humboldt described as "furious northeast and east-northeast winds," gusted from the Caribbean across the vast expanse of Lake Nicaragua to the Pacific, where the wind's energy fueled rich marine life.[75] As they crossed the lake, "a gale commenced."[76] Narrow and shallow, the bongies were designed to navigate the river, not an undulating inland sea. Blunt and Parker's bongie "managed" to land on an island and, when the wind died down a few days later, arrived at the city of Granada.[77] Lyman's bongie never reached the city. Nine of the ten men aboard the boat—the captain, the Colombian merchant, the Boston dandy, and six crew members—drowned in the shark-filled lake. The only survivor—who Blunt described as "an Indian" and who was probably a Rama man who knew how to swim—"escaped to tell the news."[78] Like Clossey the translator, Lyman the dandy was dead.

One man lost to illness and another to the wind. What else could go wrong?

EVEN BEFORE THEY BOARDED the bongies to ascend the river, the men on the *Mary Livingston* had heard rumors that Nicaragua was "in a state of revolution."[79] When the survivors of the papagayo arrived in Granada, they found themselves traversing a war zone. Amidst the tiled roofs protecting the bleached peat buildings from sun and rain, cannons guarded Granada's central square; earthen breastworks blocked its streets.

The survivors soon realized that the stop in Mexico, which had delayed the trip by three months and cost Clossey his life, proved worse than worthless. The letters of introduction were signed by enemies of the current "Governor" of Granada. Despite his distaste for their recommenders, the republican leader—whose ideals motivated both his ousting of the conservative de la Cerda and refusal to join the new country forming in Guatemala City—offered to read and promised to "correct" the "topographical description" that had been provided by the Mexican politicians.[80] To foil his predecessor's plan, the republican never returned it.

Within a week and without their map, Blunt and Parker headed north for León with hopes of obtaining permission to begin surveying the route from the Mexican politicians' contacts in that city. Avoiding the scorching sun by riding on horseback through the "fine moonlit night," the men and their guide made their way to Managua. Arriving at three in the morning, they found the city closed to them and slept "on the bare stone."[81] The next day, as they struggled to replace a lame horse, Managua's conservative alcalde refused to help. Neither Granada's republicans nor Managua's conservatives supported the surveyor's mission.

After a day of riding muleback, they slept the next night in a village barracks garrisoned by "Republican troops," perhaps the vanguard of San Salvadoran forces sent to support the new government in Guatemala City's effort to subdue all of Nicaragua.[82] Starting at sunrise, the men and mules were forced to wait out the "heat and dust" of the middle of the day. Passing through more "very dry" land before reaching León, Blunt and Parker arrived in the "desolate" city at dusk. Here amidst "destroyed" houses, a military leader that Blunt described as "the General" welcomed them, explaining that "he had received information of our project from the Government of Guatimala."[83] In contrast to the governor of Granada and the alcalde of Managua, Blunt thought the general of León "treated us very politely." Nonetheless, this leader also stymied their mission by requiring them to wait for "the determination of the Government of Guatimala" before they could begin surveying.[84] After three nights—each spent with a different side of Nicaragua's civil war—Blunt had not found a government fully supporting his mission.

Blunt lacked both his surveying instruments and permission to use them. But the friendly general did not prevent the surveyor from climbing to the top of León's newly completed cathedral to view the landscape. Built to survive earthquakes, the white building's neoclassical and baroque elements made it rather square and squat. From the roof, Blunt gained his first glimpse of the Pacific Ocean. He could also see a nearby lake that, during the rainy season, drained into Lake Nicaragua. Toward the ocean and the lake, Blunt observed, "the land appeared very level." To the north of the city, he noted a river flowing to the coast and a "good road" from the city to the busy Pacific port of Realejo.[85] It was far from Lake Nicaragua, but the countryside around León looked promising for a canal.

All Blunt could do was look. The next day, he returned to "the General who spoke very favorably of our undertaking, but requested us to wait until he had heard the determination of the government, and not make any examination whatever until then." The general provided Blunt and Parker with "passports" to ease their return to the brig and obtain the scientific equipment.[86]

Setting out before dawn on February 6, 1825, the men rode all day. Stopping for dinner at the town that had been garrisoned by republicans on their way to León, Blunt noted that it was "greatly altered since we passed there, as all the troops had left it." Continuing toward Managua, they stopped for the night in a "miserable" small town. "About midnight," the duo were awakened and forced out of bed to make room for "the troops that were then coming from Managua." Getting back on their mules, they passed "a great many soldiers on the road in a very bad condition." When they arrived in Managua "at daylight," the city was unrecognizable.[87]

Blunt and Parker had missed the final standoff of the civil war, which had taken place while they were looking out from León's cathedral. They likely did not meet the victorious General Manuel José de Arce, who had once pursued US annexation of San Salvador. Since his return to the region, Arce had served as a member of the Central American government's executive triumvirate, but he resigned this post to lead Salvadoran soldiers to Nicaragua in support of the Guatemalan troops. Defeating the conservatives in Managua and recruiting the republicans in Granada to the Central American cause, Arce would be credited with ending the civil war, pacifying the province, and ushering Nicaragua into the new country. If Blunt met this important man, he made no note.

When Blunt and Parker arrived in Granada on February 8, they expected their passports to speed their return to the brig. But documents did little to motivate people who knew the river's condition this deep into the dry season. It had been about a month since they started their ascent of the San Juan and slept on the river's pebble islands. The bongie men knew the sedimentation had increased. Blunt had trouble "getting bongies to go down the river." After days of negotiations, he recruited six vessels to arrive at the river's mouth by the month's end.

No sooner had he secured the boats than Granada's leader summoned him to convey orders from the general in León that Blunt and Parker were "to remain here until he heard from Guatimala." Furious, Blunt refused: "We told him we should start and if brought back, it must be by an armed force." So much for the polite general and his passports. They struck a deal. Blunt could return to the brig, but Parker would stay behind. Recording the man's words, Blunt underlined in his journal "*we must not consider ourselves prisoners.*"[88]

When Blunt tried to get the boats going the next morning, he found "the bongie men all drunk."[89] They were celebrating the war's end. On Sunday, February 13, he "Witnessed the swearing to the Constitution." The streets "were strewn with leaves and flowers" as a statue of the Virgin Mary paraded through the city.[90] By the evening of the next day, Blunt managed to get a bongie to depart for the brig, but despite his deal, the boat was "so full" the surveyor "could not get on board."[91]

Three days later, Blunt and Parker informed the leader that they would leave the next day regardless of whether permission had been received from Guatemala City. Calling the surveyor "very malicious," the man "ordered a guard placed on the Plaza to prevent any bongie starting."[92] Blunt wrote a seething letter to his employers informing them of the mission's many setbacks from Lyman's death to his own quasi-imprisonment. "Had no person but myself been interested," Blunt conceded, "I should have considered all business at an end."[93] Perhaps thinking of his dead crewmates, Blunt decided to soldier on. It would be another ten days before he was finally at "liberty to go."[94]

Less wind and less water defined the return voyage. The now placid lake's water level had dropped, enabling the easy harvest of shellfish. As they passed the fort and entered the river, Blunt spied large schools of alligators. He noted the blistering sunburns of the men who had rowed across the lake and the ease of drifting downriver overnight. On March 8, almost two full months after the brig's arrival in Nicaragua, the surveyor was reunited with his equipment.[95]

One week later, the surveyor started his third trip on the San Juan River in a bongie full of surveying equipment and goods from the brig's hold. The dry season had nearly reached its climax; the pebble islands had become nearly unpassable peninsulas. Absent any easy drifting, Blunt's bongie "grounded often." Landing the cargo each time, the crew "had to dig a passage" through the sedimentation.[96] Traveling 100 yards took half a day. Blunt marveled at the "remarkable" birds and grumbled about "moschitoes" that attacked him through his clothes.[97] Water levels had "fallen about a foot in two months."[98] He wondered what the river looked like "in the rainy season."[99] Could such a "very dry" river support year-round transit?[100]

BY THE END OF MARCH, Blunt had returned to Granada, where still no word had been received from Guatemala authorizing his surveying. Two weeks later, on April 11, "it commenced raining very violently." The city's streets flooded into impassable streams leading straight to the lake. Out of the fog of this first wet day of 1825, Curtis Bolton emerged.[101]

Prohibited from proceeding with precise surveying, Bolton joined Blunt and Parker on informal investigations of the land between the lake and the Pacific Ocean. They expected to follow "a carriage road for the whole distance," but no such road existed.[102] They traveled south across dry riverbeds and over "soft white stone" and dark volcanic rock—all seemingly "easily cut through."[103] When they turned west toward the Pacific, their guide took them through a sloping forest with views of the ocean. Without a trail, they got lost, sleeping on the floor of the jungle before reaching San Juan del Sur, the potential Pacific terminus of the waterway. Good for pearl fishing, the town's small harbor, adverse winds, ten-foot tides, and offshore reef had probably been the reason why, as a resident informed Blunt, it had been "five years since a vessel was here."[104] It was hardly a booming port.

Blunt was eager to continue exploring, even without his equipment. On April 25, Bolton and Parker returned to Granada, leaving the surveyor "to pursue my inquiries." "The season is now so dry that the wells have but little water in them," he remarked as he watched children using a "crow bar" and a dried squash to dig for water.[105] Adults knew their thirst would be quenched very soon.

The anticipation of rain might explain why Blunt could not find anyone to help him make his way through the woods. Getting stuck in the forest could be deadly. Besides, the local people who lived between the lake and the ocean might not want to assist a foreigner who aimed to turn their land into a waterway. The Spanish and Aztec descended people of the west rooted their lives to their villages, towns, and haciendas. Rural Nicaraguans might not share the canal dreams of urban elites like de la Cerda.

For perhaps all these reasons, Blunt failed to find a guide. The day after Bolton and Parker departed, he succeeded in hiring "a servant to carry provisions and water" but, as he later recalled, within the first three miles, "the boy became afraid and ran off with everything, leaving me without water."[106] Perhaps the piercing call of howler monkeys or growls of jaguars frightened the young man. More likely, he did not want to get stranded by the *temporales* amid poisonous frogs, venomous snakes, and an imperious English-speaking surveyor. Sunburned, parched, and alone, Blunt tried to make his way through the thick trees and bushes but could not cross the isthmus.

Hoping that he would find news that, seven months after signing up for the mission, he could begin his measurements, Blunt returned to Granada. When he arrived, he learned that the government still had not corresponded, that the river had become an impassable "bed of dry rocks," and that Bolton had departed for Guatemala City.[107]

TRAVELLING HUNDREDS OF MILES north and west into the highlands of Guatemala, Bolton quickly realized that he was not the only capitalist dreaming of constructing a canal. Joining throngs of foreign agents in the temperate highland city, he found Baily and his British competitors "besieging" the government to obtain the canal.[108]

But he did not find his own British partner, Col. Bourke. The footloose veteran had sized up the situation and split. As Blunt later explained, "after obtaining all the money he could," Bourke "has given up the enterprise." The surveyor saw Bourke as "guilty of duplicity in more than one instance."[109] A more charitable interpretation would suggest that Bourke realized that his Mexican imperialist contacts were no use in the new republic, which was being constructed by men who had opposed annexation. In fact, Bourke was already en route to Mexico where he would soon pitch a Tehuantepec plan to British bankers and the resident US diplomat.[110]

Bolton submitted a canal proposal to the Central American government. But he realized that given the competition and the country's incomplete formation no decision would be immediately forthcoming. "As I could not perceive or understand that the Canal would be taken up by the Congress at any particular period," he later explained, "I remained but 15 days in Guatemala after putting in my proposals."[111] He headed home.[112]

By mid-July, US newspapers announced Bolton's return. Anticipation grew that he would provide "an official report" to the public on the feasibility of the waterway, which seemed "every day more near and certain."[113] But the merchant would do no such thing. He and his partners had hired Blunt—at great expense—to write a report solely for their eyes. Moreover, the report remained to be written; Blunt would not compose it "until I have finished my examination."[114] When Bolton last saw the surveyor in the hilly uncharted forests near the Pacific, Blunt did not yet have permission to even begin his survey.

NEXT TO THE WORD "MAY," Blunt matter-of-factly noted in his diary a much anticipated and yet unexpected event: "This day received license from the Congress of Leon to examine the country."[115] Never hearing from the government in Guatemala City, Blunt owed his long-awaited permission to begin surveying to the new provincial Nicaraguan government. The new head of state was none other than Granada's ousted alcalde Manuel Antonio de la Cerda.[116] With a canal dreamer commanding the province and facilitating its integration into the Central American Federation, a government finally supported Blunt's surveying.

Writing to the older Bolton brother upon learning the good news, the surveyor confessed he was "fearful it is now too late in the season; as the rain here is so violent that it will be very difficult to get anyone to accompany me into the woods." Describing the "natives" as "indolent and timid," the surveyor refused to recognize the wisdom of the local people, who shaped their lives around the extreme seasons. He informed his employer that "should the business proceed," he would want "men from the U.S. to assist me" because he thought they could be "depended upon."[117]

On May 13, Blunt headed for the southern lakeside city of Nicaragua (now Rivas) to "come to some conclusion" about the route's potential.[118] He eagerly raced ahead of the pack animals transporting his cherished "instruments." Arriving just before midnight, no one in the city would provide him "shelter for the night," not even a man he recognized from his most recent bongie voyage, who brought Blunt's horse feed but left the surveyor to sleep "in his yard."[119]

Even with the assistance of the local alcalde, recruiting men to help with his investigations proved nearly impossible "on account of the season." When finally, men and mules carted Blunt's equipment into the woods, the surveyor found a "dry bed" of "gravel and stones" in place of the river he had seen flowing toward the Pacific only a few weeks earlier. That night, it "Rained hard" continuing well into the next day. Under his tent, Blunt fended off "Lice, ticks, moschitoes, fleas, crabs" and "fire ants." He started to feel "unwell." The men Blunt employed refused to fetch water and returned to the city.

Avoiding lethal coral snakes, cutting through bushes, and setting fallen trees ablaze, Blunt scouted the parched riverbeds alone. He kept track of how high above sea level he walked, but he could not get very far. "Rain every day," he recorded when he returned from a hike "wet to the skin" finding everything in his tent covered in tiny red insects. Even when he cleared the infestation and the hired men returned, the rain made it "impossible to use the instruments." All this rain, and yet Blunt observed, "the ground is still dry" because the water was "absorbed the moment it falls." The rain slowly saturated the soil and refilled the rivers.

Meanwhile, high up in the rainforest in what is probably now Costa Rica, Blunt ran out of food. The men he sent for provisions did not return. As the rain fell steadily, the soaked surveyor spent several nights "supperless" until an "Indian, passing, supplied us with some cakes of meal." On the first dry day in weeks, when measurements might be possible, the surveyor focused instead on acquiring sustenance because they had "nothing to eat." Eventually, he broke camp and returned to the city. Walking barefoot through standing water puddling on the now saturated soil, the soles of the surveyor's feet were bruised from stones, the skin broken by thorns. He found refuge in a farmer's "house" that consisted of "a roof standing on posts, about 40 feet square" where "pigs, fowls, calves, and men, live together." The generous owner of the house may not have realized that the surveyor thought this land was the most level in southern Nicaragua; the home stood on his favored path for a canal.

On June 1, Blunt recognized that the rain had defeated him. "The lower country was so covered with water," he explained, "that I thought it best to give up the design of finishing until the wet season was passed."[120] He later lamented to his employers, "the country was impassable."[121] More than six months behind schedule, the surveying mission lost its race against the rain.

Blunt needed a break. He was "lame" from the thorns in his feet and still had to trudge through knee-deep mud to reach the closest village. Unable to obtain corn along his journey, a frustrated Blunt described the families living between Lake Nicaragua and the Pacific Ocean as "the most miserable people under the sun."[122] The refusal of the "natives of the country" to share their food and geographical knowledge fueled his racism as he pronounced them "scarcely more instructed than the very monkeys who were inhabitants of the woods with them."[123]

Occasionally the "hot sun" peeked through the clouds, but all such moments ended in rain.[124] Confined to his bed in Granada during two long months of illness, he waited for news of the arrival of the brig, which had departed for New York after offloading its cargo. In early September 1825, Blunt wrote to his employers, "we have no intelligence of the arrival of the Brig in the Boca, and feel very anxious, as the time calculated for her arrival has gone by two months."[125]

In mid-October, as the rains began to diminish, the *Mary Livingston*'s captain ascended the river to bring the surveyor home. Blunt never returned to the field. Boarding bongies laden with hides, indigo, and dyewoods, his trip down river was the fastest yet. The river roared over rapids and falls; no sedimentation stopped their progress. Less than a week after leaving Granada, Blunt boarded the brig anchored in what he had assumed to be a "healthy" harbor at the boca to find "only one well man." The second mate had died, the mission claiming yet another life.[126]

Feverish himself, Blunt became numb to the difficulties of his return trip.[127] At long last, on January 7, 1826, *The New York Evening Post* announced his arrival and reported: "very severe weather in the passage, had been blown off twice." Blunt's journal made no mention of these hardships. Clearly, the surveyor had a new definition of "very severe weather."[128] What was a little wind when he had survived the rain?

ALTHOUGH HE MADE FEW MEASUREMENTS, Blunt worked hard for the $992 in salary that he earned over the seventeen months between August 1824 and January 1826.[129] Embracing challenging field work, he would go on to lead a three-decades-long career as first assistant to the US Coast Survey.[130] But after arriving in New York City in early 1826, he still had one task to complete to receive his pay. It was time to write the report.

For such a wet mission, the report was rather dry. Blunt detailed the San Juan River's sedimentation and rapids confirming, "I do not consider any part of the river susceptible of being improved 'to admit Steam Boats.'" Without mention of either the Rama or Miskitú inhabitants, he recommended "a Canal for the whole distance," estimating the artificial river would be about seventy miles in "a straight line." Suggesting a return to Nicaragua "between December and May" to resume his measurements, he urged "the survey of it as soon as practicable."

Passing quickly over navigable Lake Nicaragua without mentioning the fatal wind, he turned to the "Part between the Pacific and Lake." Unable to locate a natural channel between the lake and the sea, he sought a level, narrow route for a canal. But these two criteria did not exist simultaneously. Mountains split the smallest spans; the flattest routes would require significant construction.

At the narrowest point of the isthmus, he could not imagine the water collected in a man-made reservoir surviving the "loss from evaporation and filtration" during the dry season. He assured his employers, "such loss here would be more than that in any canal ever made." To engineer a workaround, he envisioned a "tunnel, or deep cut." Impressed by the "easily worked" softness of the region's stone, he thought such solutions "plausible." But if the arid air's thirst in the dry season made a tunnel necessary, the overwhelming moisture of the rainy season "prevented" him from "finishing" his exploration in the wettest part of the Pacific rainforest.

Considering the most level land between the lake and sea, Blunt relayed his observations from the León Cathedral. But he did not mention that the general had prevented Blunt from any on-the-ground exploration of this more northern, war-torn region as he awaited Guatemala City's permission. In fact, his only mention of the civil war was a brief reference to the "unsettled state of the country," which he blamed for delaying "my making any examinations until the commencement of the rainy season." Echoing his other recommendations, he suggested for the northern routes, "it would be well to have them surveyed."

As this statement suggests, Blunt argued for his return to Nicaragua. Despite the deaths, the weather, the war, and his disdain for the people, he reported favorably on the prospect of a canal. He opined, "here a canal may be easily formed between the two seas and the undertaking compared with the benefits to the commercial world sinks to a cipher."[131] Although Blunt claimed the mantle of science to justify his appraisal, he reported few numbers. His surveying mostly consisted of surviving for almost a year in Nicaragua, a feat that set him apart from most canal dreamers.

Dry and wet seasons threatened any canal with evaporation or flooding, but the Nicaragua route's water cycle left few months of easy transit. Sanguine in his support for the project, Blunt did not even consider what papagayos would do to sailboats on the waterway. He left out the alligators, sharks, snakes, and insects. He made no mention of the epidemic disease that killed his crewmates, active volcanoes along the route, or the earthquakes which had shifted the river and shaped the architecture. He even mostly ignored the violent political instability, which seemed to have resolved in sync with the rain.

Nicaragua's pacification, however, was incomplete. Within the next half decade, civil war would return. De la Cerda would twice be deposed by coup. The second time, the lawyer-turned-shoemaker could not cobble together a new career. In 1828, he was executed.[132] But canal dreams did not die with the *Plano Ídeal*'s creator. The map inspired Curtis Bolton and others to keep de la Cerda's plan alive.

THE CONGRESS OF LEÓN may have granted Blunt permission to survey the route, but a different government nestled along the Potomac River, two thousand miles northeast of Nicaragua, would play a decisive role in the denouement of Bolton's canal dreams.

Just before Blunt's departure for Mexico, the first diplomat from the new government forming in Guatemala City arrived in Washington. This representative of the new Central American country planned to negotiate the terms of a canal. But first, he would need his country to be officially recognized by the United States, and for this, he would require the attention of the always busy Adams. The secretary could barely distinguish between Nicaragua and Panamá; the diplomat had his work cut out for him.

CHAPTER FIVE

Recognition

On the cool morning of August 4, 1824, fifty-seven-year-old John Quincy Adams woke up before six and walked a mile from his Washington, DC, residence to the Potomac River. Upstream from the putrid flow of the city's sewage, the balding Adams stripped off all his clothing and joined his valet and one of his sons for an hour-long swim in the strong river currents. Refreshed, Adams dressed and walked home to eat breakfast and write. Around noon, he would take the short stroll to his office in the State Department building adjacent to the White House. Would-be appointees, diplomats, and a pile of unanswered correspondence awaited him in his second-floor office. It was going to be a long day.[1]

The day was typical for the secretary of state. It began with his early morning skinny-dip and ended late at night, because even after an evening at the White House, he came home to find a line of officeholders and office-seekers keeping him from his bed. Between the swim and sleep, Adams joined the president in meetings with three vastly different sets of diplomats: one representing a powerful European monarchy, a second representing a newly independent American republic, and a third representing seven Indigenous nations from the Mississippi Valley. The secretary led this day-long diplomatic waltz while also running for president.

Adams was a man in motion, and his movements on this very long day reveal how officials of the US government perceived Central America's position in a hierarchy of nations. Without contiguous territory to yield, established markets, or known mineral wealth, Central America was seen by some as worthy of little more than recognition. Nonetheless, recognition by the United States as a sovereign foreign nation was not enjoyed by every delegation of would-be diplomats. Recognition made the new country's treaty negotiations possible and its contracts justiciable; importantly, it enabled these options for US canal dreamers who recognized the new nation as the sovereign power over the route through Lake Nicaragua.

To Adams, Central American recognition was part of just another very busy day; Central Americans, however, might recognize August 4, 1824, as a day for the history books. Remarkably, few have devoted much ink to the story of this event.[2] Adams's diary entry for this cool Washington summer day provides the only known firsthand account. Peering over the secretary's shoulder, we can glimpse how this diplomatic event fit within the era's conflicts between republicanism and monarchy, continental struggles over land, and political schisms within nations. Squeezed into Adams's busy day, Central America's recognition happened quickly, quietly, and just before supper.

DURING THE MORNING of August 4, 1824, a notice was delivered to Secretary Adams announcing the arrival in the nation's capital of Don Antonio José Cañas, the first envoy extraordinary and minister plenipotentiary from the recently formed nation that Adams described as "the United Provinces of the Centre of America."[3] Adams knew that the diplomat was making his way to Washington. He had been expecting him when writing Mann's diplomatic instructions, but Adams could not predict which day Cañas would arrive.

It had been a long trip. In early April 1824, Cañas and his Secretary of Legation Fernando Valero journeyed from Guatemala City to Omoa, Honduras. Three months later, newspapers announced their arrival in Newport, Rhode Island.[4] The trip soon stalled when Valero got sick. When the Central American diplomats arrived in New York in early July, Cañas composed letters to President Monroe and Secretary Adams apologizing for the delay in announcing his US arrival. He explained that he was appointed by "the Supreme Government of Guatemala or of the Federal States of the Center of America."[5] Providing two alternative names for his country, Cañas wanted to ensure that the president knew exactly where he came from. Recognition of Cañas's country would be the first goal of his mission.

Referencing the ideals embodied in the United States's founding documents that had contributed to antimonarchical and anticolonial revolutions for a half-century, Cañas described his new country in his introductory letter as having "assimilated its ideas with those of this happy nation."[6] Tall and thin, Cañas's personal history attested to his upright faith in republican principles—at least for European-descended men.[7] Good with both words and guns, Cañas held a law degree from a Guatemalan university; he put it to use in the Salvadoran junta as it proclaimed opposition to imperial domination by both Mexico and Guatemala. As a colonel, he also served as second in command of the Salvadoran army behind General Arce.[8] When Arce left to pursue Salvadoran annexation in the United States, Cañas attempted to prevent a Salvadoran surrender long enough for the Mexican Empire to collapse. While Arce's annexation mission left a lasting influence on Adams's thinking about hemispheric policy, Cañas responded

Portrait of Don Antonio José Cañas (1785–1844) from an early twentieth-century Spanish encyclopedia. *Enciclopedia ilustrada Seguí* (Barcelona: Centro Editorial Artístico de Miguel Seguí, 1907), 3:314.

to Central American independence from Mexico by putting republican ideals into action. In 1823, he won a seat in the Guatemala City legislature that drafted the constitution.[9] This provisional government appointed him chargé and sent him to Washington.[10] Envisioning future negotiations about a treaty and a canal, Cañas hoped to refresh Adams's memory of the special place the Salvadorans—and by extension Central Americans—earned in US diplomatic history. Before closing with the national motto of "God, union, liberty," Cañas expressed his eagerness to receive "personally your Excellency's orders."[11]

Four days later, in Washington, Adams penned a brief reply inviting the meeting that would result in the official recognition of Cañas's nation: "It will give me pleasure to see you at this place, whenever it may suit your convenience."[12] Lingering in New York another month, the men finally arrived in Washington on August 3. The next morning, Cañas sent Adams an announcement of his arrival.[13] Adams did not immediately respond; his attention was focused on facilitating a meeting with agents of a more powerful country.

AT ONE O'CLOCK, Adams officially presented to President Monroe the new envoy extraordinary and minister plenipotentiary from France. In early June, the diplomat along with his wife, four children, and considerable staff left Paris.[14] Terrible food and seasickness plagued their fifty-day transatlantic voyage, a short trip compared to Cañas's trek.[15] Traveling via steamboat from Norfolk to the capital, the entourage was greeted by the diplomat's brother, a French consul.[16] Washington impressed neither of the brothers who joked: "it would be a beautiful city if it had any houses, a beautiful countryside if it had any trees."[17] The US capital was no Paris.[18] Without an established embassy, the diplomat moved into the former residence of a Russian minister.[19]

In 1824, Russia and France shared more than a Washington address. No longer a revolutionary republic or Napoléon's empire, France under the Bourbon Restoration saw a resurgence of royalism, now in a more limited constitutional monarchy. King Louis XVIII, like the Russian tsar and other monarchical leaders of Europe, disapproved of republics. The French regime, nonetheless, recognized political and economic value in cultivating relations with the United States, regardless of its form of government. In fact, the United States partly owed its own diplomatic recognition to France's 1778 alliance during the fight for independence.[20] The France of 1824 was not the same as that of 1778. But with Bourbon monarchs at the helm, the first ally of the United States was closer to the monarchy that supported the American Revolution than it had been in decades.[21]

This meant that the new French minister's visit to the White House carried diplomatic significance but little drama. For two years, a lawyer—the US-born son of exiled French nobles—had been serving as a temporary chargé d'affaires but intended to return to France.[22] Monroe expressed his hope "that happiness and prosperity would attend him wherever he might go."[23] The new minister presented his official documents to Monroe and, as Adams recalled, "made a very short Address to the President, assuring him of the friendly dispositions of the King of France towards the United States, and of his own earnest desire to promote the good understanding between the two nations."[24]

"Good understanding" would be helpful as the United States and France had become stalled in a dispute over payments to US citizens for property losses during the many wars of the Revolutionary and Napoleonic regimes. Although both sides could agree to the justness of this compensation,

French officials tied the payment of claims to French trade rights in New Orleans that, they argued, had been conveyed in the 1803 treaty that also transferred French rights to the Louisiana Territory.[25] One of the Louisiana Purchase's negotiators in Paris two decades earlier, Monroe knew all the terms of that treaty and disagreed with this interpretation.[26] A new minister offered promise for resolving this dispute. Before the minister and chargé departed, Monroe, Adams, and the diplomats exchanged reciprocal pleasantries in French.[27]

FOR ADAMS, THE NEXT MEETING was less pleasant and more personal. Adams was running for president. In fact, in the 1824 presidential election, three out of the five members of Monroe's cabinet were competing against each other as well as two outside candidates. The nation's politics had not settled into a two-party system. It was a multicandidate free-for-all. Yet presidential aspirants were not supposed to publicly run for office; this would look shamefully ambitious in a republic that was supposed to be led by disinterested men. Instead, candidates operated behind the scenes and depended on newspaper editors and friends to burnish their reputations and tarnish those of their rivals.

Continuing with their day jobs, the secretaries of state, war, and treasury subtly sought to steer Monroe's policy to serve their own electoral strategies. Unlike some presidents, Monroe did not want to handpick his successor. His disinclination to show favoritism left the secretaries scheming.[28]

Although the cabinet did not officially meet that Wednesday morning, Treasury Secretary William Crawford engaged Adams and Monroe in an hour of discussion. Long presumed to be the presidential front-runner, Crawford had suffered a year of both stroke and scandal. Temporarily blind and often too sick to attend meetings, he nonetheless refused to resign his post or end his presidential aspirations. Accused of corruption, the treasury secretary plotted the political demise of rivals who argued that Crawford illegally wielded the power of his office to further his presidential ambitions.[29]

In slurred speech, Crawford informed Monroe and Adams that he would soon depart for Pennsylvania and New York, states where his campaign enjoyed significant but susceptible support.[30] The threat to Crawford's electoral support in each state was different, but to some extent, Adams was responsible for both.

In New York, Crawford was losing directly to Adams. New York state's electoral votes were controlled by a few powerful men. Adams's New York support surged after DeWitt Clinton—former New York governor, Erie Canal commissioner, and losing 1812 presidential candidate—confirmed that he was running for governor and not for president. Clinton's supporters got behind the secretary of state. Adams was not a popular man in New York, but in the Empire State in 1824, the legislature—not the people—voted for president.

The source of Crawford's susceptibility in Pennsylvania was only indirectly Adams's fault. In Pennsylvania, the state's white men voted for electors who were pledged to particular candidates. Crawford's challenge came from a man who did not serve in the cabinet: newly elected US senator and former US General Andrew Jackson. Although nominated by friends in Tennessee, Jackson's meteoric rise in the presidential race had been facilitated, in part, by Adams.

Just a few months earlier, shortly after Jackson began his first Senate term in Washington, Adams hosted a ball celebrating the anniversary of Jackson's victory at the Battle of New Orleans, which occurred as the War of 1812 ended. On January 8, 1824, Adams recorded that a "thousand" guests arrived at his residence, which "could scarcely contain the company."[31] Adams hoped the gala would turn Jackson's popularity as a war hero to his own advantage. Despite his daily naked dips in the Potomac, Adams was a bookish career politician and diplomat from New England. His father, President John Adams, had led the elitist Federalist Party, which crumbled after the War of 1812. Although Adams had broken with his father's party before the war by supporting the Louisiana Purchase, he still had a reputation for being an elitist insider.[32] The gala offered Adams the opportunity to literally change his image.

Adams stole the sartorial politics of Thomas Jefferson, his father's opponent and the founder of the Democratic-Republican Party, the only nationwide party to survive the divisiveness of the war. Eschewing imported silks, Adams declined to wear the formal attire that cloaked his guests.[33] He looked the ideal republican: humbly dressed and magnanimously honoring a rival.[34]

Alternatively, Jackson did not need such theatrics to look like a republican hero. To many, he was one. But the general displayed autocratic tendencies. Without a political pedigree but with a reputation for defeating the Spanish, British, Seminoles, and Creeks, sometimes without government sanction, Jackson enjoyed support from the enslavers of the Southwest and those who despised the professional politics of Washington. If Adams could convince the general to serve as his running mate, the secretary of state could gain votes from Jackson supporters and win the election. The lavish event in the general's honor may have been a party enjoyed by a thousand, but it existed to win over one.

As a campaign strategy, the party failed.[35] By August, Jackson had become a legitimate presidential candidate in his own right. The general could win some of Crawford's electors, but Adams did not want him to win too many and gain a majority in the Electoral College. According to the Constitution's Twelfth Amendment, if no candidate received a majority of the electoral college votes, the result of the election would be determined by the House of Representatives. This was Adams's path to victory, so he needed Crawford to hold on to Pennsylvania's electoral college votes. With Jackson as a common enemy, the recovering Crawford was now oddly on the same side as Adams, at least regarding Pennsylvania.[36]

If the sickly man blamed Adams for his campaign's decline, it might not be a pleasant meeting, but it brought Adams good news. One of his opponents was leaving town, and better yet, the effect of the trip might be an Adams presidency.

WITH CRAWFORD'S DEPARTURE, Adams prepared to return to his office and its pile of unanswered mail, but before leaving, he informed Monroe of the arrival of Cañas. Monroe reminded Adams that he was "extremely anxious to return to-morrow to Loudoun." Monroe wanted to escape to his newly constructed brick mansion in Virginia's Bull Run Mountains that overlooked 4,000 acres of his land worked by some of the people the president enslaved.[37] Just the day before, he had requested that Adams schedule the French minister's visit with only one day's notice.[38] Now he wanted, as Adams recorded, "to get through the presentation of Mr. Cañaz [*sic*] this day."[39] This language—"to get through"—implies a hasty completion of an inconvenient task. Monroe's desire to squeeze Central America's recognition into his schedule perfectly captured the tone of US diplomacy toward the new country.

For Cañas and his country, being presented to President Monroe was no mere task to be got through. Just as France's diplomatic recognition of the United States had provided the young republic with legitimacy as a polity among the nations of the world, the United States's recognition of Central America would be the diplomatic debut for another young republic.

By 1824, recognizing Spanish American nations had become routine, but this had not always been the case. During the 1810s, many US citizens wanted to recognize the independence of the new Spanish American republics to express solidarity against European monarchy and open new markets to US trade.[40] With Adams as secretary of state, the acquisition of contiguous land trumped the support of other American republics.

The Monroe administration waited to recognize the independence of the former Spanish colonies until after the 1821 ratification of the Spanish-American Transcontinental Treaty, which conveyed to the United States all Spanish claims to Florida and Oregon.[41] Sometimes called the Adams-Onís Treaty, this deal—like the Louisiana Purchase—reflected the secretary's belief that the territorial expansion of the United States was key to the country's survival.[42]

After the ratification of the Adams-Onís Treaty, the administration yielded to the popular call for the recognition of the hemisphere's new countries. The president acquired a $100,000 budget from Congress to outfit new US diplomats to send to Spanish American capitals.[43] Although these funds were proof of legislative support, Monroe determined when and which countries he would recognize by inviting their credentialed representatives to meet at the White House.[44]

When Monroe received the Colombian minister in 1822, the United States became the first country in the world to recognize any of the newly independent Spanish American nations.[45] Although eager to trade with the former Spanish territories, Britain would not officially recognize any as countries until 1825.[46] France waited for Spain, its fellow Bourbon-controlled monarchy, to recognize the new nations.[47] For another decade, Spain refused to consider recognition. In fact, the Spanish government plotted with other monarchies to reconquer its American empire.[48]

Two years after Monroe received the Colombian minister, Adams arranged a similar meeting for Cañas.[49] Cañas's letter jumped to the top of the secretary of state's pile, as Adams penned a response: "The Secretary of State presents his compliments to Don Antonio José Cañas, appointed Minister Plenipotentiary from the Republic of Guatemala, and will be happy to see him and the Secretary of Legation at this office immediately."[50]

Easier said than done. No one in the State Department knew where to find the Central American legation. Farcically, it took Adams's men hours to locate Cañas, who had rented rooms only a few blocks away at "Gadsby's," a nickname for the genteel National Hotel located near the White House.[51] Adams wrote in his diary, "it was so long before his lodgings were found that when he came it was past four O'Clock."[52]

When Cañas and Valero finally did arrive at the State Department, Adams made a striking discovery: neither man spoke English, and they did not bring an interpreter. Adams, although a polyglot, lacked Spanish. He switched to French, but Valero spoke "only very little French," just enough to understand

Adams's request for Cañas's official documents. It would be a quiet trip to the White House. Adams recorded, "I went with them immediately to the President, and presented them—Mr. Cañas delivered his Credential Letter but made no speech—The President assured him of the friendly feeling of the United States toward his Country."[53]

This was not at all like the early afternoon meeting with the new French minister. Cañas was unprepared to converse with the men with whom he was to negotiate. Clearly, he had not had enough time in Washington to hire an interpreter. And Monroe was so eager "to get through" this meeting and retreat to his mountaintop that he did not delay the recognition to find one. Mutually incomprehensible, the meeting was brief. Nonetheless, the minister accomplished his mission's first goal, an almost silent historic event; the United States officially recognized the new government of Central America.

But what was the name of "his Country" exactly? No one knew what to call this political entity that had hastily been recognized into international existence. In documents written on August 4, Adams alternately referred to Cañas's government as "the United Provinces of the Centre of America" and as "the Republic of Guatemala."[54] A precise man, this inexactitude was atypical for Adams; his inconsistency found its source in Cañas's documents, which referred to his government in four distinct ways. Only adding to the confusion, the seal affixed to Cañas's official credentials contained a fifth Spanish name.[55]

Had Monroe or Adams been able to ask, Cañas could have explained that his country's name was in flux because his country's government was still being established. The country had been trying to form, in fits and starts, for three years.[56] When a Central American congress, the Asamblea Nacional Constituyente (ANC), met for the first time in the summer of 1823, it declared independence from Spain and Mexico for the "Provincias Unidas del Centro de América."[57] As an ANC representative of a Salvadoran district, Cañas signed the document; he knew the United Provinces of the Center of America was a new name for an old place, known for centuries as the Kingdom of Guatemala.[58] The new regional government would not be a "kingdom." For nearly fifty years, Central American *ayuntamientos*, or local governments, embraced elections.[59] By combining these ayuntamientos, the ANC created new provinces. To unify and equalize the provinces of Guatemala, El Salvador, Honduras, Nicaragua, and Costa Rica, the ANC rejected the confusing name "Guatemala," which referred to the capital (Guatemala City), the capital's province (Guatemala), and the entire region between Mexico and Colombia (Kingdom of Guatemala).

Fearful of a single leader who might revert the region to a kingdom, the ANC created an executive triumvirate. Unbeknownst to him, Manuel José Arce was the first man selected to serve on what became known as the Supremo Poder Ejecutivo (SPE).[60] Before Arce returned from his mission to Washington to seek Salvadoran annexation, the still-forming government experienced its first coup. A new SPE was appointed (again including the absent Arce), but the United Provinces' government remained unstable.[61] In October 1823, a committee provided the ANC with a draft of a constitution that would require new elections of a single president and a bicameral legislature. Changing the government's name to "Estados Federales del Centro de América," the new federal system—modeled on the United States—included an elected central government and elected state governments.[62]

As the constitution gathered support, the ANC made some big decisions. In December 1823, the ANC abolished slavery and declared Central America an asylum for foreigners. Coupled with these humanitarian policies, the ANC also signed a deal with John Baily to sell its national debt to London investors.[63] As canal dreamers swarmed to the capital, it gathered proposals for the construction of an interoceanic waterway. And it officially launched the diplomatic corps.[64]

In March 1824, two weeks after Arce finally took his oath of office as a member of the SPE, Cañas received his credentials and diplomatic instructions.[65] While the diplomat was traveling to Washington, Arce resigned from the SPE to lead Salvadoran troops into Nicaragua to quell the civil war and convince the province to approve the constitution.[66] Arce's success in Nicaragua made him a front-runner for the first presidential election, but he faced stiff competition from one of his former fellow members of the SPE. By the end of 1824, Adams and Arce were both engaged in hotly contested presidential elections. One man sought the leadership of a central government that had survived nearly fifty years of independence; the other aimed to be the first president of a not-quite-formed but nonetheless internationally recognized nation that lacked even a definitive name.

When the constitution became law in November 1824, months after Monroe received Cañas, the very first article declared the people of "la República federal de Centroamérica" sovereign and independent.[67] But a subsequent article denominated the country "Federación de Centroamerica."[68] Even the constitution lacked consistency. Like the country's name, sovereignty in Central America was plural and shifting.

Had Monroe officially recognized the Republic of Guatemala or the United Provinces, Supreme Government, Federal States, or Federation of Central

America or the Center of America?[69] It all happened so quickly and so quietly; the details got lost in the day.

THE SUN HAD NOT YET SET on August 4, 1824. Adams had facilitated the transfer of representation for one foreign power and acquired recognition for another, but his very long day was far from over. After an "early dinner" at his residence, Adams returned to the White House, accompanied by his wife and son.[70]

At half past five in the evening, the Washington elite gathered for a second conference with agents from seven Indigenous nations of the Mississippi Valley. In his diary, Adams described the men, women, and children who formed the delegation: "They were Saukeys or Sturgeon's, Musqukeys or Foxes, Piankashaws or Miamias, Pah-a-geser Ioways the people seen in a fog—Menomine or Wild Oats, Chippeways, and Nacatas or Sioux's, the amiable people."[71] Days earlier, at the first meeting, Adams noted that some of the delegates were "all but naked" and "were mostly painted red; but one chief had his whole face coloured with yellow Ochre."[72] At this second meeting, their appearance had changed: "They were now all dressed in the clothing furnished them here."[73]

Although the cool night might have made the multilayered European-style attire appealing, the Indigenous delegates' costume change, like Adams's party outfit, was meaningful.[74] In donning trousers and waistcoats, the Indigenous nations' male representatives looked like their elite white hosts. According to the democratic ideals established during the American revolution, equality as men implied equal political power.[75] But race mattered. Since the end of Adams's father's administration in 1801, the United States refused to recognize the Black male leaders of Haiti; free men of color lost voting rights.[76] US law recognized enslaved men only as property, even as their labor facilitated the diplomacy transacted in the White House.[77]

Monroe's Indigenous guests were not seen as human property, but neither were they recognized as US citizens. In 1824, these polities and the people who composed them were regarded by the federal government as foreigners.[78] But not all foreign nations were seen as equal. The secretary of war, not the secretary of state, orchestrated the evening's event because the delegates were not recognized as diplomats. Their clothing change might be seen as symbolizing US attempts to exert control over the Indigenous polities inhabiting the center of the continent. This is hinted at in Adams's use of the passive voice suggesting they were "dressed" by the US government, which "furnished them" with new clothes. The viewing of Indigenous people wearing corsets and collars reflected the centuries-old strategy that colonizing Europeans used against Native peoples of North America: recognize Indigenous sovereignty only enough to enable them to sell their sovereignty away.[79]

While Monroe was busy meeting with the new French minister who represented a nation of unquestioned sovereignty and the minister from the still-forming Central American country whose sovereignty was now recognized, the Sauk, Meskwaki, and Ioway agents signed treaties ceding sovereignty over lands in Missouri and what would become Iowa to the United States in exchange for commodities and cash.[80] More than 2.8 million acres changed hands that day for mere cents per acre.[81] But this was not the only cost of these lands. Through the Louisiana Purchase two decades earlier, the United States had paid France for the right to buy land in the Mississippi Valley from the Sauk and Meskwaki.[82] Led by territorial expansionists, the United States was so eager for sovereignty over contiguous land, the country paid for it twice.

The land-cession treaties were a boon for the federal agents who had invited the Indigenous delegates to Washington with the goal of brokering peace between warring nations. The French diplomats saw American cities as underdeveloped villages, but US agents in the War Department and its newly formed Bureau of Indian Affairs thought the sight of Washington, Baltimore, Philadelphia, and New York might overwhelm the delegates and bring them to the negotiating table.[83]

Far from altruistic, US agents sought pacification of the Mississippi Valley to entice white settlers to the region. Western land sales filled Washington's coffers and confirmed its territorial control. Brokering peace was barely disguised imperialism, but it was also ignorant. Demanding reciprocal deaths, the region's mourning wars were decentralized family affairs. Because Indigenous nations were not patriarchal and neither monarchies nor republics, the male delegates in Washington lacked the power to stop the fighting.[84]

But this did not stop the nearly two dozen Indigenous men, women, and children from pursuing their own goals in Washington. Six years before the passage of the Indian Removal Act made Indigenous expulsion the law of the land, the Sauk, Meskwaki, and Ioway agents agreed to their own dispossession to secure US support against neighboring enemies.[85] The final White House meeting of Adams's long day recognized foreigners' diminished sovereignty.

Or did it? From the perspective of Keokuk (or Watchful Fox), a Sauk delegate, negotiating with Washington and ceding overhunted lands provided his people with a powerful ally.[86] In speeches he made during his visit to the US capital, Keokuk appreciated the "opportunity of speaking to you on the subject of our claims" against a neighboring nation that had illegally ceded Sauk lands. Although he did not "want the land," Keokuk wanted recognition of his nation's territorial sovereignty in the form of compensation for what "is ours."

Just like the other diplomatic representatives Monroe and Adams met that day, Keokuk acted as if he was an agent of a unified population who "have clothed me with authority."[87] But the Sauk nation—like the United States, France, and Central America—was divided. This did not stop Keokuk and other delegates from agreeing to cede to the United States their claims to all their land "within the limits of the state of Missouri."[88] At the behest of one of the delegates, the treaty described the precise location of the lands ceded, putting the individual nations' former territorial sovereignty on the map.[89] Making their marks, the delegates would derive power from the concessions they negotiated by distributing the cash and commodities to their supporters.[90]

The Ioway, however, yielded more than land; they signed away their diplomatic independence. This was explicit in the treaty between the United States and two "Chiefs and Head Men of the Ioway Tribe of Indians," who agreed to place their nation "under the protection of the United States of America, and of no other sovereign whatsoever."[91] This upset Keokuk, who explained about the Ioways, "when they were weak we took [them] under our wing, and have ever since protected them."[92] Transferring this allegiance to the United States, the Ioway's treaty weakened their Sauk neighbors.[93] Moreover the Ioway delegates agreed not to make "any treaty with any foreign powers, individual state, or with individuals of any state."[94] Making their marks, the Ioway agents signed away the capacity to negotiate with any government but Washington.[95]

Contrast the Ioway's diplomatic position with that of Central America. Cañas also wanted to acquire a treaty with the US government; it was the second objective of his mission. But his country, whatever it called itself, *could* make treaties with other countries. In fact, Bolívar's Gran Colombia would be a party to Central America's first treaty.[96] Cañas was not the only minister plenipotentiary sent out from Guatemala City to foreign courts; ministers sought Central American recognition in Mexico City, London, and elsewhere. The Central Americans could turn negotiations with multiple nations into leverage. So even if US officials did not see Central America as a valuable trade partner or a future site of territorial expansion, Washington's representatives might engage in diplomacy with Central America designed to exert influence over other nations with more global power—like Great Britain, Russia, or France—as well as nations with more coveted resources—like Mexico or Colombia. Central America's diplomatic hand might be relatively weak, but US recognition meant that it was joining the international game.

And as Cañas knew, his nation held one important trump card: a shortcut through its land could link the globe's waters and provide a shortcut to the Oregon Territory on the Pacific coast. Such a possibility fit Central America into Adams's grand strategy of expanding the United States across the continent. This meant that Central America was worthy of US recognition, however hastily it might be performed. Therein lies an essential difference between Monroe's quiet meeting with Cañas and the evening's event, which was anything but a silent affair.

President Monroe and the representatives of the seven tribes spoke plenty of words. At their first meeting, Adams recorded that "The President made a very short speech of welcome to them which was answered with like brevity, by a principal chief of each tribe." Each brief speech was interpreted, some of them twice. As Adams explained, "They speak five different languages and the discourse between the President and them was rendered by as many interpreters—For the Sauks and Foxes there was a double interpretation, first into French and thence into English."[97] Monroe could not meet the Indigenous nations' delegations without hearing them.

But hearing is not listening. Recalling the first meeting, Adams wrote, "In the speeches of the chiefs there was much gravity, and painful earnestness."[98] Adams recognized the tone but not the topic. Of the second meeting, he noted, "Short speeches were made again to them by the President, and by him to them in return."[99] Again, he did not record the content but just the length. Perhaps, he thought newspapers would print transcripts.[100] But unlike the conversation between Monroe and the French diplomats, the secretary of state did not deem the Indigenous delegates' words worthy of recording in his diary.

As the presence of the families of the officials suggests, this meeting was viewed by the Washingtonians as a spectacle. Adams called those in attendance "Spectators," a term derived from the Latin word for "to look."[101] What they saw mattered more than what was said. This was confirmed by the presence of another White House guest to the meeting, the painter Charles Bird King, who would, over the course of his career, paint portraits commissioned by the US government of more than a hundred Indigenous people.

When Adams visited King's studio the next day, he "saw the Portraits he is painting of the Indians now here."[102] At least fifteen members of the twenty-three-person delegation sat for King. The War Department's Bureau of Indian Affairs paid King $320 to capture the likenesses of twelve men, but King also painted one woman, which would likely be the most profitable work when he sold reproductions to the public. The portraits were completed before the end of the month, and King earned an additional $193.50 for duplicates sent to the delegates after their departure from Washington.[103]

Although few originals survived an 1865 fire, lithographs of the portraits depict none of the sitters wearing the clothing "furnished them" in Washington.[104] Most appear as they did at their first meeting—adorned with paint, feathers, and furs. But many of the portraits include one souvenir distributed by the president on the evening of August 4, 1824: a colorful ribbon laced through a silver "peace medal" minted with the profile of James Monroe.[105]

When he visited the White House earlier in the day, Cañas did not receive a medal. Neither did the departing French chargé or the arriving French minister. Regarded as men representing independent sovereign nations, the Europeans and Central Americans would not wear the likeness of a foreign leader around their necks. Nor would the wearing of such a medal be a symbol of personal power when the diplomats returned to Paris or Guatemala City.

By contrast, Keokuk's medal became a life-long adornment. Shirtless in his original portrait, the leader is pictured in fuller attire and with a child at his feet in an 1836 lithograph.[106] One large medal clearly hangs from the man's neck on top of an elaborate collar of furs, claws, and feathers. A second slightly smaller presidential medal hangs from the neck of the child. To the Washingtonians, the medal might be a claim to the man's allegiance or even obedience. But to Keokuk, the gift symbolized his personal relationship with a powerful ally; it marked him as a diplomat owed promises by the federal government.[107] Arguing in 1829 for the continuation of the minting of these metals, a federal agent described them as indicators of "Government Friendship, badges of power to them, and trophies of renown."[108] Moving frequently from ceded territory to soon-to-be-ceded territory in what became Missouri, Iowa, and Kansas, Keokuk held on to this sign of his power as a diplomat. In a gilt-framed daguerreotype produced more than two decades after his 1824 visit to Washington, an aging Keokuk stares out at the viewer, his medal still resting prominently atop beads, claws, and furs.[109]

AS THE END OF Adams's very long day drew near, his diplomatic pecking order was clear. At the top, France had recognized the United States and through the sale of its Louisiana preemption rights facilitated the territorial expansion of the young republic. At the bottom, the Ioway became dependent on the United States and fell out of the international hierarchy altogether.

Central America's diplomatic rank was somewhere in the middle. San Salvador had tried to offer the United States its land, but Washington avoided annexing it. Too distant, too Catholic, too Spanish, with too many volcanoes

In this 1838 portrait, both Keokuk (c. 1780–1848) and the child seated at his feet wear peace medals. John T. Bowen, "Keokuk, chief of the Sacs & Foxes" (Philadelphia: F. W. Greenough, 1838), LCCN 95502203, LC-DIG-pga-07519, Prints and Photographs Division, Library of Congress.

and alligators, Central American land was not of interest to the leaders of the United States, who wanted to expand the nation westward across the continent, not southward down the isthmus. Monroe just wanted to "get through" any interaction with the new nation. But getting through might be the most valuable thing Cañas could offer the US government.

As he turned toward his second goal of negotiating a treaty, what if Cañas bargained not his nation's land, but the avoidance of his nation's land? As we have seen, land was at the center of much of US foreign policy in this era, and thus territorial expansionism is the focus of most of the history of US imperialism during its first century. But imperialism could also be accomplished through trade.

More subtle, commercial expansionism depended on access to untapped or lucrative foreign trade. For US merchants located on the Atlantic or Gulf coast, the trip to Asia's coveted markets depended on long and dangerous sailing voyages around Cape Horn into the Pacific Ocean. US voyages stopped in Spanish American ports for water and food, but the trade with most of the former Spanish Empire remained small.[110] China was the goal. What better way to shorten the route and avoid interactions with Spanish Americans than by building an interoceanic canal? Moreover, what if this new waterway sped up the expanding US continental empire's communication with its Pacific territories? With neither desirable land to sell nor valuable markets to open, Cañas could offer the United States the opportunity to construct a global shortcut, a means to "get through" the continent. The promise of a canal offered the United States a provocative power: an imperialism of avoidance.

"BETWEEN 8 AND 9 IT WAS OVER," wrote Adams about the evening at the White House. As the guests departed, Adams was still working. He pressed Monroe for "directions upon various points; but he was not prepared to give them."[111] Eager for Loudoun, Monroe was exhausted. Adams could not be.

When he arrived home, Adams found an old friend waiting for him who had just returned to Washington as a member of the French diplomat's staff.[112] Three more men were, in Adams's words, "afterwards here."[113] The first was a late chief justice of the Michigan Territory who felt he had been wrongfully deprived of his post and was now pursuing a nomination as a Florida territorial judge.[114] The second was the federal agent appointed to administer US citizens' claims against the Spanish government under the Transcontinental Treaty.[115] The first man sought an office; the second owed his office to Adams. A constant "swarm of visitors," like Consul Savage and the men seeking to replace the late Special Agent Mann, overwhelmed the secretary.[116]

By the time the last late-night visitor arrived at Adams's door as August 4, 1824, finally drew to a close, he was exhausted. For the second night in a row, the "second Comptroller" came to see Adams "complaining" about the meddling of a cabinet member in his official decisions. Adams merely "advised him to see the President."[117] Soon, Adams would be that president. But, for now, his very long day was done.

CHAPTER SIX

Corrupt Bargains

In early 1825, Guatemala City offered "delightful" temperatures in the low seventies during the day. Cooler nights prompted one shivering would-be canal contractor to sleep under a "sheet, double blanket, and quilt." Dodging daily thunderstorms and strolling through the "regularly laid down" streets lined by "elegant" churches and one-story houses "adapted for resisting the effects of earthquakes," foreign agents explored the Central American capital.[1]

While some found the volcanoes on the horizon unsettling, John Baily, agent of BHRC, probably felt at home. Situated 6,000 miles away, the British lieutenant's childhood home on the island of St. Helena in the South Atlantic shared the city's moderate temperatures, tropical rains, and volcanic landscape.[2] US Consul Charles Savage, meanwhile, was homesick, or at least he would soon be both home and sick. Other agents of capitalists and countries arrived throughout the year, but Guatemala City's comfortable climate remained consistent.

The solid architecture and temperate climes did not reflect the political tensions boiling just below the surface in the new nation's capital. In fact, both Guatemala City and Washington, DC, were about to erupt in contentious presidential elections that would shake both nations' political systems. Claims of corrupt bargains split both US and Central American politicians into new factions. For the United States, the election would begin the decline of the personal patronage that defined politics in the "Era of Good Feelings" and the rise of two opposing political parties. For Central America, the delegitimization of the first presidential election shook the new nation at its moment of foundation. Meanwhile across the Atlantic in London, the desire for Spanish American stocks and securities reached a fever pitch. Here, too, charges of corrupt deals would have decisive consequences for canal dreams.

Meanwhile, in a place that felt like spring all year round, agents passed the time as events beyond their control changed the global political and financial environment.

SAVAGE HAD PERMISSION to tour the potential canal route but did not depart the capital. Perhaps he delayed because of lingering concerns about the recently ended civil war in Nicaragua, or perhaps he lingered in the capital to see the new government take shape.[3]

This late nineteenth-century portrait depicts Central America's first president Manuel José Arce (1787–1847). Ramón A. Salazar, "Manuel José Arce," *Los Hombres de la Independencia* (Guatemala, 1899). Courtesy of Harvard University.

Manuel José Arce's success in pacifying Nicaragua and bringing the province into the new republic positioned him well to win the first presidential election in Central America, but he had stiff competition. In the words of Arce's twentieth-century biographer, his chief opponent José Cecilio del Valle was "undoubtedly one of the most intelligent and learned men in Central America."[4] Raised in the Honduran countryside, Valle trained as a lawyer in Guatemala City, but his provincial roots prevented him from ascending the colonial-era ranks. During the decade of instability in Spanish rule leading up to independence, while the republican Arce was imprisoned, Valle climbed into high office with the support of royalist conservatives. In 1821, Valle drafted Central America's first Act of Independence and then quickly embraced Mexican annexation. He served as the Central American deputy in the imperial Mexican Congress and was appointed Emperor Iturbide's secretary of foreign and domestic affairs—the Adams to Iturbide's Monroe. After Iturbide's fall, Valle returned to the Mexican Congress. He served there until

This late nineteenth-century portrait depicts Arce's rival José Cecilio del Valle (1780–1834). Emilia Serrano de Wilson, "José Cecilio del Valle," *Americanos Célebres: Glorias del Nuevo Mundo* (Barcelona: N. Ramírez, 1888), Vol. 2.

he was appointed as one of the three members of the Central American SPE, which he led with little resistance until Arce returned from the United States and joined the triumvirate.[5]

Arce and Valle were opposites, and yet they ruled together until the summer of 1824 when Arce resigned to lead the Salvadoran army into Nicaragua. After the election of a federal congress, the SPE would be disbanded; in its place a single president would lead the executive branch. Valle and Arce were the leading presidential candidates. According to the rules for the election, eighty-two electoral votes would be cast, and then congress would certify the results. On April 20, 1825, congress decided to eliminate the votes of one region that had submitted two sets of returns; it also refused to count the returns from two other districts that submitted their results after the deadline. In total, seventy-nine votes were counted, and with a few stray votes going to other candidates, Valle won with forty-one electoral votes to Arce's thirty-four.

But Valle did not become president. In a power-grabbing twist, the congress decided that a majority of the eighty-two *possible* votes rather than a majority of the seventy-nine *actual* votes was required to win the presidency. According to this calculation, Valle was one vote short of victory; the election was thrown to congress.

Already an irregular election, something even stranger happened when the votes of the congressmen were recorded. Although Valle had been the voice of conservativism and Arce had been the candidate of republicanism, the conservatives from Guatemala voted for Arce instead of Valle. Some believed that a conversation between Arce and Guatemalan conservatives resulted in a clandestine deal that swung the legislators' votes in Arce's favor. As a result of this rumor, Arce entered the presidency in an impotent position: scorned by his former friends and not quite supported by his former enemies. For a man who long dreamed of leading a Central American republic, the rumor of a corrupt bargain would undermine his ability to do so.[6]

IN MARCH 1825, as the new Central American government formed, "discharges of artillery" celebrated the news that the British government had recognized the republic of Mexico. Would Central America be next? A British agent stationed in Guatemala City reported to London: "A Consul-General has already arrived from the United States, by which they were much flattered, and they would be ten times more so by receiving one from England." Unbeknownst to this correspondent, the British government had already assigned an informal agent to investigate the new country. Coming from Mexico, he arrived in mid-May.[7]

But the US consul would not meet the British agent. On Monday, May 2, 1825, Savage addressed a letter to the minister of state and of foreign relations, informing him that "the day of my departure for the United States is fixed and that I shall leave this city for Omoa on Friday morning."[8] This was a sudden and complete change of plans. Instead of investigating the canal route, the consul was returning home after only two months in Guatemala City. Savage's reason for departing was implied in later letters; his wife Susan was deathly ill.[9] Despite Savage's speedy departure, Susan died before he got home.[10]

Even before he learned of Susan's death, it was a tough voyage. Savage's luck regarding illness ran out. On his way home, he spent six weeks in "confinement by fevers in Havana."[11] When he arrived in New England, Savage busied himself in procuring a tombstone for Susan's grave. Clearly thinking of his life through the lens of his wife's death, Savage defined Susan through his federal office: "Affection dedicates this stone to the memory of Susan, wife of Chas. Savage, Am^{n} Consul to Guatemala."[12]

His consulate never far from his mind, he rushed his mourning and his recovery. He was determined to return to Central America. On his way south, he met with Adams, who recorded that the consul "has been out of health, and lost his wife during his absence." Savage reported favorably on the "Fine Climate" in Guatemala City and shaved a hundred miles off Mann's estimate of the distance between the sea and the capital.[13] But Savage's first destination upon his return to Central America would not be to reunite with his nephew Henry at his consular post in Guatemala City; instead, Savage headed directly to the canal route.

On April 5, 1826, Savage arrived at the "Boca de S. Juan," the Caribbean mouth of the river. He never left the boat, explaining to his family, "My health is too delicate to continue on an excursion to Lake Nicaragua."[14] When he returned to the United States, Savage wrote to the State Department that "my loss of health precluded the possibility of prosecuting such a journey during the season of rain." Unlike the Central American capital, the canal route's weather was extremely seasonal. His timing was bad, and so was his initial impression of the river: "I doubt the practicability of it for a ship navigation." Far from a booster, he opined, "I hope it will not be undertaken with American capital."[15]

Regretting his choice to return to Central America so quickly, Savage confided in his family, "I left you before I should;—I was ill—and now more so—in mind as well as body—I calculated I was possessed of more firmness than I really do possess—my failings are as true as ever occasionally, my grief prostrates me."[16] His consular fees amounted to "little or nothing." Asking for government funds to support his "residence" in Central America, Savage explained "no commercial operations can be depended upon to support it."[17] The State Department ignored his request.[18] As he summarized for his family: "Business very bad."[19] Never remarrying, he described himself as "a lonesome man."[20] Looking back years later, Savage regretted his appointment as consul to Guatemala and his "ambition for place, power, rank, and wealth."[21] For Savage the bargain of office holding proved corrupt, indeed.

ON MAY 4, 1825, the day before he departed Guatemala City to race home to his ailing wife, Savage received "a letter from an American Gentleman at Omoa" that informed him of important US news. Immediately, he wrote to the Central American minister of state. The consul underlined, "I am extremely proud to say I believe the Honble [honorable] *John Quincy Adams,* is now the President of the United States."[22] Savage owed Adams for his office, and now his patron was president. When Savage left Massachusetts for Central America in October 1824, Adams's election to the highest political office in the United States was anything but a foregone conclusion. By the time the consul triumphantly announced Adams's victory, the election was mired in scandal. But Savage had no idea; he had missed more than six months of US news.

When the Electoral College voted in November 1824, Adams, Jackson, Crawford, and Clay remained in the race. None of these candidates garnered a clear majority, or 132 of the 262 electoral votes. Jackson led the pack with ninety-nine electoral votes; Adams came in a close second with eighty-four. Crawford edged out Clay, forty-two to thirty-seven. This meant that the election would be thrown to the House of Representatives where only Jackson, Adams, and Crawford would be contenders.[23]

In the House, each congressman would vote within his state delegation; the winner of each delegation would receive that state's single vote. Balloting would continue until one of the candidates received a majority of at least thirteen votes. Jackson had the support of five states. Adams could depend on six; Crawford had only three. This left the votes of ten states in play.

In addition to continuing to serve in their offices in the cabinet and Senate, the three candidates and their friends ardently wooed congressmen from undecided states and tried to convince members from decided states to change their votes. For the first six weeks of 1825, rumors of secret meetings and hushed promises swirled around Washington.

During the general election, Jackson's supporters claimed he was the people's choice. But he did not win a majority in the Electoral College, and many of the states he won undemocratically provided enslavers with additional representation. He hardly had a truly popular mandate. Regardless, congressmen were not required to cast their votes on the basis of the popular will.[24]

One of those congressmen, the most powerful man in the House, was Henry Clay, who was no longer a candidate. He could not vote for the ailing Crawford, who openly disavowed Clay's signature platform: the American System, a policy of national economic development, which included constructing canals. He could not vote for Jackson; Clay saw the general's autocratic and militaristic tendencies as a threat to the republic. He was left with Adams, whose tepid support for Clay's American System could hopefully be bolstered with a well selected cabinet. To put the New Englander into office, Clay would have to convince other congressmen, especially Westerners who also favored the American System.[25]

Informing only a few men of his support for Adams, Clay kept his choice a secret for some time. On New Year's Day, seated side-by-side at a dinner, the two men—the slave-owning, gambling Speaker of the House from Kentucky and the bookish, moralizing, Yankee secretary of state, who was suffering "with influenza"—agreed to meet for a "confidential conversation."[26]

Before meeting with Clay on Sunday, January 9, 1825, Adams attended church for two different sermons. The first took inspiration from Ecclesiastes 7:23: "I said I will be wise; but it was far from me." This was a caution of the fallibility of human judgment. The second, which Adams backhandedly praised as "not uneloquent," built from the scripture of Hebrews 11.1: "Now faith is the substance of things hoped for, the evidence of things not seen." This text suggested the human propensity to believe things without proof. True believers called this faith; skeptics called it conspiracy.[27]

Was the secret meeting with Clay wise? Perhaps wisdom failed Adams when he agreed to meet confidentially with one of his former opponents. Would it look like a conspiracy when the meeting became public knowledge? This conversation, like Arce's discussion with the Guatemalan conservatives, would enjoy a long life in partisan rhetoric and history books.

"Mr Clay came at 6. and spent the Evening with me, in a long Conversation explanatory of the past, and prospective of the future," wrote Adams in an uncharacteristically short and vague diary entry. Adams recalled that Clay "wished me as far as I might think proper to satisfy him with regard to some principles of great public importance, but without any personal considerations for himself." This last clause was key because Clay next professed, as Adams recorded, "In the question to come before the House, between General Jackson, Mr. Crawford and myself, he had no hesitation in saying that his preference would be for me." Clay's decision to vote for Adams ended Adams's description of the "confidential interview." Leaving a page and a half blank in his diary, perhaps Adams intended to return to the subject, but he never did.[28]

This is Adams's version of events. His opponents would suggest that, on that chilly January night, the two men engaged in a backroom deal: if Clay delivered the necessary votes in Congress to elect Adams, Adams would appoint Clay secretary of state, the presumed heir to the presidency. Jackson's supporters suggested that Clay and Adams stole the White House. Jackson later asked, "Was there ever witnessed such a bare faced corruption in any country before?" He clearly did not know about Arce's election in Central America. Jackson's supporters cried "corrupt bargain," and the 1824 presidential election has been remembered by this catchphrase ever since.[29]

Nevertheless, most of the evidence suggests that the "corrupt bargain" was merely a conspiracy theory. After all, Clay had already announced his decision to vote for Adams to a few friends in writing before the meeting. Moreover, in his short version of a "long Conversation," Adams described no quid pro quo, no promise of an appointment in exchange for Clay's vote.[30]

But what if, in front of Adams's fire, Clay made the same bargain as Savage and so many other would-be office holders? Perhaps when push came to shove, presidencies and cabinet posts were no different from clerkships and consular posts; they were all negotiations exchanging one kind of profit for another. Was it really corruption if the entire consular system, the majority of the agents representing the United States overseas, depended on patronage to get a post and private business to do public work? Perhaps all government offices were corrupt bargains.

But if any politician could act without worrying about calculations of patronage, it might have been the man who cast the tie-breaking vote in Adams's favor in the delegation of the nation's most populous state. Stephen Van Rensselaer III was known simply as the Patroon because he was the wealthiest landowner in New York. The Patroon had no patron; at various times, he had supported each of the candidates. No one—not Clay, not Adams, perhaps not even Rensselaer himself—knew whom he would vote for during the House election.[31]

In the middle of a snowstorm on February 9, 1825, the House members of the Eighteenth Congress gathered in the Capitol. Many expected that the election would take time and multiple ballots to reach a result. Instead, when all the representatives placed their ballots in their respective state boxes and the results were tallied twice, the bare minimum thirteen states had voted for the secretary of state. Adams won.

The congratulatory messages immediately started pouring in. When Adams returned home from a celebratory dinner at the White House, "a Band of Musicians came and serenaded me." From a future president to a past president, Adams recorded that he wrote "a Letter of three lines to my father asking for his blessing and prayers on the event of this day; the most important day of my life." He knew however that he would need more than his father's blessing. "May the blessing of God rest upon the event of this day," wrote Adams in his diary.[32] The election was so close and so contentious that the New Englander struggled to win the blessing of the nation. Like Arce's, his would be a challenged and challenging presidency.

BUT MONTHS LATER in Central America, Savage knew none of this as he quickly passed along the news of Adams's election on May 5, 1825. Before the end of the day, the minister responded to Savage's announcement: "The

President of the Republic has with the greatest pleasure, heard the news, that you have been so polite as to communicate to me in your letter today." The minister conveyed Arce's joy: "He is so much more pleased being personally acquainted with the talents & virtues of the Honble John Quincy Adams." Arce interpreted Adams's election as "a new link" uniting "the American Nations & a prop that will support the Liberty of the Continent." For Arce, Adams's election turned his Salvadoran annexation mission into a diplomatic dream.

Recognizing that Savage would soon be back in the United States, the Central American president asked Savage "to intimate the sincere expression of his sentiments" to the new US president. He would also express them "directly through the medium of the Minister of this Nation."[33] Minister Cañas would do more than congratulate Adams. He was already busy proposing to the State Department a commercial treaty and a plan for constructing a Nicaraguan canal.

By the time the sick and grieving Savage arrived in the United States in the late summer of 1825, he had a new boss. The new secretary of state was working on sending an official US diplomat to Guatemala City. Explaining his hasty departure from his consulate, Savage addressed a letter to the State Department; he abbreviated "Hon^{l}. Henry Clay, Sec^{y} State."[34] Clay was surely the new secretary of state, but many believers in the corrupt bargain would dispute that he should be addressed as "honorable."

IN A SPANISH COLONIAL BUILDING that a canal agent described as "superior to that in which the British Parliament assembles," the first "federal congress of the Republic of Central America" sat along both sides of an elevated platform to consider the proposals of "various foreign houses and trading companies" with the goal of "opening a navigation canal between the two Pacific and Atlantic seas, in the State of Nicaragua."[35] Instead of weighing the terms offered by the various proposals, the congress decided to set its own.

On June 16, 1825, the congress decreed that "A canal will be opened in the State of Nicaragua, for the navigation of ships of the largest possible size." The government decree echoed some of the terms proposed by BHRC's lawyers. For example, it planned to reimburse the foreign contractor for "the opening of the canal" through "public debt." The decree also offered would-be contractors additional services: it would assist with surveys, make maps, waive the duties on imported machinery, defend the canal, and grant logging rights to the contractors. In return, the decree demanded more control. Its laws would govern the contract and control the price for "navigation or transit of the canal." The decree promised the opening of the waterway "to all friendly and neutral nations." But it also reserved its right to pay less for a canal that could not be navigated by seagoing vessels, and nothing at all "if the project cannot be carried out because of invisible obstacles."

Following its new governmental procedure, the lower house transmitted the decree to the upper house. About a month later, both the senate and the president had agreed to its provisions. The president ordered it to be communicated to the public on July 12, 1825.[36]

The foreign agents gathered in the capital gasped at the audacity of the new country to dictate its terms. One British agent decried the decree to his diary as "rather a preposterous document." He condescended, the decree's drafters "appear so puffed up with the competition which exists in Europe and America, in reference to this highly desirable object, that they seem to imagine any terms they choose to propose will be acceded to." The term he most objected to was not even in the document. When construction of the canal was completed, the British agent anticipated that "the government will take it into their own hands, allowing what they consider a fair remuneration." It was unthinkable to him that the country could name its price for buying the canal after it was built and yet refuse to pay "any part of the expenditure" if the waterway proved unbuildable. Exporting both work and risk, the new country's canal dreams emphasized its control.[37]

Designed to benefit Central America, the decree's conditions likely differed from those Baily had already proposed, which surely tilted control of the canal to British capitalists. Baily would have to inform his employers of the decree's demands and receive new instructions as to how to proceed. One contemporary estimated that by the fastest means, news traveled from London to Guatemala City in "seventy-five days."[38] Baily and other foreign agents likely appealed to the Central American government to pause its consideration of the various proposals until they could communicate with their employers.[39]

On August 1, 1825, Arce issued an amendment to the decree that would balance desire for the quick completion of "the enterprise of connecting both oceans" with enough time "so that foreign businessmen can make their proposals." Setting a six-month deadline, Central America postponed its awarding of the canal contract until after February 1, 1826.[40] For the Guatemala-based agents of would-be British contractors, the delayed decision kept British canal dreams alive.

MORE THAN 5,000 MILES from the mild climate of Central America's mountainous capital, the center of the British Empire broiled in an August 1825 heat wave. While British agents' requests for revised instructions slowly descended from the Guatemalan highlands, anonymous extracts—likely from Baily's letters of April and May—appeared in London newspapers.

On August 23, 1825, the *Times* published a prediction that "should the canal be made," Nicaragua would "unquestionably be the richest and most thriving part of America either North or South." The author described the new constitutional government in equally glowing terms, concluding "there will remain no question of Guatemala being the most favoured part of America." Moreover, the country was "exceedingly desirous of standing well in the opinion of Great Britain." Just months earlier, the British government had finally recognized the sovereignty of Mexico and Colombia. Like these neighbors, Central America would try to confirm its claims to sovereignty through the credit market.[41]

By mid-August 1825, banker David Barclay and his partners in BHRC were preparing to sell the bonds derived from the loan contract Baily had concluded with the interim Central American government. BHRC designed the initial sale of the "Guatemala loan" to be an unusually private affair.[42] For only one hour, the partners would open their quiet office on a narrow road a few blocks away from the bustle of the Royal Stock Exchange and the Bank of England to receive written bids or "tenders" from brokers who wanted to buy bonds in bulk.[43] Compared to the previous wild hullaballoos over Spanish American bonds, the city's reception of the Central American loan was even colder than the relief after the heat wave.[44] "Only one tender was made," the *Times* reported, but "a few members of the Stock Exchange attended at the Countinghouse of Messrs. Barclay, Herring, Richardson, and Co., to learn the result."[45] "There being no competition," the article explained, the public would not learn the details of the deal struck by the lone bidder: "J. and A. Powles and Co."[46]

With an angular nose, well defined chin, and a peak of fair hair dipping into his furrowed brow, the head of the house that had been the only bidder for the Guatemala loan cut quite a figure.[47] John Diston Powles's private affairs were filled with drama and descendants. Born in 1787 to an English artist's family residing in Denmark, Powles moved to London as a child. Before his twenty-first birthday, he married a gentleman's daughter. After the birth of three children, Powles discovered his wife in an affair with her dancing master. To dissolve the marriage, Powles obtained from Parliament a "private act" that, ironically, made the lurid details public. Three years later, he married the daughter of a British officer; she died a decade later after giving birth to six children. His third and final marriage in 1841 produced two more sons.[48]

Between his first two marriages, Powles began selling arms and ships to Simón Bolívar's agents. In 1820, as the revolutionaries failed to pay their bills, Powles declared bankruptcy.[49] He restored his fortunes by joining with future BHRC partner Charles Herring to create the first Colombian loan. He put these profits to work for J. and A. Powles and Company, a banking house he ran with his brother.[50] Like Barclay and Herring, he also served on the boards of joint stock companies linked to Spanish American mines.[51] To promote these ventures, Powles orchestrated publicity campaigns; he even employed a young Benjamin Disraeli to author propagandistic pamphlets. In 1826, the future prime minister included a pastiche of John and his second wife as the nouveau riche characters Mr. and Mrs. Millions in his first novel.[52] Mocked as one of "The South American Jugglers" trying to keep the prices of bonds soaring, "Don Juan de Rowley Powley" was linked to "Don Carlos de Herring-Guts."[53]

The "jugglers" kept the Spanish American bonds floating through the first half of the 1820s. In early 1825, the stock prices for Spanish American mining companies surged.[54] In a March 1825 debate in the House of Commons about one such company, some legislators lamented "the spirit of gambling that now existed in the city."[55] The "gambling mania," Alexander Baring complained, "had seized upon all classes, and was spreading itself in all parts of the country." Baring lamented, "many innocent persons, who had embarked their little capital in them, with the expectation of realising large fortunes, would be awakened some day unpleasantly from their dreams of grandeur, by the intelligence that their all was lost."[56] Powles refuted Baring in print; this buoyed stock prices for a little longer. But the bond market had already started a gradual slide downward.[57] By the time the Guatemalan loan reached the market in the late summer of 1825, the jig was up.

And so, during the hottest and driest summer in recent memory, bond sales were languid when Powles submitted his company's bid for the Guatemala loan. Powles offered to buy the bonds at a steep discount and pay for them in several installments. Upon payment of the full sum, BHRC would deliver the official bond "Certificates" but, if Powles failed to make a single installment payment, "all the preceding payments were to become forfeited."[58]

Powles immediately marketed the securities to "intimate friends," including William Thompson—a member of Parliament, London alderman, and fellow director of a Mexican mining company.[59] Thompson later recounted that the Powles brothers "strongly advised" him to buy Guatemala bonds because the price was likely to go up and "bear a Premium." Convinced, Thompson made a down payment of £1,000 with nine more installments to be paid over the next year.[60] The contract between Powles and individual investors included the same promise for delivery when fully paid and the same penalty for failing to make a payment.[61]

These terms were nothing new. They had become standard in Spanish American loans, but the times were changing. Powles found few buyers. Instead of selling at a "Premium," the price plummeted.[62]

A WEEK AFTER THE INTRODUCTION of the Guatemala loan to the market, newspaper reports described "panic among the holders of Government securities."[63] The "panic" would spread. The causes of what would later become known as the "Panic of 1825" were not limited to the bonds of Spanish America. The entire British economy contributed to the collapse of London's financial markets in the second half of 1825.

With expectations of increased demand from Spanish American consumers, the price and quantity of wool and cotton imported to be manufactured into textiles had increased tremendously. As merchants realized that the citizens of the war-torn new American countries could not afford to buy British goods, prices dropped. This led to the failure of several large merchants in northern England, which triggered other failures as the companies' creditors became unable to pay their debts. Drawing specie from the Bank of England, banks and merchants throughout Britain depleted the nation's gold and silver reserves. To protect itself, the Bank of England restricted its lending, making installment payments on stocks and foreign bonds nearly impossible to meet. Soon, bankers refused to accept foreign bonds and stocks as collateral; this dried up the market for new Spanish American shares, which had been leveraged by speculators as security for other investments. As engineers' reports arrived revealing the flooded condition of many of the mines, stock prices plummeted. The directors of these companies withheld dividends, further diminishing demand for their companies' stock.

The more shareholders and bondholders sold off their securities, the lower the prices sank. By the late fall, Mexican mine shares had plummeted from £1,550 to £200. Investors who had made initial installment payments began cutting their losses. If they could not find buyers for their shares, they refused to complete their purchase. As the terms agreed upon by BHRC and Powles suggested, failure to promptly pay a single installment often forfeited the previously paid capital. With little money coming in and no demand for new stock sales, some companies dissolved. After deducting expenses—including upfront fees paid to directors—the boards of defunct companies returned to shareholders tiny fractions of the sums invested.

In mid-December, on a densely foggy day, the failure of a "reputable London bank" led to significant bank runs in the city and throughout the country. People accepted only gold or Bank of England bills as payment. The Bank of England hired clerks and printed small notes to keep the currency circulating; the Mint worked round the clock producing coins out of gold borrowed from the Rothschilds. By Christmas, the acute panic had ended. The bubble had burst.[64]

Spanish American bond prices continued to decline. An investigation into the failure of a Mexican loan contractor revealed the way bond sales buoyed stock prices. Mortified by the exposure of his financial dealings, the forty-nine-year-old loan contractor "threw himself on the sofa in despair, and remained for three hours in a state of inanimation." Without a "struggle or groan," he died, supposedly without the observation of "his relatives, who surrounded him."[65] While the doctors who examined the corpse ascribed the man's death to "apoplexy" or "the bursting of a blood-vessel in the head," reports circulated that "the real cause" was "a broken heart."[66] "After filling for so long a period a very high rank in the commercial world," the *Times* surmised, "he could not summon fortitude enough to bear up against the loss of reputation."[67] Barclay agreed to serve as a trustee for the settlement of the man's affairs.[68]

In the spring of 1826, Barclay stood for election to the House of Commons as the representative of Penryn, a small town in Cornwall with a history of piracy and a reputation as a "venal borough"—a corrupt legislative district that might be purchased by would-be politicians.[69] In a race with three other candidates, the two-term Bank of England director won—or more likely bought—the seat with a plurality of the votes.[70] Although he did not reside in the borough, Barclay's dealings in Spanish American stocks and bonds made him a reasonable representative of a town rumored to have been a pirate haven.

Barclay's businesses were in trouble, but he had already secured significant personal profits through upfront fees and commissions. Presiding over a "meeting of the shareholders" of a Mexican mining company, Barclay blamed the stock's drop in price on "the embarrassment of the times." And yet, the company was in an "awkward predicament" of needing to raise funds from shareholders to continue "the works of the company." Making matters worse, several shareholders failed to pay their installments and forfeited their stock, so the pool of people who could contribute to the company's coffers had shrunk. Despite Barclay's gloom, the shareholders expressed unshaken faith in the dream of the company. "The concern was certain to proceed most prosperously in the future," one prophesied as they voted to contribute the necessary sums and "carry on the concern."[71]

The same spirit did not carry BHRC through the aftermath of the Panic of 1825. Reprinted from the *London Gazette* of Friday September 15, 1826, the *Times* published a tightly kerned paragraph of tiny print announcing, "Partnerships Dissolved." More than halfway down the list could be found the names of the BHRC partners.[72] Formed to sell the bonds of Spanish America, the men who made up BHRC dissolved the ties that bound them.

SOME STILL BELIEVED IN THE PROMISE of Central America's not-quite-sovereign debt. As the bond market tumbled, William Thompson obtained the signature of Powles on the receipts documenting his installment payments. By mid-April 1826, when his sixth installment was due, the investor had paid in £4,000, more than half the total sum he would have to pay to receive his bond certificates. He "offered to pay" the sixth installment, but according to his lawyers, "was prevented from doing so by *Powles & Co.*" Thompson recalled that Powles "advised him not to make any more payments, saying that there was a disagreement between *Barclay & Co.* and the Government of *Guatemala*, respecting the Loan." Powles supposedly told Thompson that it would not be "safe" to make payments "until such difference should be settled." Of course, the terms of the contract for the purchase of the loan still applied, and Thompson's nonpayment triggered the forfeiting of his paid-in capital. Thompson would later argue that Powles's goal was not to protect him but to force him "to commit a forfeiture of the Instalments already paid."[73] J. D. Powles, for his part, would deny that any of this had occurred.[74]

Thompson believed, and his lawyers would later argue in court, that Powles and BHRC had "clandestinely arranged" during those hot days of August 1825 to defraud would-be bondholders through a scheme of forcing forfeitures.[75] Although J. D. Powles would deny "any previous concert" with BHRC and called the theory "an entire fabrication without one particle of truth," the partners of BHRC and Powles could have arranged such a deal.[76] Herring might have invited Powles, his fellow engineer of the Colombia loan, to join this more nefarious iteration of drawing personal profit from Spanish American debt. The men had made a killing on the Colombian loan; perhaps they salivated over the prospects of *not* receiving payments for the Central American bonds. Worse than their usurious loan sharking, this alleged scheme suggested outright fraud.

Thompson later came to believe that the April 1825 "disagreement" between BHRC and the government in Guatemala City was actually a discovery by

Marcial Zebadúa, that government's newly arrived London agent, of the fraud. Indeed, funded initially by Baily's advance to the Central American government, Zebadúa set up his Central American Legation at 68 Baker Street around the same time as Powles advised Thompson not to make his payment.[77]

Looking back several years later upon his arrival in Britain, the Central American agent described London as a scene of "panic terror" in which the "bonds of the new republics began to fall rapidly until reaching a state of complete nullity." He continued, "Houses without number interested in the commerce of America, loans, mining, colonization, canals, roads, and so many giant projects, all collapsed, and finally sank among their ruins, for lack of the foundation on which they had been built." Guatemala City's structures were built to survive earthquakes; the British capital proved less prepared for and more vulnerable to the shocks of panic. Disappointed in London, he found "the capital of the political world, and the center of universal wealth circulation" to no longer offer "the fruits"—of finance and diplomacy—he had been sent to harvest.

Zebadúa described BHRC as having "failed to meet its most solemn commitments," which left his country lacking "the resources that this negotiation offered us." For a government agent who found himself personally financing his mission to secure his country's diplomatic recognition, he cast the loan debacle in a surprisingly positive light. He saw his country as "liberated" by the "general collapse." BHRC's failure meant that "instead of millions" his country's "foreign debt was limited to a reduced sum."[78] Indeed, only bond certificates worth a little more than ten percent of the loan contract ever made it into circulation.[79] The panic may have saved Central America from significant debt, but it did not save its bid for sovereignty. Despite Zebadúa's best efforts, the British government refused to recognize Central America.

BRITISH COURTS COULD NOT consider claims arising out of loans to not-quite-sovereign countries, even loans that might be frauds perpetrated on purported friends. When Thompson sued the Powles brothers and former BHRC partners, the defense harped on Central America's failed bid for diplomatic recognition. "The whole of this transaction," they argued, "arises out of a Loan to a Government which is not recognized by this Country" and, as the Peruvian precedent had determined, "such a transaction is illegal." Whether a fraudulent scheme or a legitimate failure, the loan's illegality made it nonjusticiable.[80]

Powles's lawyers interjected into this familiar argument historical references to previous foreign loans and diplomatic incidents. Recalling the beginnings of the Age of Revolutions, they cited France's loan to Britain's rebellious North American colonies, which demonstrated the close relationship between the creation of nation states and the creativity of capitalists.[81] Achieving independence at the very end of half a century of fluid sovereignty and speculative investments, Central America and its promise of an interoceanic waterway entered British minds and markets as resources and revolutions became exhausted. The opportunity to find investors in a truly revolutionary project of changing the physical geography of the world had passed. Born as the era ended, British dreams of a Central American canal suffered from terrible timing.

Thompson's lawyers tried to reframe Central America's late independence as an asset. The argued that "*Guatemala* is a Sovereign and Independent State, and has been recognized as such by his Majesty."[82] To make this claim, they questioned the very definition of "what is meant by the recognition of a State." They turned to recent history to raise doubts about the standard of "a Treaty" and "a resident Minister" to qualify as a recognized "Country." They argued "the independence of Mexico"—of which Guatemala was at one point part—"was recognized." And they asserted consuls had been sent throughout Spanish America, constituting "a distinct, unqualified recognition of the independence of the whole of *Spanish America*," including Central America.[83]

Intrigued by these arguments, the judge wrote to the Foreign Office for confirmation of the status of the sovereignty of Central America. The Foreign Office assured the court that "the Federal Republic of Central America has not been recognized, as an independent Government, by the Government of this country."[84] The judge ruled that he could not permit the suit to continue because the case "bottomed on the original representation that certain Persons were the agents of the Government of the Federal Republic of Central America, which then was and is an independent State, the fact being that it was not then, has not been, nor is now an independent State acknowledged by the Government of this Country."[85]

The Central American government's lack of sovereignty in the eyes of the British government allowed Barclay, Herring, Powles, and their partners to keep Thompson's money. Loan sharks or worse, neither Barclay nor Powles lost their personal profits from the Spanish American speculations they directed. Ordinary bondholders, stockholders, and the new nations that sold their debt as a bid for diplomatic recognition would not be so fortunate.

Not-quite-sovereign bonds proved easily broken by the British capitalists who created them, but the corrupt bargain of these loans entrapped the new countries who contracted them.

IN FEBRUARY 1826, as the deadline for canal proposals arrived, Baily and his competitors sitting in the not-quite-sovereign capital high above two seas had not yet learned of the Panic of 1825. They had no idea that British investors could no longer compete for the contract to construct the interoceanic waterway. "The unfortunate money crisis," reflected one observer, "put a stop to these plans."[86]

In the late 1820s, most British investors stopped dreaming of constructing an interoceanic waterway through Central America. In an investigation of the "curious record" of the 624 British joint stock companies formed in "the speculations of 1824 and 1825," the Atlantic and Pacific Canal Company was included in a table titled "Abandoned." Half a million shares of stocks designed to support infrastructure projects were abandoned or remained only "Projected" and never traded.[87] Some of the mining stocks lasted longer, but never produced a profit for shareholders. Many investors—like future Prime Minister Disraeli—lost money they could ill afford to gamble.[88] Thousands of British canal dreams turned to nightmares.

But British investors were not the only canal dreamers. The Central American government would have to seek a different foreign contractor to construct the canal. Its attention turned to the country whose fight for independence launched the Age of Revolutions. The fulfillment of 1820s canal dreams would hereafter depend on the US government, its citizens, or some combination of the two.

CHAPTER SEVEN

Climate Changes

After nightfall on July 21, 1824, roughly six months before John Quincy Adams was elected president, and on the same day that the secretary received confirmation of Special Agent Mann's unexpected demise, the pale and gangly Augustus Brevoort Woodward waited in the dim light of the crescent moon outside Adams's house. Woodward wanted to be first in line "for the appointment vacated by the death of T. N. Man [*sic*]"; he managed to be both awkwardly early and inconsiderately late.[1] Over the next few months, the job of filling the Central America diplomatic post would exhaust Adams as Woodward and his competitors adopted Consul Savage's strategy of fatiguing their way into office.

A disgraced judge, Woodward had lost his nearly two-decade-long appointment to the Michigan Territory's bench due to accounts of intemperance circulated by local political rivals.[2] This was not Woodward's first attempt to gain a new post in a new land; he had already unsuccessfully sought the governorship of Florida.[3] Determined not to be passed over again, he reappeared at Adams's house the next morning "repeating his application for the appointment to Guatemala."[4] He returned three more times in as many weeks including the evening of Central America's diplomatic recognition. Eventually, Adams gave the former judge the verdict, "I told him I thought it doubtful whether the President would send any more Ministers to South-America." Summing up the climate at the White House, Adams explained that Monroe's "principal object was to wind up his Administration."[5]

But Woodward still wanted an office; he returned a few weeks later and acquired a spot on the bench in middle Florida.[6] Unimpressed with the region's barely constructed capital in Tallahassee and frustrated with the prospect of building another territorial government, he soon sought a different post. Adams described Woodward as "an intelligent, learned and public spirited man, with defective judgment; and so strange in his dress and deportment, that he passes with many for insane—and is within a thin partition of it in reality."[7] Was it crazy to want to go to Guatemala? Finding a man with the temperament, strength, and immunities to resist both the temptations for private gain and the infectious diseases of the tropics proved challenging.

In the nine months following Mann's death, while the isthmian diplomatic appointment remained a low priority for President Monroe, US public interest in a Central American canal swelled. Even without a diplomat on the ground in Guatemala City, and perhaps because the available information on Central America was so slim, US newspapers stoked a brief interoceanic canal mania. Far from a crazy scheme, the waterway through Central America increasingly appeared less like a dream and more like a certainty that would change the world's history, geography, and even climate. To make this widely imagined future come to pass, however, someone had to go to Guatemala. If not Woodward, who would it be?

UNDOUBTEDLY A SINGULARLY strange man, Woodward was not alone in seeking the Guatemalan post in the shadow of Mann's death. Adams knew that Monroe sought a "cool" candidate, not "a very ardent South-American Patriot" because the job demanded "impartial observation." Diplomats also had to have "discretion," which was "a quality quite indispensable" but maddeningly absent from many of the applicants.[8]

Some candidates were unimpressive. Adams praised a frequent applicant's "perseverance in pursuit of place" as "exemplary," but found him too "dull" for "the appointment of Agent to Guatemala."[9] Others were too sharp. Adams described a serial applicant—who had already been dismissed from one diplomatic appointment—as "a shallow, inflated coxcomb, meaning to be honest, fancying himself profound and eloquent, and making himself every where ridiculous in the superlative degree."[10] But perhaps the joke was on Washington. Although Monroe deemed the man "not fit for any appointment, which required the exercise of discretion," his "powerful friends" won him the office of "Secretary and acting Governor of East Florida."[11] As this appointment as well as that of the nearly insane Woodward suggest, the newly acquired territory of Florida served as the Monroe administration's dumping ground for less-than-ideal clients of powerful patrons.

Patronage and private profits combined with disastrous results for diplomacy. Unlike consuls, appointees to the diplomatic corps received salaries to discourage them from trying to profit from their posts. Nonetheless, Adams described most Spanish American office seekers as "continually crossing one another; and all masking interested projects under the garb of South-American patriotism."[12] In the patronage-based politics of the "Era of Good Feelings," Adams found it difficult but necessary to hire disinterested men.

After the recognition of Central America, the next man sent to Guatemala City would be a fully credentialed chargé d'affaires with greater authority than a special agent. Two days after the infamous "corrupt bargain" meeting with Clay, as seemingly countless politicians courted candidate Adams at his home, office, and on the walk between the two, a North Carolinian congressman solicited "the diplomatic appointment to Guatemala for Mr. Miller."[13]

Losing his parents at a young age, William Miller inherited a nearly 1,000-acre North Carolina tobacco plantation. A practicing lawyer and champion of improving the state's transportation infrastructure, he spent the 1810s climbing state government ranks, ultimately becoming the first governor to live in the new executive mansion.[14] His home emptied by the recent death of his wife and only child, Miller had "no family" and was "ready at any moment to set out on his mission." One of his recommenders described him as "a man of respectable abilities, undoubted integrity, and great worth." Another partially disagreed, claiming Miller was "poor" and therefore needed the appointment.[15] Whether he was wealthy or not, the forty-one-year-old widower was well-connected, convinced of the value of canals, and ready to go. He might be just the man for Mann's job.

Despite his uncertainties about whether Monroe would fill the post before the end of his term, Adams agreed during his final weeks as secretary of state to "recommend William Miller of N.C. as Chargé d'Affaires to Guatemala."[16] With Adams now president-elect, Miller's appointment looked to be a certainty.

But then state politics intervened. Just two days before his inauguration, Adams learned that the current governor of North Carolina intended to "oppose the nomination of Miller to Guatemala" citing "Miller's former intemperance."[17] As with Woodward in Michigan, the "too free use of ardent spirits" provided a cover for sinking a local rival.[18] But if alcoholism ruled out nominees, the United States would struggle to find enough men to serve the government. In the 1820s, the average person in the United States consumed approximately seven gallons of alcohol per year.[19] Miller's recommenders assured that he had "entirely abandoned" intoxicating drinks and "was thoroughly reformed."[20] Miller's nomination regained momentum.

On March 5, 1825, the day after President Adams's inauguration, the same day that he officially nominated Henry Clay as secretary of state, Adams nominated Miller as chargé d'affaires to Guatemala.[21] Two days later, without any discernable debate, the US Senate—meeting in a week-long special session—consented to the appointment.[22] The new secretary of state would be responsible for preparing Miller for his mission. In late March, Clay sent him his "commission" and alerted him that as "soon as your Instructions are prepared, which will be with all possible dispatch, the President hopes that you will be prepared to set out upon your mission."[23] With an eager new administration, the political climate in Washington changed.

A LITTLE OVER A MONTH after Miller's appointment, a wave of discussion of a Central American interoceanic canal swelled in the US press. Newspapers in the 1820s circulated between editors for free, and text composed in one town would be reprinted throughout the country.[24] In columns of minuscule type on enormous pages, popular support for the idea of an interoceanic canal spread.

For years, newspapers had been covering small stories about potential canals. In the fall of 1822, US newspapers reported that the newly independent nation of Colombia was "cutting a canal" across the "Isthmus of Darien" or Panamá. "All Europe and America are greatly interested in this great project," suggested the article, "it will be, in particular, of incalculable advantage to the people of the United States, as it will at once throw open a wide field for Yankee enterprise." It would also unearth South American lands "rich in the precious metals" and composed of "a luxuriant soil." Even more valuably, it would "greatly lessen the danger and facilitate our intercourse with the East Indies and China, by shortening the distance about 10,000 miles."[25] The effects of an interoceanic canal, then, would combine Columbus's fifteenth-century dream of a fast water route to Asia with nineteenth-century desires for commercial, mineral, and agricultural wealth.

Articles reported on several British commercial agents in Colombia pursuing canal contracts, but Simón Bolívar's government demanded British diplomatic recognition before it would consider awarding a contract to a British company.[26] Citing its treaties with Spain, the British government refused to recognize any of the new Spanish American nations. The plan for a canal through Panamá stalled.

While British diplomacy got in the way in Colombia, canal dreamers conjured other interoceanic routes on the pages of US newspapers comparing Humboldt's proposed routes in Mexico and Central America.[27] Some argued that the "immense advantage" of an interoceanic canal was "apparent to every one who looks at a map of the world."[28] But authors rarely acknowledged their evidence in proclaiming the flatness, narrowness, or simplicity of specific routes.[29] One article hid its lack of evidence behind the passive voice, claiming "it is asserted, that even now, there is a natural communication between the two oceans by means of the river St. John, lake Nicaragua, and the river of Mandinga."[30] His mission perhaps inspired by such anonymous and unfounded assertions, surveyor Edmund Blunt learned the hard way that no "natural" interoceanic waterway existed in Nicaragua. Blunt's valuable firsthand experience, however, was not public knowledge. Most US citizens had no way of discerning fact from fiction as calls for a canal increased.

Despite the lack of verified facts, newspapers imagined enormous potential effects of an interoceanic canal, even for distant communities. An article from a small Massachusetts island expounded, "to no portion of N. America could the establishment of an intercurrence through this narrow tract, be of greater importance than to the inhabitants of Nantucket." Arguing that a shorter route to the Pacific whaling grounds would halve the time, cost, and danger involved in the island's dominant industry, it argued that "an inquiry" into an interoceanic canal ought to be a priority of the US government.[31] But before Congress could even read the article let alone begin any investigation, other whalers disagreed, imagining the canal as a nightmare leading to the "utter ruin" of their "lucrative business." Once the canal was built, a critic predicted, "the danger would be so trifling and the distance so short, that vessels of every description would immediately engage in it; the consequence of which would be, that there would soon be no whales in the Pacific to hold spouting intercourse with each other."[32] A canal would make whaling too easy to be profitable and make whales too scarce to survive. Whale extinctions added to a growing list of imagined canal effects.

Easier access to the Pacific might also enable the territorial expansionism driving most of US foreign policy in this period. By "shortening the distance to our own possessions in the Pacifick," the interoceanic canal might provide advantages "incalculable, both in a commercial and political point of view."[33] A transcontinental water route might accelerate US settlers' access to Oregon in the race against Britain and Russia for sovereignty over this territory.

Dreams of a continental nation were part of the culture of canal promotion even where no connection to the Pacific was possible. On October 8, 1823, the Erie Canal, which connected the Atlantic Ocean to the Great Lakes via an internal waterway composed of rivers, lakes, and manmade canals, enjoyed an elaborate opening ceremony. Channeling the produce of the vast western territories of the United States to New York City, the state-sponsored Erie Canal turned previously isolated areas in the Mississippi Valley into Atlantic hinterlands. The waterway transformed US economic and political life by increasing the desires of white settlers to dispossess the Indigenous nations whose once remote homelands became more accessible to world markets.

The Erie Canal's effects inspired competitors. Other states raced to compete with New York; Congress debated support for federally sponsored canals. Even New York's own state legislators proposed additional waterways.

Politicians at every level of government—and the speculators who lobbied them—projected limitless possibilities for canals in Ohio, Indiana, Pennsylvania, and throughout the nation.[34]

Enabling the flow of commodities between the Mississippi Valley and the Atlantic seaboard, the Erie Canal was a monumental achievement, but its celebrants extended its significance beyond the eastern half of North America. The Erie Canal did not cross the continental divide. Nonetheless, at its opening ceremony a participant "poured into the Canal a bottle of water from the Pacific Ocean, and another from the Atlantic Ocean." This "meeting of the waters" was purely symbolic, but the desire for a more permanent "meeting" of the seas intensified.[35] The US "spirit of canalling" was expanding beyond the nation's boundaries.[36]

The arrival of Minister Cañas fed the fury. Before Washington's recognition of Central America, articles reporting on the diplomat and his new country asserted that "The Envoy has brought a plan of a contemplated Canal, from Lake Nicaragua to the Pacific Ocean."[37] Cañas and Central America were immediately linked to the already feverous canal boom. The proposals for a Nicaraguan route joined the competition among proponents of a Colombian canal and those who wanted a Mexican canal.[38]

But with every day, the prospect of the construction of at least one of these interoceanic canals seemed to become more of a certainty. One short article employed the future tense: "The splendid project of uniting the Pacific and Atlantic oceans by a canal will now be attempted."[39] Another asserted that "a junction of those vast bodies of water, will soon be effected."[40] Sparse on detail, short on evidence, certainty about the imminent construction of an interoceanic canal grew, especially in New England where reports of Blunt's surveying mission to Nicaragua circulated in late January 1825.[41]

But what would happen to the waters themselves? Would a marriage between the seas be an equal partnership or would one ocean dominate the other? This question provoked a widely circulated discussion in late April and early May 1825 about the human-created environmental change that an interoceanic canal might produce. The debate began when nearly insane, would-be Guatemalan agent A. B. Woodward sent to the press some private correspondence.

Although for most of his life he made his living as a federally appointed judge, Woodward had also been actively engaged in scientific research, publishing, and institution founding. During his career as a territorial chief justice, he had been instrumental in founding the University of Michigan.[42] Only a few months into his tenure as a Floridian judge, he was already involved in the Agricultural Society of Middle Florida, which was founded in March 1825.[43]

Perhaps this explains why, the next month, Captain Isaiah Doane wrote to Woodward. Born to a prominent New England family, Doane enjoyed a reputation as a daring naval hero of the War of 1812.[44] Like so many veterans of the wars of the Age of Revolutions, he struggled to find his footing after 1815. Living in Pittsburgh, Pennsylvania, in 1819, he served as an agent selling land in the projected town of Hindostan, Indiana; interestingly, in Lexington, Kentucky, future Consul Charles Savage also served as a Hindostan agent.[45] But for Doane, Savage, and a thousand other speculators, Hindostan proved an utter failure. In 1822, Doane's first wife was among the many who died in the disease-ridden and soon-to-be abandoned settlement.[46] By the spring of 1825, Doane was in Washington looking to transition from land speculator back to federal ship captain.[47] By late May, he had secured a federal post commanding a customs enforcement vessel assigned to patrol the Florida coast.[48]

But about a month before receiving this commission, Doane's thoughts drifted to the interoceanic canal, and he composed them in provocative prose for Woodward. Perhaps he wrote to Woodward because of their western connections or the judge's interests in Spanish America and science. Or perhaps Doane was hoping that Woodward, who had recently won a federal job, would help him do the same. Whatever Doane's rationale, his letter to Woodward cited inspiration found in recent articles "in the National Journal, relative to the projected canal to unite the Atlantic and Pacific Oceans."[49]

In the spring of 1825, the Washington-based *National Journal* offered nearly daily reporting on interoceanic canal plans. In early April, it published a translation of a November 1824 decree from the Mexican Congress inviting proposals "to undertake a communication between the two Oceans, through the isthmus of Tehuantepee [*sic*]."[50] The next day, the newspaper declared this route "decidedly preferable" to the Nicaragua route "on account of its more convenient location."[51] Perhaps sensing that readers had no idea where Nicaragua was located, the next paper contained a lengthy description of the "Province of Nicaragua" which was written by a Nicaraguan and "Translated for the National Journal." The piece contained a great deal of geographic information as well as puffery. An example of the latter claimed, "There is, perhaps, no part of America that possesses such good and capacious ports as this province." This was not what Blunt found. The article also attempted to soften the truth of its "humid and hot" climate by suggesting that "this may be somewhat remedied by clearing the land."[52] True, humans might alter the climate, but we now know that destroying rainforests would do the opposite of cooling the land.

But where did the paper get a local booster's account of Nicaragua? In the United States of the 1820s, information about Central America was rare; the newspaper credited its source in a subsequent article as it acknowledged "the politeness of the Envoy from Guatemala." Cañas supplied the newspaper with more material including a translation of Central America's decree abolishing slavery.[53] But he could not place Central American promotional pieces into every paper.

In numbers of the *National Journal* that did not include accounts of Central America, promotion of domestic canal projects filled columns. The newspaper advocated "A canal to unite the waters of the *Gulf of Mexico* with the *Atlantic*" by cutting through Florida.[54] In another article assessing the progress on several domestic canal projects, the newspaper praised speculation and canal "ardour." "By the enterprise of our ancestors," it asserted, "the forest has been felled; it is for our enterprise to plant artificial rivers in the wilderness."[55]

Like other newspapers, however, the *National Journal* recognized that other countries could also construct "artificial rivers."[56] Printing London news whenever it became available, the *National Journal* suggested the perils of British investment in Spanish America as part of a "gambling mania."[57] It explained British news stories about Spanish American investments as detrimental to US interests. Such was the case on April 27, 1825, when the *National Journal* devoted two columns to articles reprinted from London papers about a "Bill" that "was about to pass the House of Commons for incorporating a company, whose object is to unite the Atlantic and Pacific Oceans by navigable canal" through Nicaragua. The *National Intelligencer* rued this development. Having "indulged the hope" that the canal "would have been accomplished by the Government of Central America, or the individual enterprise of the United States," the newspaper regretted the idea of British construction of the canal. Citing the threat of British connections at the "Mosquitos Shore," the editors preferred the closer Mexican route. Incorrectly suggesting that "our citizen Mr. Blunt" was currently surveying Tehuantepec, the editors hoped that the United States would control a superior interoceanic waterway.[58]

Although Doane did not specify which *National Journal* articles inspired him to write to Woodward, his letter was probably prompted by the two columns of canal coverage in that day's paper. He complained that in the paper, "The importance of this great work is but slightly touched on." Whereas previous writers had mostly considered the shorter route to Asia as the chief effect of the canal, Doane confessed, "My ideas on this subject go beyond these considerations." Far beyond.

Citing the British explorer Captain Cook, Doane asserted that the waters of the Atlantic Ocean were "nineteen and a half feet higher than the Pacific."[59] A topic of debate among scientific thinkers, Humboldt described the idea of the seas as anything but level as a "vulgar opinion" derived from ancient texts, but the era's technology could not yet measure the relative heights of the oceans.[60] Imprecisely echoing Humboldt's explanation of ocean currents, Doane argued that this supposed height differential contributed to the rapid current in the Florida Straits between the Keys and Cuba that he reckoned were part of the Gulf Stream.[61] In Doane's view, the isthmus between the American continents that separated the oceans kept the Gulf Stream churning. "When this canal is opened," he imagined, "the rush of water into the Pacific will be immense." It would cut away the land creating "a passage for itself equal in magnitude to the Straits of Gibraltar," which separated Europe from North Africa. Ships would easily pass between the seas.

But there was more to Doane's vision. "It follows, of course," he asserted, "that all those places on the Atlantic side of the continent . . . will reclaim from the ocean all banks that have 19 feet water thereon." In other words, sea level along the US eastern seaboard would fall. This would have the anticipated beneficial effect of eliminating "dangerous shoals" along the coast. "The Gulf Stream," he exclaimed, "will be done away; navigation rendered safe and easy." There would be no more shipwrecks along the Florida Reef and travel to Cuba would be faster. Moreover, the canal would feed the hungry United States with new land along its Atlantic Ocean and Gulf of Mexico coastlines.

"But these are minor considerations to what I am now coming at," he transitioned. Doane's next prediction: the Mississippi River would suddenly gain a deep and safe mouth and its "unproductive and unhealthy" marshes would be drained. "Reclaim thousands of acres from the ocean," he projected, "and, in fine, make the states of Mississippi and Louisiana high and healthy." Meanwhile a change in the winds would chill Cuba's "climate" producing the same "severe frost and ice" that prevented the "coffee tree" from growing in New Orleans. For Doane, the human action of cutting through the isthmus would produce global environmental change in terms of air, land, and sea.

The War of 1812 veteran's global visions took nationalist form. Referencing the reports of a London-based canal company "soliciting Government protection, and supported by British capital," Doane feared, "I should not be surprised if our flag was excluded, unless prompt measures are taken to insure us a fair participation with the British." Calling for the US government to accelerate its entry in the canal race, Doane closed his letter to Woodward explaining, "I have thus, Sir, suggested my views on this subject to you, to be used by you in any manner you may think proper."[62]

Woodward immediately replied to Doane and sent both letters to "a distinguished press." In his reply, also penned in Washington on the same day, the Floridian judge offered to send Doane's letter to the Agricultural Society of Middle Florida, where the members had apparently already been discussing this topic. Woodward suggested that the water differential might be smaller, perhaps only as little as "five feet," and he was less optimistic about what benefits a fall in sea level might produce. "I would anticipate severe deleterious sickliness, in the first instance," he opined, "gradually succeeded by the consequences you mention, and eventual healthiness." He was willing to consider the destruction of the Atlantic's ocean currents, but he thought that these effects might be diminished by the choice of route. "If the operation should be conducted through the Lake Nicaragua," he wrote, "perhaps the effects and results as relates to physical changes would be greatly reduced." Advocating for the Central American route, Woodward agreed with Doane's concerns about British control of the canal: "some movement and exertion are necessary on our part is too obvious to be denied."[63] With this implied request to US policymakers and with a plea for a canal through Florida, he closed his letter.

A theory of human-created climate change and a short reply advocating the Nicaragua route thus began their circulation through US newspapers. First printed in Washington in April, the pair of letters made their way to Boston by early May.[64] Doane's letter was translated into German in Reading, Pennsylvania.[65] The responses started pouring in. Arguing that the sea level differential had "often been urged as a reason" for not constructing an interoceanic canal, an author in the *U.S. Gazette* praised Doane's positive reframing but suggested that "the *draining* referred to" might produce new "ugly shoals."[66] Newspapers around the country reprinted this critique and wrote others, which were themselves reprinted.[67]

Some saw significance beyond US coasts. Situating an interoceanic waterway among other "magnificent schemes for internal improvement" like the Erie Canal, a Maine paper argued "the effects of a canal to unite the Atlantic and Pacific Oceans between North and South America, will not be felt by a single State alone, nor by one nation, nor even by one continent."[68] An undeniably global project, the interoceanic canal accrued nationalist undertones that suggested it was in the interest of the United States to try to control the project.

Other responses critiqued the science behind Doane's suggestions. The contrarian *Richmond Enquirer* questioned whether the Pacific might not be higher than the Atlantic.[69] This too would produce "a marine revolution of a contrary and less beneficial effect than if the Atlantic was higher than the Pacific." Concerned by the uncertainty of a potential rise in sea level, the article asserted in all italics, "*No time should be lost in ascertaining this important point of altitude.*" As the voice of Southerners demanding free trade and protection of slavery, the *Enquirer* would not directly advocate for the federal government taking on the project. Instead it employed a backhanded call to action: "In these times of speculation, and let us add, of great enterprize, a more important and useful project could not possibly present itself to the consideration of any government." But the *Enquirer* did not want just "any government" or private concern to build the canal. "To make so vast a project the speculation of a private company," the article opined, "would ill comport with the general benefits to be produced; and to permit Great Britain to cut the canal, and to demand Sound duties, or close the great short-cut or avenue to the Pacific at pleasure, would give to that power the key to both seas." If neither private companies nor the British government should hold "the key to both seas," who ought to pay for and own such a valuable canal? Against federal internal improvement projects, the *Enquirer* ignored the question. It imagined a "free" waterway where US ships could travel "unquestioned and unmolested," never mind that building a canal was anything but "free."[70]

Even more critical, a lengthy article written for a Salem, Massachusetts, paper encouraged readers to rethink Doane's math. If the Atlantic was nineteen feet higher than the Pacific, the sea level would drop by only half the difference, or nine and a half feet. Even this smaller drop in sea level, the author suggested, would have cataclysmic short-term results. Until the water leveled off over "several years," the canal might be "no more navigable than the Falls of Niagara."[71] Predicting that the longed-for waterway would temporarily be a waterfall, this critic favored the Nicaragua route, which was removed from the Gulf Stream and, therefore, would probably not interfere with it. Whatever the canal's location, the critic argued that humans lacked the power to produce such massive global change. "It is certain," the critic asserted, "that it is not in the power of art to change the Gulf Stream, any more than to change the trade winds." Only "a great convulsion" like the biblical flood could have created the ocean currents, and only a similar force could make a deep enough cut through the continents to channel the Gulf Stream into the Pacific. "In which case," he ridiculed, "would not the southern part [of the American continents] . . . float away, or tip over?" The fanciful imagery of a continent adrift implied that only God could stop the Gulf Stream's gyre. "I do not know who Mr. Doane or Judge Woodward are," the Massachusetts author concluded, suggesting that both needed to understand that no canal was going to alter the divinely "ordered" environment.[72] Others would agree, "it is not within the reach of human power to 'disturb the economy of nature's realm.'"[73]

Condemning Doane's notion of human-caused climate change did not preclude supporting the construction of an interoceanic canal. One such critic explained, "almost every great and brilliant enterprize has to encounter the ridicule and the opposition of the weak, the timid and the selfish all over the world."[74] Believing that the "art" of building a canal could have environmental effects, Woodward and Doane were cast as starry-eyed dreamers, but with the same ink, critics who condemned the idea that humans could transform nature spread the dream of an economically and politically transformative canal.

But the ink was what mattered. As more and more newspapers printed and reprinted first the coupled letters and then their many critiques, the idea of a transatlantic canal approached the status of a fait accompli. Speculations about the potential waterway's effects on the Gulf Stream were carried by the current of newspapers to the public in every corner of the nation well into the summer of 1825.[75] The high tide mark of 1820s US popular support for an interoceanic canal, Doane's theory enjoyed a long news cycle and spread canal dreams across the country.

MEANWHILE, IN LATE APRIL 1825, as Woodward and Doane's words began to circulate and popular enthusiasm for a Nicaraguan canal swelled, the chief clerk of the State Department sent Miller a letter confirming that his official instructions "are prepared, and that it is the wish of the President you should proceed upon the mission with all convenient dispatch."[76]

It is surprising that Clay needed more than a month to prepare Miller's instructions as he copied much from Adams's instructions to Mann. Clay included verbatim the entire passage about the Salvadoran annexation mission and the "superior" claim of Central America to the "interest and regard of the United States." Miller's goal would be identical to Mann's "to obtain and to communicate to this Department, by every opportunity of conveyance that may occur, information."

One variation between the two instructions, however, indicated how Central American recognition altered the job. Miller was specifically "authorized to propose" a commercial treaty to promote what Clay called "fair competition," which meant eliminating "discriminating duties" that put the United States at a disadvantage compared to other countries. Clay conveyed Adams's preference that the treaty's negotiation "should take place in Washington."[77]

Miller's official instructions could be boiled down to two orders: obtain information and favorable trade relations. But these were not the only instructions sent to the new chargé d'affaires. A lengthier letter of the same date provided the practical details to accompany the policy priorities. The letter contained a twelve-item list of "papers, documents, and books" that were to be shipped by the US government for Miller's mission. The papers were practical: his official commission, a letter of introduction to the minister of foreign affairs, a passport, his official instructions, an engraving of the required dress uniform, and a "Letter of Credit upon the Bankers of the United States at London," which would enable the chargé to receive his salary and pay his expenses. He would also receive the tools for fulfilling his information-gathering order: two reams of "Despatch paper" and a "cypher" to write encoded messages. This paper was especially important to the State Department because it had begun to standardize its record keeping. To bind the numbered "despatches" in uniform volumes, the letter specified the paper dimensions, margins, and line spacing with "these instructions" providing "an example."

The bulk of the items on the list, however, were books. The State Department would ship forty-five volumes: twenty-six indexed volumes of the newspaper *Niles Weekly Register*, twelve volumes of Watt's *State Papers*, six volumes and two pamphlets containing the Laws of the United States, and a volume summarizing "the Commercial Regulation of the Foreign Countries." Hoping to pay the freight charges for shipping the library only once, Clay cautioned Miller that the books were "for the use of the mission," should remain in Guatemala, and would "pass" to Miller's "successor." As this suggests, the United States intended Miller's mission to be the first of many. These were not just instructions for one man; they were meant to establish a permanent US diplomatic presence in Central America.

But there would be no mission without money. Clay detailed Miller's salary, how and when it would be paid, which expenses would be paid by the US government, and the method of keeping accounts. In the collection of information, he cautioned Miller "to discriminate between that which is authentic and that which is spurious" by writing to other US diplomats posted elsewhere as well as through "friendly social relations" with other nations' diplomats posted to Guatemala City. Required to socialize, perhaps Miller's commitment to sobriety would keep him clear-eyed while others drank.

Regardless of how he obtained his information, Clay urged Miller "to collect and to transmit information of every kind." Unlike consuls who were provided a small budget for sending publications mostly about epidemics, the diplomat was to acquire "historical works," travel guides, "authentic maps," and scientific publications. Clay ordered Miller to correspond "with the consuls of the United States in Guatemala," and authorized him to fill consular vacancies with "a temporary appointment." The plural was unnecessary, as Clay explained, "The only Consul of the United States at present in Guatemala is Charles Savage." Whereas Savage was prohibited from providing US citizens with passports, this was among Miller's explicit duties. Miller, however, was prohibited from accepting "presents of Jewelry and other articles of pecuniary value" from the Central American government; no medals with Arce's face would hang around his neck.[78]

With so many "minute" details enumerated, both sets of instructions remained silent about how Miller was to transport himself and his considerable luggage to Central America.[79] The State Department left the choice of route to the diplomat.[80] Eager to leave North Carolina and "enter upon the duties of the mission," Chargé Miller accepted this challenge.[81] His first stop would be Washington.

IN THE US CAPITAL, the Adams administration was eager to send a diplomat to Guatemala City. But there was already a Central American diplomat in Washington. Cañas was hard at work attracting attention to his newly independent country. In addition to feeding the press with fodder to generate public interest, he pursued a diplomatic agenda with the government. After recognition, the canal was the centerpiece of his campaign. Through public debates and private communications, Cañas found a climate in Washington more amenable than ever to learning about his new land.

CHAPTER EIGHT

Diplomats

On February 8, 1825, the day before the US House of Representatives voted to elect John Quincy Adams to the presidency, Minister Cañas penned a letter that would give the secretary of state and soon-to-be president-elect a reason for haste in appointing a chargé to Central America. In flowing Spanish cursive, the gaunt diplomat offered Adams his country's most prized resource: the right to build an interoceanic canal along the Nicaraguan route.[1]

Cañas curiously waited six months after his country's recognition to convey this offer to Adams. The delay meant that his proposal got lost in the shuffle between US administrations. Too busy preparing to be president, Adams left Cañas's correspondence to be answered by Clay. Two eventful months passed between Cañas's February offer and Clay's April response. In Guatemala City, a new government formed. Cañas's credentials became questionable, his instructions outdated. The diplomat in Washington did not know that Arce favored a canal constructed not by treaty but by contract. Although this ultimately turned Cañas's offer into a dead letter, he effectively wielded the canal as a diplomatic carrot that heightened Adams's interest in Central America. The new president nominated Miller to the Guatemala City diplomatic post on his first full day in office.

All diplomats' powers depended on paper. The word "diplomat" derived from the French adaptation of the Latin word "diploma," meaning "an official document" or "a state letter of recommendation."[2] Meant to be a solution to the problem of slow communication between capitals, governments issued credentials and instructions to state agents sent to distant countries. But sometimes conditions changed too quickly for the documents to keep up. The communications lag between the United States and Central America required diplomats to make their own decisions.

IN HIS LETTER TO SECRETARY ADAMS of February 8, 1825, Minister Cañas revealed a portion of his diplomatic instructions. His government had "particularly recommended" that the diplomat discuss with the US government the "interesting subject" of the "opening of a canal for the communication of the Pacific and Atlantic Oceans in the province of Nicaragua." According to Cañas, the construction of an interoceanic waterway would "be a most glorious act" because the "general prosperity" it would produce would be "the most vast which had ever been conceived." A canal would literally change the world's fortunes.

Cañas was authorized not only to discuss this "interesting subject" but also to make a deal. As he explained, the "inestimable benefits" of such a "great enterprize" demanded resources Central America did not yet possess. Conceptualizing the canal as the culmination of the Age of Revolutions, he conveyed that his government would be "grateful" for the "cooperation" of "your generous nation, whose noble conduct has been a model and a protection to all the Americas." Recognizing that the canal would be revolutionary in its transformation of the earth's waters, Cañas explained that his government wanted the United States to be "a participator, not only of the merit of the enterprize, but of the great advantages which that canal of communication must produce." Proposing joint control over the waterway, the diplomat offered fluid sovereignty over the route in exchange for a commitment by the United States to participate in the canal's construction "by means of a treaty which may perpetually secure the possession of it to the two nations."

The diplomat enclosed a "plan" to demonstrate the "possibility of the work."[3] If the map had been provided by Cañas's government, it would have been a copy of de la Cerda's *Plano Ídeal* sent to Guatemala City. But it was more likely a copy of the Mexican version, which was at that moment in Washington in the hands of Curtis Bolton.[4] Later in life, Bolton recalled receiving Cañas's "countenance & support" for his canal proposal.[5] The men likely coordinated the timing of Cañas's proposal to accompany Bolton's request for support for his journey to Nicaragua to save Blunt's surveying mission. In his offer, Cañas assured Adams, "A company of respectable American merchants is ready to undertake the work, as soon as it is secured by a treaty between both Governments." Bolton was, of course, not the only US citizen "ready to undertake" the canal. By the time Cañas wrote his offer of joint canal construction to Adams, Guatemala City was quickly filling with agents of eager foreign capitalists. In part to manage these men, Cañas's government urged "a diplomatic Agent" be sent from the United States to Guatemala City.[6] Cañas had dangled just the right prize in front of Adams to ensure that a diplomat would be nominated immediately after his inauguration.

Adams may have been motivated to get a diplomat to Guatemala City but neither he nor Clay felt the need to respond quickly to Cañas's offer. Blaming the more than two-month delay on the change of administration, Clay penned a response on April 18, 1825. Expressing Adams's "very great sensibility" to Cañas's "expression of sentiments of consideration and friendship towards the

United States," Clay assured, "they are most cordially reciprocated." Viewing Cañas's "highly important proposition" as a manifestation of the good feelings between the two countries, Clay acknowledged a long history of ideas about "uniting those two seas by a canal navigation." He agreed, "The execution of it will form a great epoch in the commercial affairs of the whole world."[7]

But was the "execution" of such a global and epochal project even possible? "The practicability of it can be scarcely doubted," Clay wrote, acknowledging that public opinion about the "Various lines for the proposed canal" seemed to favor the Nicaragua route. Nonetheless, the Adams administration did not put its faith in the existing "evidence" about the canal route. Clay hedged, "on a project of such vast magnitude it is necessary to proceed with the greatest caution. A false step, taken in the first movement might lead to the most mischievous consequences." Clay conveyed Adams's plan "to instruct the chargé des affaires of the United States whom he has just appointed, and who will shortly proceed upon his mission to the Republic of the Centre, to investigate with the greatest care the facilities which the route through the Province of Nicaragua offers."[8] The Adams administration punted. It would send a diplomat, and it would empower that diplomat to assess the canal. It would not trust the *Plano Ídeal*.

Even if the chargé d'affaires confirmed ideal conditions for the construction of a canal, the president could not act alone. It would be "necessary to consult Congress as to the nature and extent of the co-operation which shall be given towards the completion of the great work," Clay explained.[9] Congress had just voted Adams into office, but it had been an unusually fraught election. The new president could not count on a congressional majority to vote for his policies. The legislature might not support Adams's ambitious agenda to plow the proceeds of western land sales into domestic infrastructure development. They might especially scoff at a foreign drain on the nation's resources. Debates raged throughout Monroe's presidency about the limits of the federal government's powers of "internal improvement"—the right to build canals, roads, and other public works.[10] Such a project of what we might call "external improvement" was uncharted ground. Clay could not predict the result in the nation's legislature. Whether the United States committed to build the canal or not, Clay assured the diplomat that his offer to include the United States in the canal's construction was a "friendly overture" that carried, in and of itself, significant influence.[11]

Clay explained the new administration's prioritization of Central America in a striking new passage in his instructions to Chargé Miller. To the diplomat, Clay described the canal offer as "new, and highly interesting proof of the friendly sentiments" of the Central American government toward the United States. The opportunity "to share" in the "important object of uniting the Atlantic and Pacific Oceans by a Canal navigation through the Province of Nicaragua" established the diplomatic mission's top priority: "the acquisition of further information." Elaborating, Clay outlined exactly what information the United States wanted: "ascertain if surveys have been made of the proposed route of the Canal." The secretary demanded answers to a flurry of specific questions: "what is its length; what the nature of the Country, and of the ground through which it is to pass; can the supply of water for feeders be drawn from the Lake Nicaragua or other adequate sources." He summarized, "in short, what facilities do the Country and the state of its population afford, for making the Canal, and what are the estimates of its cost?" Privately, Blunt had been sent by Bolton to answer similar questions. Now the US government was investing in its own search for "full information."

Answering these questions was only one part of Miller's mission; he also had to set the appropriate tone for further negotiations. Clay cautioned, "It is not intended that you should inspire the Government of the Republic of Guatimala with any confident expectation that the United States will contribute, by pecuniary or other means, to the execution of the work, because it is not yet known what view Congress might take of it."[12] Before Adams gambled on asking Congress to consider a bill supporting such a large work of external improvement, he needed more information.

Miller was instructed to be discreet about the US government's interest in the canal, but the urgency of Miller's appointment said it all. Adams was seriously considering Cañas's offer.

LESS THAN A WEEK after Clay finalized Miller's instructions, the new chargé appeared in Washington, met with Adams, acquired his instructions, and headed north to New York City to find passage on a ship heading to Central America.[13] But few US ships sailed there in the mid-1820s. Although he was unsuccessful in finding a vessel, he did find Cañas who recommended a fellow Central American to help locate transportation to Guatemala.[14] Cañas's contact informed Miller that "I have used every practicable endeavor to find a passage suitable for us to pass to Guatemala." He ruled out the only vessel currently headed to the region as one in which he "would never risk the crossing," because it was too small and would not be able to protect itself from the "numerous pirates, unfortunately infesting the coast of the Island of Cuba." The contact recommended that the chargé reach out to the US government to gain passage on "a Public vessel cruising on the Coast of Cuba, which vessels, frequently sail from Norfolk."[15]

Eager to get the diplomat to Central America, and with Clay out of town, Adams discussed Miller's predicament with Samuel Southard, secretary of the navy. Southard suggested that Miller take passage to "Thompson's Island in the *Decoy*, Store Ship, which is about to sail, about a fortnight hence for that place, from the port of Norfolk in Virginia." Thompson's Island was the name given only two years earlier to what the Spanish had called *Cayo Hueso*, or Key West, a strategically significant island with a deep harbor on the Florida Straits. The *Decoy* was a small vessel that brought supplies to the West Indies Squadron, which suppressed piracy off the Florida coast. In Key West, Miller would find "passage" on one of the squadron's pirate-hunting ships "to some convenient and eligible port."[16]

Responding hastily from New York, Miller asked the State Department to forward to Norfolk his cypher, passport, other papers, and a locked "Trunk" full of books with a doctor who would serve as his private secretary on the mission.[17] With the diplomat still absent on the date scheduled for departure, the navy delayed the *Decoy*'s sailing so Miller could catch the ship.[18]

Unfortunately, when Miller arrived in Key West, he also caught yellow fever. Epidemics of yellow fever had plagued US and Caribbean human populations for over a century. Borne by mosquitoes, the virus typically proved lethal for adults who had never previously contracted the disease. Named for the tell-tale jaundiced yellow eyes of its victims, its cause was unknown and all treatment ineffective.[19]

Once bitten, even Miller's doctor/secretary could do nothing to save the diplomat. The prey of something much smaller than a pirate ship, Miller died after three days of illness on September 10, 1825. Writing from the Cuban port of Havana, the doctor planned his return to the United States "with all the papers &c. left by Mr. Miller, Esq. Dec[d] [deceased]."[20] The mission's books had sailed to Key West and Cuba but not to Guatemala; they would have to be reshipped. The State Department would be forced to start all over again in its doubly fatal attempt to get a diplomatic agent to Central America.

WARM WEATHER BROUGHT tropical diseases to North America. That summer, Cañas fell ill visiting New York City. He traveled to nearby Saratoga Springs for its mineral waters, but his health remained precarious. Only in early September, around the same time that Miller died off the coast of Florida, did Cañas feel well enough to return to Washington.[21]

As Cañas gathered his strength, Clay also suffered. The secretary had spent the early summer at his home in Kentucky. As his large family traveled back east to the nation's capital, Clay found himself a month delayed in Ohio—not far from Hindostan, Indiana—by the illness and death of Eliza, his twelve-year-old daughter.[22] The secretary survived the disease that took his child, but when he arrived in Washington, Adams described Clay as "unwell" and unable to leave his lodgings.[23]

Cañas blamed both men's prolonged absences from Washington in explaining his not "proceeding to the adjustment of the treaties which, as you know, are the objects of my mission." With recognition accomplished and canal negotiation stalled, Cañas had proceeded to his third goal: acquiring a commercial treaty between the United States and his nation. Planning his return from New York, Cañas wrote to Clay inquiring whether the US government "finds itself disposed to enter upon negotiation."[24] Under the weather and overwhelmed with the "accumulation of business" during his absence, Clay responded, "I shall be glad to see you here on any business connected with your mission, when it may be altogether convenient to you."[25] The diplomat need not rush.

As temperatures cooled and they recuperated, Cañas and Clay finalized the treaty's terms, which were largely based on a recent treaty with Colombia.[26] In late November, Adams recorded in his diary, "Mr Clay informed me that he was nearly ready to sign a Commercial Treaty with the Minister from the Republic of Central America Cañaz [*sic*]; but seemed to think it best to postpone the signature till after the commencement of the Session of Congress."[27] A treaty could wait. Central American commerce was basically nonexistent; few citizens were clamoring for improved duties on Central American goods.

Waiting to finalize the commercial treaty, Cañas extended another offer to the US government. In response to rumors of a plan for European reconquest, Simón Bolívar had called a "General Congress of the American Republics" to meet in Panamá.[28] When the liberator decided not to invite the United States, other nations sought Washington's participation. Cañas offered "an invitation from the Government of the Federation of the Centre of America to that of the U. States to send deputies to the contemplated Congress at Panama."[29] "I am anxious," Cañas wrote, "to know if this Republic which has ever shewn itself the generous friend of the New American States, is disposed to send its Envoys to the General Congress, the object of which, is, to preserve and confirm the absolute independence of these republics."[30] As Clay informed the diplomat, this too would have to wait "a few days" for

Congress to convene and for the Senate to give its consent. A longtime supporter of Spanish American independence, Clay hoped a delegation would be sent to Panamá "without any unnecessary delay."[31]

As with the proposal for US involvement in a Central American canal, all Clay could do was hope and wait. In Congress, the topic would prove incredibly controversial, and would rupture the support for US hemispheric leadership that Clay had spearheaded in the 1810s and early 1820s. By the time the Senate gave its consent to the appointment of ministers to Panamá and the House funded the mission, the men were so delayed that they missed the Panama Congress entirely.[32]

But this was in the future. In the late fall of 1825, the treaty was the higher priority. The "Treaty or general Convention of Peace, Friendship, Commerce, and Navigation" outlined "the rules" governing relations between the nations.[33] The countries agreed that, in all manner of dealing, they would treat each other as "the most favoured nation do or shall enjoy."[34] With a few exceptions, they agreed that "the Citizens of each may frequent all the coasts and countries of the other, and reside and trade there" with the same rights as "native Citizens."[35] Duties or tariffs would be the same for merchandise shipped on either country's vessels. Many articles were devoted to the rules governing property, people, and paperwork during times of war and peace.

The treaty defined its own terms. For twelve years from the day of the exchange of ratifications, the commercial aspects of the treaty would be "in full force and virtue." The "parts which relate to peace and friendship" would be "permanently and perpitually [*sic*] binding on both powers."[36] Perhaps most importantly in terms of turning the treaty into the law of two lands, the document would have to be "approved and ratified by the President of the United States of America, by and with the advice and consent of the Senate." Then a ratification procedure would be followed by "the Government of the Federation of the Centre of America."[37] For the treaty to go into effect, the two nations' ratifications were required to be "exchanged in the City of Guatemala within eight months."[38]

On December 5, 1825, as the Nineteenth Congress convened for its first regular session, Cañas and Clay signed the bilingual document. Under an "injunction of secrecy," it was submitted to the Senate ten days later.[39] When the chairman of the Senate's Foreign Relations Committee visited Adams the next day, he had no harsh words about the treaty, but "intimated that he should be against" the appointment of ministers to the Panama Congress.[40] The treaty sailed through the Senate and was officially ratified by the United States on January 16, 1826.[41]

But its clock was already ticking; the deadline for the exchange of ratifications was August 5, 1826. It was time to get a living US diplomat to Guatemala City.

THE FIRST TWO MEN APPOINTED to serve as US diplomats in Central America–Agent Mann and Chargé Miller—had hailed from North Carolina; the third was born there but moved west to Knoxville, Tennessee, in the first decade of the nineteenth century.[42] Through Central American appointments, Adams sought to woo men from North Carolina who had supported a rival candidate with the prize of public office.[43] But the Guatemalan post would simultaneously relocate these one-time opponents to a distant and dangerous place.

For Colonel John Williams, the third man chosen for the job, the Central American post was a prize, a punishment, and an exile all in one. A Crawford man, Williams had not supported Adams in the 1824 election. But the president understood that Williams's campaign for Crawford manifested an all-consuming loathing of Andrew Jackson.

Williams had not always hated Jackson; the men had a lot in common. Exposed to backcountry violence at an early age, both started their adulthood as soldiers, read law in the same town, and moved to newly settled Tennessee where their practices facilitated the dispossession and removal of the region's Indigenous inhabitants to enable the replacement of this population with enslaved people of African descent and their enslavers. Both Williams and Jackson drafted land treaties with the Cherokee Nation. Jackson bought three enslaved people from Williams in 1810.[44]

One in the eastern and one in the western part of Tennessee, the men honed their political skills in a state divided into two factions. Williams learned the rhetoric of local politics and printed a letter in a newspaper disparaging a rival for frequently "staggering through the streets of Knoxville with intoxication."[45] In his late twenties, Williams married a teenage Matilda White, daughter of the founder of Knoxville.[46] Matilda made him kin to one of Jackson's oldest friends.[47] At this point, the men were on the same side.

Then came the War of 1812. They collaborated to fight "our British and Indian foes," as Williams described them.[48] Waging total war against the Seminole Nation in Florida, Williams and his men killed people, burned hundreds of homes, and seized animal livestock as well as thousands of valuable deer skins.[49] As a colonel in the US Army, he gained fame at the Battle of Horseshoe Bend where he fought the Creeks alongside Jackson. After the battle, Jackson called Williams "my friend."[50]

This early twentieth-century portrait depicts John Williams (1778–1837). S. G. Heiskell, "Colonel John Williams, Commander 39th Regulars, Battle of the Horse Shoe," *Andrew Jackson and Early Tennessee History* (Nashville, 1918).

The friendship faded fast. When Williams refused to provide a state militia regiment with federal supplies designated for army troops, Jackson interpreted Williams's actions as a form of criminal disobedience. Believing that he was being unfairly rebuked for following army orders, Williams resented Jackson's questioning of his loyalty.[51] A smoldering feud commenced.

Williams's success during the war led to political office. Elected initially to fill a midterm US Senate vacancy, Williams subsequently won his own full six-year term during which he cast one of only four votes against Adams's Transcontinental Treaty.[52] Adams explained Williams's vote as "from party-impulses, connected with hatred of General Jackson."[53] During the treaty negotiations, Williams circulated rumors that Jackson's invasion of Florida served the general's personal pecuniary interests; he could not vote to put ill-gotten money in Jackson's pocket.[54] But two men played this game. Jackson called the senator a "subtle fiend" and vowed to "punish him" because "he has, I know, in dark innuendoes and secrete [*sic*] and confidential information endeavored to injure me."[55]

Jackson was not Williams's only target. As chair of the Committee for Military Affairs, he led a movement to reduce the size and cost of the army to undermine Secretary of War John C. Calhoun. By weakening Calhoun, Williams and his congressman brother sought "to promote Mr. Crawford's election to the Presidency."[56] The Williamses might support Secretary Crawford, but it was not because of his policies. The treasury secretary advocated limiting the powers of the federal government. On the other hand, Williams supported tariffs, voted for the federally chartered Second Bank of the United States, and sought federal sponsorship of Tennessee's internal improvements.[57] Williams's positions more closely aligned with those of his fellow westerner Henry Clay, but the rival faction in Tennessee politics were Clay men. Williams would rather support Crawford and his antithetical policies than empower his local enemies.

When he ran for reelection to the Senate in 1823, Williams's rivals pursued extreme means to defeat him. Although they supported Clay in the presidential election, the rivals nominated Andrew Jackson as a presidential candidate with the goal of inducing Williams to sink his own senatorial campaign by not endorsing the general for president. This strategy would ultimately prove incredibly consequential for US political history, but in the 1823 senatorial election, it failed. As the election neared, it became apparent that the only way to defeat Williams was for him to run directly against Jackson, who promptly entered the Senate race and won Williams's seat.[58] As the feud intensified, Jackson was so successful at "punishing" Williams that the former US senator even lost a campaign for the state legislature.[59]

And then Henry Clay's letter arrived in Knoxville. Clay offered Williams the "mission from the United States to Guatemala" at the rank of "Chargé des affaires, with its emoluments of outfit and salary." Clay stressed Central America's "friendly and flattering" relations with the United States and reminded the former senator of the visit of the Salvadoran commissioners who proposed annexation. "We wish to give extension and strength to these relations," explained Clay, "and great reliance would be placed on your zeal, discretion, and patriotism, in accomplishing that object." Williams had zeal and patriotism in spades. For a man who spent much of his political career spreading rumors and intriguing against rivals, discretion was not his strong suit. Nonetheless Adams and Clay thought he was the man for the job. Clay concluded his offer by stating that he was "Happy to be the organ of communicating this distinguished proof [of] the President's confidence in you."[60] This unusual closing suggests that Clay and Adams, both potential candidates in 1828, saw Williams as a valuable ally in what was already brewing: a fight against Jackson.

Williams quickly penned a terse response: "the mission to the Republic of Guatemala is accepted."[61] Desperate for a political resurrection, perhaps the forty-seven-year-old did not care that his younger predecessors had died trying to get to Central America. The diplomatic post offered the old soldier a new field of glory far from Washington, Tennessee, and Jackson.

But first, the Senate would have to consent to Williams's appointment. The Senate read Williams's nomination into the record on the day after Christmas 1825.[62] Two days later, Stephen Van Rensselaer, whose vote earlier in the year had decided the presidency, visited Adams to lobby on Williams's behalf. According to the president's diary, the Patroon "came to urge that Mr. John Williams should be appointed Minister Plenipotentiary to the Federation of Central America, instead of Chargé d'Affaires." Adams described Williams's partisan struggles in Tennessee and his having been "very solicitous to obtain this appointment of Chargé d'Affaires to Guatemala." Only after his official nomination, Adams explained, fellow Crawford supporters "have whispered to him that this Office of Chargé d'Affaires is not of sufficient dignity for him, and that he is degrading himself by accepting it." Adams refused to reconsider Williams's title or promise a future promotion, explaining that "the nomination was made," that Congress would not provide a greater allowance for a higher ranked diplomat, and that he "could make no promise for futurity, other than of goodwill and a friendly disposition."[63] On the same day that it consented to the Central American treaty, the Senate confirmed Chargé Williams.[64] The treaty and the diplomat became a package deal.

In late January, Williams met with Adams and "asked for advice."[65] In early February, Clay sent Williams his formal and personal instructions. These documents were almost the same as those sent to Miller and Mann. In the formal instructions, the few deviations reflected the existence of the newly ratified treaty.

Clay opened with a new paragraph explaining that the chargé's "first object" would be to exchange ratifications of the commercial treaty with "the Government of the Central Republic." Clay assured, "No difficulty is anticipated as to the ratification of the Treaty at Guatemala" because it was negotiated "in a spirit of great amity, and both the negociators appeared to be sensible that the Treaty was founded on the equitable basis of perfect reciprocity." Along the same lines, the instructions concluded with a short new paragraph exerting the United States's claim to "fair competition" should any other nation attempt to receive "peculiar concessions" for their "Commerce and Navigation" in Central America.[66] Apart from this new priority, the document reiterated the previously composed history of Salvadoran annexation, the discussion of Cañas's canal proposal, the profession of US ignorance of the region, and the instruction to acquire information.

Aside from adding two extra volumes containing the last year's *Niles Weekly Register* and one new sentence about how to keep account of publications sent to Washington, Williams's informal instructions were identical to Miller's.[67] Even the port of departure would be the same. On February 11, 1826, Williams and his congressman brother met with Adams before he set out for Norfolk. Leveraging Williams's imminent departure, the brother recommended a fellow North Carolinian and Crawford man to be appointed a diplomat to Peru. Adams recalled, "I told him I would take into consideration and I assured him it would be very agreeable to me that a Citizen of North-Carolina should be appointed upon one of those Missions abroad." Agreeable, indeed. For years, Adams had been trying to send North Carolinians to Central America. Williams was getting close.[68]

By early March, Williams had arrived in Norfolk.[69] Mann, the first US diplomatic agent assigned to Central America, died without ever leaving the port. Miller, the second, made it to the United States's southernmost naval base. Williams would get all the way to Guatemala City, but never to the canal route.

WILLIAMS DID NOT TRAVEL on the *U.S.S. John Adams* alone. Although diplomats' wives and children often joined missions, Williams's family did not. Matilda planned to surprise her husband by overseeing the building of a new mansion. Constructed of thousands of clay and mud bricks, individually struck nails, hand-hewn timber, and horse-hair infused plaster, all formed by the hands of the men, women, and children that the Williams family enslaved, the hilltop mansion would symbolize the family's elevation in Tennessee. Overlooking a river descending from the Smoky Mountains, Matilda's domestic mission paralleled her husband's diplomatic goal: to reassert control over land, water, animals, and people.[70]

While his family remained in Knoxville, Williams traveled with a personal secretary. He would also be accompanied by the West India Squadron's commander and a less decorated but no less duty bound government agent named Gustavus H. Scott.[71] Offered the post on March 8, 1826, the Virginian Scott agreed to serve as a "Bearer of Despatches" for the Department of State.[72] Temporary government agents whose appointments would not need Senate approval, "Bearers of Despatches" were paid to deliver documents on the government's behalf.

The lowest ranking man among the *John Adams*'s passengers, Scott would be delivering papers to the US minister in Colombia, who had recently been confirmed to serve as a US representative at the Panama Congress. After a few days' rest in Bogotá, Scott's mission should continue with a trip to Guatemala City, "where you will receive from Mr. Williams the Chargé des Affaires of the United States at the Republic of Central America, such despatches as he may confide to you." Clay hoped that "such despatches" would be the treaty ratified by the Central American government. Scott would then return "in any vessel in which you may be able to procure a passage."[73]

With Williams personally transporting the treaty to Central America for that government's ratification, the hope was that one courier could be responsible for circulating two important diplomatic documents. As Clay explained to Williams in a separate letter, "as there will be ample time while [Scott] is gone to Bogota for deliberations on the Treaty, it is presumable that the decision of the Government of the Central Republic will have been made by the time Mr. Scott reaches you." But if the ratification were unexpectedly delayed, Clay would allow Williams to decide "whether you will employ any other person to bring the Treaty to the United States."[74]

If it worked, Scott's mission smacked of government efficiency. He would be reimbursed "actual expenses of traveling," as long as they were "reasonable," and was "allowed six Dollars per day" in compensation, "supposing that your time is not unnecessarily wasted abroad." Considering that Williams would be paid $4,500 per year, or a little over twelve dollars per day, Scott's time was cheap. But compared to an average laborer paid a dollar a day or even more starkly to a free consul, a confidential courier was costly. The State Department depended on men like Scott when the physical movement of paper required the most direct route. Nonetheless, Clay urged Scott to "observe due economy." The federal government was not paying Scott to take a luxurious Caribbean cruise.[75]

The trip would feature neither luxury nor leisure. By the third week of March, the *John Adams* had set sail on the Atlantic Ocean.[76] Two weeks later, the ship reached Cuba. As John Williams reported on April 10, 1826, temporarily anchored in Havana's harbor, plans were rolling along: "This ship will sail tomorrow for Omoa & after landing me will proceed with Mr. Scott to Carthagena."[77] Scott would have liked to be moving faster, as he informed Clay, "When I have control over my own movements, you may rely on it, no time shall be lost."[78]

With efficiency as his motivation, Scott informed Williams that on his return from Colombia he did not want to travel inland to Guatemala City. He had learned that it would take five vessels of various sizes and an "enormous expense" to get him to and from Guatemala City. "So tedious," he reported, "is the operation of conveying cargoes to & from the City of Guatemala."[79] Respecting this decision, Williams decided to bring "Midshipman Marshall," one of the *John Adams*'s officers and a nephew of the chief justice of the US Supreme Court, with him to Central America's capital so that Marshall could convey the treaty back to Washington.[80] As Scott explained, Marshall should be able to transport the treaty by "a Philadelphia schooner expecting to obtain the balances of her cargo in six weeks."[81] US trade with Central America had clearly begun.

From the decks of the *John Adams*, Scott did not like what he saw of the Honduran port of Omoa. Scott bore his prejudices along with his dispatches, informing Clay, "Omoa is a trifling little village containing perhaps two or three thousand souls, nine tenths of which are blacks & Indians." He described, "their huts are built of bamboo poles plastered over with mud & thatched with palm leaves; the floors are of earth, except the Governor's, which is constructed of undressed mahogany plank laid loosely on the earth."

If the people and the buildings were not to his liking, the land was worse. He saw little arable land, and the ground that could be tilled remained "wholly uncultivated." There were no inns or provisions to be purchased. Omoa was, to Scott, barely a place. And to make matters worse, the port was surrounded by land "equally mountainous & uninhabited for a distance of sixty miles from the coast." To Scott, much of the Honduran and Miskitú lands he spied along the isthmus's Caribbean coast seemed "uninhabited" and unworthy of inhabitance. He saw no value in venturing ashore. Hence, the lowest ranking government agent employed by the State Department embodied in both words and deeds the policy Monroe had reflected at the moment of recognition of Central America—a diplomacy of avoidance.

But as Adams realized early in his presidency, even a place to be avoided had value. Negotiating a canal required prioritizing the deployment of a diplomat, even if the goal of the canal was to avoid interacting with Central America and Spanish America more broadly. By the time Scott's ship was back at sea headed to Colombia, he confessed to Clay, "I am heartily tired of the sea & uncomfortable & arduous as my prospects on land are, I should have been glad to encounter them long since."[82] In his forties, Scott was not a sailor. Recognizing the ugliness of his penmanship, he apologized for not being "sufficiently accustomed to the irregular motion of a ship at sea to write legibly."[83]

Scott was not the only man aboard the *John Adams* with poor handwriting. He was also not the only man aboard the *John Adams* who, like Mann before him, refused to ride muleback on the Omoa road. "Mr. McIntosh who sailed as my private secretary has become terrified of the description of the road," Williams confessed, "I have consented to his return."[84] And so, with the dismissal of the chargé's secretary, the State Department and later historians would be consigned to the fate of scrutinizing Williams's nearly illegible scrawl for the information they so desperately desired.

Undaunted by weaker men's fears, the chargé continued to Guatemala. Accompanied by Midshipman Marshall, Williams arrived on May 2, 1826, almost exactly six months from Clay's letter offering him the job. After more than two years and two deaths, the US government finally sprinted to its goal of placing a diplomatic agent on the ground in Guatemala City.

THE PACE SLOWED CONSIDERABLY once Williams reached the new nation's capital, where President Arce was at odds with his government. Williams immediately recognized the country's political factionalism and personal vendettas from his experiences in Tennessee. Delays were tools of dispute. It took more than two weeks for Arce to officially meet Williams, and the treaty ratifications that were expected to be a mere formality would take much longer. Although the treaty's clock ran perilously close to invalidating the US government's ratification, canal contract negotiations quickened. As sales in London of the new nation's bonds disappointed, the Central American government was growing increasingly desperate for funds from a canal.[85]

Ordered to remain noncommittal about his nation's plans for the canal, Williams saw opportunities to impress people at home if he wielded his unofficial support for projects in Central America. Healthier than his predecessors and more fortunate than his rival office-seekers, Williams faced a new challenge as an agent on the ground in Central America: deciphering the best interests of the United States from 2,000 miles away. Despite the public support for the canal in US newspapers, was the world's most anticipated external improvement project in the US government's best interest?

The future of US involvement in the canal rested largely on the choices of its diplomat. Williams might have been less passionate and less financially interested than his rivals for the post, but he was far from politically disinterested. It cost lives and years to get a US diplomat to Guatemala City, but after all this effort, could he be trusted to make his own choices when his instructions became outdated?

CHAPTER NINE

Nation Divided

Tall, dark, and handsome in his military regalia, Manuel José Arce reportedly tripped over a hog walking to his presidential inauguration.[1] Figuratively and perhaps literally, the mild-mannered new president was mired in mud: his election besmirched by scandal, his new republic splitting along provincial seams, and his government's coffers empty.

But watery earth could also be the key to the new president's success. Rather than negotiating with a nation for a treaty-built Nicaraguan canal, as Cañas had proposed in Washington, the new president preferred a contract with capitalists. Within the first two months of his administration, the new constitutional congress had passed a resolution inviting canal proposals that Arce eagerly signed into law. Implored by the swarm of competing foreign agents for time to communicate with their overseas employers, Arce extended the deadline.

The ideal contractor of Arce's imagination was not limited by nationality but by speed. He set a six-month deadline for proposals by "any person or company, whether national or foreign, who wants to be in charge of executing the enterprise of connecting both oceans." The government would award "the contract" to the proposal that solved the greatest portion of Arce's problems.[2] Hoping to redeem his reputation, he wanted terms that would quickly infuse the government with cash. Arce saw in the canal the potential to unite the country by dividing the land with a profitable waterway.

As Arce stumbled his way into office, José del Valle retreated to his study. A man "passionately addicted to literature," Arce's rival surrounded himself with books—on shelves, in piles on the floor, and spilling off his manuscript-laden desk.[3] Valle had been researching plans for an interoceanic canal for years. During his time in office both in Iturbide's Mexican Empire and as a member of the SPE, he had copied old Spanish hand-drawn maps and manuscript tables. He had studied the *Plano Ídeal* sent to both governments by de la Cerda. He corresponded with Alexander von Humboldt and Jeremy Bentham. As a member of the SPE, he may even have drafted the instructions to Cañas to negotiate a US canal treaty.

Valle's canal dreams followed a different timetable on different terms from what Arce proposed. Although he believed that an interoceanic waterway would transform his nation, Valle vocally opposed Arce's plans for the Central American government to sign a canal contract with a private company. As a member of the legislature, he hurled criticisms at the proposed contract, but his greatest fear was that building the canal before the nation's political system had become stable would end Central American independence by turning the region into a target for greedy foreign empires. His critique of the waterway was not whether it should be built, but when and by whom. Dramatically divided in their politics, both rivals envisioned the future of their country through canal dreams.

ELECTED IN EARLY MAY 1825, Arce had recently been inaugurated when British Special Agent George Alexander Thompson arrived in Guatemala. During his three-month visit, Thompson seized every opportunity to gather information about the potential value of the new country for the British Empire.

Having participated in the negotiation of a British treaty with Mexico, Thompson was "ordered to leave Mexico" and head to Guatemala "to report to the British Government on the state of that Republic." As Thompson explained in the travel narrative he published four years later, "I spared no pains in endeavouring to obtain the most authentic information respecting CENTRAL AMERICA; especially, as no correct or adequate account of it had hitherto been received in Europe."[4] Britain, like the United States, hungered for reliable information about the region.

Thompson's data collection started with those in power. Upon his arrival in Guatemala City, Thompson met with former Secretary of State Marcial Zebadúa, who had resigned to serve on the supreme court and would soon be heading a diplomatic mission to London. Zebadúa introduced Thompson to the current secretary of state and together they met with President Arce. Unable to present credentials, the informal agent could not engage in diplomacy. To the leaders of the new republic, Thompson made clear his desire to "report favourably" on Central America.[5] Arce warmly acknowledged the agent, hoping that Thompson might be the key to British diplomatic recognition for his country. At a later meeting, Arce promised to provide "complete statements of the finance, the commerce, and the military resources of Guatemala."[6]

After Arce, Thompson met with John Baily, agent of the British bankers who had contracted to sell Central America's bonds in London. They attended a session of the first federal congress, where Baily pointed out "the most enlightened" legislators who might provide "points of information."[7] At a ball, Thompson met the secretary of the treasury who, despite the social setting, "promised to draw up for me a report on the state of their revenue and finance."[8] He even crossed what would soon become violently divided party lines to obtain information. Thompson spoke with wealthy elites and religious leaders who opposed independence altogether.[9] He also met with Arce's opposition who supported independence but not the current administration. In fact, aside from the president, Thompson's principal informant would be Arce's chief rival, José del Valle. "These two exalted characters," Thompson later explained, "were equally assiduous in furnishing me with every information which I was seeking to collect."[10]

With books "in large masses, not only around the walls but on the floor," Valle's library overwhelmed the British agent, who could barely walk through the room.[11] An Anglophile who described Great Britain as "the first power of the earth," Valle was eager to share his knowledge with Thompson, especially after realizing that the British agent was himself an author of Spanish American history.[12]

Valle provided Thompson with access to documentation on the nation's trade, its laws, and a draft of his soon-to-be-circulated plan for settling foreigners along the Nicaraguan canal route.[13] The first step of this plan, which aimed to attract foreign investors to build a canal among other infrastructure projects, was to "form an association with the precise aim of sending to this republic a scientific expedition of geographers, botanists, mineralogists, etc." who would gather statistics, create accurate maps, and publish their findings.[14] Explicitly lamenting European—and especially, English—ignorance of Central America, Valle cited Thompson's 1812 book *A Geographical and Historical Dictionary of America and the West Indies* as an example of the work of European "sages" who lacked "facts or documents to make honest additions to the respective articles of this republic."[15]

Valle seized the opportunity to remedy this. As Thompson later described, "He gave me paper after paper and document after document, till I began to feel my appetite satiated at the very sight of them; they were more than I could have duly digested even had I delayed my stay in the country twice as long as I intended."[16] He physically could not carry all the documents. Kindred spirits, Thompson recognized Valle as an "Andean Cicero." The two authors swapped publications and became friends who met frequently during Thompson's stay.[17]

Perhaps the most valuable documents that Valle shared were copies of his collection of canal maps.[18] As Thompson explained in an appendix to his confidential government report, the maps "vary from each other, both in their delineations and their corresponding descriptions."[19] But Thompson found value in each document. The oldest two maps, both dating from the Spanish period, Thompson judged to be "very incorrect." But even these documents had redeeming features. One provided "the best plan . . . of the Port of San Juan"; another provided "the better notion" of "the Western side of the Lake."[20] He believed the *Plano Ídeal* was the most accurate. Valle also provided him with a table listing 347 surveying levels between the lake and the Pacific Ocean. Together these four documents represented the cutting edge of intelligence on the potential canal route. Except for Central America, Spain, and Mexico, no other government had access to these depictions of the potential waterway. By sharing this information with Thompson, Valle fanned the flames of British interest in his nation's most valuable prospect.

Thompson agreed with Valle's evaluation describing the canal as "a business of such incalculable importance, and one which, if effected, will certainly produce a new era in the Commercial transactions of the world."[21] Failing to visit the potential route in person, he solicited information from Baily. BHRC's agent introduced Thompson to a legislator who gave him "a sketch of a road" projected to connect the interior of the nation with the Pacific Ocean. In early June 1825, Baily told Thompson that his employers would be forming a company to build the road. Baily also confided that "there was every probability that the same firm would get the privilege of opening a water communication between the two seas at the lake of Nicaragua." Thompson later recalled his gladness to believe that these works of infrastructure "would be carried into execution by British energy and British capital."[22]

Baily's confidence and Thompson's glee were misplaced. Within the month, Baily would learn that the Central American government was soliciting new canal proposals. Thompson regretted that Arce's short deadline would likely foreclose additional "British capitalists" from submitting proposals. Expressing hope that Baily's plan would be accepted, Thompson conceptualized the canal as a boon to private "British enterprize" and "a great National policy." As an opportunity "destined to fix and rivet a new link to the chain of the political & commercial connexions of all future generations," Thompson saw the long-term interests of the empire at stake in the expedited canal race. But the timing of the deadline, ironically, posed less an obstacle to "British Capitalists" than the Panic of 1825, which would dash 1820s dreams of a British-built canal.[23]

AS HE TRAVELED TO THE COAST IN LATE JULY, eager to return home with the valuable information he had gathered, Thompson encountered the first

British consul making his way to Guatemala City.[24] After Thompson transferred to the consul his horse, his servant, and his sense of "the exact state of affairs in the republic," the British agent boarded the consul's schooner.[25] After an adventure-filled return trip to London, Thompson's extraordinary reconnaissance was recognized by the British government with the payment of not only his salary of more than a thousand pounds but also a hefty bonus.[26]

Meanwhile, about a month after his rendezvous with Thompson, on August 24, 1825, the consul met with Arce and officially opened British commercial relations with the republic. The consul acknowledged that his posting was a "first step toward friendly relations" between Central America and the British Empire. Eager to turn this commercial relationship into diplomatic recognition for his nation, Arce listed the many positive attributes of his country, including "the isthmus of Nicaragua that may be the envy of the other nations of the new world." The president pressed the consul for official "relations with the Cabinet of St. James," and prepared to send a diplomatic envoy to London.[27] Valle had already rejected this appointment; in January 1826, Zebadúa would be appointed to the post. Five months later, Zebadúa met with the British foreign secretary to discuss a never-to-be-drafted treaty. British consular agents would continue to represent the empire's economic interests in the region without the Central American republic ever receiving formal British diplomatic recognition.[28]

Although many in Central America prioritized Britain, the new nation attracted the interest of other European countries. In 1825, the Netherlands officially recognized the republic. A Dutch chargé arrived in Guatemala City in early February 1826, making him the first credentialed European diplomat to reach the region.[29]

Arriving even before Thompson and certainly ahead of the Dutch chargé, US Consul Charles Savage had won the race to get government-authorized boots on the ground in Central America. Nonetheless, Savage had already departed for home when the British consul reached Guatemala City. The next US government representative to arrive in the Central American capital would reflect the fuller diplomatic relationship that Minister Cañas had achieved in Washington. When US Chargé d'Affaires John Williams rode into Guatemala City in early May 1826, he was a fully credentialed diplomat carrying a treaty in need of Central American ratification.[30] By the time of Williams's arrival, the deadline for canal proposals had passed. A canal contractor had been selected, and the terms of the contract were being debated in the congress.

TWO MONTHS BEFORE WILLIAMS'S ARRIVAL, the subject of the canal featured prominently in the speeches that opened the second session of the federal congress. Delivered on March 1, 1826, Arce's message provided a relatively brief overview of "the state of our relations with the powers of Europe and America" as well as his domestic plans for the nation.[31]

Like Adams, Arce prioritized Europe. He started with Spain because "it should occupy the first place in our consideration." His account of Central America's former colonizer could be summed up with his description of King Ferdinand VII as a "criminal."[32] Arce turned from Central America's Spanish "enemy" to its most coveted ally: Great Britain. Awaiting expected news of the formal recognition of Zebadúa, Arce asserted that with the British consul's arrival, "we are in a certain way recognized by Great Britain." Despite Arce's confidence, the "certain way" the British government recognized the value of Central America was exclusively commercial.[33]

Even the commercial value of the republic to the British would prove dubious. Later in his speech, Arce minimized the unsold Central American debt languishing on the collapsed British bond market by misleadingly suggesting that the lack of funds "has hardly been felt." To cultivate an image of a prosperous future with a balanced government budget, Arce emphasized continued British interest in private investments. He asserted that companies had formed and were forming "aimed at mining, agriculture, trade, and industry." Specifically, he mentioned "proposals from another company in London that seeks permission to fish for pearls, hawksbill, and coral in our rivers and seas, and to collect and extract the gold that forms the sands of the Guayape."[34] If only Arce could turn sand into gold. Implied from these proposals is the need for a source of money for the republic's coffers. Because much of the federal government's budget was dependent on contributions from the constituent states, its source of funds was woefully unstable; it could barely afford to print the constitution, let alone pay the salaries of soldiers and statesmen.[35] The solution to this budget deficit, however, would not be found in London. From the British, Arce wanted to obtain recognition or at least capitalization, but the best he could muster were proposals for extraction.[36]

The actual European recognition of the republic by the Netherlands won third place in Arce's hierarchy. US recognition of the republic followed a panoply of recently created Spanish American nations. He discussed the arrival and departure of Consul Charles Savage, the tragic death of Chargé Miller, and the successful negotiation of the treaty by Minister Cañas.

Despite the United States ranking rather low in Arce's hierarchy, he prioritized a project that would depend upon this relationship. "The great work of the communication between the two oceans through the isthmus of Nicaragua has had the privilege that it deserves in my attention," Arce assured the legislature as he prepared to reveal good news. Expressing almost palpable excitement for "this project, which can be called a spring of wealth," he trumpeted, "with pleasure I announce to you that the contract is being concluded under the most promising prospect for the Republic."[37]

Arce did not provide more details. Quadruple the length and significantly more nuanced, the "exposition" delivered to the legislature by Arce's secretary of state filled in the details.[38] The secretary announced the departure of Savage to "return with his family" and the delayed return of Cañas, who had "carried out the main objects of the Legation" and was awaiting the arrival in Washington of his replacement. Clearly the Arce administration no longer expected or even desired Cañas to negotiate the construction of the canal with the US government; recognition and the treaty were enough.

Calling the US government "our sincere friends," the secretary explained to the legislature the remaining steps for the treaty to become law. First, the actual treaty needed to arrive in Central America. Then, Arce would "present it to Congress for its examination and approval." Finally, "the exchange of ratifications will take place in this city."[39] In this confident phrasing, the treaty seemed to be a done deal.

His next paragraph, however, hinted at one of the many problems that would make the treaty's ratification a more complicated process. "Unfortunate incidents," he explained, "have deprived the Executive of the satisfaction of receiving the Minister of the United States before now." Elaborating, he traced the fatal history: "Two were appointed in succession, and both perished before arriving in Guatemala." With hope, he continued, "The third has been appointed, and will not be long in presenting himself."[40] Two more months would pass before Williams and the treaty arrived in Guatemala City.

With confidence, the secretary anticipated the arrival of the US chargé, but he expressed even more certainty about the canal. Although the secretary lumped together "Roads and Canals," these two types of public works had opposing objectives.[41] Whereas better roads might serve the domestic interest of uniting the nation, an interoceanic canal would physically divide the nation's land to turn the country into the oceanic crossroads of the world. For good or ill, the canal was the Arce administration's higher priority.

"Six different proposals have been made to the government by as many English and Anglo-American houses or companies," he announced. The proposals had been submitted "to the secretary of the treasury office, for the examination of the one that offers the greater advantages to the Republic." He provided no further details about how the secretary of the treasury evaluated the "advantages" of the proposals or which proposal from which country had won the contract. "Within a few days," he matter-of-factly declared, "the contract will be closed." He confidently conveyed, "within a few years, we will see the great project of connecting the seas carried out, whose practicability is better known every day, and whose establishment will give a different direction to the commercial business of the world."[42] Again, it sounded like a done deal, and one in which the legislature would have no further role.

JOSÉ DEL VALLE disagreed with the Arce administration's canal plan and made it his mission to mobilize the legislature to vote down the contract. Denied the presidency, Valle had been elected the nation's first vice president, but he refused this post. He also refused an appointment to serve as a diplomat in London. In late 1825, three different districts elected him as their deputy in the second federal congress. Twice Valle attempted to refuse to accept these results claiming ill health, but the congress denied these declinations.

And so, on March 28, 1826, a few weeks after the commencement of the session, Valle took his seat as the deputy representing the capital city, historically the most powerful place in the region. Committed to the existence of a Central American nation and yet personally opposed to the Arce administration, Valle found himself in a congress where the majority opposed the president for a wide range of reasons. In this tense environment, Valle claimed the high ground, casting himself as a voice of reason, prudence, and erudition. Eager to document his speeches for history, Valle published them. Although other delegates surely debated the canal contract, their words were not as intentionally preserved.[43]

On April 27, 1826, Valle opened the first and lengthiest of four speeches by defining his subject: "It is the Nicaraguan canal that has been the object of geographers, economists and politicians for more than two centuries: it is about connecting the waters of the Atlantic with those of the Pacific, and making ocean what is dry land: it is about changing the destinies of the Republic, America and the whole world."[44] Even more glowing than the Arce administration's pro-canal rhetoric, Valle began his criticism with a striking and seemingly incongruous recognition of the canal's potential for revolution. His praise for the canal would be flabbergasting without the knowledge of Valle's vast research. His opposition was not to a canal; it was to this particular contract.

Celebrating the "beautiful prospect" that the "great communication canal" would "inspire projects, stimulate enterprises, and excite speculations," Valle hoped that when "enthusiasm ceases, and reason begins to calmly ponder the project" a more critical perspective could be applied to the specific plan being considered by congress. To lay bare the potential "difficulties" and "consequences" of the proposal under consideration, he asked four interrelated questions. "Can a communication canal be opened between the two oceans by making the San Juan River navigable and cutting out the land between Lake Nicaragua and the Pacific Sea?" If so, "Should it be opened?" When? And finally, "should the enterprise be trusted to a foreign company?"[45]

Valle's answer to his first question depended on science. "To know if the opening of the Canal is possible, it is necessary to gather a multitude of facts," argued Valle. He called for surveys of the land and the creation of precise maps. "None of this has been executed so far with the necessary accuracy," he reported. Drawing on the evidence in his personal collection of canal documents, he discussed the flaws of each of the existing maps of the region. Only with the necessary "reconnaissance done" and only if "the result of all of this convinces the possibility of the project," could Valle consider his second question of whether the canal ought to be opened.[46]

Supposing that the science supported the canal and that "no other canal" had been opened in the Americas, Valle allowed himself to begin to dream of the "immense" good and "infinite" consequences that could be wrought by the waterway. "An extraordinary revolution," he predicted, "would suddenly take place in the fate of Nicaragua and in the destinies of this Republic and the new and old world." Like so many other canal dreamers, he anticipated benefits for trade that would save lives, leagues, time, and money. He anticipated an increase in agriculture, industry, and trade with a fall in "the price of all merchandise." Many envisioned the same economic benefits, but Valle's predictions went considerably further: "The world's population would double or triple. The intelligence of Europe would pass to India and America. Universal civilization would make infinite progress. The races would be improved by crossing each other. The human species would be more beautiful, more enlightened, richer, and more powerful."[47] Immense and infinite, indeed.

Zooming in, Valle imagined, "Nicaragua would be the great center from which wealth would flow to our Republic in particular, and to America and Asia in general." This might sound like a good thing, but as Valle turned from the question of should to the question of when, he raised a "point more delicate than the others." "I was once one of the most exalted in this project," Valle confessed, recalling arguments he made as a member of the SPE to increase the defense of Nicaragua in preparation for the canal. "Later I thought more carefully about it," he continued. And now, as he addressed the congress as a mere deputy while his rival occupied the presidency, he judged, "it is not advisable to open the canal at the present moment. I believe its opening should be deferred to other times and circumstances."[48]

Eager to appear above domestic politics, Valle's criticism drew on global and historical fears. Citing past fights over other key transit points, he warned, "The entire history of the settlements of Europeans in America and the East Indies constantly shows that every country that becomes advantageous for trade is the object of jealousies, rivalries, wars and conquests." Citing recent publications, he suggested that the English government was already being encouraged to "seize the Isthmus of Nicaragua by force or by negotiation." He queried whether it would become even more desirable "by having a communication canal between the two oceans and thus becoming the most important point of the globe?"[49]

Valle argued that the republic was not "yet consolidated" enough to defend itself. It was not recognized globally; the nation's resources were not monetized. The army was not organized; the port and river of San Juan were located in territory still under dispute with Colombia and adjacent to lands controlled by unconquered Indigenous nations allied with Great Britain. Nicaragua was still healing from a "painful revolution." "Our Republic is still tender. To open the canal now," he summarized, "is to sow the seed of foreign jealousies and rivalries when we have not yet developed our strengths." If they could just seize the waterway, how long would foreign nations pay canal tariffs set by the weak new republic?[50]

He called for the imitation of Mexico and Colombia's hesitation to pursue their own interoceanic canal plans. In the meanwhile, Central America could fortify Nicaragua and further develop its institutions and resources. Concluding his negative answer to the question of whether this was the time for building a canal, Valle summarized, "A canal that connects the two oceans is brilliant: it is flattering: it is full of attractions. But under that brilliance there are dangers, there are risks, there are chasms."[51]

In answer to his final question of who should build the canal, Valle was blunt: "its execution should not be contracted with a foreign company." Instead, he asserted that the canal should be built by the government or at least by the nation's citizens. He laid out his plan for government construction of the canal: obtain a loan from London, employ prison and military labor, and import engineers and equipment from the United States or England. "A foreign company does not make proposals to serve the republic," he cautioned, "It makes them to advance its interests." He cited evidence that, if BHRC signed a contract with the republic, it might be willing to sell the contract to another company. Moreover, disputes with a foreign company might "make its government take part." Fearing invasion, he continued, "if, unfortunately, some revolution occurred in Nicaragua, the company would say that it should be allowed to bring foreign troops to continue its work" and "to defend the State of Nicaragua" from invasion by another foreign power. With this fear of invasion and with a summary dismissal of many of the terms of the contract as proposed, Valle ended his first speech with a request that the contract be reconsidered and that the congress not be called upon to vote on the proposal.[52]

Valle failed in removing the canal plan from the congressional docket. On May 2, he addressed a second critique of the canal proposal to congress. Trained as a lawyer, Valle read the canal contract closely.[53] In its broadest strokes, the contract conveyed a reciprocal arrangement where the company would be responsible for supplying capital, engineering expertise, and management, and the country would supply military defense, most of the labor, and ultimately the repayment of the project's expenses plus an annual interest of ten percent. As with any contract, the devil was in the details, but the draft Valle reviewed does not survive. The final contract included many of the provisions he found problematic as well as terms that may have been added in response to his criticisms.

Valle saw risk where others saw reward. The contract channeled two-thirds of the revenue from the canal to the company. This money would be used to repay the costs of its construction plus interest. The remaining third of the canal revenue would be channeled into the country's coffers. According to Valle, the contract's champions argued, "The Republic is going to create a new income without having made any outlay." Valle disagreed. He argued that such celebration of imagined revenue streams was irrational because the Central American government had made no "approximate calculation of the costs." "Without numbers," he insisted, "no work of any kind should be decreed." He put the administration's lack of data in context: "There is not a single government in the educated nations of the world that contracts or undertakes the execution of a public work without first forming approximate budgets of expenses and calculations of profits." Without this data, Valle believed the government "cannot know" the cost of building the canal, amount of interest that will be due each year, appropriate tariff rate, whether the duties received would cover the payments of capital and interest, how many "centuries" would pass before the debts were repaid, or whether any government income would ever be generated by the canal. "I cannot form exact or approximate calculations because, having not made any surveys, or worked on budgets," he bemoaned, "I lack the basis for making them."

In such "dense darkness," he envisioned a nightmare scenario of low canal fees. In Valle's vision, other "Republics of America" constructed their own canals, forcing Central America's fees into a race to the bottom. In such a competitive scenario, the canal debts would linger perpetually unpaid. He imagined, "the foreign company that has opened the canal will be eternal in the State of Nicaragua." Imagining these terms as "more or less ruinous," Valle saw the canal contract as an unintended license to foreign imperialists.[54]

He also attacked the many terms of the contract that, he argued, did not conform to the congressional decree of June 1825, which had set the acceptable terms of proposals. The decree prioritized repaying the cost of the canal's construction by applying *all* the canal revenue to this debt, but the contract channeled one-third of this revenue into the country's treasury. Clearly, the Arce administration wanted canal revenues to provide government liquidity and make up for the lethargic bond sales in London. For Arce, bringing the canal dream into reality under this contract would solve near-term economic problems; for Valle, the canal's construction under these terms would be a source of long-term fiscal nightmares.[55]

Beyond the payment of the canal debt, Valle found other provisions that he read as contrary to the congressional decree, including the extended payments to the company after the canal's completion and the granting of a twenty-year steamboat monopoly. And yet, according to Valle, unnamed supporters of the canal argued that the "decree should not be cited, and that Congress can revoke it."[56] A man of law and letters, Valle demanded adherence to a law already on the books; he again asked for the contract to be revised before being put to a vote.

Perhaps some of the final contract's terms reflect his concern about the canal as a source of eternal debt and his desire for data-based decisions about construction. One provision that may have been added in response to Valle's concerns was the demand for the contractor to provide engineers to conduct a survey of the route within eight months of the contract's signing. These engineers would determine whether the construction of the canal would be "practicable." At the same time the engineers arrived in Nicaragua, the contractor was required to deliver a $200,000 loan to the country. If the engineers declared "the canal is not feasible," the $200,000 loan, "together with the interest due" at the rate of 10 percent per year, would be repaid. If the engineers approved the project, construction was required to begin within a year. Time was of the essence.

So was money. The $200,000 loan was so important that its terms appeared twice in the contract. If "insurmountable obstacles" prevented the canal's construction, the country would be responsible for repaying this loan but no other costs. The contract's terms allowed for the repayment of the initial $200,000 investment plus interest in the form of "bills on London out of the loan contracted with the company of Barclay." This tied the contract to Baily's unsellable bonds. Negotiating with a US company, the Central Americans kept British capitalists in the picture.[57]

If these provisions were added in response to Valle, he succeeded in providing his country with a means to save itself from committing an untold fortune to a project that might not be feasible. But in terms of his goal of sinking the contract, he lost.[58]

FROM THE FLOOR OF THE LOWER HOUSE of the legislature, Valle continued his effort to cancel the contract. He questioned the identity of the agent and the capacity of the capitalists dealing with the Central American government. Nonetheless, buoyed by Arce's pitch for the canal as a panacea, the contract proceeded through the congress.

But was the lower chamber's approval enough to ratify the contract? In his fourth and final anti-canal speech on May 18, 1826, Valle argued that the canal contract had not followed the right legal procedure. After quoting the constitution, he expressed exasperation, stating that he could not "fathom the reason . . . that a decree of this kind should not pass to the Senate." Undoubtedly hoping that one more layer of legislative review might scuttle the canal contract, Valle made his last unsuccessful plea to stop what he saw as a canal nightmare.[59]

Muddied from the beginning, the Arce administration did not stop to consider the constitutional consequences of contracting a canal without following the country's lawful procedures. Speed—not stability, science, constitutionality, or strategy—guided the country's contract negotiations in the spring of 1826.

CHAPTER TEN

Contract

On Wednesday, June 14, 1826, in Guatemala City, two men signed a contract to construct a waterway connecting the Atlantic and Pacific Oceans via Lake Nicaragua. One represented a country; the other, a company.

The first signatory identified himself as "Secretary of State and of the Treasury of the Supreme Government of the Federal Republic of Central America." Two days later, three notaries certified his signature. They identified the second man's signature as "that of Mr. Charles de Beneski, agent of the company of New York." This was a vague company name, especially for an entity executing one of the globe's most coveted contracts.

Although the US government was not a party to the contract, its newly arrived diplomat also witnessed the document with his "hand and seal of legation." US Chargé d'Affaires John Williams identified the parties differently. Williams certified the first as "acting minister of finances in and for the republic of Central America."[1] The "acting minister" was in his first month on the job and was the fourth to fill the secretaryship in as many years.[2] For the second signatory, Williams provided even less information than the notaries, referring to Beneski only as "agent, &c."[3] Agent of whom? Williams did not elaborate.

Charles de Beneski was the perfect man to negotiate a valuable contract with a volatile nation for a vague entity. By 1826, he had already shown himself to be a master at manipulating his identity. A European soldier of fortune with falsified credentials, Beneski had been Mexican Emperor Iturbide's right-hand man, a witness to his death, and a banished survivor. A liability in post-imperial Mexico, Beneski's tie to Iturbide proved an asset in Central America. To negotiate the canal contract, Beneski needed to win over President Arce's new conservative allies in the legislature, as well as the president's former republican friends. Beneski could shape his vague past to appeal to all of them.

To succeed at negotiating the contract, Beneski also needed to garner support from the new US chargé, who was explicitly instructed to obtain information about the canal but *not* to commit the United States to its execution.[4] Drawing on their common military background, Beneski encouraged Williams to become his ally in the fight for the contract. Like Arce, Valle, and so many others, Williams dreamed of an interoceanic canal as a solution to his problems. Recouping his political fortunes at home, the contract could be Williams's diplomatic triumph even though—or perhaps because—the US government was not officially a party to its terms.

Beneski skillfully used his vague biography to woo Central America's partisans; he deployed his employer's vague identity to garner US diplomatic support. Whatever the fate of the waterway, negotiating a contract proved a doable dream for the man who called himself Charles de Beneski.

WE DO NOT KNOW when Beneski arrived in Guatemala City. But he entered the United States at least twice before the canal negotiations. In April 1822, two months before Agustín Iturbide was crowned emperor of Mexico, Beneski boarded a brig in the Spanish colony of Cuba and sailed to New Orleans. In an era without photographic identification cards or birth certificates, ship officers recorded "passengers" on slips of paper that tracked the navigation of foreigners across US borders.[5] Aside from name, age, sex, and occupation, the form requested information about the passengers' present and future national identities. In the Age of Revolutions, the answers to these questions could be complicated. While the brig's other passenger planned to become an "inhabitant" of the United States, Charles de Beneski indicated that his allegiance remained with Poland. He played his migratory cards closer to his chest; in fact, he kept several documents up his sleeve.[6]

Beneski's answers to the form's questions were not entirely true. His original name was Karol Benecke. Although he listed his age as twenty-nine, he was only twenty-five years old. And his "occupation" was certainly not "gentleman"; he was a soldier.[7] Although Beneski had been born in Poland, he carried documentation of more than a decade of decorated service in the Prussian army fighting in Spain, France, and Russia.[8] He had no desire to return to Poland. Like many Napoleonic war veterans, Beneski was looking for a lucrative new fight.[9]

In the spring of 1822, Beneski quickly departed the United States for the court of the newly crowned Mexican Emperor Agustín I, formerly Agustín Iturbide. In his application for admission to the Mexican army, he lied again, informing Iturbide's general inspector of cavalry that "he was of Polish descent, a retired lieutenant-colonel of the Prussian army, who had emigrated to the United States, but decided to move to Mexico after having heard of the country's independence." He presented mostly falsified documents attesting to his career: his entrance into the Prussian army, his honorable discharge, letters confirming his vast experience, and commendations including Iron

Crosses of the first and second class and a nomination to the French Legion of Honor.[10] In reality, Beneski's career ended when he was demobilized in 1820 as a second lieutenant, a junior officer, whose sole decoration was a second-class Iron Cross.[11]

So why did Beneski lie? For a mercenary, a longer and more glorious military past in Europe could create a brighter future in the Americas.[12] And initially, his future in Iturbide's Mexico sparkled. Beneski quickly rose to prominence, traveling with the newly crowned emperor.

Being close to Iturbide, however, soon proved dangerous. Rebellion brewed. As the emperor spent lavishly, consolidated power, and claimed monarchical prerogatives, his republican and provincial foes plotted his overthrow. By the end of 1822, the military revolted in the Caribbean port of Veracruz, and another rebellion broke out in the south. In early 1823, the peripheral provinces, including Central America, declared themselves independent. Soon, Iturbide's vast empire, which spanned from just south of Oregon to just north of Colombia, had been reduced to Mexico City. On March 19, 1823, as troops approached the capital, Emperor Agustín I abdicated. The Mexican Empire was formally abolished.[13]

Beneski became a wanted man. The army inspector now reported that the Polish soldier was "an adventurer and a creature of Iturbide who, in order to have him at his elbow and use him as a tool of tyranny appointed him to a totally unmerited position."[14] Beneski refuted the accusations but was sentenced to deportation. He followed his former Mexican sovereign who had already departed for a pensioned exile in Italy.[15] Fearful of assassination attempts, Iturbide soon moved his entourage, including Beneski, to London.[16] When Spanish agents sought Iturbide's support for the reconquest of Spain's American colonies in early 1824, he planned a return to Mexico "to secure the independence and freedom of the country."[17] When news of this plan reached Mexico City, the new government declared the former emperor and his supporters traitors who would be executed if they returned.[18]

Unaware of their condemnation, Iturbide, Beneski, and others boarded a British brig bound for Mexico. When the ship arrived off the Caribbean coast, Iturbide sent Beneski ashore to do some reconnaissance, but the province's commander immediately recognized him. Foreign agents had become so common in Mexico that Beneski justified his return with the claim, "I came on commercial business, being commissioned by several mercantile houses of London."[19]

Over the next several days, Beneski and Iturbide participated in a series of complicated decoys and double crossings that ultimately led the former emperor to a firing squad. As the setting sun illuminated a stifling public square, Iturbide proclaimed his martyrdom, "I die for having come to help you. I die with honor: not, as a traitor."[20] Blindfolded, the kneeling former emperor "received two balls in his forehead, and two in his breast." Condemned under the same law but spared execution, Beneski begged for death, recalling "the distress of mind I suffered in the idea of surviving my friend and benefactor." In October 1824, he was tried and sentenced to "perpetual banishment from the Mexican territory." He received a "certificate" from the Mexican officer documenting his loyalty to Iturbide.[21]

Armed with this new evidence of his past, he departed Mexico. During Beneski's imprisonment, Iturbide's very pregnant widow, youngest children, chaplain, and several servants made their way to Baltimore.[22] Beneski followed. His arrival was documented on another passenger list. This time, the Polish-born Mexican soldier honestly listed his occupation as "military," but otherwise, he continued to lie. The two years since Beneski last entered the United States must have felt like four because he reported his age as thirty-three. Dispensing with his Polish birthplace, his Prussian service, and his allegiance to the Mexican Empire, Beneski claimed to "belong" to the place of his previous exile: Italy. Beneski had lived there for less than a year, but his entry on the passenger list suggested he was ready for a change. He proclaimed his intention to "become an inhabitant" of the "U. States."[23]

In the United States, Beneski disliked the "equivocal statements" he read in the "public prints" about "the death of Don Augustin de Iturbide, ex-Emperor of Mexico." He decided "to step forward in vindication of his memory." In New York City, on November 14, 1824, Beneski signed his name to a document he composed in Spanish. Translated into English and published the next year, Beneski's *A Narrative of the Last Moments of the Life of Don Augustine de Iturbide, Ex-Emperor of Mexico* provided a gripping eyewitness account of Iturbide's violent end.[24] Far from hiding everything up his sleeves, Beneski decided, upon his second entry into the United States, to publish his most recent past.

Sometime after the book's publication, Beneski became the agent of the party described by the notaries as "the company of New York."[25] The details of this negotiation have disappeared, but Beneski had already imagined himself as an agent of capitalists. We have no evidence of when, how, or under what alias Beneski traveled to Central America. We do not know the contents of his canal proposal or when he submitted it. And we have no record of Beneski's negotiation with the government. In late 1824 with the publication of his *Narrative*, Beneski vanished until his name entered the official record of the Central American Congress in the spring of 1826.

ON APRIL 24, 1826, when canal critic José del Valle was not in attendance, the Central American Congress approved a motion: "*The government will contract the Nicaraguan canal enterprise with Mr. Carlos Beneski as representative of the house of Palmer.*" "After I saw it," Valle explained, "I stated that I did not know who Palmer is, nor what the circumstances of his House are; and that Beneski's powers are not sufficient."[26] Interestingly, Valle did not say that he "did not know" Beneski; he merely doubted the legal power of his credentials. Valle likely knew more about the Polish-born soldier than he cared to say.

A wealthy member of the aristocracy who had been a loyal Spanish subject in the 1810s when others like Arce pushed for independence, Valle supported the annexation of Central America by Mexico.[27] In March 1822, the Honduran capital elected him to the Mexican Congress.[28] Valle's trip from Guatemala City to Mexico City took about three months. He arrived one week after Iturbide had crowned himself emperor and began dismantling Mexican republicanism.

The Mexican Congress quickly elected Valle vice president, but two days later, Valle was arrested. For nearly six months, as Iturbide faced increasing challenges to his reign and sought to silence opponents, Valle found himself imprisoned. Eventually recognizing that the Central American was not an enemy, Iturbide's personal secretary offered Valle the office of Mexican secretary of foreign and domestic affairs. Valle recognized this invitation as an avenue to freedom that led directly into the heart of the problematic Mexican court. After twice attempting to be excused from this appointment, Valle became one of the highest-ranking officials of the short-lived Mexican Empire.

When he was two weeks into what would be a six-week term, Valle explained to the Mexican Congress, "I defy the most distinguished talent to learn in such short time all that there is to know in the ministry in my charge. I have not rested; I have the satisfaction of having worked day and night."[29] His round-the-clock travails did not end when Iturbide abdicated. He helped to plan the terms of the emperor's exile, navigated accusations of intrigue, and then resumed his post in the revived Mexican Congress, where he became an ardent supporter of independence for Central America. In the fall of 1823, he resigned his Mexican congressional post to serve as a delegate in the newly formed ANC—the provisional legislature in Guatemala. Before he left Mexico, he gathered scientific instruments, a portrait of "Jorge Washington," and copies of documents, including sources on the Nicaraguan canal.[30] Before he arrived home, he was elected to the SPE—the new country's provisional executive triumvirate.[31]

During their time in Mexico City, the Polish soldier must have crossed paths with the Central American politician. Both dealt intimately with the emperor during his last weeks in office. Valle planned the details of Iturbide's Italian exile; Beneski joined it. From his position as a member of Central America's executive triumvirate, Valle would certainly have learned of Beneski's return to Mexico, his role in the events that led to Iturbide's execution, and his second banishment.

Even if they had never met, the two men at the very least knew of one another, but Valle had good reason not to share this knowledge with the legislature. Expressing his reasons for doubting the credentials of Beneski would have reminded his fellow legislators of his own participation in Iturbide's government. Since the controversial presidential election of 1825, many of the opponents of the Arce administration were devout republicans who had opposed Mexican annexation. These men were important to the anti-canal coalition that Valle sought to build, but Valle's participation in Iturbide's regime was anathema to them. Meanwhile, many of Arce's supporters in congress had monarchist preferences that would make Beneski's closeness to the former emperor an asset. Too much attention drawn to Beneski's past would rally both Arce's supporters and Arce's opponents against Valle. If he wanted to sink the canal plan, Valle needed to take the high road and make arguments based on reason and law.

Instead of alluding to Beneski's past, Valle demanded more information. He asked that congress read into the record "the documents relating to Palmer's credit and circumstances" and the documents that empowered Beneski to act as Palmer's agent. He also asked whether "the documents relating to Palmer's credit and circumstances are sufficient to prove one and the other," and if Beneski's documents "prove the legitimacy of his personage."[32] No one besides Beneski knew who Palmer was and whether this man and his associates had command of enough capital to build the canal. Moreover, Valle doubted Beneski's "legitimacy" as an agent. In the speech, he twice drew attention to Beneski's self-characterization as Palmer's agent: "Beneski (I repeat) has presented himself as Palmer's representative." But how was the Central American government to know that this Polish-born soldier had the authority to commit an unknown US company of indeterminate capital to a contract that would determine the nation's future? Valle proposed adding an addendum to the motion requiring "*the legitimacy of his personage and the credit and circumstances of his grantor be confirmed.*" Again, Valle was unsuccessful. These reasonable demands for investigation were brushed aside by a congress eager to approve the contract.

No investigation of either Beneski or the mysterious "house of Palmer" took place. The US company Beneski represented remained as vague as his past.[33]

EVEN THE OFFICIAL representative of the US government did not know exactly who Beneski represented. Williams arrived in Guatemala City on May 2, 1826, the same day Valle railed against the financial terms of the proposed canal contract. The chargé carried the commercial treaty. According to his instructions, the "first object" of his mission should be the ratification of the treaty before the deadline on August 5, 1826. Describing the treaty negotiations with Cañas as having been "conducted in a spirit of great amity," Clay and Adams anticipated "no difficulty" in Guatemala City.[34]

Beyond ensuring the treaty's exchange of ratifications, Williams's second goal was to gather information, especially regarding the potential for the waterway proposed by Cañas. Clay told Williams "to ascertain if surveys have been made of the proposed route of the Canal, and if entire confidence may be placed in their accuracy." The State Department also wanted to know the route's length, the water supply, "the nature of the Country, and of the ground through which it is to pass." Clay summarized, "in short, what facilities do the Country and the state of its population afford, for making the Canal, and what are the estimates of its cost?"[35] This was the same information Valle demanded of the Central American Congress.

Without this information and a better sense of how a canal treaty might be received by the US Congress, the State Department was unwilling to commit to a negotiation. Clay cautioned Williams, "It is not intended that you should inspire the Government of the Republic of Guatimala with any confident expectation that the United States will contribute, by pecuniary or other means, to the execution of the work." According to Clay, President Adams wanted "such full information as will serve to guide the judgement of the constituted authorities of the United States."[36] Williams was explicitly denied the power to negotiate a canal.

And yet, Williams did not hesitate to jump into the Central American Congress's canal debate at his first opportunity. When Williams arrived in Guatemala City, he announced himself to the secretary of state, who reviewed the diplomat's documents the next day. Williams's official presentation to President Arce, however, was postponed to "some subsequent day."[37] The congress had granted Arce a significant budget for receptions of diplomatic ministers, and it took his office more than two weeks to make the "considerable preparations" for the "ceremony."[38] While Williams waited, he learned the state of the congressional canal contract negotiations. He realized that the contract would go to a private US company, which meant that Cañas's canal treaty proposal was a dead letter. During the six months since their drafting, his instructions had become obsolete. The US government might still value information about the canal, but it could no longer count on a treaty to build a canal as a public work.

On May 19, 1826, one week after Valle demanded more information about Beneski and his employer, Williams finally met Arce. The Central American republic's official newspaper, the *Gaceta del Gobierno*, published the day's speeches. Initially given in English, Williams's speech was first translated into Spanish and then, months later, back into English by a newspaper in the United States and separately by one in British Honduras. Whatever precision might have been lost in this "double translation," the chargé's support for the canal could not be clearer.[39]

Williams began with a lengthy celebration of independence, republicanism, and the promise of hemispheric unity. Drawing on language originally written by Adams for Special Agent Mann, the chargé turned praise for the "circumstances" of the Salvadoran annexation mission into personal support for the canal plan. He expressed his "great satisfaction" that the busy Central American government devoted time "to discuss a plan, which ensures the success of the project to open a communication between the Atlantic and Pacific ocean by means of lake Nicaragua." Williams's praise was absolute: "This is the greatest enterprize ever yet projected by any community." It was confident: "and its accomplishment, which from the means adopted may be considered as certain, will be hailed as an epoch in the commercial annals of the world." It was historical: "it will also exhibit in the most striking colors, the contrast between the old government and the actual legislators of this country." And it was diplomatic: "This canal will not only produce incalculable benefits to the commercial world, but will also pour out upon Central America indescribable sources of prosperity, attracting to its shores the capital, the industry, the enterprise, and the arts of all nations."[40] The translator in British Honduras chose waterier words, suggesting the canal would "shower down unheard of torrents of prosperity on Central America."[41] Swimming in canal dreams, Williams forgot to mention the treaty ratification, the "first object" of his mission.[42] Securing the canal contract for a US company became his priority.

Arce followed Williams's lead; he did not discuss the treaty. Proclaiming that "the republics of Central and North America should be sisters," Arce emphasized the "friendship" between the two nations before explaining that "the first authorities of the republic" were "bringing to a point" negotiations over "the enterprize of connecting the two seas by the lake of Nicaragua." He agreed, "the advantages of this great work will result in the benefit of all the commercial powers of the globe." And he envisioned an important benefit for the hemisphere: "it will constitute a new link of fraternity and union between all the sections of the American continent and this republic." Gambling on the canal to save his country's finances, Arce depicted his nation's policy—especially the canal—as altruistic, "She does not limit her wishes to her own felicity—she extends them to all other nations; and on this occasion she makes very sincere ones for the aggrandizement and prosperity of the U. States of the north."[43] The version from British Honduras toned down this expansionist language, substituting "greatness" for "aggrandizement."[44] Either way, Arce suggested that the canal would be beneficial to Williams's nation. It might be a contract with a private US company, but it had diplomatic significance.

WHY DID WILLIAMS IGNORE THE TREATY and support the canal plan when his official instructions directed him to do the opposite? This question cuts to the heart of the conundrum of office holding in the Era of Good Feelings, when public servants with private interests were creatures of personal patrons. Serving many masters, Williams failed them all.

The origins of Williams's support for Beneski's contract can be traced back to surveyor Edmund Blunt's boss, would-be canal contractor Curtis Bolton. Bolton had sent Blunt to Nicaragua in the summer of 1824 and, in the first half of 1825, traveled himself to Guatemala City to submit a proposal.[45] He left Central America before the Arce administration issued its decrees calling for new proposals.[46] Back in the United States, he met with Cañas.[47] Neither man knew about the Arce administration's decrees when they formulated a plan for obtaining the rights to construct the canal under Cañas's proposed treaty.

In March 1826, Bolton wrote to Secretary of the Navy Samuel Southard, who had arranged the merchant's travel to Central America and who was a vocal advocate of federally funded "canal navigation."[48] Encouraging support for Cañas's proposal, Bolton informed Southard of his "well founded belief that an American Company could be made up on reasonable terms." He wanted to relay this information directly to the new chargé, so he enclosed an unsealed letter for Williams "on the subject of the Canal."[49]

In his next letter, Bolton asked Southard if the government would "instruct the Chargé to endeavor to influence the Govt. of Central America to refer the whole subject of a Canal to Mr. Cañas." Shifting canal negotiations to Washington would help Bolton determine whether a US company could be formed "for completing it." He reported, "Two Englishmen were besieging the Gov't of Guatemala when I was there in opposition to each other & to me for the canal." Citing "the pecuniary distress in England," Bolton recognized that the English would no longer be in the canal race, but new competition might be found in "Europe." Bolton thought that the US government should assist "by urging its speedy reference to Mr. Cañas" so that "an American Compy [Company] can probably secure it."

Although Bolton was correct about the result of the Panic of 1825 on British canal plans, he was wrong in assuming that the Central American government would empower "Mr. Cañas" with canal negotiations. By the time of Bolton's April letter, the canal contract proposal period had already closed, and the Central American government no longer aimed to negotiate the contract through Cañas or with the US government. The Arce administration was considering several US proposals; Bolton did not anticipate this competition from other US companies. Imagining that the canal contract was his for the taking, Bolton closed his letter to Southard, "If I did not think the Canal very practicable & very important I should not feel justified in asking one moment of your precious time to be devoted to its consideration."[50]

Southard's reply closed one door and opened another. In a short letter marked "private," the cabinet member wrote bluntly, "I do not perceive that it would be proper for the Govt. U.S. to make a formal & official appeal to the Govt. of Guatimala on the subject of the Canal." He believed Adams shared this "opinion." Official avenues closed to canal negotiations, Southard hinted at an alternative and informal approach for Bolton. "But private letters might properly be written to Mr. Williams," Southard suggested, "& he might, in his private & informal intercourse, with the officers of the Govt. there, present the subject in such way as to produce a salutary effect in accomplishing your object." Southard was, in sum, sanctioning Bolton's overtures to Williams in a "private & informal" capacity.[51]

According to Southard's suggestion, Williams could choose to serve both privately as an agent of canal contractors and publicly as the agent of the US government. For consuls, this blending of private and public affairs was expected. With his response to Bolton, the secretary of the navy suggested that salaried diplomats might also act on their private interests. As if to prove this for government agents in any post, Southard had marked his letter containing this suggestion "private," indicating his own division between his public decisions as a cabinet member and his "private & informal intercourse."[52]

Whether the advice came from the secretary of the navy or citizen Southard, Bolton responded by writing another unsealed letter for Williams. "I have written the inclosed agreeable to your suggestion for which I am obliged," he explained in his cover letter. Although it appealed to the chargé's private interests, the secretary forwarded the unsealed letter to the Department of State to be forwarded to Guatemala City via government channels.

Southard kept Bolton's cover letter, which on its reverse side conveyed the conundrum of government agents acting simultaneously in both public and private capacities. While the letter containing Southard's suggestion to Bolton had been marked "private," Bolton addressed his response to the "Honorable S. L. Southard, Sect. of the Navy, Washington." In red capital letters, a clerk in the post office had stamped the letter, "FREE." This meant that Bolton's private, unsealed message to Chargé Williams traveled at no cost through the mail. Free postage was designed to subsidize official government correspondence but was not supposed to be applied to officeholders' private mail. Southard might try to intimate that his suggestion to Bolton was "private," but addressed with the secretary's title, Bolton's response was paid for by the public. This minor corruption hints at the bigger problem of segregating the private from the public for government agents.[53]

SOUTHARD'S NUANCE BETWEEN PUBLIC AND PRIVATE DUTIES was lost on John Williams. On the very same day that Williams was formally introduced to President Arce, he received Bolton's first unsealed letter. It had taken three months for the paper to make its way first from New York City to Southard's office in Washington and then on to Williams's legation in Guatemala City.

Writing on June 13, 1826, more than a month before he composed his first dispatch to the State Department, Williams excitedly responded to Bolton, reporting on the canal contract negotiations. His descriptions are evocative, enthusiastic, and evident of a significant and blatant error. "On my arrival in this city the 2nd of last month," Williams recounted, "I met Col. Beneski agent for yourself and associates to negotiate for the canal between the North & South seas thro' Lake Nicaragua." Beneski was not Bolton's agent. When he had written the letter, Bolton still thought the canal rights would be decided by treaty and not through a private contract. Bolton believed "that an American Company *could* be made up on reasonable terms."[54] He was not yet involved in any such company. And he had no connection to the entity that the Central American congress described as "the House of Palmer."[55] Beneski was not Bolton's man, but Williams clearly presumed that Palmer and Bolton were associates and that Beneski represented them both.[56]

Whose fault was this misconception? Perhaps the misidentification derived from Bolton's letter. Bolton believed that a singular "American Company" might be formed to construct the canal; he did not anticipate competing US companies. Beneski's vague characterization by the notaries as "agent of *the* company of New York" confirmed the idea that there was only one.[57] Williams's misconception of Bolton's relationship to Beneski was no doubt fed by the Central American Congress's failure, despite Valle's haranguing, to demand more information about Beneski and his employer. And certainly some of the fault lies with Williams who, distracted from the treaty, lost sight of the details while reveling in the big picture of a diplomatic coup. With Bolton's letter arriving through government channels, Williams may even have believed that his patrons, Secretary Clay and President Adams, supported Bolton's quest for the canal. Williams may have interpreted fulfilling Bolton's private request for assistance as both payback of patronage and part of his public duties.

Blind to his errors, Williams depicted the contract negotiations as a triumphal victory of the United States over Britain. "The English," he snickered, "were extremely desirous of obtaining this contract. Their agent, who is still here, at some time supposed he had it & it's said wrote home to that affect." Enter the unlikely US hero: "Before my arrival, Col. Beneski had fought the principal battle with the English & gained a signal victory in the House of Deputys." Williams continued with his military metaphors, "The Colonel has followed up his first success with the skill & ability of a field Marshall of France & has totally put the enemy to rank."

Aware of how uniquely positioned Beneski was to win Arce's supporters and his adversaries, Williams lauded the former Napoleonic soldier: "I doubt whether any other man could have effected what Col. Beneski has done. He merits & no doubt will receive the thanks of our commercial community." Angling for credit, Williams cast himself as a soldier in this fight: "I came in as a reserve corps to the Colonel's aid." Despite Beneski's assurances that Williams "contributed to his final success," Williams humbly assured, "the laurels are all his." Although Beneski's acquisition of the contract served the interests of a private company, Williams cast the benefits as national: "It is fortunate for the commerce & navigation of the United States that this canal has not fallen into European hands." The diplomat suggested Beneski had served his employers well. "The terms of the contract are highly advantageous to the company," he praised, adding almost as an afterthought, "And beneficial to the Republic of the Center." Williams closed the letter with a glorious prediction: "Stock on this company cannot fail shortly to become the most valuable of any in our country or perhaps in the World."[58]

If the chargé had been writing to the correct New York investor, this message should have been music to the capitalist's ears. But he was writing to Bolton, whose goal of turning Williams into his private agent and making his acquisition of the canal contract into US policy had backfired. The agent of the wrong New Yorker enjoyed Williams's support.

Beyond believing that supporting Beneski in the contract negotiations served his nation and his patrons, Williams dreamed of the canal contract as personally beneficial. As many imagined, a canal through Nicaragua would be beneficial to the United States, and particularly profitable for the Mississippi Valley, including Williams's home state of Tennessee. Claiming the canal as his personal diplomatic victory might revitalize Williams's political career. Moreover, by imagining the contract negotiations as a battle with British interests, Williams could cast his diplomatic victory in the same militaristic and Anglophobic terms that had launched his rival Andrew Jackson to national honor in the aftermath of the War of 1812. If the canal fulfilled its potential, Williams could claim the contract as his Battle of New Orleans.

And if the canal failed, Williams had an out. He had, after all, only assisted Beneski as a member of the "reserve corps." The US government was not a party to the contract. Although Williams recognized the diplomatic potential of the canal, the contract was ultimately a deal between the Central American government and a private company. Williams had signed and sealed the document as a witness, not as a signatory. It did not commit the US government to anything. Williams could interpret his actions as in accordance with his instructions.

WILLIAMS WITNESSED THE CONTRACT in late June but curiously waited until August 3, more than a month, to send his first dispatch to the State Department. Whatever his interpretation of Bolton's letter, the chargé clearly did not think that the signing of the canal contract required official communication to his superiors.

On the day between the signing and witnessing of the canal contract, the chargé wrote a letter to Clay. It did not even mention the canal. It focused instead on the case of the missing consul. Williams informed Clay that Savage "has not arrived." Williams reported that he had met with Savage's nephew Henry, who had "inquired whether his uncle had resigned, saying he had heard such a report." Williams informed Clay that if the rumor was true, he had found a replacement for the wayward consul: "I take the liberty of recommending Capt. William Phillips as his successor." A Philadelphian who had been sent to Guatemala on mercantile business one year earlier, Phillips had quickly become a friend and housemate of the diplomat. Williams conveyed his qualifications, "Capt. Phillips has been engaged in commerce & navigation for near *thirty* years," emphasized Williams, "He possesses extensive information on those subjects & is well qualified to discharge the duties of consul."[59]

The housemates caught canal fever. If Williams's infection led him to prioritize the waterway over the treaty, Phillips's strain turned him into an agent for "the New York Company." As Phillips would later explain, "At the recommendation & with the approval of Col. Williams, I accepted the agency for the company." The diplomat did not become the agent of the canal company; he got his friend Phillips to take the job.[60]

Neither the conclusion of the canal contract nor the absence of the consul induced Williams to compose an official dispatch to the State Department. The triggering event for Williams's first dispatch, labeled "No. 1." in its header, was his mission's official "first object": the exchange of ratifications of the treaty between the United States and the government of Central America. In a long letter composed of a single paragraph with large margins and little punctuation, Williams recounted the difficulties of accomplishing this goal. In the evening after Williams's formal reception by Arce at which he gave the speech that ignored the treaty, he informed the Central American secretary of state that he "was prepared to exchange the ratifications of the treaty between our governments." The secretary responded that "he had been only five days in official possession of the treaty. And so soon as it was ratified by Congress he would proceed with me in the exchange of ratifications."

This sounded deceptively simple. There was a fundamental difference in the treaty ratification process between the two countries. In Washington, a treaty negotiated by the executive branch need only be approved by the Senate. "The Constitution of this Republic requires that a treaty should be ratified by both houses of Congress," explained Williams. This meant more deliberation.

But Williams did not think this fully explained the situation. "It is difficult to account for the unreasonable delay which has taken place," confessed Williams. He elaborated, "They have all been profuse in their professions of regard for the United States, & of esteem for me individually—In conversations with those in authority on the subject of the treaty, they expressed their unqualified approbation of it."[61] The problem of the leaders of the Central American republic was not with the United States, Williams, or the treaty. It was hostility between President Arce and his opponents in the lower house. This hostility would lead to civil war before the end of the year.

Arce and the provincial government of Guatemala had been engaged in a complicated and occasionally lethal dispute for nearly a year. As tensions escalated, some deputies called for the relocation of the congress to El Salvador. In support of this, the president's friends withdrew from the congress, forcing its adjournment. The congress reconvened only when the president's opponents assured that they would not impeach Arce. Even then, the deputies from Costa Rica and El Salvador refused to return.[62] Most of the president's supporters ultimately "voted for the treaty."[63]

Searching for reasons related to the treaty to explain why what was supposed to be so easy proved so hard, Williams learned that in "secret discussions" deputies argued "that although the treaty on its face was reciprocal, there was in fact no reciprocity in it." Williams learned that the treaty's critics wanted more of a military alliance against European foes and less of a trade deal that might deny Central America the power "to grant peculiar concessions to Mexico & the other Spanish Republics." Espousing a bias in favor of their fellow former Spanish subjects, these critics also wanted to postpone "treating with the U. States" until after the "Congress at Panama," which was meeting that summer. Despite these critiques and perhaps attesting to the bipartisan support for cultivating diplomacy with the United States, the treaty passed the house as one of the last acts before it again adjourned.

The senate received the treaty for ratification on July 3, but that body did not ratify it until July 29. This also confounded Williams because "They had little else before them during all that time." The chargé reported, "I have not yet learned the precise objections in the Senate." He was convinced that the delay was "not ascribable . . . to any motive disrespectful or unfriendly to the U. States." He blamed the delay on his anti-Hispanic prejudices: "an inherent disposition for procrastination & an undue caution in the transaction of business."

Narcissistically focused on the United States, Williams could not see the internecine tensions that were about to lead to bloodshed. The Central American government would become embroiled in a decade-long and very complicated civil war. The ratification of the treaty with the United States would be one of the last actions of Central America's legislature in its constitutionally defined form.

For Central America's government, foreign policy trumped the domestic agenda. The treaty was ultimately ratified, but as Williams noted, "The House of Deputies adjourned without passing the appropriation bills." Relaying the news of the failure of Barclay & Co. and the inability of the bond sales to provide the nation with capital, Williams observed, "The present state of their finances is most unpromising." Without a budget or a hope of an influx of money, the Central American government could barely function. Williams relayed rumors that a "forced loan" or the seizure of "Church property" might be on the horizon. Noting of the nation's military that "most of those in service [are] without pay," Williams recognized that "The troops are maneuvering." Although he was unable to see the implications of these facts for the treaty ratifications, even Williams could sense a gathering storm. He observed that "there are restless spirits ready to seize on the discontent of the army & put others out & themselves into power." Partisanship, fiscal failure, military rebellion, religious disputes, and provincialism would all contribute to the central government's collapse. Ultimately, the federal republic would yield to the centrifugal forces demanding a separate sovereignty for each province.

Unable to see the delayed ratifications as a part of these bigger problems, Williams accounted for his own actions. "I hastened them as much as propriety & decorum would permit—But could not procure an earlier decision," he confessed. The treaty became law a mere four days before the deadline.[64]

As he wrote his dispatch, Williams prepared to send the treaty back to Washington in the hands of US Navy Midshipman John Marshall, nephew of the Supreme Court chief justice of the same name. The naval officer had accompanied Williams specifically for this duty. Events that occurred on Marshall's trip from Guatemala City to the Caribbean coast would lead to diplomatic controversy, but as Williams sought to negotiate a resolution, he had to deal with an increasingly powerless government unable to control its agents.[65]

Before concluding his dispatch, Williams provided general observations about the "public men here." The Tennessee enslaver's prejudices colored his views. Although he acknowledged the leaders' classical educations, he criticized their lack of knowledge of "the science of free Government." He blamed the problems with the "administration of justice in this country" on "those habits which mark the character of all enslaved people." Alluding to the Spanish Empire, he elaborated: "The utter abhorrence for their former oppressors, sustained by a majority of them, a resolution to live under a free government & a wish to improve their institutions will in the progress of time rescue them from those embarrassments, which ages of ignorance, superstition & oppression have engrafted on all their social institutions." He described the Central American "code of laws" as "little else than a collection of superstitions." He reported condescendingly that he had "taken the liberty of making some suggestions in relation to the improvement of their code, which have been well received." Williams's intervention in their legal system was not enough; he also reported, "I have been requested by some of their most distinguished men to aid them in their financial system."[66]

With his "first object" accomplished, Williams's next object according to his instructions was supposed to be gathering information. Again, he ignored his orders. Rather than passively collecting data about the government, Williams took an active role in its construction.

IN HIS LENGTHY FIRST OFFICIAL DISPATCH, Williams did not mention his role in the canal contract negotiations. By then, the waterway was no longer a topic of significant discussion in Guatemala City, but it was still on Arce's mind. In late August 1826, the president signed confidential instructions for Cañas's replacement in Washington.[67] As it was no longer a high priority, Arce mentioned the canal in the middle of the document. The president commanded Central America's diplomatic agent to investigate whether "the house of Palmer" was disposed "to conclude the canal contract" according to "the terms and conditions" negotiated with the house's "representative." Clearly, in late August 1826, Arce still dreamed that the canal might solve his woes.[68]

By the time Arce composed these instructions, it had been over a month since Beneski departed Guatemala City. Due to the contract's short deadline for engineers and money to arrive in Nicaragua, he was racing against the clock.

In early July, the Polish soldier turned Mexican revolutionary turned US canal agent arrived in British Honduras. A local newspaper reported, "Col. Charles de Beneski . . . as agent for Messrs. Parmer [*sic*] and Co. of New York, has concluded a contract with the Government of Central America, to open a Canal, from the Lake of Nicaragua to the Pacific Ocean, by means of which the Atlantic and Pacific Oceans will be united." While readers of the paper puzzled over "the reason" why the proposal of "Barclay, Herring, Richardson & Co. of London" had not been selected, Beneski boarded a schooner bound for Rhode Island.[69] In late July, while the schooner was still at sea, Beneski transferred to a brig bound for Philadelphia.[70] His ultimate destination was New York City, where he would deliver the contract to his employer and Williams's letter to Bolton.

No official record exists of Beneski's arrival in the United States, but news of the agent and his canal contract began circulating on the treaty deadline, August 5, 1826.[71] This time, Beneski did not need to invent his laurels; he had won one of the world's most coveted contracts.

CHAPTER ELEVEN

The Race to Quincy

In July 1826, Charles de Beneski raced from Central America to New York City, transporting the world's first contract to build an interoceanic canal. To whom would he hand over this valuable paper?

Despite José del Valle's warnings, the contract imprecisely defined Beneski's employer as both "the New York Company" and "Aaron H. Palmer and associates."[1] Were these the same? A jumble of conflicting nouns and pronouns suggested that the man and the company were distinct entities that were required to work together: "Mr. Palmer will keep this contract in the company, and cannot sell, make over, or transfer the same to any other company or house, unless under their own responsibility." Beneski reinforced the separation between the man and the company by declaring, "Aaron H. Palmer and the company are likewise bound, henceforth, to carry into effect everything covenanted in each of the foregoing articles."[2] This legalese bound both a man *and* a company to the terms.

But evidence outside the contract suggests that this plural language was imaginary, the company a fiction, and Palmer merely a singular man without identifiable associates. While Beneski raced to New York, surveyor Edmund Blunt's family published the latest edition of *The New American Practical Navigator,* which contained an advertisement in English and Spanish for "Aaron H. Palmer's Stock Exchange, Agency, and Loan Office" located at "33 Wall-Street, New-York, (Up Stairs.)." Here papers related to finance were "bought and sold," "negotiated," "collected," and "recovered."[3] The passive voice elided the work of Palmer and any business partners or employees. In the Spanish version of the ad, the passive phrasing turned the bonds, bills, debts, and more into the subjects of the sentences, as if the shares sold themselves. Echoing the canal contract, the only identifiable person mentioned in either the Spanish or English advertisements is Aaron H. Palmer who, at least in the English version, claimed possession of the office. Was this also a one-man enterprise masquerading as more?

Uninvestigated in Guatemala City and almost invisible in his advertisement, Palmer was an unlikely person to win the right to build the communication between the seas. In the summer of 1826, in his mid-forties, Palmer had already lived several different lives—none of which were especially lucrative or powerful. He was always, however, a master of language. If ever there was a man who could convince the world to read him as plural, it was Palmer.

But he would need help to turn the contract into a canal. In August 1826, he called on the most powerful man in the country. But in the middle of this semicentennial summer, when the United States celebrated a half-century of independence, John Quincy Adams could not be found in Washington. Racing home to his family's estate in Quincy, Massachusetts, shortly after Independence Day, the president found himself reckoning with profoundly changing times. His father's revolutionary generation gone, the Era of Good Feelings collapsing into partisanship, and his own presidency increasingly impotent, Adams was in a fog.

If Palmer could make himself seem like more than one man, the president was doing the work of many. Preoccupied with present concerns, Adams and Palmer both drew on their pasts as they found themselves holding a canal contract that might reshape the globe's future.

BORN DURING THE AMERICAN REVOLUTION, the descendant of several generations of excommunicated Quakers, Aaron H. Palmer's childhood combined his father's financial foibles with his mother's success as a schoolteacher and grammar textbook author.[4] While Palmer's father faced serial insolvencies, his mother Mary taught "Reading, Punctuation, Writing, Arithmetic, English and French Grammar, Geography, Tambour, and all kinds of Needle Work."[5] Bouncing between the Hudson River Valley and New York City, Palmer absorbed his mother's cutting-edge lessons about language systems and the science of measuring, navigating, and knowing the globe. Encountering people from around the world traveling through New York's port, he became a polyglot. But the same Age of Revolutions ships that brought opportunities to learn languages from and teach English to foreigners also transported the "prevailing epidemic" that took his father's life in 1803.[6]

These currents of oceanic circulation also gave Palmer new and more worldly kin. Mexican-born prodigy Mariano Velázquez de la Cadena had served the Spanish king, attended the coronation of Napoléon, discussed the world with Humboldt, and got stranded in New York City during the Mexican fight for independence. A Spanish speaker in a primarily Anglophone land, Velázquez hired Palmer to teach him English. The Catholic and the Quaker shared a love of language and of learning. They also both loved Mary. In July 1809, a Jesuit priest—himself a refugee of the French Revolution—married Mary to the much younger Mariano.[7]

One year later, Velázquez registered his copyright for a book with the translated title of "Elements of the English Language for Use by Spaniards."[8] Between the copyright page and the prologue, Velázquez dedicated the book in multiple affectionate paragraphs and all capital letters to "AARON H. PALMER, ESQ." who "gave me my first English lessons."[9] Receiving no public acknowledgment until decades after her death, Mary also assisted her new husband with his publication and the development of his career as a translator, prolific author, and language teacher to boys sent from what was once the vast Spanish Empire to live with the scholar who would become Columbia University's first Spanish professor.[10]

At first, Palmer planned to follow his mother and stepfather's path. Operating out of his mother's schoolrooms, he became a "teacher and translator of languages," proposing books designed to teach English, French, Italian, and Spanish, and offering translations of the "Portuguese, German, and Dutch Languages."[11] Soon he would add Danish, Swedish, Latin, Greek, Hebrew, "Persian, Arabic, Sanscrit and Chinese."[12] When President Jefferson's 1807 embargo shut down the cosmopolitanism that fueled Palmer's linguistic work, he found opportunity assisting a Chinese merchant stranded in New York.[13] With letters of recommendation from leading New Yorkers that claimed Palmer "is perhaps already master of more living tongues than any person among us," the polyglot traveled with the Chinese merchant to Washington to plead the man's case and to pursue a government job.[14] But presaging his later attempts to turn his skills into a government salary, Palmer did not find work in Washington.

Undaunted, Palmer's Quaker principles led him toward engagement with a broader humanitarianism within the intellectual and political patronage networks that had supported his first application for a federal post. In 1808, he joined the New York Manumission Society.[15] He wrote to the White House appealing to the president for a job in which his "knowledge of several languages would be requisite," and to the first lady for her intercession on behalf of someone in need.[16] In 1811, perhaps with his stepfather's encouragement, he unsuccessfully applied to serve as chargé to the Spanish court.[17] Petitioning under a "new Insolvency Law," Palmer followed in his father's footsteps. He successfully employed the legal system to manage his debts but, by doing so, found himself following the family tradition of being disowned by the Quakers.[18]

In his life's second act, Palmer turned toward his financial savior: the legal system. With his insolvency case settled in June 1811, he opened a new translation business inside a law office.[19] He learned a new language—law—and he built new networks that rejected Quaker pacificism and egalitarianism for masculine hierarchy.

He advanced quickly through the ranks of Freemasonry, joined elite Democratic-Republicans on the "Iron Grays" militia roster during the War of 1812, and built his legal career cleaning up the loose ends of the war.[20] He served as a judge advocate in army proceedings, vouched for travelers seeking passports, negotiated claims of investors in privateering ventures, notarized documents for former prisoners of war, and requested pensions from the navy for sailors.[21] Always interested in increasing communication, he facilitated a loan to build a local bridge.[22] He enabled clients' land sales and litigated creditors' claims.[23] By the spring of 1816, he had parlayed this private work into a patronage job with the state government in his appointment as master in chancery.[24] He became fluent in collections law.[25]

Pursuing claims and collecting bad debts required tenacity. Some might see this as stubbornness. In fact, the polyglot lawyer's most famous case centered on a portrait of himself literally depicted as an ass. A dispute over a badly rendered likeness escalated into several trials that featured a who's who of the city's most prominent lawyers, foreign diplomats, politicians, and artists. Although a jury found that the disgruntled artist maliciously libeled Palmer by exhibiting his portrait with the man's ears replaced by those of a donkey, the case proved precedential. The portrait eventually vanished, but the image of Palmer as a donkey stubbornly enjoyed widespread and long-lasting fame.[26] Too funny, too novel, too memorable, the case made an ass of Palmer.

And yet his tenacity as a master in chancery and as a lawyer pursuing clients' claims for "LAND WARRANTS, PATENTS, and PENSIONS" brought him success.[27] The work done in Palmer's New York office contributed to the dispossession of the continent's Indigenous nations and facilitated hemispheric change. Before the US government recognized the new Spanish American republics, Palmer's practice supported the claims of these nations' revolutionaries in the US legal system.[28]

In 1819, during a triumphant moment, Palmer sat for a second portrait, this time by a friend, who painted Palmer as a man looking up.[29] On top of a silk vest and spotless white shirt with lace ruffles, his navy coat's brass buttons shine, as do his hazel eyes. Focused slightly up and to the right of the viewer, he appears to be confidently looking into the future. In his clean uncalloused hand, he casually holds a slip of paper, folded in the shape of a legal filing. With curly mutton chops, a slight afternoon shadow, and a dimpled chin,

Palmer's face is fuller than his slight frame might suggest. His slightly unkempt hairline has receded, revealing a prominent forehead. A few wrinkles at his brow and a hint of gray bags under his eyes show signs of aging, but the forty-year-old Palmer looks young with flushed cheeks and a mouth that betrays the smallest of smiles.

His hand is remarkably clean for a man who spilled so much ink. His signature was bold and thick, his penmanship distinctly heavy-handed. And yet, the perfectly manicured fingernail of his left pointer finger shines. It lightly rests on the paper as he points to the source of his power: words. We can almost see the cultured linguist's passion for communication combined with the lawyer's practical implementation of paper and ink. Here is not an ass but a visionary.

The 1819 portrait captures a moment of prominence and promise for Palmer, but his livelihood still depended on local debt collection cases.[30] Extending the work he could do in Chancery Court, Palmer was "admitted to practice" as a counselor of the Court of Chancery at the end of 1820.[31] Outside of work, he served as treasurer and chairman of the Board of the New-York Atheneum and contributed to the New-York Historical Society.[32] At a national Masonic meeting, Palmer served alongside New York Governor DeWitt Clinton.[33] He associated with New York's leaders.

In late February 1821, as the Transcontinental Treaty between the United States and Spain became law, Palmer saw opportunity. Hoping to apply his pen to the mountain of paperwork that the treaty created, Palmer applied for "the Secretaryship of the Board of Commissioners under [the] Florida Treaty."[34] This application differed significantly from Palmer's previous attempts to secure a government job. In 1809, he was vague in his request for a job "either in the foreign or home department"; in 1811, he was overreaching in his desire to be appointed "Chargé d'Affaires" to Spain.[35] By 1821, he sought a middling post between a commissioner and a clerk.

Whereas a single letter composed his earlier applications, Palmer's 1821 application was a sheaf of papers. It consisted of a cover letter, six letters of recommendation, and a calligraphed petition signed by twenty-three individuals and companies. Prominent men, Palmer's recommenders were Democratic-Republican politicians, federal office holders, leading Freemasons, members of cultural institutions, senior officers in the military, and even the sitting US vice president. These "respectable citizens" enumerated Palmer's "qualifications" for the job.[36] Palmer had transformed from Quaker linguist to networked lawyer; he had learned that to obtain a government post, patronage trumped personal pleas.

On the morning of Friday, March 16, 1821, he hand-delivered his application to Secretary of State Adams at his Washington office.[37] In a diary entry a few weeks later, Adams complained, "There are perhaps fifty applicants for it, and there is difficulty in making the selection." Thinking about the task of staffing the federal government, Adams elaborated, "The problem to solve in such cases is the highest degree of qualification for the place with the most urgent want of it." Adams weighed applicants' merit and need.

Palmer's application full of esteemed men exhorting his talents certainly testified to the "highest degree of qualification" but did not convey "urgent want." Adams's nephew had submitted the application of the former assistant surgeon general of the US Army who had lost his job in the military's postwar retrenchment and had six children to support. The army doctor was a candidate in need, but he was not atop Adams's list. In his diary, the secretary recalled, "There was a person by the name of Palmer, who came with very strong, numerous and respectable recommendations from New-York, and whose knowledge of language was said to be very uncommon." Adams continued, "I had much inclined to the appointment of him, and had already mentioned him to the President." The application had been so perfect that Palmer's name made it all the way to the White House. Adams told his nephew that the doctor's application was "too late."[38]

But on May 15, 1821, Washington newspapers reported that the doctor was "appointed Secretary to the Commissioners under the Florida Treaty."[39] The news arrived in New York three days later.[40] Too busy to write full diary entries, Adams did not explain why Palmer lost the post. Perhaps the secretary decided that need trumped merit.[41] Or perhaps, nearly a dozen visits with his nephew fatigued Adams into deciding that kinship trumped all.[42]

Even without a government job, the treaty created work for Palmer as he represented US citizens "before the commissioners for settling claims under the late treaty."[43] While Palmer was defending Spanish American revolutionaries and representing claimants, his stepfather and mother built a business instructing and boarding sons of the Spanish Empire.[44] Adams's kinship may have caused Palmer to stand before the claims commission rather than sit behind the bench, but his own kinship invited him into Spanish America.

In the 1810s, boys from families that remained loyal to Spain lived and learned in Mary and Mariano's home. The parents wanted their sons exposed neither to the Spanish American revolutionaries who traveled through New York City, like Palmer's clients, nor to the opportunities for licentiousness that the rapidly expanding city offered.[45] One father wrote a scathing letter about a recently dismissed teacher of "Castilian grammar," asserting that "he did a lot of damage to the young people with his bad advice." Whether this teacher was a revolutionary, a libertine, or both, the father believed this "individual lacked moral principles" and worried about "the faults that were noticed in some students."[46] Threatened but not undermined, Mariano's reputation spoke for itself through the multilingual boys who returned to their homes prepared for commerce and politics.

By the 1820s, Mary and Mariano welcomed Spanish speakers of all persuasions.[47] They even continued to communicate with the dismissed teacher, who by 1826, had become a translator for a merchant operating in Central Mexico.[48] Looking back, Palmer fondly recalled the family's "collegiate institute, in which a great number of young gentlemen of the first families in Mexico, Central and South America, Cuba and Porto Rico have been educated."[49] In their letters, former students and pupils' parents reported on politics, trade, and hurricanes. In the summer of 1825, had Central American families sent their new government's call for canal proposals? Around the same time, had Mexican monarchists introduced the banished Beneski? This might explain how Palmer and Beneski met and, moreover, how they planned a canal proposal that fit the Arce administration's decree when fellow New Yorker Curtis Bolton did not even know that the decree had happened. Here kinship advantaged Palmer.

Around the same time that the Central American government issued its call for proposals in the summer of 1825, the woman who had taught Palmer to bring the world into communication "suddenly" passed out of it.[50] Perhaps Palmer saw the opportunity to send Beneski to acquire the contract to build the coveted communication between the seas as a glorious tribute to his mother, whose life work had been teaching across languages and cultures, whose home facilitated connections throughout the hemisphere, and who had reared a man with the necessary combination of language, legal, and networking skills to become the only individual identified as a party to the world's first interoceanic canal contract. Although they were not his business partners, Mariano and Mary were certainly among Aaron H. Palmer's most valuable associates.

Before his mother's death, Palmer was already looking to leave the law for a new career as a banker. In early 1825, he rallied his network to petition the New York State Assembly to incorporate a bank.[51] This time, he was not applying for an existing federal job; instead, he was trying to use the state government to create a new career. But distracted by more urgent issues, the legislature failed to approve the proposed bank's charter. If Palmer wanted a new job, he was going to have to create it himself.

"The undersigned hereby announces to the public," Palmer wrote in a widely circulated newspaper advertisement dated July 6, 1825, "that he has formed an establishment in the city of New-York, for the purchase and sale of public securities." This would be only one "department" of his business. The "Stock, Exchange & Loan Office" at "NO. 33, Wall-Street" also included "an Agency for the collection and recovery of bills, notes, dividends, interest, debts, claims &c." Palmer actively described his work: "*He* is prepared to make loans," and "*He* will also receive all sums of money that may be offered to him, on deposit."[52] Channeling the lesson of his 1821 application, Palmer soon devised the passive voice language to remove himself from his description of his business. With this last step of extricating his personhood from his work, Palmer became the "company of New York."[53]

From his frequently excommunicated family, Palmer learned to push beyond the constraints of the community. Inspired by his mother, he had a polyglot's vision of a world of increasing communication. An interoceanic canal perfectly fit this desire because it would expand US diplomacy and might even ultimately result in his dream of a government job. His father's experiences with trade taught him the power of law. His own legal career was built upon contracts and larger context. Through his stepfather, the Spanish American world became familiar, and its monarchist and republican rifts navigable. His assumption of leadership roles in the New York Manumission Society, Freemasons, militia, and cultural institutions cultivated an arsenal of powerful contacts whose names he learned to wield at will. His petition for the bank suggested he could create a government job for himself, but it also taught him about the precarious process of incorporation absent an urgent need. And finally, in his advertisements, he had formulated the language that would transform his labor into the work of an abstract and impersonal office.

Motivated by his mother's worldly vision, Palmer would deploy lessons learned from his father's commercial and legal entanglements to draft a canal proposal that could be negotiated by an agent who had been both a monarchist and a revolutionary and who was hired through his stepfather's network, his own Spanish American client base, or both. Inspired by his recent experience with the bank, Palmer would reimagine himself as a company *before* he sought incorporation or acquired the canal contract. He empowered an agent to negotiate a contract on behalf of the imaginary New York Company with confidence that he could depend on his elite network to incorporate and fund the company *after* the contract made it an urgent necessity.

When Beneski traveled to Guatemala City, negotiated the contract, and returned to New York with the signed agreement in early August 1826, the

"New York Company" existed only in Palmer's imagination. Beneski was Aaron H. Palmer's only associate. And together these two men took their contract and departed New York to knock on the president's door.

THE DOOR IN QUESTION was just becoming the property of the president. In Washington, on July 4, 1826, President John Quincy Adams presided over the nation's "Independence Jubilee"—the celebration of the fiftieth anniversary of the Declaration of Independence, which launched the Age of Revolutions.[54] Two days later, Adams learned that, while the country celebrated, Thomas Jefferson—the declaration's principal author and the nation's third president—died.[55]

While Adams was deeply engaged in planning Jefferson's memorialization, the mail brought "quite unexpected" news. Adams learned that his "father's end was approaching." The family doctor thought the nation's second president "would probably not survive two days, and certainly not more than a fortnight." In his diary, Adams recorded, "I immediately took the determination to proceed as speedily as possible to Quincy."[56]

At five the next morning, accompanied by his son John, Adams raced home. Stopping for breakfast, they learned the news that the ninety-year-old John Adams had died on July 4, outliving Jefferson by about four hours. The president was prepared; as he confided to his diary, "this event was so much expected by me, that it had no sudden and violent effect on my feelings." Adams interpreted the coincidence of the two founders' deaths on the fiftieth anniversary of independence as "visible and palpable marks of divine favour." He and his son—two men named John Adams now grieving a third man with the same name—kept traveling at a breakneck pace.[57]

For four steamy summer days and nights, they made their way north in carriages, stagecoaches, and steamboats.[58] As they made "rapid progress" across Long Island Sound on July 11, John Quincy Adams reflected "upon this return of my birth-day, and the peculiar circumstances with which it is attended."[59] Peculiar indeed, but not as peculiar as the birthday of his traveling companion. The day of the oldest John Adams's death and the nation's fiftieth anniversary had been the youngest John Adams's twenty-third birthday.[60]

When they arrived in Boston on the evening of July 12, the thermometer read ninety-six degrees. The family doctor relayed to the president "the circumstances of my father's last moments, and of those attending the funeral." His corpse drew a crowd: "About two thousand persons took a last look, at his lifeless face; and all that was mortal of John Adams was deposited in the

Tomb."[61] All along the sweltering journey, the president kept his cool, but his response to his father's house surprised him.

Just as the heat broke on July 13, Adams arrived in Quincy. Surrounded by family all day, he initially noticed no change. But as he entered his father's bedroom, the president felt overwhelmed: "That moment was inexpressibly painful, and struck me as if it had been an arrow to the heart." He connected the lost people with the physical place: "My father and my mother have departed. The charm which has always made this house to me an abode of enchantment is dissolved: and yet my attachment to it, and to the whole region round is stronger than I ever felt it before." He contemplated his own mortality through a domestic metaphor: "it is time for me to begin to set my house in order, and to prepare for the Church-yard myself."[62]

As a career diplomat and civil servant, Adams had never owned a house.[63] "My father by his will," the president explained, "has given me the option of taking this House." Weighing the opportunity to buy his parents' home from the estate, the president confessed, "It is repugnant to my feelings, to abandon this place where for near forty years he has resided, and where I have passed many of the happiest days of my life." Contemplating his own retirement from public life, he wondered, "Where else should I go"?[64]

But the house was not vacant. In his last years, John Adams shared his home with another son's large family, a widowed granddaughter, and her nine-year-old daughter. John Quincy Adams resolved to allow all these relatives to continue to live in the house at least until the end of his presidency when he hoped, "I should come to reside here myself."[65]

For the next month, much of the president's time was devoted to answering questions about his father's will, organizing the estate, replying to condolence letters, and meeting with a stream of mourners.[66] Required also to continue to fulfill the "public business" of the presidency, Adams signed many Western land grants for white settlers—sometimes hundreds per day.[67] He seems to have missed the irony of this dispossession of Indigenous people's homelands as he sought to protect his own ancestral property.

On the foggy morning of August 17, 1826, three appraisers assigned by the probate court "to take the Inventory of the Estate" arrived at the house.[68] They did not finish listing "the furniture" before lunch. After their meal, two of the three men weighed all the silver. Satisfied for the day, they planned to "finish the appraisement of the personal Estate to-morrow."

Just as the appraisers walked out the front door and into the fog, a stranger approached the president. Adams recorded the encounter in his diary: "A Col. Beneski, who told me that he was a native of France, born at

Marseilles but of a Polish father, came and delivered me a Letter of Introduction from John Williams, Charge d'Affaires of the United States at Guatemala." Claiming to be French, Beneski invented another past for himself. In his European accent, the canal agent delivered "a verbal message" from President Arce. Adams invited Beneski and Palmer into the family home that was becoming his house.

If he remembered meeting Palmer as a job seeker, Adams made no mention in his diary, which is our only source for the canal contractors' meeting with the president. According to Adams, Beneski and Palmer began their pitch by handing the president the fully signed and sealed contract. Adams recalled, "To this contract Col. Beneski and Mr. Palmer solicited the Protection and Patronage of the United States; which I assured them should be given so far as my personal influence and Constitutional Power could assure it."

Palmer wanted more from the president than his "personal influence"; he either desired the government to assume responsibility for the contract or incorporate his canal company with a federal charter. As Adams recalled, "Mr. Palmer said an Act of Incorporation of the Company would be indispensable; and a question was whether it should be obtained from the Legislature of New-York, or from Congress." Palmer was asking Adams whether this globally significant canal ought to be controlled by a state or the federal government. As the leader of the latter, Adams confessed, "I thought that Congress was the only proper authority to grant an act of Incorporation, for objects thus interesting to the whole Union, and even the whole World." The president "advised Mr. Palmer to consult with the Representatives and Senators from New-York on the Subject." With this advice, Adams yielded the federal government's role in chartering the company to New York state's patronage politics. Could Palmer muster enough political capital to win over New York's divided delegation, let alone the entire Congress?

To the extent that the executive branch ought to be involved, Adams directed further canal inquiries to his secretary of state. "I told them," the president confessed, "Mr. Clay purposed returning to Washington at the close of this or the beginning of the next Month, and advised them to address their future Communications to the Department of State."[69] Whether in Quincy or the White House, Adams wanted to avoid future interviews with the canal contractors.

If Palmer and Beneski caught the president's innuendo, Adams had made three arguments. First, he thought the construction of the Nicaraguan canal was historically significant not only to the United States but also to the "whole World." Second, amid a campaign to nationalize the infrastructure projects the period called "internal improvements," Adams preferred that the federal government retain control over what might be called an "external improvement" that transcended the nation's borders. Third and finally, despite the transnational and historical significance of the canal and the federal jurisdiction of the project, the canal was not going to be Adams's pet project. Support would have to be garnered from the New York congressional delegation and the State Department. This last fact was, no doubt, disappointing for the canal contractors. Although Palmer had met New York Governor DeWitt Clinton, many of the state's representatives in Washington were Clinton's rivals. Once again, Adams failed to provide Palmer with a federal job.

The interview at an end and Adams's plan for their next steps clear, Palmer and Beneski walked out the door of the president's soon-to-be home and into the eerie August fog.

WHAT DID THEY MAKE OF THE MEETING? They had not transferred responsibility for the contract to the federal government. Instead, they gained the president's promise of his "personal influence." Unfortunately, the president had been steadily losing power since his election. Tainted by the accusation that he had won his office through a "corrupt bargain," Adams faced increasingly organized opposition from supporters of Andrew Jackson. In the year and a half since his election, Adams had been able to accomplish few of his ambitious domestic goals to build the nation's economy through federal power.[70]

In terms of his support for domestic road and canal projects, the president privately pledged to support "every particular undertaking which may be proposed."[71] This meant that Adams supported infrastructure projects, but he did not coordinate a centralized plan. This universal support offered to haphazardly proposed projects proved more expensive than all the previous federal spending on such projects in the nation's history.[72]

The diary's account of Adams's interview with the Central American canal contractors implied that the president might support federal expenditure for a canal beyond US borders. But presidential support could take Palmer and Beneski only so far. The president was limited by his "Constitutional Power," which was among the topics vehemently debated in Congress during the exceptionally long session that ran from December 1825 to May 1826. The policy that sparked this intense congressional debate was directly related to Central America and was even tied to the canal itself.

In mid-November of 1825, Minister Cañas invited the United States to send a delegation to a hemispheric conference planned to be held in Panamá during the summer of 1826.[73] In late November, Adams instructed Clay to accept the invitation with the caveat that the Senate must provide its consent.[74] Clay had already begun drafting letters to the two proposed ministers, one of whom was currently serving as minister to Colombia.[75] He also extended an offer to William B. Rochester of New York, a stalwart Clay supporter, to serve as secretary of legation.[76] In all three of these letters, Clay acknowledged that the appointments would not be official until the Senate consented.

In his letter to the chargé in Bogotá, high in the Andes Mountains, Clay provided specific details of how he thought the mission to Panamá would unfold. The US-based minister and secretary would "leave here between the Middle of December and the middle of January, in a public vessel, and proceed to some port of Colombia or the Central Republic." The legation would meet on the Caribbean coast and travel together "to the point of your common destination." The plan still depended on the Senate's approval, which Clay "confidently anticipated."[77] This confidence was sorely misplaced.

The congressional response to the Panama Congress was one of the first organized campaigns of Adams's opposition. After all the congressional pressure to recognize the new Spanish American republics, Adams did not expect US participation in a meeting designed to facilitate hemispheric friendship to provoke controversy.[78] The lengthy congressional debate united Jacksonians in opposition to Adams, challenged the president's power, reinvigorated calls for US diplomatic neutrality, reshaped US perceptions of the hemisphere's republics, and fueled racism against Spanish Americans and their nations' emancipationist policies.[79]

It also delayed the US legation. The Senate officially confirmed the nominations at 3:00 A.M. on March 15, 1826. Debate continued for nearly two more months in the House of Representatives, which was asked to appropriate funds for the mission. Meanwhile, Clay composed a "confidential" letter updating the distant chargé of the continued delay in his colleagues' departure.[80] Sending the letter with Gustavus Scott, who sailed out with Chargé Williams on his journey to Central America, Clay anticipated that his letter would take nearly as long to reach the chargé in Colombia as the House debate over funding the mission.[81] Given this timing, Clay informed the diplomat to leave Bogotá "as soon as may be after the receipt of this dispatch." He was to make his way to the Caribbean side of the isthmus where he should await his colleagues' arrival. But Clay recognized a problem with this plan; the Caribbean port "may be unhealthy, and you may be exposed to some danger by waiting there." Hoping to keep his diplomat alive while Congress deliberated, Clay authorized the minister to "go to some more healthy position in the neighborhood."[82]

Nowhere "in the neighborhood" was particularly healthy and, as the congressional deliberations continued, the administration revised its instructions. "Considering the advanced state of the season, and the consequent danger," Clay wrote to the two men waiting to depart the United States, "the President has determined to leave it to the option of each of you, whether you will proceed now or wait until the fall."[83] Both the minister and the secretary decided to stay stateside.[84] But the chargé in Colombia was already making his way to the coast during "the sickly season."[85]

The minister and secretary's choice to stay in the United States meant that a bearer of dispatches would "speedily" need to make the dangerous trip to transport to the Colombian coast a "large sealed pacquet [*sic*]" of confidential papers from the State Department, including the news that the mission's schedule had changed. Unfortunately, in mid-June, this State Department agent was shipwrecked. Writing from the British colony of Turks and Caicos, he reported, "From a situation of the most imminent peril, I had the good fortune to escape with what I believe to have been the most important of the papers entrusted to my care. Everything else, the clothing I had on at the moment and my sword excepted, I was obliged to resign to the violence of the waters." Although he saved the "pacquet," the paper was "so perfectly saturated with water as to render it necessary, with a view to their preservation to expose every page to the Sun and air." What had been among the most confidential papers in the US diplomatic corps became public knowledge. "I could not but learn their nature & importance," he confessed, assuring he would be discreet. But some of the papers—especially the diplomat's commission, credentials, and key to the department's secret code—were so damaged that the agent asked for replacements.[86]

New documents would soon prove unnecessary. On July 22, 1826, when the shipwrecked man finally arrived in Cartagena, Colombia, he found the chargé "extremely ill at the residence of the US Consul." Less than a week later in a letter to Clay, he reported, "I am sorry to add, that he is now no more, having expired on the night of the 24th." Congress's delays had deadly consequences.[87]

The bearer of dispatches summarized recent Panamanian newspapers that reported "no adjournment" of the Panama Congress regardless of the "present sickliness of the place where the session is held."[88] The chargé's death in Cartagena meant that, despite all the danger and debate, no US representatives would attend the Panama Congress. The United States would not be the only country to miss the meeting. Brazil's ministers failed to arrive. Also delayed by legislative foot-dragging, Chile's representatives did not arrive in time. On June 22, 1826, delegates from Mexico, Central America, Colombia, and Peru met. Britain sent an agent, and the Netherlands sent an unofficial observer.[89] Hardly continental in its composition, the congress was cut short. Planned to last months, it ended after three weeks.[90]

ALTHOUGH THE MISSION to the Panama Congress was a disaster—deadly for the chargé, politically poisonous for Adams, and unable to accomplish its purpose of hemispheric unity—the lengthy instructions Clay composed for the ministers provide insight into the administration's ideas about an interoceanic canal.[91] Despite what he said to Palmer and Beneski, Adams and his cabinet disliked the idea of a canal contract between a country and a company.

"A cut or canal for purposes of navigation, somewhere through the Isthmus that connects the two Americas, to unite the Pacific and Atlantic Oceans will form a proper subject of consideration at the Congress," Clay predicted. Although such a waterway would be globally significant, the secretary believed that it would benefit "all America," and especially "Colombia, Mexico, the Central Republic, Peru, and the United States." Against turning the waterway into a national project, he argued that it "should be effected by common means and united exertions, and should not be left to the separate and unassisted efforts of any one Power."[92] These instructions suggested that Central America's unilateral contract with Palmer's company was contrary to the administration's canal dreams. Adams hinted at this when he described the project as interesting "to the whole World," but Palmer and Beneski probably did not perceive the full implications of this phrase.[93]

Built jointly, Clay explained in the instructions, the canal should not benefit one country over others. "If the work should ever be executed, so as to admit of the passage of Sea-vessels, from ocean to ocean," Clay advised, "the benefit of it ought not to be exclusively appropriated to any one Nation, but should be extended to all parts of the Globe, upon the payment of a just compensation, or reasonable tolls."[94] To the Adams administration, the canal offered a greater diplomatic prize than US domination of the region: the opportunity for international unity.

Adams's opponents disparaged such prioritization of cosmopolitanism over nationalism and would likely doom any multinational project in the legislature. Predicting congressional challenges, Clay instructed his ministers that "it would not be wise to do more than to make some preliminary arrangements." The project, Clay was suggesting, would occur in the future. "What is most desirable at present," the secretary directed, "is to possess the data necessary to form a correct judgment of the practicability and the probable expense of the undertaking, on the routes which offer the greatest facilities." Echoing the diplomatic instructions to Mann, Miller, and Williams, and with the same goal as Blunt the surveyor and Thompson the British agent, Clay wanted the United States's Panama Congress delegates to collect information. The secretary, however, wanted the diplomats to avoid any commitment to canal construction. Clay ordered, "You will state to the Ministers of the other American Powers, that the Government of the United States takes a lively interest in the execution of the work." Curious about whether the project could be accomplished with "reasonable human efforts," he nonetheless wanted other countries to invest in research: "Their proximity and local information render them more competent than the United States are, at this time, to estimate the difficulties to be overcome."[95]

The administration was even fearful of committing to a multilateral scientific agreement. From a draft written before the acrimonious congressional debate, Clay cut several sentences empowering the ministers to commit the US government to a portion of the cost of surveys of the potential routes.[96] In the final instructions, he limited their actions to collecting "any proposals" or "plans" for "its joint execution."[97] This reduction in the ministers' powers reflected Clay's growing concern about congressional backlash. Here the interoceanic canal's future was actively saddled by the nation's recent past; hemispheric and global dreams were sunk by rising domestic partisanship.

Clay's instructions on the potential waterway also reflected other recent history. In the middle of his long canal paragraph, Clay recalled Cañas's "liberal offer" to the US government to jointly construct the canal. He even enclosed copies of Cañas's letter, and his "answer." He interpreted Cañas's offer as "manifesting high and honourable confidence in the United States." Nonetheless, the United States could not agree to the "friendly overture" without "information necessary to enlighten their judgment."[98]

Despite this lack of information, Clay informed the ministers that "the best routs [*sic*] will be, most likely, found in the territory of Mexico or that of the Central Republic."[99] But as any reader of Humboldt knew, the potential routes ranged further. In fact, the location of the congress in Panamá was not an accident. Simón Bolívar had been dreaming of convening an "august assembly" there for over a decade.[100] In 1815, before he solidified independence from Spain for the territories that would become the nations of Venezuela, Colombia, Ecuador, Peru, Bolivia, and Panamá, the liberator dreamed of a future pan-isthmian "confederation" that would "become the emporium of the world" owing to its "magnificent position between two mighty oceans."

He prophesied that isthmian "canals will shorten distances throughout the world, strengthen commercial ties between Europe, America, and Asia, and bring to this happy area tribute from the four quarters of the globe." The future Panamá of Bolívar's imagination married commerce to the politics of international union: "There some day, perhaps, the capital of the world may be located."[101]

Despite its reputation for summer sickliness, Bolívar had chosen to convene the Panama Congress in the place he hoped would one day lead the world. Perhaps the most powerful man in the Americas at that moment, Bolívar aimed to promote his potential waterway by requiring the hemisphere's diplomats to tour the route. A good idea in theory, Bolívar's dream proved undoable. The Brazilian, Chilean, and US agents never got there and, even if the US ministers had arrived, their instructions encouraged negotiation for a Mexican or Central American route over that of Panamá. At this point, in August 1826, Palmer's contract for a Nicaraguan waterway was closer to fulfilling Bolívar's expectation of connecting the oceans than the liberator's foiled plans for a Panama Canal.

But internal US politics proved problematic for Palmer. Adams and Clay could hardly contemplate generating support for the chartering of an external improvement project when policies of internal improvement and Spanish American diplomacy generated enormous congressional opposition. Southern enslavers especially excoriated the idea of working with republics that had emancipated and enfranchised people of color. Even without knowledge of the civil war brewing in Central America, the Adams administration refused to marshal its waning political capital to charter a private interoceanic canal company.

DRAWING ON HIS PAST, Palmer won the contract, but its terms demanded quick future action. And the present changing political times complicated what might have been a more popular project only a few months earlier, when the newspapers' interoceanic canal mania crested. By the summer of 1826, the contract faced opposition not only from the nationalist Jacksonians but also within the Adams administration. Could Washington turn the man into a company before the deadline?

CHAPTER TWELVE

Cancellation

In June 1826, as Charles de Beneski prepared to depart Central America for New York City, Chargé John Williams entrusted him with hand-delivering two letters. Both would eventually make their way to President John Quincy Adams.

Addressed directly to Adams, Williams's first letter was designed to open the president's door for the canal contractors, which it did for Palmer and Beneski on that foggy August afternoon in Quincy.

The second letter was not intended for the president but ultimately ended up in his hands. It was a report of Beneski's triumph in Guatemala City addressed to Curtis Bolton, who Williams incorrectly assumed was affiliated with Palmer's New York Company. Given that the chargé believed that Bolton and Palmer were working together, the delivery of both letters was supposed to be simple, but Williams's confusion sent Beneski on a tour of Manhattan.

Beneski's first stop was Palmer's office. He strolled a half mile up Wall Street from the wharves along the southern tip of Manhattan. About midway between the East River and Broadway—just past the city's oldest bank at number thirty-two and diagonally across from the New-York Insurance Company at number thirty-four—Beneski climbed the stairs to find the headquarters of "the New York Company."[1]

To deliver the second letter, he would continue westward past Broadway to the docks along the Hudson River. Here amid ferry piers and grocers, he would find Bolton's out-of-the-way office. The would-be canal contractor's home was even further afield. Two miles north of the city's bustling downtown, Bolton lived where street names gave way to numbered rural roads. On the map, his home was a tiny square in a block full of trees and grass.[2]

With his office amid the city's leading capitalist institutions, Palmer might appear better situated to recruit canal investors. But Bolton had the inside scoop. With his brother serving as the president of a recently incorporated canal company, Bolton did not even have to leave home to find a model for his canal plan.

Both Palmer's and Bolton's dreams ran through a Central American waterway. Whereas Palmer wanted to turn the canal contract into his government dream job, Bolton wanted to build a canal more glorious and globally significant

Aaron H. Palmer's Wall Street office was located near the tip of Manhattan on this 1817 map of New York City. By contrast, the Bolton family lived near the upper right-hand side of the map, at the corner of Herring and Hammond Streets, where the house is depicted as a small black square amid trees and fields. David Longworth, "This actual map and comparative plan showing 88 years growth of the city of New York" (New York, 1817). Courtesy American Antiquarian Society.

than his elder brother's. Instead of joining together, Williams's letters launched the men on a collision course. Would the rivalry cancel out the canal?

IN AUGUST 1826, CURTIS BOLTON was not expecting his dreams to be upended by a letter delivered by a stranger with a thick foreign accent.[3] A resident of Manhattan for more than a decade, Bolton had become a New Yorker, but like Beneski, he did not sound like a native.[4]

On the Eastern Shore of Maryland in 1784, when Bolton was less than two years old, a fatal illness claimed the lives of both of his parents and two of his five siblings. A wealthy paternal cousin from Georgia rescued the toddler and his surviving siblings from a neglectful guardian. The orphans were integrated into the cousin's family. Upon adulthood, the Bolton brothers became partners in the family's prosperous Savannah mercantile house, and through marriage they intensified their kinship. John Bolton married his cousin's oldest daughter Sally, and Curtis married her next younger sister Ann.[5] In 1802, when the cousin died, the daughters each inherited money, real estate, and enslaved people; the Bolton brothers inherited wharves and other business interests.[6]

After the War of 1812, the two brothers and their growing families moved north and founded "John and Curtis Bolton of New-York."[7] Although Curtis Bolton had been raised in Georgia, he easily integrated into northern society. In 1820, he was elected a director of the Bank of the United States.[8] The next year, he joined the board of the New-York Institution for the Instruction of the Deaf and Dumb. The president was a longtime friend of Aaron H. Palmer.[9] Bolton and Palmer's networks overlapped and intersected through many of the city's most powerful men.

In the early 1820s, despite the abolitionist aims of some of Palmer's friends, New York City proved a welcoming place for wealthy, white Southerners like the Boltons. Partners in trade, the Bolton brothers shared an estate—and perhaps a single house—along what was then the northernmost edge of New York City.[10] In the 1820 census, their households totaled eighteen people: the brothers, their wives (who were themselves sisters), more than a dozen children, and servants, including two unnamed enslaved adults and one enslaved child.[11] New York's gradual emancipation law of 1817 would legally allow the Boltons to enslave the two adults in New York City until 1827. In the form of a prolonged indenture, the child's bondage might last into the 1840s.[12]

The Boltons also invested in nonhuman property: a sawmill, a wide range of dry goods, real estate, and several ships.[13] One of these was the Brig *Mary Livingston*, which in 1825, transported Edmund Blunt on the canal surveying mission.[14] By the time Curtis traveled to Nicaragua to save Blunt's mission, John had entered the local canal business.

Unlike Curtis's dreams for contracting a Central American canal, John Bolton could not claim to be the founder of his canal company. In March 1823, a Philadelphian named Maurice Wurts obtained a charter from the Pennsylvania legislature "to improve the navigation" on a river with the goal of floating Wurts's newly discovered coal from the interior of the state to the border. Here another canal built in New York state would transport the expensive and typically imported fuel to the Hudson River and the New York City market.[15]

Wurts recruited prominent New Yorkers to petition their legislature to charter a company that would enable Wurts's coal to heat New York City's houses. When the New York State legislature incorporated "the Delaware and Hudson Canal Company" (DHCC) and granted it the rights to construct a "water communication" to transport "stone coal," it authorized eleven prominent New Yorkers to oversee the capitalization of the company.[16] Although the goal was to raise $500,000, purchasers would initially pay only a five dollar down payment per share; the balance would be due when the DHCC officially became "a body politic and corporate" that would be "capable of perpetual succession."[17] Governing this immortal, state-chartered corporation, thirteen elected managers would appoint "a president, a secretary and treasurer, to hold their offices during the pleasure of the board."[18]

The DHCC hired the surveyors of New York state's in-progress Erie Canal to examine the proposed route.[19] After the surveyors dragged the chains and did the math, the New York legislature amended the DHCC charter, recognizing that "it appears from an actual survey and examination of the route, that it will require a larger sum to make a canal." The corporation would now be authorized for a capitalization of up to $1.5 million, making it one of the country's first million-dollar, publicly traded corporations.[20] But as in London, stockholders paid for their shares in installments; this left the DHCC without immediate cash to pay for construction. In the fall of 1824, the DHCC sought another amendment to its charter to ease its liquidity issues by allowing the company to circulate bank notes up to the value of $1.5 million.[21]

After a demonstration of the warming power of Wurts's anthracite coal in January 1825, stock sales soared.[22] Capitalists invested in the DHCC's energy revolution, thus enabling the incorporation of domestic fossil fuel into Manhattan's energy regime.[23] Over the next few years, the canal company used its bank notes to pay the estimated 10,000 laborer workforce to dig and blast a 108-mile waterway that used locks to scale more than 1,000 feet of elevation.[24]

In 1828, the waterway opened and the DHCC sold its first ton of coal in New York City, but for three years, the canal company had already been doing business as a bank. The board of the DHCC initially appointed Philip Hone as president and John Bolton as treasurer.[25] Hone's presidency did not last long. He was elected New York City mayor in January 1826, and he resigned his DHCC office.[26] John Bolton ascended to the canal company's presidency.[27]

A few months after John took on this new role, the brothers dissolved their mercantile firm, moving out of their wharf-side "handsome Counting Room."[28] Perhaps some sibling rivalry set in. Hoping to preside over his own more ambitious canal company, Curtis Bolton wrote to Secretary Southard seeking Chargé Williams's support for his Nicaraguan waterway. By early August of 1826, when Beneski delivered Williams's letter, the younger Bolton was a solo merchant with interoceanic canal dreams operating from an out-of-the-way office.

BY THE TIME BENESKI KNOCKED ON THE DOOR, Curtis Bolton had been chasing his canal dream for two years. As he held the unopened letter in his hands, Bolton believed Beneski was merely a messenger; he quickly realized Beneski *was* the message.

As Bolton unfolded the paper and began reading Williams's scrawl, nothing could have prepared him for the news the letter conveyed. The middle of the poorly punctuated second sentence dropped a bombshell: "On my arrival in this city the 2nd of last month I met Col. Beneski agent for yourself & associates to negotiate the canal between the North & South seas thro' Lake Nicaragua." Somehow, Williams had come to believe that the stranger who delivered the letter was Bolton's agent.

As he kept reading, Bolton learned that Williams's mistake about Beneski's identity had cost him the canal. As he discovered that the chargé had helped this foreigner win the contract, Bolton's shock turned to fury. All Bolton had risked in traveling to Guatemala City, his investment in Blunt's surveying mission, his cultivation of a relationship with Cañas, and his lobbying of Southard and Williams to support his canal proposal let the wrong man reap the reward.

Awash in emotion, Bolton skeptically read the chargé's assessment that "The terms of the contract are highly advantageous to the company." He would have to see the contract for himself.[29]

Beneski obliged. He returned with Aaron H. Palmer and Palmer's English translation of the contract. "They alone appear to be the parties concerned," Bolton later remarked, providing confirmation that at this point the "New York Company" was a fiction. Bolton recalled that the two men "offered to me & my associates to unite with them in interest." Deferring this decision until "we have had an opportunity of conferring together," Bolton nonetheless reviewed the contract, and came to his own decision.

Writing to Samuel Southard on August 14, 1826, a few days after first meeting Beneski, Bolton explained that "my own mind is made up not to join with them because Capitalists will not put out their money on those terms."[30] In reviewing the contract's thirty-four articles, four "additional articles," and five "explanatory articles," Bolton reduced the agreement to three problematic terms.[31]

First, Bolton did not approve of the idea that the government of Central America might purchase the canal from the contractors after its construction. He explained: "if the Canal turn out to be a good thing, a pledge of the Canal itself would enable that Govt. [Government] to raise the money in London & thereby divest the Compy [Company] of possession; if it prove a bad property, it would be left in the hands of the Compy until it might become otherwise."[32] Whereas Valle had worried that the Central American government would never be able to afford to buy the company out of its canal, Bolton thought the sale of the canal would come all too quickly, thereby limiting the company's potential as a long-term investment.

No doubt, Bolton was comparing Palmer's contract to the DHCC's Pennsylvania charter, which placed a thirty-year horizon on the canal rights granted to Wurts. The DHCC's New York charter and various amendments were even more favorable, providing a twenty-year limit on the DHCC's banking privileges, and granting the company canal rights "forever."[33] Palmer's contract promised no such perpetuity.

Second, Bolton bristled at the idea that a canal that moved goods but not ships "from Sea to Sea" was prohibited by the contract. It was bad enough, according to Bolton, that the company had to pay for the canal route's survey. What happened if the survey revealed that building a canal for oceangoing vessels would require "a ruinous expenditure," but a canal constructed for smaller barges "might be rendered advantageous"? According to Bolton's interpretation, the contract foreclosed the possibility of building a "trans-shipment" canal—like the DHCC and the Erie Canal—and yet it required "a sort of bonus or loan" of $200,000 to be paid before the survey was even conducted.[34]

Bolton knew from his brother's experience that this was an insufficient amount of money to construct a canal, and that the surveyors would likely estimate an orders-of-magnitude larger sum to engineer the moving of deep-water ships rather than shallow-hulled barges. He knew all too well that the DHCC's survey of its route necessitated the tripling of the company's capitalization to seven and a half times the amount of the loan required by Palmer's contract. He may also have known that the DHCC's nearly unprecedented capitalization at $1.5 million was already proving inadequate for constructing a "slack water navigation" of locks and pools designed to enable small barges to ascend and descend the waterways of Pennsylvania and New York.[35] Within a year, the New York State legislature would "Loan the Credit of the People of the State of New York" to the DHCC to back another $500,000 stock issue.[36] The price to build the DHCC was proving astronomical, and it was designed for small, shallow vessels. Palmer's contract precluded this less costly but still capital-intensive option in Nicaragua where Blunt's report suggested a costly tunnel might be required to accommodate the starkly seasonal climate.

Third and finally, Bolton objected to the Central American government reserving "the right of levying transit duties." The lack of limitation on the government's ability to raise the price of transit duties might "drive the trade around Cape Horn." Bolton imagined that by diverting the ship traffic away from the canal, the Central American government would then "force the Company to sell out their interest at a great sacrifice at which the Gov't might become the purchaser." This criticism suggested that the country might sabotage the canal's purpose to gain its possession.[37]

Bolton's brother did not face this problem. Tolls on both the New York and Pennsylvania canals of the DHCC were specified in the charter, keyed to profits, and exclusively the property of the company.[38] Clearly designed to drive investors toward the canal, the state did not expect any payment from the DHCC besides property taxes.[39] Similarly, the New York charter specified an upper limit on tolls.[40] The state was not entitled to a percentage of the tolls, and after the 1827 loan, New York state even exempted the DHCC from paying taxes for the next six years or until it realized an income of six percent on its investments.[41]

All this suggests that the state governments of both Pennsylvania and New York sought little if any direct revenue from the DHCC. The state legislatures expected the canal to increase economic activity and thereby indirectly swell state coffers. The DHCC's deal with both states reflected a theory of political economy in which the government's role was to create corporations that would "improve" the state's natural resources without directly controlling or profiting from the improvements.

The state might not receive cash profits from the DHCC, but the politicians who voted for the incorporation expected a different kind of profit: political capital. State legislatures doled out corporate charters, in part, to win the support of key constituencies. If they wanted to be reelected, the legislators could not ignore Phillip Hone, John Bolton, and the other powerful men they represented. In the 1820s United States, the profits from state-chartered canals were paid in patronage.

This was not the case in Central America. The government in Guatemala City sought immediate cash and a revenue stream from its canal to solve the country's fiscal problems. The contract did not empower individual Central American citizens with the rights to profit from the "improved" waterway; it did not build political support for the nation through payoffs to powerful constituents. Although Arce's government might have benefited by deriving patronage from the canal contract, the country desperately needed the money.

Bolton read this governmental priority—this alternative political economy—as problematic. All three of Bolton's criticisms—of the country's ability to buy the canal, of the exclusion of a trans-shipment canal, and of the country's unrestricted ability to set tolls—implied that he did not believe the Central American government was negotiating in good faith. He interpreted the contract as unacceptably tilted in favor of the country.

Trying to persuade Secretary Southard to stop the federal government from supporting Palmer's canal contract, Bolton did not consider any of the provisions that benefited the company—like its twenty-year steamship monopoly, consideration for military contracts, or continued cut of the profits after the country reimbursed the company for the canal. He did, however, hint that there were "other objections to the Contract." To Bolton, the other concerns merely confirmed the contract's "impracticability." The three "vitally important" terms that he outlined were enough for Bolton to condemn the contract and anticipate its failure.

"On those terms," Bolton stewed, "it would be far better that the English or any other Foreigners should have the contract than our own Countrymen, for it must be a losing concern." This damning interpretation was designed to undercut Williams's triumphant tone. Perhaps the chargé should have stayed out of Beneski's battle and let the British win. Because Bolton anticipated that the contract would not produce a canal, he dismissed any diplomatic concerns and judged, "no danger could arise from such a contract as this."

It may not have been dangerous, but could it become so? Bolton presented the cabinet member with his analysis of whether the perceived flaws in the contract could be repaired. Unconvinced, he predicted, "finding Palmer & Co.

indisposed or incapable of fulfilling their present contract that Govt. might become disgusted & refuse any further negotiation under that name." With this "probability" in mind, Bolton wanted to distance himself from Palmer and Beneski.[42]

Bolton had his own plan in the works. Since his return from Guatemala, he had been cultivating a relationship with Central America's Minister Cañas. Suffering "ill health," in late June 1826, Cañas officially announced his impending return to Central America.[43] US newspapers reported, "He seeks in the equable temperature of his native mountains of St. Salvador the restoration of that health of which he has been deprived by the rigors of our climate."[44]

Before he departed on Bolton's *Mary Livingston*, bound for the mouth of Nicaragua's San Juan River, the ailing Central American official agreed to convey Bolton's revised proposal to his government.[45] As Bolton explained to Southard, "I sent by him, with the concurrence of my associates, modified propositions. These we shall yet further modify since the perusal of the present contract gives us insight into the view of the Govt. of Guatemala, which shall be consulted as far as practicable." As this plan for continued revisions suggests, despite Palmer and Beneski's contract, Bolton still hoped to win his own Nicaraguan canal contract from the Central American government.[46]

These hopes depended on the huge assumption that by the time Cañas returned to Guatemala City, there would still be a government to award a contract. Around the time that Beneski delivered Williams's letter to Bolton, the *Mary Livingston* with Cañas on board landed in the British colony of Jamaica to replenish its water supplies.[47] When he arrived in Central America a few weeks later, the minister would not find much of a government to debrief. On June 30, 1826, shortly after approving the canal contract and without approving the federal budget, the Central American congress adjourned.[48] On September 2, 1826, the Central American senate also adjourned; it would never meet again.[49] President Arce called a special congressional session in early October, but the congress could not gather a quorum.[50] When the special session failed, Arce attempted to call for new elections to a wholly new congress, but the superior court of Guatemala found this action unconstitutional.[51] With the Central American government resting entirely on his shoulders, Arce found himself embroiled in escalating and violent conflicts with the state governments of both Guatemala and his native El Salvador.[52] Nicaragua had already begun reverting to civil war.[53]

In late November 1826, after only seven months in the country, Chargé Williams penned his penultimate dispatch from Guatemala City, planning his return to the United States and reporting on the chaotic descent of the republic into anarchy. Criticizing Arce's substitution of "the bayonet for the influence of the Magistracy," Williams universalized the problem of entrusting national leadership "to a person whose education & habit have been exclusively military." A dig at Andrew Jackson, Williams saw Central America's political violence as a warning.

Williams penned this dispatch upon his return from a thirty-seven-day tour of Guatemala and El Salvador. His description of Cañas's homeland confirmed it as "temperate, salubrious, & fertile." Scorning Humboldt's failure to visit the region, he judged much of the land "probably superior in fertility to any other tract of the same extent on this or on either of the other continents." So impressed with the potential for US trade, he imagined vast markets for US wheat when "the Nicaragua canal shall be completed."

On his journey, Williams had encountered Cañas, who the chargé reported "returned from the United States by the river St. John & Lake Nicaragua." This route enabled Cañas to form his own opinion of the potential for an interoceanic waterway. Ascending the river during the rainy season, his timing could not have been better. "He entertains no doubt of the practicability of the contemplated canal," Williams reported. The US diplomat could make no further comment as he never visited the canal route himself.

Although Cañas had justified his departure from the United States as necessitated by his poor health, the minister found himself unable to simply retire from public service. As Williams confirmed, "He is appointed to the Treasury Department by President Arce."[54] Managing the failing state's starved coffers would be anything but recuperative; Cañas ultimately declined the post. Climate aside, Cañas's retreat home to a country on the brink of civil war might not be as restorative as he hoped.[55]

NOT KNOWING ANY OF THIS, Bolton believed both that, through Cañas, he had a foot in the Central American government's door and that there was still a door to wedge open. Bolton strategized that if he united "with Palmer & Co., the ground I now stand upon might be thus lost." Bolton envisioned that the cancelation of Palmer's contract—because it failed to meet the deadlines, raise sufficient capital, or both—would lead to his own triumphal negotiation of a new canal contract.

Bolton also surmised that although Palmer had temporarily won the canal contract, the timing worked in his own favor. Waiting out what Bolton saw as the contract's inevitable failure would enable "an opportunity to hear at Guatemala the report from London that Barclay, Herring & Co. of London have failed." Not only would this failure eliminate Bolton's "principal competitor for the canal," but the related failure of the Central American government's loan on the bond market would also "embarrass their fiscal resources & abate their pretentions with regard to the Canal." Without alternatives and unable to negotiate with the confidence of British capitalization, the government might award "an American Company" with "a grant" composed of "fair & practicable terms."[56] Of course, Bolton's definition of "fair"—based on the ideas of political economy governing Pennsylvania and New York—might be entirely and irreparably different from the definition in Guatemala City.

Nonetheless, Bolton continued to dream of becoming the Nicaraguan canal contractor. This explains why he forwarded Williams's letter to the US government. "And here it becomes necessary," he confessed to Southard, "to notice a remark in Col. Williams' letter here enclosed." Bolton continued, "you will perceive he calls Col. Benesky [*sic*] my agent. How Col. Williams could have fallen into this mistake, I know not; but it is proper for me to declare that I never knew or heard of such a person as Col. Benesky until now." Worried that "in Col. Williams' report to you on this subject, he may have fallen into a similar mistake," Bolton justified, "I have felt bound to make these explanations to you as it were in self defense."[57] Bolton here made an incorrect assumption. Williams had chosen *not* to report the canal contract negotiations to the federal government. Writing to Southard, Bolton wanted to protect himself, but correcting the record also served as a convenient pretext to bring the canal to the cabinet's attention and attack Palmer's contract.

Justifications aside, the entire tone of Bolton's letter was offensive, not defensive. To promote his own self-interest and foreclose federal support for Palmer and Beneski, Bolton wrote to one of the nation's most powerful men. Surely, Bolton expected Southard to share his views with the president. Using the excuse of correcting an error and defending his honor, Bolton contrived to cancel the contract.

Bolton strongly disagreed with Williams's letter's closing assertion that "Stock on this company cannot fail shortly to become the most valuable of any in our country or perhaps in the World." To Bolton, Williams's confidence in the stock was sorely misplaced. Bolton believed that no capitalist would want to invest in Palmer's company, and moreover, he would do everything in his power to sink the contract before a single share was sold.[58]

When Bolton's packet arrived in Washington, Southard jotted his own brief cover letter and put the packet back in the mail. Sending it to Quincy on August 23, 1826, Southard summarized, "I enclose to you a letter received from Curtis Bolton, Esq. upon the subject of the contemplated Canal to connect the Gulf of Mexico with the Pacific Ocean." With a subtle cue that Bolton had persuaded the secretary, Southard drew Adams's attention not to the diplomat's correspondence revealing his entanglement in the canal negotiations but to Bolton's cover letter.[59]

Bolton's circuitous route to Adams—sending his packet south before Southard forwarded it north—enabled his criticisms to already be circulating in Washington when Palmer arrived.

PALMER SPENT MUCH of September peddling his contract in the nation's capital. His timing was terrible for pursuing federal patronage. The Nineteenth Congress was in recess. Having adjourned in May, its next session was set to convene on December 4, 1826. Eager to get out of the swampy, sickly city, most congressmen and senators returned to their home districts for the summer. The president would not return from Quincy until mid-October.[60] Clay was also out of town but was planning to return in mid-September.[61]

Although few agents of the federal government could be found in Washington, the diplomat representing the British government lingered at his post. On October 2, 1826, Sir Charles Vaughan wrote to his superior in London: "Mr. Palmer of New York, who calls himself the 'general Agent of the Central American and United States Atlantic and Pacific Canal Company,' has lately been at Washington."[62] Clearly, Palmer gave himself this title and endowed the company with a more geographically expansive and descriptive name. Never mentioned in Vaughan's correspondence, Beneski may not have accompanied Palmer to Washington.

Vaughan reported that articles "appeared in the newspapers, purporting to give an abstract of the terms and conditions of the contract lately entered into by a company at New York and the Republic of Central America."[63] Indeed, press coverage of Palmer and Beneski's pursuit of federal incorporation began within a week of their meeting with Adams. The canal would receive "considerable attention."[64]

On August 24, 1826, a Massachusetts newspaper reported that "Colonel de Beneski had delivered to the President of the United States at Quincy, despatches from Colonel Williams, the United States Commercial Agent at Guatemala." Laden with errors, the article misrepresented Williams's office—he was a diplomat and not a consul—and mischaracterized his communication with the president—he had provided a letter of introduction and not an official dispatch. It even erroneously reported that the contract had been "made in June last, in New York." The article more correctly reported on the company's intention "to apply to Congress for an act of incorporation," but it offered a different name: "the Central American and United States Atlantic and Pacific Junction Canal Company." Announcing a capitalization of more than triple that of the DHCC, the newspaper put a favorable spin upon "this important enterprize." Hoping the company would be "a national concern," it asserted without evidence that the canal was "known to be practicable."[65]

The misrepresentations multiplied. One Boston paper suggested that the "whole extent of excavation" would be seventeen miles and would require only "a lockage of 200 feet."[66] Such an estimate assumed that the San Juan River was navigable by oceangoing vessels. But as Blunt found, the San Juan River was barely navigable by "bongie," especially in the dry season.[67] This would certainly mean more miles of canal construction. Minimizing the undertaking and maximizing the payout, the article surmised the contract "can scarcely fail to be a source of wealth to the company, and advantage to the whole commercial world."[68]

Other papers sought to correct the record. Announcing the arrival of a bearer of dispatches from Central America sent to recall Cañas, an article circulating in South Carolina introduced new errors, claiming that "the canal is to be commenced within 10 months, and two years allowed for its completion."[69] The actual contract allowed a year for "work" to begin and set no target for its completion.[70] Beyond errors, the articles spread rumors: "It is said that Col. de Beneski, the agent of the company, who negociated [*sic*] the contract receives $50,000 for his services." Although crediting Williams for his "great service in this business," Beneski's gigantic bonus of more than ten times the diplomat's salary implied that personal profit was the real driving force behind Beneski's success.[71] Another newspaper argued that the Central American government's "partiality for our republican institutions" had really defeated the British. Recalling the "flattering attentions" paid "three years since" to the Salvadorans sent to annex their country to the United States, an article argued that Arce awarded the canal to the United States as "return for the good offices he and his co-patriots received during the short time they staid [*sic*] in our country."[72]

A pan of the project argued that Spain would never have "neglected canalling her empire, and joining the Atlantic to the Pacific, had it been practicable—nay had it been even possible." Deeming the canal "hardly worth pursuing," a Massachusetts paper predicted, "No Indian merchant would think of sending his vessels to Bengal and China through the range of all the West Indies, to the deadly climates of Central America, for a passage across the Pacific with only the Sandwich Islands between America and India." Suggesting instead that the longer route around Cape Horn offered advantages, the article praised the opportunity for merchants rounding South America to take "the pulse of the markets of Brazil and La Plata." Dismissing the dangers of the longer route through Antarctic waters, the article asserted "no seaman thinks any more of doubling Cape Horn than of Cape Cod." "In short brother Yankees," the article advised, "if the New Yorkers choose to add this to the late batch of bubbles that have burst, let them have it all to themselves."[73]

By late September, Palmer tried to take control of his canal contract's image in the public sphere. He offered the *National Journal* the opportunity "of reading the contract itself."[74] Reprinted across the country, the *National Journal* article provided readers with "a brief abstract of the terms and the conditions of the contract." The article also reported on the contract's progress in Washington: "We understand that it has been submitted to the inspection of the Secretary of State and Secretary of the Treasury." The article reported that "they have both expressed their decided approbation of the great object of uniting the two oceans by means of a canal for ship navigation." The secretaries hid the administration's preference for an international treaty-based canal in what sounded like laudatory language that confessed "their great satisfaction" that if the canal "should be executed by any company, that company should be composed of citizens of the United States."[75]

Oblivious to this subterranean critique, the paper reproduced Palmer's confidence in "the practicability of the enterprise." It deemed the cost "insignificant, when compared with the incalculable advantages which must be derived to commerce in general, and particularly to that of the United States." Informed by Palmer, it credited the contract "To the activity, intelligence, and persevering zeal of Col. D. Beneski, a gentleman formerly attached to the Mexican army, and personally held in high respect by the members of the Central American Government, most of whom had been his associates and companions in arms." From Palmer's perspective the contract was not secured based on Williams's diplomatic influence, Arce's feelings for the United States, or Beneski's greed. It was, instead, Palmer's clever selection of a well-networked agent that led to his success over the British and everyone else.[76]

HAVING READ MUCH OF THE PRESS COVERAGE of the contract, Vaughan provided the British government with a summary. He reported, "the canal across the isthmus of Panama by the lake of Nicaragua, is to be navigable for ships." The "Republic of Guatemala" agreed to grant the company timber rights, "furnish plans and charts, to procure workmen, and to indemnify the owners of lands." Unlike Bolton, the British agent highlighted the potential long-term profits to be derived from the payment of 10 percent interest on the capital invested in the canal, the company's continued share of canal duties even after the loan had been repaid, and the twenty-year steamboat monopoly. Recognizing potential diplomatic concerns, Vaughan reported, "the navigation of the Canal will be completely in the hands of the Company formed in the United States, though the Contract provides that the navigation shall be common to all friendly and neutral nations, without any exclusive privilege."

Beyond this newspaper account, which the diplomat enclosed, Vaughan reported on rumors: "It is said that the estimate of the expence to be borne by the Company, does not exceed half a million of Dollars, and that the subscription has been filled up at New York." Both halves of this rumor were false. Given the newspaper's estimates and the real cost of the DHCC, Vaughan's price tag seems unrealistically low. The subscription rumors were equally bogus. As Palmer's company—whatever it was called—had not yet received either a federal or state charter, it was unlikely that stock sales had even begun let alone "filled up."[77] The company was still just Palmer and Beneski, or as Vaughan's letters' omission implied, maybe just Palmer.

Time and a more intensive investigation would allow the diplomat to return to the subject in an October letter: "Having observed, that the Agent of the Company was at Washington, about the time of Mr. Clay's return, I took an opportunity of asking him [Clay] what countenance this Govt. was likely to give to that scheme." The secretary of state's interview with Vaughan offered good news for the British government. "Mr. Clay informed me that the agent of that Company had been indefatigable in his endeavours to engage through himself and other ministers, the Government of the United States to take part in this contract," described Vaughan, "but that it was resolved that the Govt. should have nothing to do with it in any shape." Despite his best Sisyphean efforts, this result was a predictable Washington defeat for Palmer.

Moreover, Clay explained to Vaughan the administration's position on an interoceanic canal. "If the Canal was to be made by any foreign power," Vaughan reported Clay's words, "he should not regret that it fell to the lot of Americans to effect it, but that he was convinced that it must be carried into effect with the consent of all nations, studiously avoiding any privileges reserved for any one."[78] Even if the United States might benefit from building the waterway, the Adams administration wanted the construction of an interoceanic canal to be an international project. Ironically, Palmer's contract was so good for the nation that Clay saw it as bad diplomacy.

And the president did not direct Clay otherwise. Adams was not in town to provide his promised "personal influence."[79] Despite abundant opportunity, Adams did not mention the canal contract in correspondence with his cabinet. His promise had been empty, and it left Palmer empty-handed as he departed Washington.

ADAMS COULD OFFER PALMER such empty promises because he knew that he would never have to make good on them. In another article that Vaughan sent to his government, the political problem with Palmer's contract was laid bare. "While we heartily wish success to this splendid project," the editors confessed, "we would rather hear of its failure than be assured of its success through an act of incorporation by the Congress of the United States." Confident in Congress's opposition to Adams's attempts at creating a strong federal government, the article concluded, "such an act will never be passed."[80] Whatever support Adams promised, he could not wield enough political capital to create a compliant Congress.

Despite arriving before Palmer, Bolton's term-by-term critique of the contract's faults would be only one factor in the cancellation of Palmer's federal incorporation. The Adams administration, despite its professed support for improving infrastructure, did not support the construction of an interoceanic canal unless it became a hemispheric project. The opportunity for such diplomatic negotiations died with the minister to Colombia. And the Panama Congress debate had revealed an overwhelming antipathy by the administration's opponents to US entanglement with its southern neighbors. With diminished political capital and his own critique of the contract, Adams was not going to try to push Palmer's charter through the increasingly dammed channels of federal power. And if Palmer tried to work around the president, to somehow recruit support from the New York delegation, Congress's schedule—with its next session not set to begin until December—would force him to fail to meet the contract's deadlines.

Giving up on the federal government, as September rolled into October, Palmer heard the tick of the contract's clock. With less than four months before $200,000 and an engineering team were due in Nicaragua, he turned to his second choice for incorporation: New York state. There, Aaron H. Palmer's network was wide, but Curtis Bolton's was deep. Awash in the glow of the Erie Canal's success, would the Empire State be a font of capital or a patronage quagmire?

CHAPTER THIRTEEN

Visionaries

On Sunday, September 3, 1826, a warm rain fell outside DeWitt Clinton's home in Albany, New York.[1] Cloudy skies darkened the governor's writing chair, high-backed and black with a desk attached to its right arm.[2] Increasingly sedentary in the aftermath of an 1818 riding accident, Clinton tried to combat his growing girth with daily walks. But he did more sitting than walking. On and off during the previous month, he had "sat for" portraitist George Catlin, whose more famous later works featured leaders of Indigenous nations. Catlin's portrait of the governor depicted a jowly Clinton balding, full-bellied, and seated—perhaps in his writing chair. The weather scuttling his walk and the calm of the Sabbath quieting the usual storm of visitors, the governor lowered his double-chin and, in his nearly inscrutable hand, drafted a letter to Aaron H. Palmer.[3]

Full of insertions and strikethroughs, this was no quick draft. Clinton sought the right tone, balanced between a defense and a demand. Marking it "*Confidential*," the governor knew that the letter—even the draft—was a private plea, a father's request.

The letter opened with a heavily edited clause suggesting that by early September, while Palmer pursued federal incorporation in Washington, the canal contractor had already been in touch with New York's most powerful politician. Palmer needed names of men who could begin the survey of the canal before the deadline. Clinton recommended an engineer who had "competent skill for the survey of the Canal between the Atlantic and Pacific." But for this mission, candidates also needed to be hungry for experience. Slashing through the word "young," Clinton searched for phrasing that suggested healthy men early enough in their careers to be induced to depart quickly for the notoriously deadly isthmus. Settling upon "of not an advanced age," perhaps the Erie Canal commissioner recalled the exertions of his own exploring mission through Haudenosaunee homelands when he was a younger man.[4]

After nearly two decades of work promoting and overseeing the construction of the recently completed Erie Canal, Clinton was the perfect source for recommendations. For nearly fifty years, his cousin had been the New York state surveyor general, converting the hunting, fishing, and farming territory of Oneida, Seneca, and others within the Six Nations of Iroquoia into parcels

In 1826, DeWitt Clinton (1769–1828) sat for portraitist George Catlin (1796–1872). This undated lithograph may have been "drawn on Stone from the life" while Palmer and Clinton formulated their plan for the Central American canal. George Catlin, "DeWitt Clinton" (New York: Imbert, c. 1826), LCCN 2003670628, LC-DIG-pga-04613, Prints and Photographs Division, Library of Congress.

of private property to be disposed of by the state.[5] A celebrated contributor to both the humanities and sciences in his own right, Clinton knew the most prominent engineers in the country.[6] Less than two years earlier, he had signed the charter incorporating the nearby Rensselaer School, designed to train scientists and surveyors to meet the growing demand for this expertise.[7] Earlier in the summer, he had even sent nineteen-year-old George Washington Clinton, the fifth of his ten children, to participate in its "experimental traveling summer school" designed to train students in geology, botany, and engineering as they ascended and descended the Erie Canal.[8]

George was the reason for Clinton's rainy-day letter. When he made his initial recommendations, the governor confessed to Palmer, "I had no idea that my son would think of the appointment, being already most amply provided for—but I find that he is ambitious of securing his name associated with this stupendous enterprise." Surprised that his son wanted to risk his life to survey the interoceanic canal, Clinton expressed confidence in his son's "entire competency" in the laboratory and, more importantly, "in the field."

Often on the receiving end of entreaties, Clinton appealed to the canal contractor for a favor. "All I request," he enjoined, "is that you will keep this ~~subject~~ in mind and avail yourself of any favourable opportunity to furnish his object—so far as you deem proper." The letter was a golden ticket of patronage. All Palmer needed to do was offer one boy a job, and he could count on the support of one of the nation's most powerful politicians and the world's most successful canal dreamer.

That is, if the governor could remember the interoceanic canal contractor's name. At the end of the page, Clinton scribbled what might be the name "Aaron" diagonally down the page between "A" and "H," and crossed out his first attempt at a last name before penning "Palmer" above the line.[9] By 1826, the governor had already been a New York City mayor, a US senator, a presidential candidate, a founder of the New-York Historical Society, and an officer in countless associations. From astride his position at the apex of a pyramid of patronage, the governor might not remember meeting the polyglot lawyer six years earlier at a Masonic event.[10] He was a busy man about to become even busier.

Despite the governor's full schedule, Palmer's "stupendous enterprise" won Clinton's attention. The governor would come to know the canal contractor's name so well that, in the lists of visitors in his bare-bones diary, he reduced it to one name. "Palmer" met with Clinton at least nine times in both Albany and New York City during the fall of 1826.[11] Such investment of time suggested the canal's appeal to Clinton. Despite his assertion that George was "most amply provided for," the governor found himself falling short of his family's financial needs. Palmer's contract promised the kind of lucrative compensation that did not flow from his many government and associational offices. His Erie Canal dreams generating affluence for his state, Clinton hoped the Nicaraguan waterway would be profitable for his family. The governor, like his son, became ambitious to secure his name to Palmer's canal.

AFTER DRAFTING HIS REQUEST to Palmer on that quiet Sunday, DeWitt Clinton enjoyed a busy month of travel and triumphs. On September 16, 1826, in New York City, Clinton sheathed his slender sword in its decorative scabbard and, in a secret ceremony, enjoyed election to one of the highest Masonic offices in the nation.[12]

Like Clinton, the Masons were at the peak of their power, but this had already begun to change. Earlier in the same week, near the western terminus of the Erie Canal, a former Mason preparing to publish an exposé of the organization's "secrets and mysteries" disappeared. Newspapers would blame his abduction and presumed murder on local Freemasons.[13] As the scandal intensified, an anti-Masonic political movement formed. Although meant to be an honor, Clinton's Masonic office would prove a political problem.[14]

A few days after the secret ceremony, a statewide convention of Clinton's faction of the Democratic-Republican Party unanimously voted to nominate him for reelection to the New York state governorship.[15] Unlike in his first gubernatorial race in 1817, Clinton would face serious opposition in his bid for reelection, but the rival faction of the party, commonly called the Bucktails, would not hold a convention until October.[16] For the moment, Clinton was the only candidate in the 1826 race.

Without pausing for celebration, the fifty-seven-year-old left Albany on a ten-day trip to examine the potential route of the Oswego Canal, a proposed expansion of the statewide waterway that earlier critics had derided as "Clinton's big ditch."[17] Hardly the fit explorer of his youth, Clinton refused to let his heft or his hobbled leg hold him back. The nation's preeminent Mason, the executive of the country's most economically powerful state, the leader of a partisan faction, and the face of the first and most successful of North America's early nineteenth-century infrastructure projects, Clinton was at the apogee of his career.

AT TEN IN THE MORNING ON OCTOBER 5, 1826, Clinton steamed back into Albany with his surveyor son George. As the scrawled names in Clinton's diary attest, the governor's day quickly filled with a dozen men who sought his attention.[18]

The most surprising name on the list was "Wm B. Rochester." Less than a year earlier, Rochester had been appointed secretary of legation to the Panama Congress, but the congressional debate over US participation took so long that Rochester never left New York.[19] Earning a salary from the State Department, he awaited the end of the isthmus's sickly season at his home on a street bisected by an aqueduct of the Erie Canal in the booming city that bore his family's name.[20] Meanwhile, he pursued a government job closer to home.[21]

At noon on October 4, 1826, Bucktails from across the state converged on another Erie Canal town. By a vote of 103 to 1, they selected Rochester as their gubernatorial candidate.[22] News of his nomination traveled quickly. Toward the bottom of his October 5 diary entry, Clinton scribbled this rival's name.[23] He would prove a formidable opponent. The temperature was rising to an unseasonably high seventy degrees, and the race between the two Democratic-Republican candidates was just warming up.

CLINTON'S EARLIER MEETINGS WERE COOLER. The previous nine visitors offered collaboration, not confrontation. After talking with some political allies, Clinton met with Aaron H. Palmer.[24] As Clinton's earlier letter on his son's behalf suggested, the governor and the canal contractor had already been in conversation. The effects of these discussions were visible to one of the governor's other visitors on October 5.

With a full head of curly dark hair and brown eyes set beneath thick brows, the thirty-six-year-old historian Jared Sparks met with Clinton and Palmer that afternoon.[25] Like Palmer, Sparks reinvented himself in his thirties. After graduating from Harvard, Sparks edited the *North American Review*, a literary magazine with a national readership. In 1818, he resigned to pursue his calling as a Unitarian minister. In 1823, at thirty-four years old, Sparks abandoned the pulpit, purchased the *North American Review*, resumed his role as editor, and embarked on a mission to collect, preserve, and write the history of the American Revolution.[26]

In mid-September of 1826, Sparks set out from Massachusetts "to examine the archives in Rhode Island, New York, and New Hampshire."[27] Waking up in Manhattan on October 3, 1826, Sparks boarded a steamboat "at 6 o'clock in the morning, and arrived in Albany at 7 in the evening, a distance of 150 miles in 13 hours." Sparks flew. The speed impressed Sparks, as did the Hudson River's scenery, which he described as having "no parallel of the kind in this country."[28] Indeed, the riverine vistas and increased steamboat traffic since the opening of the Erie Canal attracted artists, including Romantic landscape painters and portraitist George Catlin.[29]

When Sparks arrived in the New York State capital at Albany, he quickly moved indoors—from the wonders of the natural world to the archival. He consulted revolutionary era documents, interviewed revolutionaries' descendants, and "Passed half an hour with Gov. Clinton, who is just returned from the interior of the state, where he has been making examinations for a canal." In his diary, the historian elaborated, "He is very much taken up with things of this sort at the present moment."

Clinton had canals on his mind. Sparks explained: "Mr. Palmer is here, and concerting a scheme with Gov. Clinton in regard to the Mammoth Canal of Central America. The plan of an active company is forming, of which Gov. Clinton is to be the president."[30] Sparks already knew the canal contractor. The historian first met Palmer in New York just a week earlier. About Palmer's "contract for the great canal through Central America," Sparks judged, "He is very sanguine in the project." Sparks believed Palmer was overly optimistic; the historian was more skeptical.

In his diary, Sparks echoed Palmer's story about winning the contract: "The grant was obtained wholly through the influence of Col. Benesky [*sic*], a Pole, who was an aid to Iturbide, and with him when he was shot." The canal's connection to the history of Mexico's revolution intrigued the historian. Sparks did not record meeting Beneski, suggesting that the agent may have already departed, leaving Palmer with the task of turning the contract into a canal. The clever lawyer recognized an opportunity. As Sparks explained, "Mr. Palmer offers me materials for a review on the subject of this great Canal."[31] This was the first of several attempts to convince Sparks to publicize the canal in the *North American Review*.

In Albany on October 5, when Palmer and Sparks next met, they were both appealing to Governor Clinton for assistance. Although Clinton had been traveling through the interior of the state for the previous ten days and had returned to Albany only a few hours earlier, Sparks described the interoceanic canal "company" as already "forming." Palmer and the governor were mid-plan. More precisely, according to Sparks, they were "concerting a scheme." This language implies Sparks sensed something untoward.[32]

In truth, although the governor was politically powerful and culturally prominent, Clinton was also financially strapped. With the expenses of hosting elite social functions, a large family to support, and his time tied up with unpaid and poorly paid offices, Clinton's expenses exceeded his income.[33] Palmer's company might offer an ample salary to supplement his government pay. Although in the room for less than an hour, Sparks sensed that Clinton's interest in promoting Palmer's canal was not merely an act of goodwill.

Clinton could certainly empathize with Palmer's situation. Palmer desperately needed a charter of incorporation; the contractual surveying deadline was only three months away. And Washington had failed him. Clinton knew from personal experience how difficult it could be to win the federal government's support for a canal project. Two decades earlier, in 1808, Albert Gallatin, Jefferson's secretary of the treasury, recommended federal funding for the construction of a national system of canals and roads.[34] Inspired by this proposed policy, the New York State Legislature created a Canal Commission that would advise the state on the political, financial, and technological engineering of a waterway to connect the Great Lakes to the Atlantic Ocean. Having seconded the legislation creating the commission, Clinton accepted an appointment as a commissioner and explored the proposed route. In 1811, he traveled to Washington to seek the aid suggested in the Gallatin report. But President James Madison believed a constitutional amendment would be required to direct federal funds toward internal improvements. Washington was deadlocked; DeWitt Clinton's canal dream seemed moribund.[35]

But after the War of 1812, and after Madison vetoed a bill that would have funded the canal's construction, Clinton resurrected his dream through the government of New York state.[36] Rather than chartering corporations to construct the canal, a plan that had failed in the 1790s, the state retained control and financed the construction through bonds. The Erie Canal would not be beholden to shareholders; it would have no president. For his work turning 362 miles of land into a waterway that descended 571 feet of elevation, Clinton earned political capital but not a fortune. He owed his election as governor in 1817 and again in 1825 to the canal, but he never enjoyed significant remuneration.[37]

The promise of the presidency of Palmer's canal company appealed to the governor. And Clinton, in turn, appealed to Sparks to promote the canal in his magazine. As Sparks commented in his diary, "I am beset to take the matter up in the N.A. Review. It is a great work, and cannot but excite a deep interest in the community. The Review shall do what it can to help it onward." Flush in the currency of favors, Clinton loaned the historian revolutionary era sources and suggested he might have access to other documents. "I am to see him further," concluded Sparks as he parted ways with the governor and the canal contractor.[38]

AS SPARKS RETURNED TO HIS RESEARCH, Clinton moved on to other meetings. Of the dozen men Clinton scrawled in his diary, only one contains neither a first nor last name: "The Patroon."[39] When he reached the age of twenty-one in 1785, Stephen Van Rensselaer III inherited the largest landed estate in North America and his family's ancestral titles: Lord of the Manor and Patroon of Rensselaerswyck. The titles were vestiges of New York's colonial past that had empowered the Van Rensselaer family with the right to control local government, religious institutions, and the tenants who rented their land. By 1826, the feudal rights had vanished, but the titles and deeds lingered. Van Rensselaer owned entire counties, more than 200 square miles of land. 5,000 tenants paid him rent, making the Patroon one of the nation's first millionaires.[40]

Van Rensselaer invested in scientific research to unearth his land's geological value and increase his tenants' agricultural production. To train men skilled in science and engineering, he founded the Rensselaer School.[41] With similarly mingled philanthropic and personal interests, he served alongside Clinton on the Canal Commission for twenty-three years, fourteen as its president. He also joined the governor in office holding. A major general in the state's militia, Van Rensselaer served as the commander of all troops stationed in New York during the War of 1812.[42] Since 1822, he represented his district in the US House of Representatives, where he recently had cast the ballot that elected John Quincy Adams to the White House. In 1825, he was elected to the highest state Freemasonry office. Masonic brothers, Clinton and Van Rensselaer were also kin. The Patroon was a first cousin of the governor's second wife, Catherine Livingston Jones Clinton.[43]

On October 5, 1826, the sixty-one-year-old visited the governor. Although we have no record of their discussion, Van Rensselaer's name appeared in a draft of a legal document Clinton reviewed that day. Because the governor had been traveling for the previous ten days and the document was too legalistic to have been hastily penned, Palmer likely wrote the four pages that would later be described as a "deed of trust between Aaron H. Palmer and De Witt Clinton."[44] Palmer probably brought the draft with him to Albany for the men to edit together. Perhaps the Patroon joined the revision process.

THE DOCUMENT WAS AN "INDENTURE," or contract, designed to "assign, transfer, or convey" Palmer's "right, title, and interest" in his Central American canal contract to Clinton and other named parties. After a description of the history of the contract, the document claimed that "various persons in the United States of America" had already associated with Palmer as "'*the Central American and United States Atlantic and Pacific Canal Company*.'" Without naming these "various persons," the document suggested, "many others are desirous of associating themselves with him" to share in the company's "benefits."

With the goal of facilitating investment, Palmer sought to turn the company into a government-chartered corporation. The "indenture" would help Palmer accomplish this goal. The document would "in trust" turn Clinton and his associates into "commissioners" empowered to "execute" what was "necessary and proper" to "carry into complete effect the contract or charter."[45]

The "powers" and "duties" of the commissioners filled the next three pages. Anticipating an overwhelming demand by investors, the commissioners would be responsible for orchestrating the sale of 50,000 shares of "capital stock" across the United States and Central America. Each share would be worth $100 with the goal of raising $5,000,000. As a first installment, subscribers would pay ten dollars per share; this would quickly raise sufficient capital to meet the January deadline for delivering $200,000 to Nicaragua. Like the British loan contracts, the document specified that if a subscriber failed to make a payment, "all previous payments" would be "forfeited." Paid-up stockholders would "from time to time" receive "dividends of the profits" and, at an annual meeting, learn the company's "affairs."[46] The commissioners, however, controlled the company. They would "have the authority to appoint from their own number a president." Clinton would presumably fill this role. They would also designate a "treasurer, and such other officers, agents, engineers, surveyors, artists, clerks, and servants, as they shall deem necessary." The commissioners would set the salaries of employees, negotiate the contracts to build the canal, and serve as the company's "true and lawful attorneys."[47]

Ever the clever lawyer, Palmer ensured he would be contractually guaranteed the job of "secretary and general agent."[48] These titles circumvented the clause in the canal contract stipulating, "Mr. Palmer will keep this contract in the company, and cannot sell, make over, or transfer the same to any other company or house, unless under their own responsibility." With Palmer as an officer, the new company would arguably remain under his "responsibility."[49]

Beneski would also get a job: "the said Charles de Beneski shall be their agent at Guatemala." Conceivably, Beneski had already agreed to reside in Central America, but even if he decided not to return to the isthmus, Beneski benefited from a provision that empowered the company to "bestow such compensation as they may consider reasonable and just on the said Beneski, for his important services in negotiating the said charter with the federal government of Central America." Hardly enjoying the rumored $50,000 windfall, Beneski had not yet been paid for securing the contract. Moreover, in promising to satisfy the agent's expenses incurred in "procuring said charter," the document confirmed Beneski outlaid his own money to finance his work in Guatemala City.[50]

The company's next charter—"an act of incorporation" by a "competent authority in the United States of America"—would be the responsibility of the commissioners. Should they fail, the document determined how the company would persist without one. Stockholders would annually meet on "the fourth Monday of December" to elect "five commissioners to manage the affairs of the said company." With nationalist aims of limiting the power of foreign shareholders, the document stipulated, "stockholders actually resident in the United States of America, and in the federal republic of Central America, and none other, may vote in elections by proxy."[51] In this way, Palmer and Clinton attempted to thwart British, Mexican, or other foreign interests from capturing control of the company.

Hopeful of recruiting a board of powerful commissioners, the document concluded that those who signed accepted "the trust" because they were "anxious to promote an object so intimately connected with the commerce of the world and welfare of the human race." Such magnanimity would be protected through a declaration limiting the liability of the signatories, with the desired state charter ultimately providing more robust protection of their assets.[52]

With promises and protections, the document demanded the signature of particular men. Clinton's intended fellow commissioners included "Stephen Van Rensselaer, C. D. Colden, Philip Hone, and Lynde Catlin."[53] Present in Clinton's office while Palmer and the governor finalized the terms of the "indenture," the Patroon may have directly contributed to the document. The other three men—selected for their political, financial, and personal connections—may not yet have known about the "scheme."

THE LONG-FACED AND RUDDY fifty-seven-year-old Cadwallader D. Colden currently served as a state senator, but he had been a US congressman, a district attorney, and a New York City mayor.[54] He owed his mayoral appointment to Clinton, which meant that Colden was deeply ensconced in Clinton's patronage network. Like his patron, Colden held offices in the Freemasons and philanthropic associations including the Society for the Prevention of Pauperism, the Bank for Savings of the City of New York, and the New York Manumission Society.[55]

In these posts, Clinton often outranked Colden; the opposite relationship defined Colden's ties to Palmer. In his early Quaker years, Palmer joined the New York Manumission Society; Colden sat on the board. During the War of

1812, Palmer enlisted as a "private" in the Iron Grays; Colden "commanded" the state's militia.[56]

Canal dreams ran in the Colden family. Before the revolution, Colden's powerful namesake grandfather advocated improving Western navigation.[57] The younger Cadwallader shared this passion. In 1825, New York City's government selected Colden to author a "Memoir" celebrating the completion of the Erie Canal. A racist paean to "civilized man," it praised the dispossession of Indigenous people, asserted the necessity of "improvements" over nature, and argued that the Erie Canal's construction resulted from political independence. Pursuing this argument beyond the United States, Colden condemned the lack of Spanish canalization of "the Isthmus which separates the Atlantic and the Pacific." Arguing that Spain was "Jealous of her Colonies," Colden criticized, "she did not encourage any attempt to form a communication between the oceans." Colden glowed "Independent governments are hardly established to the South, before it is proposed to unite the two great seas." Praising the powers of "republican governments" to accomplish such goals, he imagined that an interoceanic canal would be completed "within a few years" and would "make an important change in the arrangement of the lands and waters of the earth, the effects of which will be felt by the whole human species."[58] Colden practically invited Palmer and Clinton to solicit his support for Central America's canal.

Lynde Catlin was another obvious choice. A generation older than his painter cousin George, the fifty-eight-year-old had been a banker for decades.[59] When the Merchants' Bank of New York opened in 1803, the Yale-educated lawyer was its first cashier. In 1816, John Jacob Astor recruited Catlin to serve as cashier of the New York Branch of the Bank of the United States, where the millionaire Astor served as president. In 1820, Catlin returned to the Merchants' Bank as president, but his son's appointment as Astor's private secretary reinforced ties to the tycoon.[60]

For Catlin, banking mingled with philanthropy. In 1824, he joined Colden as a trustee of the Bank for Savings in the City of New York. In 1816, Clinton had also been a director of this institution.[61] Founded with the moralizing mission of encouraging poor New Yorkers to save rather than spend their money, the institution actually served the interests of the Erie Canal's promoters. Gathering the resources of the poor, the savings bank generated a pool of capital, which could be invested only in government securities—such as the newly issued state bonds that financed Erie Canal construction. In the late 1810s, before European investors gained confidence in the canal, the savings bank's portfolio of New York state bonds ranked among the largest in the world. This meant that Clinton, Colden, and Catlin had channeled the collective capital of the city's poor to fund the construction of the Erie Canal.[62]

Privately channeling money to the canal, Catlin also publicly supported it. When the Bucktails removed Clinton from the Canal Commission in 1817—an event leading to his landslide first gubernatorial election—Catlin joined Colden in signing a petition conveying support for Clinton.[63] Catlin's signature—circulating throughout the nation on his institutions' bank notes—had also lent its support to Palmer's 1821 application to serve as secretary of the Spanish Claims Commission.[64]

Beyond these personal endorsements, Catlin's precise penmanship graced several other documents supporting the construction of internal improvements. He had been an early individual investor in the bonds that funded the Erie Canal.[65] In 1823, he had agreed to manage the sale of Delaware and Hudson Canal Company shares.[66] And that same year, when the Patroon petitioned the New York State Legislature for an act to charter the state's first railroad, Catlin agreed to orchestrate the sale of its shares. By the time Palmer and Clinton enlisted his support for the interoceanic canal, the banker had become the railroad company's treasurer, and the Patroon served as president.[67]

Aside from Colden and Catlin, with whom they had significant ties, Palmer and Clinton's "indenture" solicited the support of one final man: Philip Hone, the current mayor of New York City. Although he wore it fashionably and it framed his wide blue eyes and rosy cheeks, Hone's curly gray hair prematurely aged the mayor, who, compared to the rest of the proposed commissioners, was a young man approaching his forty-sixth birthday.[68]

Second to the governor, the most prominent officeholder in the Empire State was the chief executive of New York City. The port at the mouth of the Hudson River had been a financial center for over a century, but the Erie Canal transformed it into the nation's metropolis. By the end of the decade, Manhattan's population would top 200,000 men, women, and children, an order of magnitude larger than its nearest competitors.[69] In 1826, New York City's exploding population could not vote for mayor; only the Common Council—twenty-four aldermen who were elected by the white men resident in each of the city's twelve wards—enjoyed this franchise.[70] On January 3, 1826, these two dozen Bucktails could not agree on a candidate for mayor; eight ballots into this long meeting, they settled on an outsider.[71] Almost no one's first choice, Philip Hone became the leader of the country's leading city.

Fashionable and flush with cash, Hone celebrated his unexpected victory by throwing a party. "His house was literally thronged," described one newspaper, estimating that 10,000 people "of all ranks and callings and professions" and men "of all parties and sections of parties that ever existed in the State" took up the mayor's open invitation. This was most certainly a quantitative and qualitative exaggeration. Hone could not fit 10,000 people in his Broadway mansion's "splendid" parlors. And he might welcome artisans, but immigrants, people of color, the poorest New Yorkers, and some political rivals would likely feel unwelcome drinking "the juice of the generous grape."[72] Hone, like the other men named in the "indenture" had a Federalist past; they had all either been Federalist Party members—like the Patroon—or had at some point allied themselves publicly with Federalists—like Clinton in his 1812 presidential campaign. Hone opened his doors to the public, but the public that he welcomed was neither fully democratic nor Democratic.

Hardly a career political party man like Colden or Clinton, Hone knew how to throw a party. A newspaper described Hone receiving "his friends with great cordiality" next to "a huge reservoir of punch, upon a base of Italian marble." In another room guests would find tables loaded with "rounds and barons of beef, hams, tongues, corned beef, roast and boiled turkies [*sic*]." After "swallowing half a bottle of three dollar Madeira to the health of the new Mayor," the newspaper snickered, "all the people in the city are his 'friends.'"[73]

Born into a humble artisanal family, Hone had spent decades cultivating a place for himself in aristocratic social circles. Nouveau riche and without an elite education, the retired auctioneer lacked the other proposed commissioners' webs of favors, appointments, and honors. Instead, once elected to office, he depended on his personality and his pocketbook to hastily win over the city's population.[74]

Hone invested both time and money in philanthropy, but like the other men named in the "indenture," Hone was no pure altruist. In 1823, when the Delaware and Hudson Canal Company (DHCC) sought incorporation, Hone joined Catlin in petitioning the state legislature. Successfully chartered, the DHCC board selected Hone to serve as the company's first president. Shortly after his election as mayor, Hone resigned the presidency of the DHCC; John Bolton ascended to the post.[75] The mayor kept his stock and his seat on the board. Hone would later work with Colden and others to supply cheap winter heat to the poor through DHCC coal. Like the savings bank's investment in the Erie Canal, the struggling DHCC's initial profits derived from this supposed philanthropy.[76] Hone's ties to the company persisted so strongly even after he resigned the presidency that the Pennsylvania terminus of the DHCC was renamed Honesdale in his honor.[77]

In 1819, Hone joined Colden, Clinton, and later Catlin, in the directorship of the Bank for Savings.[78] He sat on the board of the New-York Institution for the Instruction of the Deaf and Dumb with Curtis Bolton; Colden's wife served on its "Visiting Committee of Ladies."[79] Whereas Hone was unaffiliated with the Freemasons before becoming mayor, a local lodge sought special "dispensation" to rapidly advance the mayor through the ranks. In one meeting, he "entered an apprentice, passed to the degree of fellowcraft, and subsequently raised to the sublime degree of master mason."[80] Clearly, Masons wanted to claim New York's accidental mayor as one of their own.[81]

Although the New York City mayoral term lasted only one year, both Colden and Clinton had strung together much longer mayoralties. Serving as mayor before New York state's 1821 constitution democratized local and state office holding, Colden and Clinton had been appointed by elite men in Albany. In contrast, to keep his office at the end of 1826, Hone would have to win over the Bucktail aldermen, who were themselves constantly wooing the voting public.[82] Hone's election party could be interpreted as an effort to win over these white male voters. Hone's new "friends"—purchased through madeira and meat—proved fickle. On Christmas Day of 1826, after only one ballot, Hone would lose his reelection bid.[83] Although he maintained his social prominence, he would never win another elected office.[84]

Of course, in the fall of 1826, Hone did not know that his political career was almost over. His resignation from the DHCC presidency suggested that he expected a longer career in politics. In listing him on the deed, Palmer and Clinton also imagined a broader horizon for Hone's office holding. Clinton would soon have familial reasons to invite the mayor when in May of 1827, Hone's niece would be married to Clinton's second son.[85] Not yet family, Clinton's and Hone's networks overlapped. Clinton and Palmer interpreted Hone's involvement in the DHCC as support for canals in general. They did not see danger in his association with the Bolton brothers.

And so, with the names determined and the "indenture" drafted, Palmer left Clinton's office. The governor continued to meet with friends and foes alike.

BRIGHT AND EARLY ON THE MILD MORNING OF FRIDAY, October 6, 1826, perhaps before Palmer—his first visitor—arrived, the governor drafted a "Private" letter to the "Gentlemen" he hoped would sign the "indenture." "Considering the importance of the grant made by the Central govt of America with Mr. Palmer, its binding nature, and authentic character (having been attested by Col. Williams our minister)," began the letter before it transitioned to his pitch: "I have considered it my duty to enter into the arrangements which will be shown to you, confidently hoping that you will associate your labors with mine in this great undertaking." Where Sparks saw the company as a "scheme," Clinton framed it as a "duty" and a "great undertaking." He assured "that no injurious responsibility can accrue, and the great good may be done." His pitch full of promise—both for progress and protection—Clinton transitioned to his plan.

The nearly illegible revisions of Clinton's heavy hand sought the perfect passive phrasing to hide the effort that would be required "to procure an act of incorporation from our legislature." Without suggesting the Patroon, Colden, Catlin, or Hone do any work, he nonetheless promised that the company would be aboveboard. Anticipating Sparks's characterization of the plan as a "scheme," Clinton ended the letter: "and the whole character of the transaction will be free from the taint of speculation."[86] One man's scheme was another's "great good."[87]

Perhaps Clinton put the letters to the three New York City residents in the mail. The Patroon's brother served as Albany's postmaster.[88] Written early on a Friday, Clinton's letters would travel by steamboat to arrive in New York City by Saturday evening.[89]

Alternatively, a courier may have hand delivered the letters. Clinton's phrasing suggested that the letters would be accompanied by a draft of the "arrangements," which, he explained, "will be shown to you." Shown but not provided. Perhaps Palmer retained possession of the single, handwritten draft and allowed each man to peruse it.[90]

If Palmer personally conveyed the draft deed and cover letters to New York City, the logistics would be tight. Rising with the sun around 6 A.M. and drafting his letter, Clinton could hand it to Palmer, who was listed as the first name in his diary for the day. Palmer could then board a steamship that departed at "9 o'clock A.M." every Friday. He would arrive in New York City late the same evening. If Palmer awoke at sunrise on Saturday, he would have about twelve hours to call upon all three men, show them the "indenture" and hopefully obtain their signatures. Just after sunset, Palmer might board the steamboat's return trip scheduled for "6 o'clock P.M."[91] This tight itinerary would get Palmer back to Albany so that he could, as he did, appear first in Clinton's diary on Monday, October 9.[92]

ON THAT SATURDAY, while the governor's letters approached their intended recipients, the governor took a morning walk and then met with nine visitors, including both a "Spanish Teacher"—a reasonable investment for the future president of a Central American canal company—and Jared Sparks.

The meeting of the governor and the historian started with a discussion of revolutionary sources and morphed into a conversation about Clinton's past. Clinton offered Sparks exactly what he wanted—copies of the governor's family members' revolutionary letters and the promise of "free access" to other papers. Transitioning from the history of the war that launched the Age of Revolutions, to the historymaker in the room, Clinton gave Sparks a "little volume called '*Hibernicus Letters*,' written by himself about seven years ago." Sparks had already read the book with admiration, believing that it "contains the best account I have seen of the canal, and of the western parts of the state of New York."

A gesture asserting his own historical significance, this gift from Clinton inspired a conversation. Trying to capture the witty repartee of mastication metaphors in quotation marks, Sparks journaled: "The Governor said to me 'These were hasty letters, written to make the canal palatable.' I replied, 'it requires no such aids now to make it go down.' 'No,' said he, 'times and things have changed; but at that time it labored hard, I assure you.'" Changing tone from documentation to interpretation, Sparks confessed to his diary, "The truth is, the merit of this great work is exclusively due to De Witt Clinton." Sparks elaborated, "He risked his reputation upon it, at a time when the voice of a great portion of the wise men of the country were against it; he made himself unpopular in his own state for pressing forward what was called a visionary project; but he persevered and was successful, and accomplished a work which is now the admiration of the world, the glory of this country, and of an immense importance to the State of New York."[93] To Sparks, Clinton's canal was clearly a triumph, but the meaning behind the diarist's choice of the word "visionary" to describe the unpopularity of Clinton's actions is less transparent.

Published two years after this conversation, Noah Webster's *American Dictionary of the English Language* provided two definitions for "visionary" as an adjective. "Affected by phantoms," this first definition evoked the era's Romantic literature. Although people died constructing the canal, Sparks was not suggesting that the waterway was haunted.

The second definition was a better fit: "Imaginary; existing in imagination only; not real; having no solid foundation; as a *visionary* prospect; a *visionary* scheme or project."[94] According to this meaning, Clinton's critics saw his plan as lacking a "solid foundation" because they believed it was an unrealizable "scheme or project." The adjective "visionary" was pejorative.

Perhaps haunted by this derision, Clinton's assurance to the would-be commissioners that the Nicaraguan canal would be "free from the taint of speculation" might have been designed to head off accusations that his new project was "visionary." But "visionary" and "speculation" were not exactly synonyms, even if they both evoked sight.

Defined only as a verb by Webster, "speculate" carried two meanings. The first was "To meditate; to contemplate; to consider a subject by turning it in the mind and viewing it in its different aspects and relations." This definition overlapped with "visionary" in that both terms depended on mental work—one involved the "imagination" and the other, "the mind."[95] Clinton's assertion that the Nicaraguan canal project would be "free from the taint of speculation" might be an assurance that it was no "visionary scheme" that existed only in Clinton's mind.

But the term "speculate" also carried a more practical meaning: "In commerce, to purchase land, goods, stock, or other things, with the expectation of an advance in price, and of selling the articles with a profit by means of such an advance; as to *speculate* in coffee, or in sugar, or in six percent stock, or in bank stock."[96] Through this definition, Clinton assured his intended co-investors that the canal company was not designed to produce quick cash but to enable the construction of a real canal, which would generate future dividends. It was to be a long-term investment. As much as a waterway can be described as "solid," Clinton wanted to convince these men that his new project's foundation was as real as the Erie Canal. Neither was "visionary."

The person who pursues a "visionary project" might rightfully be called a "visionary." But like the adjective, the noun also carried a negative valence: "One who forms impracticable schemes; one who is confident of success in a project which others perceive to be idle and fanciful."[97] So a "visionary" was confident when "others" doubted. But what happened if the visionary was right and the others wrong, when "impracticable schemes" became the "admiration of the world"? Did DeWitt Clinton redefine what it meant to be a visionary? In Clinton's case, a vindicated visionary might be seen as a hero of history.

Sparks's diary entry suggests that he thought Clinton's accomplishment of the Erie Canal was heroic and that those who called the waterway "a visionary project" were proven wrong by its triumph. But the historian echoed those wrong-minded detractors in his discussion of the Central American canal plan. About the Nicaraguan waterway, Sparks described Palmer as "sanguine"—overly optimistic—and the governor and the canal contractor as "concerting a scheme." We can almost hear Sparks sneering that the men were concerting a *visionary* scheme. Did Sparks merely lack the vision shared by Clinton and Palmer that the "mammoth canal" between the oceans would become "the glory" of the globe? Or was he a voice of reasoned skepticism doubting an "impracticable scheme"?

Whether or not the canal was doable, Sparks recognized it as dreamable. Whereas the prospect of a "practicable" project motivated the governor, the historian evaluated the canal's sources: "I spent the evening in reading the volume of '*Humboldt's Personal Narrative*' (Vol. VI.) just published, particularly that part relating to the canals of the Isthmus." Although their conversation had been about New York's waterway, clearly both men had Nicaragua on their minds.

Reading Humboldt's most recent publication, which included a more extended consideration of potential interoceanic canals than his *Political Essay on the Kingdom of New Spain* from 1811, Sparks praised Humboldt's "solid learning, and profound remark," yet he snickered "there is a great deal of pedantry in Humboldt; many loose statements, and a parade of knowledge of all sorts of things of which it was impossible for him to be well informed." A cutting critique, Sparks recognized that Humboldt knew little about the Nicaraguan route because he had never traveled to Central America. Neither had Humboldt's sources. Consulting the book's "notes & appendix," Sparks judged Humboldt's evidence as unreliable. "Time will show," the historian prophesied, "that a great many of Humboldt's statements are loose, and not to be depended on. He attempts too much." The historian might make the same critiques of the canal company, which relied upon Humboldt's "loose statements."[98]

And he would have a point. Before he "risked his reputation" on the Erie Canal, Clinton had traveled the route himself. His canal diary from 1810 witnesses the challenges of the topography, the work to be done, and the Indigenous people whom the state would dispossess to cut the canal through their land.[99] Clinton had no such personal knowledge of Nicaragua; he had not hiked the route, examined the rocks, or met the inhabitants. Neither had any of the other men named in the "indenture." There is no evidence that even Beneski had traveled to the canal route. Without journeying to the isthmus, Palmer and Clinton were relying on second- or third-hand knowledge, much of it in the form of Humboldt's "loose statements."

The only person who had been invited to join Palmer's canal company who had set foot on the canal route was Curtis Bolton. His rescue mission to save Blunt's 1824 surveying voyage brought him to the shores of Lake Nicaragua. But even Bolton had not traveled with Blunt during his drenched investigations. Bolton had not been abandoned in the forest in the rainy season, starving, shoeless, and succumbing to fever; the surveyor knew these pains but hid them in his final report. Even Bolton, then, lacked a true understanding of the challenges the project posed. The knowledge of all the would-be New York canal contractors was far from perfect.

And the man with the most information vehemently opposed Palmer's contract. If such personal experience was to be "depended upon" in preference to Humboldt's uninformed "loose statements," some of the men invited to sign the "indenture" might agree with Sparks that Palmer really was "sanguine." If Bolton's interpretation reigned, despite Clinton's assurances to the contrary, the company created by the "indenture" would be a "visionary scheme."

ON MONDAY, OCTOBER 9, Palmer was the first man to call on Governor DeWitt Clinton in his Albany office.[100] We have no record of the substance of this meeting. The canal contractor was no longer in the room when historian Jared Sparks borrowed from the governor "a very choice treasure" of documents.[101]

Sparks would spend a few more days in Albany. He met a famous Frenchman who had served as a translator at the trial about Palmer's donkey portrait. They had a "highly amusing" conversation about "a mode of sailing, or swimming through the air, as a fish swims in water." From flying fish to threatened homelands, Sparks learned of recent efforts to "christianise" Indigenous people residing both within New York and in the "Sandwich Islands," or Hawaii.[102] Sparks did not connect these discussions to the canal company he saw forming in Clinton's office, but the issues of accelerating transportation, increasing global communication, and imperialist policy toward nonwhite people could not be separated from the "scheme" to create a "mammoth canal."

Finding the governor "not at home" on his last night in town, Sparks attended a party hosted by New York's first lady and dined with Bucktail candidate William Rochester. Escaping the "labyrinth" of New York politics, on October 12, the historian rode out through the rain on an overnight stagecoach.[103] "Thus endeth my second historical tour," he reflected on October 21 upon arriving home in Boston. Pleased with his accomplishments, he summarized, "I have travelled about 550 miles."[104] In the span of about a month, Sparks traversed a distance longer than the Erie Canal and about a quarter of the distance to Lake Nicaragua.

With less than three months left before the contractual deadline, the surveyors and $200,000 would need to make similarly great time in their journey to Granada. Would Clinton's well-connected friends be as eager as the governor and his son to sign on to Palmer's vision?

CHAPTER FOURTEEN

Clinton's Ditch

On Monday, October 9, 1826, at the mouth of the Hudson River on the bustling island of Manhattan, Mayor Philip Hone penned his response to Governor DeWitt Clinton's "private" invitation to join the interoceanic canal company. "Dear sir," the letter opened with flattery. "I am so sensible of the kindness which you have, on several occasions, evinced toward me, and so desirous to propitiate your good opinion," Hone pivoted, "that I am induced to explain to you the reasons why I have not accepted the Honour which you intended for me, in naming me as one of the Commissioners to carry Mr. Palmer's Canal plan into operation."[1] In even more words and with only a day's contemplation, Hone said no.

In an era when very few people had the right to make their own decisions, a handful of wealthy and well-connected New Yorkers considered whether to join the canal company. As the autumn air chilled, the contract's deadline for supplying surveyors and cash to the proposed route demanded fast decisions and quick action. Would the accidental mayor's declination sink the governor's canal dreams?

IN HIS LETTER TO CLINTON, Hone provided four reasons for declining to join the canal company. His arguments differed greatly from those of Curtis Bolton. Instead of critiquing the canal contract, Hone's concerns all stemmed from its context.

Like Central American canal critic José del Valle, Hone started with praise. He believed, "the plan of uniting the Atlantic and Pacific Oceans, so long the subject of scientific speculation, is now about to be accomplished." Alluding to the Erie Canal and crediting Clinton, Hone argued, "The Example of our own state is too good a one not to be followed by those nations, who have been long convinced of the great results to be expected from this measure." His tone turned patronizing as he suggested the Central Americans needed "an enterprizing [*sic*] People, like us, to teach them how to overcome the difficulties which laid in their way." He sprinkled in nationalism: "I should glory in the Fame which would result from this great work being effected by my Countrymen." And then he ratcheted up from pride to profits: "Nay. I am willing to go further, and express my belief, that if it was accomplished, it might be, a very profitable stock." Phrased conditionally, it sounded like Hone was tempted.

But future "glory" could not overcome his sense that "the present is a most unfavorable time."[2] Linked indirectly to the British Panic of 1825, New York investors had spent the spring and summer of 1826 roiled by business failures and an insurance company scandal.[3] Fearing that "joint stock companies" could easily fall "into the hands of reckless speculators," Hone argued that "in this moment of excitement" would-be investors "who have the means, and the inclination to patronize works of public improvement" would be too "alarmed" to invest in an interoceanic canal company, "however tempting the object might be." Hone thought the timing was bad.

He also disliked the location. "Another cause which would operate to create a want of Confidence in timid men (and all rich men are timid)," Hone philosophized, "is the unstable nature of the Government in the Country where this great work is to be performed." Like the State Department at the moment of Central American recognition, Hone did not know what to call "the Country." One might expect him to next describe the unfortunate truth: that the country was on the brink of Civil War, that its legislature was dysfunctional, that the only remnants of the federal government were the president and the army, and that even on the provincial level, the tottering new Nicaraguan government did not control much of the proposed waterway's route, which lay in the territory of the Indigenous Miskitú and Rama nations. Instead, Hone's racism fed his doubt. He questioned the "investment of so large a sum of money in a foreign country" inhabited by people he characterized as having a reputation for a "want of sincerity" and harboring "a national prejudice against foreigners."

The mayor balanced his distrust of Central Americans with his faith in the names on the "indenture." He acknowledged, "the appointment of such a board of Trustees" would help overcome "some of the difficulties" in attracting investors. "Yourself and Genl. Van Rensselaer," Hone flattered, "have been so identified with the successful accomplishment of a similar work in this State" that, he assured, "your very names would go far to inspire Confidence." Again, this sounded like praise. When Hone's own name along with "Mr. Catlin" and "Mr. Astor" were added to the list, he predicted the faith of investors would grow. With Astor, Hone made an error of fact; Clinton had not invited the millionaire to join the company. Regardless, Hone assured that they "are known to be practical men, not likely to lead their fellow Citizens into the mazes of speculation, or to sacrifice their Interest for individual aggrandizement." The business would be built on the good names of its commissioners.

Protection for these sterling reputations undergirded Hone's concern. He saw the work of incorporation and capitalization hidden in the passive voice phrasing of Clinton's cover letter. The mayor surmised that he and the other busy men could not fulfill the "pledge of our time, talents, and labour" that would be necessary to build the company. He explained, "It may be said, that the sanction of our names only, will be required at this time and that the duties of the Trust will devolve upon others." But such a delegation of work would turn Clinton's plan into a corrupt "scheme" where investors would be duped into believing the company was run by "honest and honourable men" when in practice it was just a "borrowing of names."

The mayor did not want to loan his name without investing his time, and he could not afford the latter. Hone's ultimate reason for rejecting Clinton's proposal was personal. "As to myself," the mayor confessed, "I find that my official Duties require all my attention, and that I am frequently compelled to neglect, other concerns of a public nature, which I have undertaken to perform." Even after resigning the DHCC presidency, the mayor felt overcommitted. Expecting empathy from the governor, the mayor could have merely told Clinton that he was too busy to join the company, but Hone wanted to convey his "general" concerns as an act of respect. Honored to be asked yet privileged to decline, Hone was "anxious to convince" Clinton of his appreciation for the opportunity to be associated with the governor "in an undertaking of so important a character."[4]

Having said no to the most powerful man in the state, Hone folded the paper, warmed his bright red wax, and sealed the correspondence. A postal clerk stamped the date on the letter and marked it paid. If Hone submitted the letter before 8 A.M. on Monday, it should have arrived in Albany by Tuesday.[5]

CLINTON DID NOT RECORD the date and time of the letter's arrival. Instead, he boarded a southbound steamboat. On the morning of Tuesday, October 11, the governor noted in his diary, "went to New York with DeWitt."[6] Another of Clinton's sons, a few years older than George, DeWitt would soon be appointed the "chief engineer" of a Pennsylvania canal.[7] Two DeWitts—a canal dreamer and a canal designer—steamed down the Hudson. The trip was likely a spontaneous response to Hone's letter because later that evening, Catherine Clinton was left on her own to host the party attended by Jared Sparks before he departed Albany.[8] Arriving to find Manhattan cast in moonlight, the governor rendezvoused with Palmer at Colden's house.[9] No record exists of their conversation, but given Hone's letter, the men had much to discuss.

"A terrible storm & great rain" clouded the next day. Palmer was Clinton's first meeting. The only other easily discernible name among the day's list of six is "J. J. Astor."[10] Perhaps, Clinton sought to replace the mayor with the millionaire.

The next morning, Clinton again met with Palmer on another rainy and dark day. As the skies cleared around noon, the mayor visited the governor.[11] What did they discuss? Had Hone spoken with Bolton? Did he convey Bolton's critique of the contract? Beginning journaling two years too late to document this interaction, Hone's diary would eventually become a famously eloquent source. Removed from the room by nearly two centuries, we have no evidence of what transpired. We do know that Clinton spent three days in the city, and that he met with Palmer and others connected with the "indenture" on each of those days. On Saturday, October 14, the governor steamed back up the Hudson. He was home in Albany by eight in the evening.[12]

MOST OF THE NEXT WEEK passed before Palmer's name found its way back into Clinton's diary. On Thursday, October 19, 1826, "A. H. Palmer" appeared at the end of a long list. By the time the canal contractor arrived, the governor must have been exhausted. Beyond his "long walk" earlier in the day, he had spent two weeks working on Palmer's canal company on top of his labors as governor, as a candidate for reelection, and as a Masonic leader facing an escalating crisis.[13]

The next morning, Friday, October 20, 1826, Palmer returned. Clinton drafted correspondence suggesting lost confidence in the "indenture" and the hatching of a new plan. As he pivoted in his role from future canal company president to character reference, Clinton addressed a letter to Albert Gallatin, the aging revolutionary who had inadvertently launched the governor's own canal career.

Born to a wealthy family in Geneva, Switzerland, in 1761, the slender and balding Gallatin had immigrated to North America as a nineteen-year-old during the American Revolution.[14] As Thomas Jefferson's secretary of the treasury, he authored the report that inspired Clinton's appointment as a canal commissioner.[15]

A man who had chosen to live in the epicenter of the early Age of Revolutions, Gallatin recognized the crumbling Spanish Empire as significant for his adopted country. Early in his secretaryship, he delighted in meeting Alexander von Humboldt. Gallatin reported that in the few days spent with the explorer, he had "swallowed more information of various kinds than I had for two years past." Gallatin eagerly transcribed the explorer's maps and notes, arguing,

"He has brought a mass of natural, philosophical, and political information which will render the geography of [the Latin-American countries] better known than of most European nations."[16] Two decades later, Sparks would form a more skeptical opinion of Humboldt's geographical information. But the historian had not met the explorer in person; Humboldt's character built confidence in his science. And the knowledge that Humboldt shared with Secretary Gallatin informed the Jefferson administration's policies regarding the Louisiana Territory, a formerly Spanish borderland.

Gallatin remained secretary of the treasury during James Madison's administration. He had the unenviable job of funding the War of 1812, which he accomplished by selling US debt to Astor and others.[17] Capitalizing the war, Gallatin also negotiated the peace along with John Quincy Adams and Henry Clay. From Ghent to Paris, Gallatin represented the United States in France until 1823. He returned just in time to be considered but not selected for the vice presidency in the election of 1824.[18]

In early November 1825, Gallatin was the first choice of the Adams administration for one of the ministers to the Panama Congress. With hopes of giving the mission a "distinguished character," Clay offered Gallatin the appointment.[19] Within a week, Gallatin declined.[20] Begging him to reconsider, Clay rued the effects of Gallatin's decision "For the public" and praised the mission as "the most important ever sent from this Country."[21]

Exercising his prerogative as an elite white man, Gallatin again declined. He gave personal and practical reasons for not accepting the opportunity. "I cannot perceive that I am peculiarly fitted for that mission," he wrote to Clay, "either by knowledge of the language[,] things[,] or men of South America, or by being known to them." An experienced diplomat, Gallatin recognized in himself the absence of the traits that had made Beneski successful in Guatemala.

Gallatin also cited "opposition I would have to encounter in my family." Respectful of his second wife Hannah's wishes, Gallatin did his research. Unlike the many agents who learned of the journey's hazards only after they had accepted appointments, Gallatin investigated the dangers before responding to Clay's invitation; "men thoroughly acquainted with the country" warned him against accepting. He said no to Clay twice. But he did not want to burn his bridges. Like Hone's declination of Clinton's offer, Gallatin sought to "preserve a grateful sense" of the administration's "favorable disposition" toward him.[22] He wanted to keep his options open for a less dangerous and more desirable appointment.

Just such an opportunity came six months later when Adams and Clay sought a diplomat to send to England.[23] The graying Gallatin eagerly accepted the appointment, although he cautioned that he would like to limit his time in London because a long stay would be financially "ruinous."[24] After thirty days at sea on the packet ship *Florida*, the frugal former treasury secretary and his family arrived in Liverpool on the last day of July. By October 20, 1826, when Clinton put his pen to paper to write to Gallatin on Palmer's behalf, the diplomat had already written fourteen dispatches to Washington about his frustrated negotiations with the British government over trade, debts, and boundaries.[25]

Like the men named in the "indenture," Gallatin supported canals, understood finance, held powerful offices, and was a personal acquaintance of both Clinton and Palmer. Hannah Gallatin was a New Yorker by birth; her father had been Clinton's ally.[26] But when the governor ran against President James Madison in the election of 1812, Gallatin continued to serve in Madison's cabinet. As leading Democratic-Republicans, Clinton and Gallatin knew each other well, even if they were often at odds.

The same was not true for Palmer. Back before he was a lawyer, Palmer assisted a Chinese merchant to petition the Jefferson administration. Despite the embargo, Gallatin permitted one of Astor's ships to transport the merchant home.[27] A lifetime ago for both men, this interaction was likely more significant to the canal contractor than to the diplomat.

"Aaron H. Palmer, Esq. of this state is slightly known to you, I believe," began the governor's letter to Gallatin, reminding the diplomat of this distant encounter. Providing Palmer a solid if scanty recommendation, Clinton praised, "He is a man of fair character and good standing." The governor requested, "I beg leave to recommend him to your favorable notice."[28] He did not mention the canal. Clinton handed the letter to Palmer and handed Palmer off to Gallatin.

With this letter, Clinton ditched his plan to be president of Palmer's interoceanic canal company. It had been a busy six weeks since he begged Palmer for a surveying job for George, but in the end, the "indenture" would never be signed—by Hone, Clinton, or anyone else. Neither Washington nor Albany would charter Palmer's canal company. His interoceanic canal would not be the "glory" of the nation; in fact, it would no longer be an American project.[29] In writing to Gallatin, Clinton released Palmer to seek British capitalization of the Nicaraguan canal.

AFTER CLINTON'S BIG DITCH, the canal contractor would meet with the governor once more. On October 28, Palmer reappeared in the governor's diary for the final time. Another rainy day, the temperature had dropped nearly thirty degrees since its October high; the relationship between the two men had likewise chilled.[30]

Sometime that day, Clinton drafted a letter to Jared Sparks. The governor explained to the historian his change of heart about the interoceanic canal. Perhaps he intended it to salvage his own place in history as a successful canal dreamer.

Surprisingly, in his letter to Sparks, Clinton did not repeat Hone's criticisms. Predictions about the confidence of US investors did not drive his argument against the canal. Similarly, he did not present Sparks's own conclusions: that Palmer was too sanguine about a visionary plan or that Humboldt's statements were too "loose" and that firsthand research was required.

Instead, he analyzed the contract; his critiques closely paralleled those leveled by Curtis Bolton in his letter to Secretary Southard. As far as can be understood from the governor's scribbles, Bolton never appeared in Clinton's diary. Someone—maybe Hone, Colden, or Catlin—conveyed Bolton's concerns to the governor.

In writing to Sparks, the governor neither cited his sources nor claimed the ideas as his own. "On a full investigation of Mr. Palmer's contract with the Govt. of Central America," Clinton employed the passive voice to declare, "it was found essentially defective in many of its provisions." Ever the editor, the governor wrote and rewrote an explanation of his first concern, which echoed Bolton's first criticism of the contract. Both men interpreted the document as imprudently allowing the country to purchase the canal out from under the company. Stockholders could not count on long-term profits from constructing the canal; the shares might never produce dividends. It might be speculative, after all.

As a second criticism, the governor bristled at "the sum of 200,000 dollars" as an initial installment and worried that "further advances" might be demanded. This is a strange critique for a lawyer who had participated in devising the structure for selling the company's stock. The "indenture" was engineered to raise a quick $500,000 in capital. The 10 percent down payment of subscribers would have produced more than double the cash required to be delivered in Nicaragua in January of 1827, with enough to accommodate "further advances." Had it really taken "a full investigation" for Clinton to uncover a term repeated twice in the original contract? More likely, Clinton had become convinced of Bolton's concerns; this criticism was second in both men's letters.

Or perhaps Clinton, who had staked his whole career on an earlier "visionary" canal dream and had less personal wealth to lose, merely conveyed to the historian the more cautious concerns of the "timid" wealthy men he had invited to join him. "For these and other causes," he deflected the decision from himself, "the gentlemen who had contemplated the enterprise considered it imprudent to undertake it, until these objections were removed, which probably may be attempted." The extreme conditionality of that last clause—"which probably may be attempted"—left the door open just enough that Clinton and his colleagues could return to the indenture if the world or the words changed. The work of removing "these objections" would not fall to the governor or his friends. Palmer and Beneski might try to modify the contract or, as Bolton had asserted to Southard months earlier, a new contract might be signed with a new contractor. By sinking Palmer's plan, Bolton hoped to buoy his own. Clinton kept this dream alive.

In the letter to Sparks, Clinton next turned the conversation to the historian's favorite subject: sources. "As Mr. Palmer had borrowed Humboldt from A. V. Goodrich Bookseller in New York," the governor reported, "he took it from me in order to return it."[31] This meant that, amazingly, Palmer had never bought the book that was to inform the canal scheme; the canal contractor had only "borrowed" it. Treating a bookstore like a lending library might make sense for Palmer. Too busy to attend to the work of his brokerage office, the canal contractor was surely strapped for cash as he traveled up and down the Atlantic seaboard searching for support for his would-be waterway. A literary man, he was friends with several Manhattan-based authors and publishers; a bookseller might trust him with some merchandise.[32] But why had the governor depended on a borrowed copy?

Clinton's next sentence suggests that only one copy of Humboldt's new book containing a more extensive discussion of the potential canal routes was available in the Northeast at the time.[33] Palmer having returned the book, Clinton advised the Bostonian that his "bookseller can doubtless procure it without difficulty from Mr. Goodrich." Clinton closed with suggestions for further reading: "Permit me to refer you to the first volume of Humboldt's *New Spain* and Robinson's *Mexico* for pertinent information on this subject." Frustrated with the lack of on-the-ground research in the borrowed Humboldt, the historian would likely find these other second-hand accounts of the potential isthmian transit as "defective" as Clinton found the contract.[34]

The letter folded and sealed, the post office marked it paid on October 29, a Sunday.[35] Clinton, busy with a surprisingly close election and swelling anti-Masonic sentiment, moved on.

IT IS POSSIBLE THAT WITH PALMER out of the picture, the canal contract lingered in the governor's mind. On November 8, Clinton scribbled a name in his diary that looks like "Col. Beneski." The next morning, it appeared again, no more legible than the day before, a blurred reminder that history is constrained by its sources.[36]

Surely Clinton could have been meeting with any military officer with a long last name that began with "B." But he also might have been interviewing the agent who had been so successful in Guatemala City. The two men might have talked about empires, firing squads, and the struggles of learning Spanish. They might have gossiped about Palmer. It is even possible that they discussed alterations to the contract, which Clinton intimated to Sparks "probably may be attempted."

In sending Palmer to London, perhaps Clinton and his partners planned to ditch not the canal but the contractor. Whether or not he worked for Palmer, Beneski would be the first choice for renegotiating with the Central American government. Proven but unpaid, the agent might want a second shot at recouping his personal losses from the expenses of the first trip to Guatemala City and securing payment for negotiating the contract. If "Col. Beneski" really did make his way to the governor's office, and if the two men concerted a new canal scheme behind Palmer's back, they did not leave a documentary trail for us to follow.

CLINTON'S PENMANSHIP, HOWEVER, PERSISTED. Traveling nearly 150 miles, Clinton's letter reached Sparks on Thursday, November 2, when the historian noted in his neat black ink that he had received it.[37]

The reach of Bolton's contractual analysis did not end here. Sparks grew intrigued by the canal and the absence of knowledge about Central America. Both Palmer and Clinton had encouraged the editor to publish an article on the waterway in the *North American Review*. Sparks had assured the men that he would try. But he did not trust Humboldt as a source.

In pursuit of reliable information, Sparks wrote to the official US agent in Guatemala City. On November 22, 1826, he addressed a letter to "John Williams, Esq." Citing the rare "opportunity" of "a vessel" departing Boston for Central America, Sparks sent the chargé "a copy" of the latest *North American Review* and offered to send future numbers. "It is my purpose to embrace in it as much information about South America, as its general design will admit," the editor teed up a request, "and you will do me a great favor, if you will send me, from time to time, any papers, documents, pamphlets, or other printed materials, which will give an account of passing events in Guatemala."

Sparks expressed his comfort in calling on Williams for this assistance because, "I am sure you will be disposed to make any reasonable exertions to diffuse in this country a knowledge of the events and progress in South America."[38] Sparks implied that the more US citizens knew about Central America, the more Williams's appointment gained in prestige. This argument had persuaded other US diplomats to write for the magazine.[39] Reflecting his reading of Humboldt, Sparks confessed, "Of Guatemala we know almost nothing, and whatever comes from that quarter will have the charm of novelty, as well as the higher value of political interest."[40]

From charm to disappointment, Sparks conveyed to the chargé the scuttlebutt on Central America's most promising prospect. "It is to be regretted," he opined, "that the contract of Palmer for the Nicaraguan Canal threatens to be unsuccessful. I was in Albany a few weeks ago, when Mr. Palmer was there, and arrangements were making to form a company of which Gov. Dewitt Clinton was to be President." From this firsthand experience, Sparks turned to a written source: "I have recently received a letter from Gov. Clinton." In quotation marks, the historian imperfectly transcribed the contents of the governor's letter. In this way, Sparks sent Bolton's contractual critique—mediated through the words of New York's governor and modified by his own loose quotation—to the US government agent who had not only ensured that Beneski won the contract but also adhered his own seal to certify its validity.

Williams might not agree with the contract's perceived deficiencies. Moreover, he would be shocked at the man who had originally performed this analysis. Williams still believed that he had supported Beneski in service of Bolton. This letter would not dispel this misidentification; in fact, it would add a new irony to Williams's imperfect knowledge. Williams would have no way of knowing that Clinton's critiques also owed their existence to Bolton. Left out of the loop, Bolton may never have learned the reach of his power. Hidden from sight and beyond his knowledge, Bolton both buoyed the canal contract's existence and then sank it.

Sparks remained hopeful, however, "that this great channel of commerce will speedily be opened." Not realizing that Clinton had already sent Palmer abroad in search of capitalization, Sparks exuded national pride as he wrote, "It will be honorable to us to have it accomplished by a Company in the

United States." Encouraging Williams to write for his magazine, Sparks concluded his letter by revealing that the chargé would find enclosed an article on Colombia written by "our late lamented countryman," the diplomat who had died en route to the Panama Congress. His clear penmanship transcending space and time, Sparks revealed channels of communication across the hemisphere.[41]

Even dubious information was interesting to the historian. Writing to a friend in New York City the next day, Sparks pursued Clinton's lead on the "copy of the sixth volume (*i.e.*, the last) of Humboldt's Personal Narrative, recently from London." He confessed to his friend that he had "written to Mr. Aaron H. Palmer to send me a copy," but had not received a reply. Sparks asked his friend, "Will you take an opportunity to ask him, if he purchased such a book for me?" He provided instructions conditional upon Palmer's answer: "If he did you can pay him and send it; if he did not, you can buy it." Confident that the canal contractor knew the booksellers' inventories, Sparks informed, "He will tell you at what bookstore it is to be found. I believe at Goodrich's."[42]

Sparks's friend would have to find the book himself. By late November, Palmer was long gone.

WE DO NOT KNOW EXACTLY when Palmer boarded a transatlantic sailing vessel.[43] Given his contract's tight deadlines, he likely sought out the earliest departure for an English port after his last meeting with Clinton. He was in a hurry and so financially harried that he skipped out on at least one of his debts.

In an advertisement in the *New-York Evening Post* in late December 1826, Sarah Letts dunned "Aaron H. Palmer, now or late of the city of New York, Broker." She sought "the balance due and owing to me on your promissory note bearing date 9th January, 1826." If she did not receive payment, Letts threatened to sell Palmer's "120 shares of the Sun Fire Insurance Company's stock, and also 50 shares of the capital stock of the Farmers' Fire Insurance and Loan Company."[44] Sharing a building at 34 Wall Street, both companies were neighbors of Palmer's brokerage. The face value of the assets Letts threatened to sell were worth $5,500.[45] This meant that Palmer owed her more than Chargé Williams's annual salary.

Perhaps Palmer owed Sarah Letts for lodging. A bachelor with only a work address listed in the city directory, Palmer might have boarded with Letts. She is not listed in the city directory but is named in an 1826 law enabling "Resident Aliens to take and hold Real Estate."[46] She needed no special law to liquidate Palmer's stock. Waiting to see if the absent—or absconded—canal contractor would pay his debts, Letts advertised four times during the first week of the new year indicating her plan to sell the stock on "Saturday, the 6th day of January, 1827."[47] Palmer was not there to stop her.

In November, the canal contractor likely departed on a packet ship bound for Liverpool. What would become known as the Black Ball Line was the first among several companies to establish a fleet of ships that sailed for Liverpool every two weeks. A vessel in this fleet, the *Florida*, had transported Gallatin four months earlier. The same ship received clearance for departure on October 31, 1826. Palmer might have been on board. His name is not enumerated in the published passenger list, but given his stretched finances, he may not have paid enough money to appear in the newspaper. Steerage passengers were commonly reported as numbers rather than names. Palmer would need to save his money for the high cost of living in London, which had inspired fear in the parsimonious Gallatin.[48]

He also might not have taken the *Florida*. Two other ships that did not publish passenger lists left for British ports the same day.[49] In the event that he missed these boats, more Liverpool packets left mid-month. In 1826, the fastest record for the eastbound voyage was just over two weeks; most crossings lasted about three-and-a-half. The Gulf Stream pushed vessels across the Atlantic, but too little or too much wind could alter the trip's trajectory, adding days or more.[50]

BY DECEMBER 12, 1826, Palmer had settled into London. He could be contacted at the London Coffee House on Ludgate Hill. For safe keeping, he deposited "the original contract, under the great seal of the republic" with lawyers who had connections to the Bank of England.[51] Perhaps Clinton's network, declining to sign the indenture, had nonetheless helped the canal contractor by extending this introduction.

Almost three miles of winding London lanes separated Ludgate Hill from the US Legation at 62 Seymour Street.[52] Palmer delivered Clinton's letter of introduction to Gallatin. He also provided a handwritten prospectus entitled "Canal from the Atlantic to the Pacific."[53]

Palmer wrote the "Prospectus" to solicit "subscriptions to stock of the Atlantic and Pacific Canal Company" in London. It began with a strange history of the interoceanic canal contract that erased Beneski from the story. In this version, "Mr. Aaron H. Palmer, of New York" faced "many difficulties" before the "government of Central America, (Guatemala,)" signed the contract. It credited "Colonel Williams, the American minister to the republic of Central

General Bernard has expressed an Opinion that 6 weeks residence in the Country will be sufficient for that purpose: & Mr Palmer has also reason to believe that the Government of the U.S. will direct a National Schooner to attend himself and the Engineers during the survey, and will direct their Ambassador to afford every facility and protection to those engaged in the Service of the Company.

After the American and English Engineers, have made a general survey and pointed out the most eligible line; the English Engineer will remain as long as he may find necessary, to make accurate surveys & estimates: and Mr Palmer, who is intimately acquainted with the Spanish Language, will accompany the Engineers, and devote his whole time to procuring information on every point connected with the enterprize, without requiring any remuneration beyond mere reimbursement of the expences he may have incurred, and shall incur, untill the value of his services, can be appreciated by the result.

The Directors of the Company formed in England in 1825, under the title of "The Atlantic & Pacific Canal Company," have reported that the Company has been dissolved, or must be dissolved in consequence of the Contract entered into by Mr Palmer. Mr Palmer will be happy to communicate with any Gentleman on the subject either personally or by letter.

London Coffee House, Ludgate Hill.
December 12th 1826

The following is a Copy of Humboldt's Map

On the last page of his handwritten prospectus, Aaron H. Palmer included a tiny map of the proposed canal route. The map was a copy of a small section of a larger map of Colombia included in the book he had borrowed in New York City: Vol. 6, Part 1 of Alexander von Humboldt's *Personal Narrative of Travels to the Equinoctial Regions of the New Continent, During the Years 1799–1804* (London, 1826). "Canal from the Atlantic to the Pacific," prospectus written by Aaron H. Palmer, p. 3, included in letter from DeWitt Clinton to Albert Gallatin, 20 Oct. 1826, Albert Gallatin Papers, Box 32, F:189–199, New-York Historical Society, 101528d.

America" with being "mainly instrumental in obtaining the contract." Moving stateside, it summarized Palmer's quest for incorporation in Washington by describing "the President of the United States, and the Secretaries of State, Treasury, and War" as all having "expressed their decided approbation of it." Palmer omitted the federal government's failure to incorporate a company, Adams's desire for a canal built by multilateral treaty, and the partisan opposition to any US engagement in hemispheric negotiations. He left out everything that happened in New York. This was history filtered through the eyes of an optimist desperate for foreign investors.

Dismissing "overrated" concerns about the potential "difficulties" of constructing the canal, the prospectus summarized the canal's scientific support. Reviewing Humboldt's canal routes, the prospectus explained that the waterway under contract would be "about 185 miles; and, though not the shortest, is considered as the best." It provided the details of the route as Palmer imagined them: the mostly navigable "St John" river, the deep-water Lake Nicaragua, "and the flatness of the country through which the canal will have to be cut." Citing "accurate levels taken by eminent Spanish engineers," Palmer argued that the length of the canal would be only "21 miles" to descend "133 feet 11 inches" from Lake Nicaragua to the Pacific Ocean. Contemporary canal investors could do the math. Palmer's interoceanic canal would be 5 percent of the length of the Erie Canal and less than a quarter of the height. If the Great Lakes could communicate with the Atlantic Ocean through a long waterway, surely the smaller task of wedding the Atlantic and Pacific Oceans was possible, practicable, and capable of producing even grander effect.

Focusing attention on himself, Palmer explained that he now sought "the assistance of British enterprise and British capital." Providing a concise summary of the contract's terms, he invited "gentlemen who may feel an interest in the concern" to inspect the contract at his lawyers' office. "The sum which the contractor conceives will be sufficient to complete the work is one million of pounds sterling," wrote Palmer as he credited himself with this estimation, which approximated the amount described in Clinton's "indenture." He also reported that 20 percent of these funds were "ready to be subscribed for in the United States as soon as the contractor communicates to his friends there that his plans are organized." US investors were also willing to buy the additional 5 percent reserved for one year for "the citizens of the Republic of Central America." If these statements are to be believed, Palmer and Clinton succeeded in securing one quarter of the necessary funds. £250,000 was not zero. Perhaps this explains Clinton's willingness to introduce Palmer to Gallatin and maybe do more to keep the canal dream viable.

Proving the seriousness of his "friends" in the United States, Palmer named names: "the following gentlemen in the United States have agreed to act as directors on behalf of the American capitalists." First in the list was "His excellency De Witt Clinton, governor of the State of New York." Identified as "member of Congress for the State of New York," the Patroon appeared second. Because the men from New York City had all declined, three new names followed.

The current "cashier of the Branch Bank of the United States in the city of New York" replaced Catlin, who had held this post earlier in his career.[54] A Virginia merchant involved in the China trade replaced Hone.[55] Colden's replacement already had a connection to Central America. A former New York City mayor, US congressman, and US district attorney, "The Hon. Edward Livingston" now served as a congressman representing "the State of Louisiana" because a scandal had pushed this scion of an old New York family out to the country's edge.[56] Establishing a successful legal practice in New Orleans, the slender sixty-two-year-old authored new civil and criminal laws for the state. In 1825, Louisiana adopted his civil code, but rejected his criminal code which became famous for its reformative rather than punitive treatment of convicts. In Guatemala City, Williams successfully encouraged the new government to turn Livingston's code into Central American law.[57] Although all three men were prominent figures with access to capital, their names did not carry the same gravitas as those they replaced.

The US "directors" sent Palmer to London to raise the "remaining £750,000." Londoners would supply the lion's share of the cash and gain control of the canal. The "directors in America" would render assistance but would not "require that any measures which may be determined upon here should be previously communicated to them for approval." Palmer found men willing to lend their names without their labor.[58]

These "directors" were willing to rely on "gentlemen in England who will command the confidence of the shareholders at large." The prospectus did not identify the English gentlemen worthy of such confidence. Moreover, in its outline of how subscriptions for stock would work, a conspicuous blank held the place in the document where the name of the firm responsible for receiving the initial deposits of capital should have been listed. Clinton's connections may have supplied Palmer with introductions to a coffee house and legal firm, but not a banker. The fallout from the Panic of 1825 might render the blank unfillable.

Turning from the financial structure to the physical engineering, Palmer planned to hire "an experienced English engineer" to immediately begin surveying the route. Young George Clinton did not get the gig. The canal contractor also believed that "the chief of the topographical engineer department of the government of the United States" would be provided with a US vessel "to proceed to Guatemala for the express purpose of assisting in surveying the country and ascertaining the most eligible course for the communication between the two seas." Palmer included a job for himself in this imaginary scenario. Touting his Spanish language skills, the canal contractor would "accompany the engineers, and devote his whole time to procuring information on every point connected with the enterprise." Palmer assured that he would not receive "any remuneration beyond mere reimbursement of the expenses he may have incurred, and shall incur, until the value of his services can be appreciated by the result." Looking to build a team that reflected transatlantic science, capital, and political support, Palmer emphasized his continued role in the company but not his monetary interests.[59]

Confident that his payday would come, the canal contractor tried to relieve concerns about competition. He asserted, "The directors of the company formed in England in 1825, under the title of "The Atlantic and Pacific Canal Company," have reported that the company has been dissolved, or must be dissolved, in consequence of the contract entered into by Mr. Palmer." This English company had been a casualty of the Panic of 1825; its demise was not a good omen for Palmer's attempt to organize a new company with the same name. His contract's deadline a month away, Palmer found himself up against the clock in a foreign country that had just lost a fortune on Spanish American investments with an otherwise occupied US diplomat as his most powerful contact.

In the dispatches written to the State Department after receiving Palmer's prospectus, Gallatin did not mention the canal contractor.[60] The diplomat did report, however, that both houses of Parliament adjourned on December 13, one day after the date on Palmer's prospectus.[61] This meant that the opportunity for British incorporation of Palmer's canal company had closed. When the January deadline for the arrival of money and engineers passed, Palmer's contract would expire. So when the canal contractor handed Gallatin the prospectus, it was basically a dead letter.

DEAD BUT NOT DEVOID OF MEANING. A long document, the penmanship throughout the copy of the prospectus Palmer gave to Gallatin is perfect, suggesting that the canal contractor wrote it on land. It included a beautifully rendered "Copy of Humboldt's Map" of the canal route, which had been copied from the volume Palmer was supposed to return to the bookseller before his departure for Europe.[62] This suggests that either Palmer brought the borrowed book with him across the sea, or he drafted the document before his departure for England.

Perhaps he worked on the prospectus during the week between his meeting with the governor on October 20 and his final goodbye on October 28. It may even have been the reason for the canal contractor's last trip to Albany. Had Palmer brought the prospectus for the governor's review, Clinton could have approved the inclusion of his name as a "director" and provided Palmer with his London contacts.

In his letter to Sparks written on the same day as his last meeting with Palmer, Clinton was clear in his decision to ditch the canal, and yet in London, his name was still attached to the enterprise. Had Palmer "borrowed" Clinton's name without his permission? Or was agreeing to appear in the prospectus Clinton's way of blunting the impact of his declination? Both Hone and Gallatin employed rhetorical techniques to say no without saying never; maybe Clinton saw little harm in saying "yes" to the sanguine—if not outright visionary—prospectus that was never going to become a company.

A man who often revised his first drafts, Clinton might even have envisioned the prospectus as an improved plan that would secure his name to the "stupendous enterprise" without demanding labor from the overcommitted officeholder. A failed presidential candidate and a validated visionary, perhaps the prospectus was Clinton's last-ditch effort to preside over a "mammoth" interoceanic waterway company and fulfill a second canal dream.

CHAPTER FIFTEEN

Aftermaths

In their seven months together in Guatemala City, absent their wives and kin, Philadelphia-born captain William Phillips and Tennessean diplomat John Williams became "family."[1] The housemates climbed volcanoes and marveled at the "fertility" of fields, imagining the land bowing to the "march of improvement" and sustaining ten times the population with "not only the comforts, but the luxuries of life."[2] Dreaming of future riches, they guarded each other's property. The diplomat's "fire arms" protected the captain from "robbers." The captain's savvy prevented the diplomat from being "much swindled."[3] Williams so fervently believed "the Nicaragua canal shall be completed" that he urged Phillips to become the company's agent.[4] They trusted each other to a fault.

When he returned home at the end of 1826, Chargé Williams empowered his friend to discharge "the duties of his office until his successor arrived."[5] With Charles Savage's long absence, the diplomat had already appointed Phillips to serve as "Consul pro tempore."[6] But now, the captain also became responsible for the US legation, including opening its mail.

On January 29, 1827, a harried Phillips broke the seal on a letter from Jared Sparks, editor of the *North American Review*. For years, the historian had sent letters to US diplomats stationed in the former Spanish Empire requesting evidence of revolution. But to this stranger in a place about which "we know almost nothing," Sparks added a summary of DeWitt Clinton's canal contract critique.[7]

With Williams already stateside, Phillips sent Sparks some documents and commented on the "disgusting subject" of the canal. Phillips professed his initial pride in having "my name coupled with such a splendid monument of my dear Country's enterprize." But he confessed being "deeply implicated in that Canal bubble." Likening the plan to a Shakespearean delusion, the captain exclaimed, "but alas!!! 'like the baseless fabric of a vision' it has vanished."[8]

But this was not true. The canal dreams of Williams, Phillips, and so many others may have faded, but their quests' consequences lingered. Having advanced money to the Central American government, the captain found himself in financial trouble, the resolution of which would bring his friend's unauthorized canal dealings to the attention of the State Department. Phillips had heard from his family in Philadelphia that "Beniski [*sic*] has absconded and that Palmer is not to be found." The contract had real consequences for these canal dreamers too. Ruing "the disgrace upon the American character," Phillips judged, "what an infamous transaction." He wondered, "What can or will they think here?"[9]

What would anyone think of the 1820s quest for a Central American canal? Hardly famous enough to remain "infamous," the canal dreams of Williams and Phillips, Strangeways and MacGregor, Baily and Bentham, Barclay and Powles, Savage and Mann, Bolton and Blunt, Woodward and Doane, Cañas and de la Cerda, Arce and Valle, Adams and Clay, Clinton and the Patroon, Beneski and Palmer, and so many more faded from memory. But the links between them shaped the history of much more than an unbuilt canal.

Centering this cast of canal dreamers, new plot lines run through familiar historical events uncovering corrupt bargains at nearly every turn. Their stories show the challenges of transforming claims to sovereignty into diplomatic recognition of stable states. Foiled by their own follies as well as giant forces (sometimes in microscopic form), these people with so much power proved incapable of accomplishing their revolutionary plan to change the world.

Even without constructing a canal, the quest's aftermath proved consequential for these individuals and for the countries and companies they represented. The documents produced in response to canal dreams lingered long after the original dreamers died. Two centuries later, ghosts of the 1820s quest for a Central American canal haunt us still. Building a waterway between the oceans through Lake Nicaragua has proven too revolutionary for any age.

FOR WILLIAM PHILLIPS, unconsummated canal dreams had immediate consequences. In January 1827, when the captain wrote to Sparks, he had overdrawn his US accounts by providing the Arce administration with a loan. His creditors pursued payment. Before the captain could depart with a cargo of goods to satisfy his debts, Salvadoran troops invaded Guatemala City.[10] Phillips compared Central America to "a volcano before an eruption."[11] The captain got covered in ash.

Beginning in April 1827, civil war ended Arce's administration and turned his second trip to the United States into an exile.[12] His plan to save the Central American republic through a profitable canal echoed across generations of regional and Nicaraguan leaders, but Arce would be condemned for signing over the nation's most valuable asset to men interested only in a "daring speculation."[13] After two decades and several attempts to regain power, the first Central American president died impoverished in what had become the country of El Salvador.[14]

Arce's old rival Valle also could not save the Central American federation. After almost a decade of corresponding with Humboldt and Bentham from a university post, Valle won the presidency of the floundering nation in 1834. But he never took office. A lifelong proponent of improved infrastructure, he died on a rough road heading to the capital; the promise of a regional republic all but expired with him.[15] By 1855, the United States had recognized each province as its own country.[16]

BUT IN 1827, IN THE COLLAPSING COUNTRY of Central America, Phillips was the only man representing the US government. Meeting daily with Cañas, who had recently returned from Washington, he stayed in Guatemala City to protect US property and to settle affairs "connected with my unfortunate agency in the Nicaragua Canal Bubble."[17] But the "imperious necessity" of his debts at home required attention. Because of his "heavy losses," he could not wait for the new chargé. He had to "abandon" the legation, leaving its library locked in trunks and carrying with him the US diplomatic seal and cypher.[18]

Haunted by the "infamous *Canal Bubble*" as "clamorous" creditors demanded repayment, Phillips found no help when he arrived home in Philadelphia. During his absence, several of his "best friends" had been "unfortunate in business or deceased." Moreover, the "very influential house" that had sent him to Guatemala "withdrew its support." Rejecting the corrupt bargain of the consular service, Phillips's employers argued that his State Department appointments were "incompatible with commercial pursuits."[19] So, Phillips traveled to Washington to save his credit by pursuing payment from the State Department. The captain requested "compensation for services rendered to the U. States after the departure of Col. Williams, whilst in charge of the Legation." Phillips explained that he needed these funds "to alleviate in some measure the loss of the funds I advanced on account of the canal."

Why were the captain's canal losses Clay's concern? Phillips connected the dots. "At the recommendation & with the approval of Col. Williams," he had "accepted" the canal company agency and "every *dollar* I advanced (nearly) was after consulting him & with his approbation." Casting a diplomatic duty on his canal agency, Phillips assured the secretary of state that the chargé "emphatically" believed the canal was "too important to the Government of the U. States to fall into the hands of any other power." Conveying these "facts" to Clay without a hint of concern for backlash against Williams, perhaps Phillips did not know that his friend's support for the canal relied on a loose interpretation of his instructions. Phillips even expressed confidence that the diplomat would "bear ample testimony" to support his claim.[20] Clay chose not to involve Williams in investigating Phillips's canal debts. He just ignored them.[21]

In January 1828, Phillips despaired over his losses. He could not expect repayment from Palmer who, rumor had it, planned to escape his debts through New York's "insolvent act."[22] To wring his money out of the dry Central American coffers, the captain prepared to return to Guatemala City. He amassed a cargo to trade under the "protection" of new Chargé William B. Rochester, the Bucktail who had recently lost New York's governorship to DeWitt Clinton.[23] Phillips planned to meet Rochester in Omoa in early 1828. On the eve of his departure, Phillips offered Clay his services to support the new legation. He also reiterated his claim that Williams "induced" him to advance the Central American government funds. The captain again assured the secretary that, "if necessary," his Tennessean friend would "substantiate" this claim. This argument went nowhere. Clay had no desire to investigate Williams for corruption; he wanted Andrew Jackson's old rival's support in the already raucous 1828 presidential campaign.[24]

Clay would need all the help he could get to keep his secretaryship. Through charges of "corrupt bargain" and other attacks on the Adams administration, Jackson garnered national support. In 1828, the Tennessean's landslide victory over the unpopular Adams would transform a government staffed through personal patronage into a machine of two-party politics. Gone would be the deliberations over merit and need; Jackson's "spoils system" institutionalized Democratic Party loyalty as the chief requirement for federal posts. Supporters of Clay, Adams, and other anti-Jackson men united in opposition, forming the Whig Party.[25]

Out of office in 1829, Adams retired briefly to his parents' former home before returning to Washington as a Whig congressman representing Quincy. The only president ever to serve subsequently in the House of Representatives, he spent nearly two decades opposing slavery, Indian Removal, the annexation of Texas, and the Mexican-American War.[26] One of the consequences of not supporting a commercially oriented, water-based diplomacy during his administration was a frustrating career of fighting policies of territorial imperialism after his presidency. Not constructing an oceanic shortcut through Central America meant that federal power focused on connecting the Atlantic and Pacific by controlling the North American continent. In early 1848, as he voted against expressing gratitude to the officers of the Mexican-American War, Adams's eighty-year-old brain hemorrhaged. He sank from his chair to the floor of the house in "the agonies of death."[27]

On the other side of the capitol building, Clay earned a reputation as the Senate's "Great Compromiser." He lost a son in the war against Mexico, and dealing with the war's aftermath weakened his tuberculosis-wracked body. A different kind of Whig than Adams, Clay's final political act was to devise the "Compromise of 1850," a deal that would stave off civil war, protect legal slavery, and connect the Atlantic and Pacific through transcontinental sovereignty.[28]

WHEREAS CLAY AND ADAMS found other Washington jobs, John Williams never returned to federal office. Four hundred miles away in Tennessee, he may never have learned that Phillips reported his involvement in the canal negotiations to the State Department. In the slave-built mansion constructed during his absence, Williams spent his last decade conspiring against Jackson and rebuilding his power through state politics and railroad speculations.[29]

Glowing from a state senate victory in August 1827, Williams extolled the invaluable services of his friend Phillips to Rochester. "He knows the road" and will "guard you against many impositions," the Tennessean advised the New Yorker, assuring that Phillips would help with the "housekeeping arrangements" and "take pleasure in attending to your finances." Let the captain "have his own way about everything," Williams advised, "it will add very much to your comfort & ease."[30]

Sensing some "peculiarities" in Phillips's personality, Rochester did not give the captain the chance to ease his time in Guatemala City.[31] Rochester delayed his departure, causing Phillips to "anxiously" wait months for the chargé's arrival in Omoa's "pestilentious climate." The captain's increasingly dire reports of the civil war overstretching Central America were coupled with angry demands for explanation of "the absence" of Consul Savage and "the unaccountable non arrival" of Chargé Rochester.[32]

When Savage finally returned to his consulate in Guatemala City, he could do very little to help his countrymen.[33] The Central American government was, in Savage's terms, "little else than a dead letter."[34] Depending on his nephew Henry's permanent residence in the region, Savage would spend the next decade circulating between Central America, Massachusetts, and New Orleans. Never able to make his consulate pay, he died broken in both "health and spirit" in the Republic of Texas. Here Savage hoped to finally find wealth by forcing enslaved people to cultivate cotton.[35] No longer looking to make his fortune through Central American commerce or a canal, the consul had become a cog of industrialization.

Savage was not alone in conceding his canal dreams to territorial expansion. Henry Clay's instructions to Rochester did not include anything about negotiating a canal. Instead, as the United States and its citizens lusted after Indigenous homelands, the State Department sought information about the "actual condition of the Aborigines within the limits of the Central Republic."[36] Clay's questions betrayed his country's debates over assimilation and dispossession.[37] He sought information about Indigenous Central Americans' "advances in civilization," their "sense of the value of property," and their "civil rights or privileges" within the "government of the Republic."[38] At the State Department, dreams of communicating with Asia had been displaced by desires for colonizing the continent.[39]

WHEN CHARGÉ ROCHESTER finally arrived in Omoa, he immediately determined the "inexpediency and inutility" of traveling to Guatemala City, where he believed the government was "virtually dissolved." The presence of Consul Savage, the chargé argued, should be "sufficient" for assisting the "two or at most three citizens of the U. States engaged in business." Without sleeping a night on the isthmus, he determined his "duty" was "to return home." Sick from the port's "pestilence" and "much exhausted," the last US diplomat sent to Central America in the 1820s fared better than most of his predecessors by returning home alive.[40]

Meanwhile, in Guatemala City, rumors swirled that "personal political motives" inspired Rochester's hasty departure.[41] News had just reached Central America of the sudden death of Rochester's rival, DeWitt Clinton. On February 11, 1828, the canal visionary suffered heart failure while seated in his writing chair.[42] Although the Erie Canal had transformed New York state's finances, Clinton's personal debts decimated his estate, leaving his family to endure the public sale of their possessions.[43]

Perhaps as his heart failed him, Clinton's mind still dreamed of becoming the president of a profitable interoceanic canal company. Before the Salvadoran troops invaded Guatemala City, Phillips reported meeting an "agent" sent by "Mr. Curtis Bolton of New York with a new Canal Project." Despite the agent's elite Guatemalan connections, Phillips predicted his failure. "In the present state of affairs," the captain noted, "nothing can be done, this misgoverned Country at present is a complete political chaos."[44] Bolton's agent (perhaps Clinton's, too) would learn quickly that there was no government with which to negotiate.

But might a deal be made closer to the route? In Nicaragua, old feuds reignited, returning the Spanish-descended elites in the cities of the west coast to decades of civil war. In 1828, a firing squad executed Manuel Antonio de la Cerda, first Nicaraguan head of state and creator of the *Plano Ídeal*.[45]

On the eastern Caribbean coast, Gregor MacGregor was long gone. He would continue to peddle Poyaisian securities in Europe, survive several prison stints, and be buried with full military honors in the same Venezuelan cathedral that housed the remains of Simón Bolívar, whose once vast empire had fragmented into separate South American nation states.[46] King George Frederic was also gone. Like his father and under equally murky circumstances, the king who sought Miskitú diplomatic recognition was assassinated. During the subsequent reign of his brother, the British cultural influence on the Miskitú transformed into outright imperialism.[47] The "protectorate" on the "Mosquito Coast" facilitated British intervention in Central American governments, including thwarting canal plans of other foreign powers.[48]

Relatedly, over the next decade and a half, Rama families gradually moved northeast, away from the English-speaking merchants and military men who occupied the river's mouth. As coal-fired steam engines replaced human rowers above and below the river's rapids, foreigners traversing the proposed canal route relied less on Rama knowledge. Rama men and women turned to turtling, fishing, hunting, and farming around an island now known as Rama Cay.[49]

With civil war in the west and British imperialism in the east, Bolton's agent would not have found leaders anywhere along the canal route with the will and power to turn the New Yorker's dream into a canal.

BACK IN MANHATTAN, BOLTON INVESTED in a fleet of "packet" ships that sailed on a schedule between New York and Europe. Tied, like Savage, to US territorial expansion and industrial textile production, his financial fate rose and fell with the cotton trade. Although Bolton wanted his waterway to change the world, his brother's coal-transporting canal enabled the burning of fossil fuels that would, over the next two centuries, change the globe's climate.

In the late 1840s, in another age of revolutions, Bolton's shipping business declined. After his wife died, he "retired."[50] Applying for a European diplomatic post, he hinted at a "delicate" and "private" matter that motivated his request and confessed being "ruined in my affairs" with no hopes of travel without government sponsorship.[51] Although claiming that he had "never asked for office before," Bolton's plea for federal transportation recalled his trip to Nicaragua on navy vessels a quarter-century earlier.[52]

In 1851, the man who had both inspired Williams's support for the canal contract and advocated for its cancellation died in the home of his third son, a prominent doctor. Bolton left a legion of descendants involved in US expansion.[53] His namesake eldest son joined the Mormon exodus to Utah and, in 1850, traveled to France on a mission—perhaps prompting his father's plea for a European appointment.[54] His eldest daughter married an engineer whose work included Atlantic lighthouses, Pacific land reclamation, and surveying the Hawaiian port of Pearl Harbor.[55] The youngest of his seven children joined the gold rush to California in 1849. Although newspapers reported that the son intended to cross through Mexico, it is possible that he got diverted south on what would become known as the "Nicaragua Route," which utilized a combination of bongies, steamboats, and mule-drawn carriages to transport thousands of US citizens where his father had envisioned a canal.[56]

TWO DECADES BEFORE THE FLOOD of gold seekers descended on the route, few flocked to the San Juan River or Guatemala City. Before a Dutch agent reopened negotiations around 1830, only Bolton's agent arrived to pitch a new canal contract. "The British make no movement," reported Phillips who kept a close eye on Baily.[57]

Abandoned by the dissolved BHRC, the former British officer lost his job, but he did not leave Guatemala. For the remainder of his life, he embraced his identity as Señor Juan Baily, but he also continued to collect Lieutenant John Baily's British pension.[58] In 1850, a quarter century after Baily's arrival and the same year that the Clayton-Bulwer Treaty diffused some of the tension between the United States and Britain over isthmian diplomacy, he published in London an illustrated guide to the region.[59]

Although British capitalists moved their money into state bonds and other credit instruments that financed the expansion of US cotton production in the 1830s, Baily continued to dream of a British-built waterway.[60] In 1838, what remained of the Central American government hired him to survey the route. Enlisting the aid of a knowledgeable local partner, he measured the lake's depths before and after the rainy season, dragged the chains around the river's many turns, and built stations in the dense Pacific forests to calculate elevations and distances.[61] Translating his Spanish text into English, he sent the British government copies of his enormous charts. Like Thompson's jewel-toned copy of the *Plano Ídeal*, Baily's depictions were designed to lure British capital to the canal project. And like the earlier map, Baily's beautifully detailed drawings ended up in the National Archives. Although he worked over the next two decades with Dutch, French, and US canal agents, Baily's dream of a Central American canal survived the collapse of the never-quite-sovereign country but never came true.[62]

IN EARLY 1827, the Arce administration kept faith in Beneski and Palmer even after the deadline passed. Phillips believed that "the government will give Palmer time to do his utmost towards complying with the contract."[63] Beneski did not negotiate this leniency. He never returned to Guatemala City, but he did go back to Mexico, illegally and under a new alias. Reinforcing his claim of a French birth, Beneski added "de Beaufort" to his name.

Wherever he came from, Beneski returned to his roots as a mercenary. He made his way once again into the inner circles of the Mexican government, which was led by a series of rival military men. After several imprisonments, banishments, and a disastrous eighteen-month stint as a Mexican district's "supreme military and civilian authority," Beneski joined the Mexican army to resist Texan independence. A survivor of several death sentences who cavalierly aged himself, the footloose agent of fortune decided that his time was up. About 300 miles southwest of the Rio Grande, Beneski loaded his own pistol and "blew out his brains."[64]

Phillips also suffered "depressed spirits." Facing forced loans, seizure of his property, and imprisonment, the captain began drinking heavily. In 1829, he fell off his horse and developed a "fistula in the anus." Bedridden for six months, "chronic evacuations" eventually killed the captain.[65]

Although Williams found Phillips financially trustworthy, his depressed, disabled, and now deceased friend left his accounts in "so confused a state as to render them almost unintelligible." Besieged by creditors, Phillips's widow requested the proceeds of the sale of the dry goods in Guatemala City. But as Henry Savage discovered, many of the items were "in bad order and are unsaleable." The captain's clothes were "old" and "much worn." Even his "gold French watch" was "out of repairs."[66]

AFTER THEIR CANAL DREAMS proved undoable, Savage, Beneski, and Phillips succumbed to despair. Arce and Bolton died broken. But not the man who won the canal contract. Having reinvented himself before, Aaron H. Palmer launched his life's third act in London.

As he advertised in December 1829 on a "circular" for his newly created "American and Foreign Agency for Claims," he "visited Europe in the years 1826 and 1827, and established a correspondence with distinguished Legal Gentlemen in Great Britain and France." From his Wall Street office, Palmer turned these new acquaintances into the means of settling "Claims, Debts, Dues, Demands, Inheritances, &c., payable or recoverable in any part of Europe."[67] Replacing the capital-intensive canal with inexpensive paper as a means to bring the world into communication, he claimed in the 1840s to have sent "upwards of 140,000 large illustrated circulars" in English, French, Spanish, and Portuguese to "the West India islands, Mexico, Central America, all South America, Egypt, Turkey, Greece, Russia, the maritime countries and islands of Asia, Africa, Austral-Asia, and Oceanica."[68] Described as "father to that characteristically American method of commercial conquest by circularization," he built a world of powerful correspondents: bankers like Nathan Mayer Rothschild and Sons in London, political leaders like the sultan of the Comoro Islands, the pasha of Egypt, and the Prince of Siam, as well as officers of scientific societies in Spain, France, and the Philippines.[69] A friend described his mailbox as "the ark of newspapers" and his business as operating "with arms as long as the world's axis."[70] Never losing faith in his mother's global vision, he wrote to the US government advocating canals, transcontinental railways, and Asian trade.[71]

Serving as consul for Ecuador and vice-consul for Peru, he moved to Washington in the 1850s to promote opening trade with Japan and prepared Commodore Matthew Perry for this diplomatic mission.[72] With civil war looming, he remained doggedly determined to receive compensation for his role in the Perry Mission.[73] He needed the money; he was living as a boarder with an estate of only $150.[74] Less than a month before Abraham Lincoln's inauguration, Congress approved an act that declared "to Mr. Palmer is due the origin of the Japan expedition." Not quite the government job he longed for in his youth, this $3,000 payday demanded the lessons of a lifetime.[75]

The world's first interoceanic canal contractor was an unusually adaptable man. This saved him from despair in the aftermath of the "Canal Bubble," but it also meant that—like Henry Clay—he compromised his principles. Although he served as consul for a nation that had abolished slavery, the former Quaker and one-time abolitionist fiercely defended US slavery in racist terms during his last years. "It is impossible, under our present social system, that negroes should ever be admitted, either socially or politically, to equal rights and privileges with American citizens," he wrote in late 1860. Advocating gradual emancipation and forced emigration for Black people, Palmer preferred "the substitution of free Asiatic or acclimated white laborers in their stead."[76] When Palmer died a lifelong bachelor in February 1863, a month after the Emancipation Proclamation, he left no heirs and little estate. His legacy was a globe in closer communication—even without an interoceanic canal.[77]

PALMER WAS NOT ALONE in wielding paper as a tool. Penned in haste in Guatemala City at the end of January 1827, Phillips's letter and its accompanying documents arrived at Sparks's Boston office in June.[78] Sparks asked his friend Caleb Cushing to write an article about "Guatemala." Forwarding Phillips's documents, Sparks surmised, "The canal project has fallen thro' because the conditions were so hard that no person would risk money in the concern."[79] He implicitly blamed Palmer who, he noted, "has disappeared."[80]

Published early in 1828, Cushing's article characterized Central America as "the least known" and most "overlooked" but "by no means the least important" part of the former Spanish American empire.[81] Like so many canal dreamers, Cushing suggested that "bare inspection of a map" demonstrated the region's favorable "geographical" position for becoming "the point of union for the commerce of both oceans."[82]

But unlike canal dreamers of just a few years earlier, Cushing predicted that "the time is far distant, when the boasted utility of the canal of Nicaragua will be realized." He was "quite certain" that "this canal will not soon be made." Such a skeptical view was informed by new documents. No longer dependent only on the secondhand stories of Humboldt and others, Cushing read Valle's "strong reasons" for the government in Guatemala City to defer canal construction. He summarized Bolton's argument that investing in Palmer's "speculation" would be "extravagant improvidence." He doubted that even the British "daring speculators" at the height of their "mania" would have risked investing in the contract's terms. "These unanswerable objections," he argued, "proved fatal to the enterprise."

According to Cushing, the contract was dead, but this did not doom the dream. Concerned that the "public expectation" of a soon-to-be-constructed canal was "unduly raised," he sought to distinguish between "the acts of the nation"—which he suggested would never agree to such a foolish deal—and the acts of "its individual citizens."[83] Advocating for a government-built canal, Cushing blamed Palmer for agreeing to the worst of possible contracts for the most desirable of projects. He clearly knew neither that Palmer had tried to convince the federal government to assume the contract, nor that Cañas had proposed the project directly to an otherwise occupied Adams. Four decades later, Cushing's own canal dreams led him to negotiate one of several treaties between the United States and Colombia for the right to build a canal in Panamá.[84]

Cushing's article was a far cry from the puffery Palmer and Clinton had requested of Sparks in the fall of 1826. Published anonymously in 1828, the *North American Review* pronounced canal dreams dead or at best dormant.

DIPLOMATIC THREATS SOON revived these dreams. In 1835, President Andrew Jackson responded to European designs to control isthmian transit by sending an agent to investigate the routes in Nicaragua and Panamá. Without reaching Nicaragua and with the investigation mired in the agent's scandalous pursuit of personal profit, the prospects for a canal dimmed.[85]

Elite New Yorkers and Philadelphians petitioned Congress to open negotiations with "the leading Governments of Europe and America" to build a canal "by united means and exertions for common good, and to secure its use and benefits to the world at large."[86] Harkening back to the Adams administration's desire to turn the canal into an international project, a congressional committee gathered information from government archives. The State Department forwarded excerpts, including Cañas's canal offer. The committee chair borrowed "Thompson's Guatemala" from the "Congressional Library."[87]

Thompson, the British agent who had hand-colored his glistening copy of the *Plano Ídeal*, included in his 1829 book an "appendix" with old Spanish surveying data. The committee requested that the "Topographical bureau of the War Department" use these flawed numbers to estimate the work of constructing a canal. The lieutenant who did the math never traveled to the route, but in the 1860s, he was hired to serve under an elderly Edmund Blunt on the coast survey.[88]

Perhaps unaware of Blunt's knowledge of Nicaragua, no one from the committee sought his opinion on the canal. One of the petitioners, however, contacted both Palmer and Bolton.[89] Bolton refused to hunt down his "manuscript copy" of a letter he sent to Secretary Southard upon his return from Central America and kept Blunt's report confidential.[90] He confessed to Southard that he did "not feel at liberty" to share these documents.[91] Instead, Bolton provided the committee with a brief recollection of his trip.

Although it had been only a decade, Bolton's memory had clouded. He asserted that when he arrived in Guatemala City, "another citizen of New York had preceded me and taken the contract on the terms prescribed by that Government."[92] This timing was wrong. Bolton had arrived in Guatemala City well before Beneski; he had departed Central America before the government decreed its preferred terms. And the contract was signed long after Bolton returned to New York. Bolton's alteration of the chronology deemphasized his role in the cancellation of Palmer's contract. He protected himself by withholding documents and rewriting canal history.

Palmer took the opposite tack; he emptied his files into the committee's hands. Having left "the original contract" as well as old Spanish "maps and surveys" with his "agents in London," the canal contractor shared seven other documents including a translation of the contract, Clinton's deed of trust and its cover letter, and his London prospectus.

Publicizing his documents provided a path to vindication. Palmer blamed his failure to build the canal on the "political disturbances" in Central America, the Panic of 1825, and "a variety of other untoward events and circumstances." This shifted fault from the contract's terms and his choice to capitalize and incorporate after acquiring the contract. Moreover, as Hone had argued a decade earlier, the mere appearance of famous and wealthy men's names on Clinton's deed of trust suggested their support for the plan even though most had withheld their signatures.

Although Palmer's documents did not shed light on the physical feasibility of the canal, they were valuable to the committee because they revealed the ineffectiveness of relying on private capitalists—even the great DeWitt Clinton—to construct a global canal. This supported the committee's argument that Washington should pursue a multinational government-funded canal. Sending his "hope that your efforts may prove more successful than mine," Palmer asked for the return of his documents, but he did not prevent their printing.[93]

In 1839, as the country suffered a cotton-based financial crisis (the second in three years), the committee could not find support for a capital-intensive, diplomatically difficult canal. Its legacy was its "full and interesting report," including Bolton's not-quite-accurate history and Palmer's not-quite-signed documents.[94]

A DECADE LATER, as a result of the Mexican-American War, half of Mexico's territory—more than half a million square miles of Indigenous homelands stretching from the Rocky Mountains to the Pacific Ocean—formed a new US continental empire.[95] Congress considered whether to integrate this land into the nation or prioritize communication with its Pacific ports.

Land or water? Tasked with this question by a joint resolution, a "Select Committee" published a 679-page congressional report entitled "Canal or Railroad Between the Atlantic and Pacific Oceans." Appearing on February 20, 1849, just months after the discovery of gold in California, the report tried to answer the "exceedingly important" question about "the best mode" of integrating the nation's new "immense possessions."

Acknowledging that "an easy and rapid communication between the two oceans" had long been a topic of interest, the committee argued that expansion across the continent made it "a matter of the utmost practical importance."[96] An isthmian canal, it suggested, would be efficient and profitable; it would link established ports. In contrast, the idea of a 2,000-mile railroad through land that they described as a "perfect waste"—snow-capped mountains and barren deserts with few European-descended citizens—seemed "preposterous."[97] Reproducing the evidence supporting an isthmian canal over a transcontinental railroad, the report included Baily's survey data, excerpts from Humboldt and Thompson, and the entirety of the 1839 "exceedingly full and valuable" congressional report.[98] Twice printed by the US government, Palmer's documents kept 1820s canal dreams relevant as the United States tried to connect its empire.

During the gold rush, the committee's tome was shelved in favor of quicker solutions. For a time in the 1850s, Cornelius Vanderbilt made money moving people from the Atlantic to the Pacific along the "Nicaragua Route." Invited in 1855 by one faction in the still raging Nicaraguan civil war, filibuster William Walker tried to seize the route and build a canal as the financial centerpiece of his own proslavery country. Like Palmer, Vanderbilt, and so many others, Walker could neither capitalize the construction nor control the crossing.[99] No one could.

Even Vanderbilt's fossil-fuel-powered steam engines could not overpower the region's environment. Papagayos continued to sink vessels on the lake. Rain-driven sedimentation and an earthquake's alteration of the river shut down traffic at the Caribbean port of San Juan, forcing ships south to tributaries in Costa Rica.[100] The climate continued to incubate deadly microbes.[101] By the 1860s, these environmental challenges and human conflicts resulted in the transit's decline.[102]

In 1869, the opening of the Suez Canal undercut European interest in an isthmian canal. Baily had been dead for more than a decade; his dreams of Britons sailing west yielded to the ease of steaming east.[103] After seven contentious decades of Anglo-American isthmian rivalry, at the dawn of the twentieth century, the British basically conceded.[104]

Although the United States would continue to pursue treaties gaining rights of way across the isthmus throughout the remainder of the nineteenth century, and US capitalists would intervene in the region's politics to support cash crop production, the desire to integrate the interior of the North American continent dominated the US government's priorities. No longer seen as "preposterous" after the US Civil War, government-subsidized transcontinental railroads provided both a connection between the seas and a means of enticing white settlers to the western half of the continent without a stop in the deadly tropics.[105] US interest in an isthmian canal would not crest again until the Spanish-American War of 1898 expanded US empire across the Pacific.

IN MARCH 1899, LESS THAN FOUR MONTHS after the end of the war, as US territory stretched to include Guam, Hawaii, and the Philippines, the quest for an interoceanic canal resurged. Congress empowered President William McKinley to commission a "full and complete investigation" of a waterway that would be "under the control, management, and ownership of the United States." With a million-dollar budget, the "Isthmian Canal Commission" would be led by two navy officers. None of the commission's members were merchants or capitalists. Military might motivated McKinley's canal dream.[106]

For two years, the commissioners explored archives and existing canals before traveling to the isthmus where nearly a thousand engineers and laborers conducted surveys at Panamá and Nicaragua.[107] The commissioners praised this on-the-ground research's production of "accurate knowledge of the geography, topography, and other physical features of the isthmian country." Such new information "dispelled the exaggerations and fictions" spread by "credulous travelers and unreliable explorers."[108]

Sharing subject and size with its 1849 predecessor, the commission's report was awash in new visual evidence—photographs, tables, charts, graphs, maps, and equations. Gone were the reprintings of texts by armchair canal dreamers. But Palmer's documents did not entirely disappear. To support the argument that "the only well-grounded hope of accomplishing the desired result is through the power and resources of a great nation," they included a "history" of the desire for a link between the oceans, from the conquistadores to their own calculations.[109] In the middle of this narrative is an account of the 1820s quest for a canal. The commission quoted from Cañas's offer, Clay's instructions to both Williams and the Panama Congress ministers, and Palmer's contract. Recognizing that some readers would want to see "the contract in full," the commissioners directed readers to specific pages of the 1849 report.[110]

Palmer's unfulfilled contract had become a case study of why canal-building could not be a capitalist endeavor. A relic rather than required reading, Palmer's contract remained relevant, especially as the commission came to its conclusion. Weighing science, finance, and politics, the commission determined that "'the most practicable and feasible route' for an isthmian canal, to be 'under the control, management, and ownership of the United States,'" was in Nicaragua.[111]

But before the massive report's printing, conditions on the ground changed. In 1901, Theodore Roosevelt replaced the assassinated McKinley; the new president favored the Colombian province of Panamá. In 1902, Congress considered an act designed to authorize a Nicaraguan canal, but clever lobbying and a powerful amendment shifted the project south. In 1903, Roosevelt sent the US military to support a separatist coup in Panamá and then, echoing aspects of Jeremy Bentham's plan of eight decades earlier, basically secured US sovereignty over what would become the Panama Canal Zone. In 1904, as their report advocating the Nicaragua route reached readers, the Isthmian Canal Commission became responsible for the construction of the waterway that opened a decade later as the Panama Canal.[112]

ALTHOUGH IT CREATED AN OCEANIC shortcut to Asia, the opening of the Panama Canal did not fulfill all the dreams of the 1820s. To get the canal built, engineers abandoned the sea-level canal for a lock system that limited the size of ships. The quest for an unobstructed waterway would continue throughout the next century with some advocating the use of atomic explosions to connect the seas.[113]

For powerful Nicaraguans dreaming of a waterway providing political and economic stability, the Panama Canal was a nightmare. Some Panamanians would agree. A transit route for centuries, the land that became water had been the homes of tens of thousands. The Isthmian Canal Commission evicted Panamanians from the Canal Zone regardless of whether their land abutted the route.[114] Workers from all over the globe repopulated the zone, where the United States imported racism and sexism along with steam shovels and mosquito nets.[115] The zone became a laboratory for controlling the human and natural world. These experiments often erased the evidence of their efforts, making the landscape and society along the waterway seem "natural" as Panamá lost evidence of its past.[116]

Meanwhile, the dream of a Nicaraguan canal persisted.[117] Even after the construction of the Panama Canal, Nicaraguan politicians pitched the waterway as a national panacea.[118] Critics turned the centuries-long quest for a canal into the country's poetry.[119] Unbuilt canal plans of liberals, conservatives, and communists entered archives in Nicaragua and abroad.[120]

CANAL DREAMS PERSIST TO THE PRESENT. On June 13, 2013, the Nicaraguan government voted to grant a Chinese businessman a $40 billion canal contract. At a signing ceremony, the businessman promised to make the "dream a reality."[121] "After so many centuries fighting for this canal to come true," glowed Nicaragua's president, "at last we are approaching that historic moment."[122] Shortly after the signing, journalists found some Nicaraguans "in the thrall of the imagined waterway" with hopes that the canal would "double the national economy, triple employment, and lift more than 400,000 people out of poverty by 2018."[123]

Hauntingly similar to the story in 1826, the businessman's corporation, his financial resources, and his ties to his government appeared unclear at the time of the signing.[124] Charging that the canal was a ploy by the Nicaraguan president "to win support for unlimited re-election," opposition leaders described him as "selling dreams."[125] Critics immediately expressed concern that "every key detail of the project remains a mystery: the sources of funding, Nicaragua's share of the profits and the route it would take from ocean to ocean."[126] As Costa Rica brought Nicaragua to international court over sovereignty along the San Juan River, the interoceanic canal plan shifted northward.[127] The proposed route tracked the Rama migration. Nicaraguan laws protected Indigenous homelands, but courts refused to hear canal cases.[128] A "Peasant Movement" protested rural dispossession.[129] Once again, a global waterway might cut through the Rama's world.

As happened nearly two centuries earlier, some considered environmental effects. Discussions of damage to the region's water and rainforests attracted the attention of scientists and activists. Some environmentalists cited "rare freshwater sharks" as among the animals in need of protection.[130] No longer living in a time when the potential effects on the land and its nonhuman inhabitants could be ignored, global critics called for "an independent environmental impact study."[131]

Akin to Palmer's race, the proposed timeline was tight, but the businessman declared himself "100% sure" of the canal's 2019 opening.[132] Delays came quick. In January 2014, the Nicaraguan government announced a one-year hiatus to wait for "feasibility studies."[133] Quickly retracted, the statement proved a sanguine prediction.[134] In December 2014, at the canal's "Commencement Celebration," the businessman lauded the "on schedule" launch of a "century-old dream."[135] But eight months after the ceremony, the widening of a dirt road was the only physical evidence of construction visible to journalists. Building a new house on the proposed route, one man asserted, "There isn't going to be a canal."[136]

The only actual digging slowed down the project. Completed in 2016, an archeological study unearthed artifacts that revealed two millennia of "continuous occupation."[137] The undoing of millions of years of geological, hydrological, and biological history also demanded "two or three years" of investigation.[138]

The plan would not survive the studies. In the fall of 2015, a Chinese stock market crash wiped out much of the businessman's fortune.[139] In 2018, he shuttered his offices in Hong Kong's tallest skyscraper; within a few years, he was prohibited from managing companies traded on the Chinese stock market.[140] In 2019, the offices of the Nicaraguan canal bureau vanished.[141] In 2020, the canal company's website—once a robust portal of project documents—featured images of buxom women promoting Indonesian online gambling.[142] Perhaps giving up on the contractor but not the dream, in 2022, the Nicaraguan president—in his fourth term and having exiled the canal's critics—continued to argue, "At some point it will be a reality here in Nicaragua."[143] That point may never arrive.

IN THE PRESENT, Indigenous and rural communities continue to live in their homes, where the manifold problems of poverty swell even as the canal plan recedes. Deforestation, overfishing, pollution, and global climate change challenge life along the would-be route.[144] Extinctions are happening even without the waterway.[145] Even the shark population is declining.[146] But for now, some intrepid bull sharks still swim up to the lake to feed and down to the sea to breed.

Epilogue
The Shark

Sharks have been swimming through the earth's waters for hundreds of millions of years, since long before the Central American isthmus existed. As the land and oceans slowly shifted, the fish adapted to survive in new contexts. But as we see in our era of climate crisis, quick changes challenge these slow-breeding, ancient animals.[1]

Sharks are not alone. For the humans of the 1820s who conceived of cutting through the isthmus to reunite the world's waters at the end of the Age of Revolutions, historical change between idea and implementation prevented canal dreams from coming true. The dreamers did not calculate for a quick shift in context; their timing was terrible. Starting a half-century after the American Revolution, the work of negotiating, capitalizing, and constructing an interoceanic canal could not be concluded before the era's collapse. Political fluidity ossified into nations and parties; flows of capital evaporated. The plan was too revolutionary, even for the Age of Revolutions.

In Central America, nearly continual civil war created too much chaos for the construction of a waterway. Canal dreams, however, continued to be preached as panaceas, ignoring the Indigenous and rural people as well as the animals and plants living along the route. Although a rebellion against the British Empire had launched the Age of Revolutions, British imperialism in Central America expanded by era's end. As the government increased its interventions in the region's politics, London's capitalists rerouted their resources toward cotton textile production with its concomitant Indigenous dispossession, expansion of slavery, fossil fuel consumption, and exploitative industrialization.

For the United States, expanding over land trumped connecting through water. Interest in "external improvements," including a Central American waterway to the Pacific, crested and fell with US imperialism. The cosmopolitanism that had fueled some of the desire for interoceanic communication collapsed into essentialist hierarchies of people and places. Corrupt bargains colored nearly every choice.

Even had they somehow predicted these shifts in human history, 1820s canal dreamers did not understand the science of the setting. They had no idea how to control the seasonal epidemics. They did not comprehend the route's extreme water cycle. Their lack of on-the-ground environmental knowledge made their engineering utterly imaginary. Never even wielding a shovel, they had no idea of the technological tools necessary to deconstruct the isthmus's geology. These powerful people could not bend the world to their will. Their visions—so believable at inception—proved unviable, their contracts unfulfillable, their canal unbuildable, their dreams undone.

ONE OF THE MOST BIOLOGICALLY diverse places on earth, the flora and fauna of the potential route survived these undone dreams. Sharks continue to swim deep into the isthmus, but some also suffer from terrible timing. In early 1943, a male shark cruised the lake's rising waters in the shadow of the old fort that guarded the entrance to the San Juan River. Just shy of five feet from rounded nose to pointy tail, perhaps the immature bull contemplated following the rushing waters down the river. Instead of making his first trip to his species' saltwater breeding grounds, the pores in his snout sensed the presence of prey. His powerful jaws opened to expose five rows of teeth, but only after he clamped down on the fish did he feel the hook. On the other end of the line, an officer in the US Army Corps of Engineers reeled in his catch.

The shark would be sacrificed for science. He was the perfect size to fit in the major's "barrel."[2] The humans that requested his capture and waited for him to arrive at his new home in the Ichthyology Department of Harvard's Museum of Comparative Zoology thought he was a marvel of natural history. Since 1877, scientists believed a rare species of freshwater shark had evolved from its ocean-dwelling ancestors after being trapped in what became a lake during the formation of the isthmus. They assumed that since sailing vessels could not ascend the river's rapids, neither could sharks.[3]

The Harvard ichthyologists wanted to reevaluate this theory by examining the shark's anatomy. The Second World War obstructed this investigation. The first "pickled" shark sank in the hold of a torpedoed ship; a salt shortage prevented the preservation of the second.[4] Caught on the scientists' third strike, the long-awaited corpse landed in San Francisco and crossed the North American continent before arriving at Harvard where it was tagged and transferred to the fluid in "coffin #3" on the ground floor of a labyrinthine building built to house millions of preserved animals.[5]

Here, he made history. Rendered a line drawing, the shark's portrait and measurements would be published by the scientists. Varying slightly in his proportions from ordinary bull sharks, he defined his species. He was *Carcharhinus nicaraguensis*.[6]

Or at least he was, for a few years. After examining several additional specimens, the ichthyologists doubted their classification. The other Lake Nicaragua sharks matched a more common species that inhabited most of the world's tropical waters. In 1961, the scientists published a note entitled "*Carcharhinus nicaraguensis,* A Synonym of The Bull Shark."[7] A decade later, sharks tagged in the lake were found in the Caribbean and vice versa, confirming the reclassification.[8] For biologists, the shark's significance faded.

But for me, a historian of watery dreams, the shark remains relevant. His biography brings my story full circle. On an unseasonably warm October day eight decades after his death, two curators pulled his wrinkled body, colored green from his post-mortem exposure to copper, from a tank's pungent liquid. As I imagined how he fought the river's current and launched his cartilaginous frame over rapids to reach the lake, I could see the value of preserving the ecosystem that would have been destroyed by the dreamers' canal. If the *Plano Ídeal* argued for the ease of constructing a waterway, this archived fish conveyed the challenges of the canal route written in tissue. His unnaturally jewel-toned body suggested the struggle to survive across space and time, the hard-won treasure of linking worlds and histories.

Like the canal dreamers of the 1820s, the shark's timing was terrible. His life ended too soon for him to pass along his genes. But for a brief time, his individual characteristics spun a story of what people thought was possible. And the dream of a species evolved to survive extreme environmental change, like the dream of uniting the world, seems particularly meaningful for our own age of revolutions.

AS WE SEEK TO IMAGINE our way through the obstacles of our time, we must expect change between idea and implementation. What we learn along the way will shape the future regardless of whether we reach our destination, and sometimes the world is better off when the powerful prove incapable of achieving their goals. Dreams do not need to come true to truly make history. Our world is but countless unfulfilled quests.

Acknowledgments

At the end of a tale of unfulfilled quests, this is a story of dreams come true.

Back in 2003, Brandeis University and the Rothschild Archive funded my first trip to research my dissertation; with unanticipated scholarly efficiency, a box of letters from interoceanic canal contractor Aaron H. Palmer yielded the first research for my second book as well. As I continued to follow the trail of Palmer's scattered papers, institutions that supported my dissertation and first book—especially the Historic New Orleans Collection, John E. Rovensky Fellowship, Library Company of Philadelphia, McNeil Center for Early American Studies, American Antiquarian Society, and a US Department of Education Jacob K. Javits Fellowship—enabled the research for this book, too. Since I joined the University of New Hampshire in 2008, the History Department, College of Liberal Arts, and Provost's Office have generously invested time, money, and resources in my project, which transformed from Palmer's biography into a globetrotting narrative with an international ensemble cast. I am especially grateful for the support of Provost Wayne Jones Jr., Deans Kenneth Fuld and Michele Dillon, as well as History Department Chairs Bill Harris, Jan Golinski, Lige Gould, and Kurk Dorsey. As the book took final form, the David Rockefeller Center for Latin American Studies (DRCLAS) appointed me a Central American Visiting Scholar, which allowed me to complete the book, access Harvard University's vast archives, and join a supportive community of Latin Americanist colleagues. Since my first book manuscript landed on her desk over a decade ago, Debbie Gershenowitz has championed my work. The team at The University of North Carolina Press and its partners—including Dino Battista, Sonya Bonczek, Alyssa Brown, Kim Bryant, Mary Caviness, Alexis Dumain, Kylie Haggen, Cate Hodorowicz, Gabriel Moss, Elizabeth Orange Lane, Virginia A. Schaefer, and Lindsay Starr—have ably steered *Canal Dreamers* from proposal through publication.

For two decades, archivists, librarians, curators, and collectors have generously helped me track down sources in English, Spanish, French, Polish, and German located in ten countries on three continents at the following institutions: the American Antiquarian Society, Boston Public Library, Massachusetts Supreme Judicial Court Archives, Massachusetts Historical Society, Phillips Library, Library of Congress, National Archives (branches in Boston, New York City, College Park, and Washington, DC), Alabama Department of Archives and History, Bibliothèque nationale de France, Center for Research Libraries, National Archives at Kew, Rothschild Archive, Lloyds Banking Group Archives, Calvin M. McClung Historical Collection, Royal Geographical Society, Bancroft Library at UC Berkeley, Wilson Special Collections Library at The University of North Carolina at Chapel Hill, Benson Latin American Collection and Briscoe Center for American History at the University of Texas at Austin, Wichita State University Library, Archives of the New York County Clerk's Office, New York State Archives, New-York Historical Society, Columbia University Library, Chancellor Robert R. Livingston Masonic Library of Grand Lodge, New York City Municipal Archives, New York County Surrogate's Court Record Department,

New York Public Library, Stony Brook University Libraries, Princeton University Library, Friends Historical Library at Swarthmore College, Library Company of Philadelphia, Historical Society of Pennsylvania, American Philosophical Society Library, University of Pennsylvania Libraries, Detre Library and Archives at the Heinz History Center, Tulane University Libraries, Quidley & Company, Hemeroteca Nacional de Guatemala, Archivo General de Centroamérica, Colecciones Especiales de Biblioteca Ludwig von Mises del Universidad Francisco Marroquín, Archivo General de la Nación (Nicaragua), Archivo General de la Nación (El Salvador), and the many museums and libraries of Harvard University (Baker Library, Ichthyology Collection of the Museum of Comparative Zoology, Ernst Mayr Library, Data and Government Information Collections at Lamont Library, Houghton Library, Map Collection, Collection of Historical Scientific Instruments, University Archives, Harvard Art Museums, and Widener Library). The remarkable interlibrary loan librarians at UNH brought me a world of print evidence. Sara Schechner and Pato Winckler taught me surveying. Andrew Williston and Meaghan Sorce introduced me to sharks. Whitney Azoy kindly shared digital photographs of the correspondence of his great-great grandfather, Mariano Velázquez de la Cadena. Rocky Roberts provided images of Bolton family tombstones. When family responsibilities and COVID prevented travel to Central America, Julio David Menchú Cruz combed the archives of Guatemala City and recruited friends in El Salvador and Nicaragua to hunt for evidence. UNH History Department staff Laura Simard, Lara Demarest, Sto Austin, and Jenna Scholefield smoothed the administrative bumps. Student research assistants Joseph Juknievich, Katie Dreyer-Rowe, and Alyssa Clina assisted me with acquiring, organizing, transcribing, and summarizing sources. This book would not be possible without UNH doctoral student James Irving who, over the course of four years and nearly four hundred hours, composed Spanish to English translations of 140,000 words.

Canal dreams were often collaborative, and so has been my study of them. This book has been shaped by questions and comments from innumerable colleagues at seminars, workshops, conference panels, and talks associated with the Society for Historians of the Early American Republic (SHEAR), Program in Early American Economy and Society at the Library Company of Philadelphia, Business History Conference, American Studies Association, Society for Historians of American Foreign Relations, Organization of American Historians, American Antiquarian Society, McNeil Center for Early American Studies, American Historical Association, American Society for Ethnohistory, Early American Money Symposium at the Rhodes Center for International Economics and Finance at Brown University, New England Council on Latin American Studies, Society for US Intellectual History, Pauline Maier Early American History Seminar at the Massachusetts Historical Society, Ohio Seminar in Early American History and Culture, City University of New York Early American Republic Seminar, National Museum of American Diplomacy at the US Department of State, David Rockefeller Center for Latin American Studies at Harvard University, Lebanon Valley College, Brandeis University, and UNH History Department Faculty Seminar.

Shivering in our conference cardigans in July 2016, Emily Conroy-Krutz and I dreamed up a vision of grassroots writing support for mid-career scholars. SHEAR encouraged us to build the Second-Book Writers' Workshop (2BWW). These annual July workshops provided motivational deadlines and generous feedback (sometimes continuing long after the 2BWW) from mentors and fellow writers including Johann Neem, Justin Clark, Brooke Newman, Christine Sears, Kevin Butterfield, Caitlin Fitz, Julia Gaffield, Vanessa Mongey, Rosemarie Zagarri, David Head, Ben Park, Seth Cotlar, Kathleen DuVal, Mark Schmeller, Margot Minardi, Kara Swanson, Rebecca Brannon, Caleb McDaniel, Billy Coleman, Kelly Kennington, Allison Lange, Whitney Martinko, Serena Zabin, Thomas Balcerski, Lindsay Chervinsky, Honor Sachs, Kim Welch, Manisha Sinha, Aston Gonzalez, Robert Murray, Michael Witgen, Joe Adelman, Michael Blaakman, Kate Grandjean, and Emily Conroy-Krutz. To demystify history publishing more broadly, Emily and I also planned panels where I learned how to turn *Canal Dreamers* into a book from Kathleen DuVal, Paul Erickson, Tim Mennel, Tamara Plakins Thornton, Cathy Kelly, Caitlin Fitz, François Furstenberg, Brian Distelberg, Adina Popescu Berk, Mark Philip Bradley, William Cronon, Ann Fabian, Susan Ferber, and Debbie Gershenowitz.

The book was fed by conversations over computer screens, energizing perambulations, and delicious meals with David Díaz Arias, Silvia Arrom, Melanie Aspey, Briggs Bailey, Rose Beiler, John Belohlavek, Michael Blaakman, James Bradley, Melissa Carle, Timothy Carle, Will Clyde, Richard Conway, Denise Damico, Robyn Davis, Amanda Demmer, Kon Dierks, Dan Dupre, Ana María Durán Quesada, Jonathan Earle, David Engerman, Martha Few, Kim Frederick, Mary Fuhrer, Nathan Furey, Malick Ghachem, Jenna Gibbs, David Green, Amy Greenberg, Heather Halifax, Candice Harrison, April Haynes, Hunt Howell, Jane Kamensky, Jennifer Jacobs, Andrea Jakobs, Maya Jasanoff, Richard John, Rachel Kapelle, Brian Kinney, Gary Kornblith, Aykut Kilinc, Beth Kilinc, Daniel Chávez Landeros, John Larson, Carol Lasser, Josh Lauer, Mark Lentz, Spencer Lepler, Anne Lightbody, Gabriel Loiacono, Brian Luskey, Alison Mann, Cathy Matson, Marie McDonough, Tim Mennel, Stephen Mihm, Nina Morrison, Margarita Muñoz Piña, Brian Murphy, Sharon Murphy, Vanita Neelakanta, Priya Nelson, Scott Reynolds Nelson, Justine Oliva, Becky Olson, Jason Opal, Ben Park, Emily Pawley, Wilson Picado Umaña, Josh Piker, Gautham Rao, Dan Richter, Harriet Ritvo, Charlotte Robertson, Jackie Rockel, Jessica Roney, Emma Rothschild, Brian Rouleau, Jonathan Sadowsky, Richard Salvucci, Ricardo Sánchez-Murillo, Lindsay Schakenbach Regele, Eric Schlereth, Jay Sexton, Andy Shankman, Mary Beth Sievens, Lisa Singleton, Gene Smith, Scott Smith, Mike Sonza, Christina Snyder, Tom Stanley, Alan Taylor, Tamara Plakins Thornton, Jonathan Truitt, Chris Thurber, John Van Atta, Margarita Vargas-Betancourt, Mike Verney, Scott Weintraub, Michael Willrich, John Winters, Nezahualcoyotl Xiuhtecutli, Lynda Yankaskas, Serena Zabin, Michael Zakim, and the late Jim Broussard.

Long ago, the dedicated staff and my fellow fellows at the American Antiquarian Society, Library Company of Philadelphia, and McNeil Center for Early American Studies helped me begin this project. At its end, I gained a footing in the vast history, politics, and hydrology of the broader Americas thanks to the many members of the DRCLAS staff (especially Sol Carbonell, Jimena Codina, Andrew Elrick, June Erlick, Eugenia Garduño, Tiago Genoveze, Darinelle Merced-Calderon, Lisia Caldeira Robert, and Vanessa Salas Fuentes) and my cohort of fellow fellows (Angela Alonso, Patricia Ames, María Bjerg, Laura Gamboa, Álvaro Hofflinger, Claudia Urrutia Hoppe, Fernando Limongi, and Patricio Winckler). Since 2020, Aaron Chin, Ann Daly, Josh Greenberg, Hannah Farber, Dael Norwood, Ariel Ron, and Emily Pawley have graciously indulged my digressions on Central America, sharks, and more when we were supposed to be discussing other people's books. For more than a decade and a half, this project has benefited from interacting with my UNH students and has been nurtured through insightful feedback by my present and former UNH history colleagues: Funso Afolayan, Kimberly Alexander, David Bachrach, Jeff Bolster, Alexis Broderick, Kurk Dorsey, Molly Dorsey, Ellen Fitzpatrick, Cathy Frierson, Jan Golinski, Lige Gould, Nicky Gullace, Bill Harris, Clay Howard, Mike Leese, Greg McMahon, Addis Mason, Fred Meiton, Liz Mellyn, Janet Polasky, Julia Rodriguez, Lucy Salyer, Jason Sokol, Sara Wolper, Lu Yan, and the late Jeff Diefendorf and Cynthia Van Zandt.

Since our Cassatt House potlucks two decades ago, my dear friends and mentors Marla Miller and Cathy Kelly have helped me surmount obstacles big and small while always making me smile. Jordana Dym's thoughtful feedback on the book proposal and several chapters informed important revisions. The book benefited from encouraging anonymous reviewers who read the proposal and full draft of the manuscript. Beyond our 2BWW projects, my writing buddy Emily Conroy-Krutz waded through swollen early drafts of this entire book. Allan and Michelle Lepler indulged their daughter by reading a slightly less bloated version. Two of the kindest souls in the history profession, Scott Sandage and Kurk Dorsey, swooped in to read the full manuscript as it neared completion. Before and after I wielded the scalpel, Michael Dube's many readings—on paper and screens as well as over earbuds and speakers—improved this book in innumerable ways. Improving my life as well as my work, he has helped me transform this project from "The Lawyer Imperfect" to "The Visionary and the Ass" and finally *Canal Dreamers.* I could not do this work without the care provided by my family: Michelle and Al Lepler, Marcia Dube, and many other folks in the Dube, Feingold, Gratz, Lepler, and Zagier families. Eggy Dube has spent his entire life with 1820s dreamers haunting his mother's office. As a "geography kid," he has marveled over maps of places with names that no longer exist, imagined worlds into being, and taught me much about the globe as it is currently configured. He is my greatest dream come true.

Notes

List of Abbreviations

AAS	American Antiquarian Society, Worcester, MA
AFP	Adams Family Papers, Massachusetts Historical Society, Boston
ANC	Asamblea Nacional Constituyente
BHRC	Barclay, Herring, Richardson & Company
BLAC	Benson Latin American Collection, LLILAS Benson Latin American Studies and Collections, The University of Texas at Austin
CCNYC	Chancery Court, New York County Clerk's Office, New York (now held at the New York State Archives, Albany, New York)
DHCC	Delaware and Hudson Canal Company
DWCD	Reel 3, DeWitt Clinton Diary, New-York Historical Society, New York
DWCP	DeWitt Clinton Papers, 1785–1828, Rare Book and Manuscript Library, Columbia University, New York
EBFP	Folder 1, Box 1, MSS 467, Edmund Blunt Family Papers, Phillips Library, Peabody Essex Museum, Salem, MA
EBJ	"Journal," Folder 1, Box 1, MSS 467 Edmund Blunt Family Papers, 1824–1933, Phillips Library, Peabody Essex Museum, Salem, MA
HBB	Henry B. Bigelow Papers, University Archive, Harvard University
JQADD	John Quincy Adams Digital Diary, Massachusetts Historical Society, Boston, www.primarysourcecoop.org/jqa/
JSPP	Jared Sparks Personal Papers, 1808–66, Houghton Library, Harvard University, Cambridge, MA
LBGA	GB1830 BOS/2/6/3/16, Lloyds Banking Group plc Archives, London
MHS	Massachusetts Historical Society, Boston
NA2	US National Archives and Records Administration, College Park, MD
NAMA	US National Archives and Records Administration, Waltham, MA
NARA	US National Archives and Records Administration, Washington, DC
NYHS	New-York Historical Society, New York
PUL	Special Collections, Princeton University Library
SLSP	Samuel L. Southard Papers (C0250), Manuscript Division, Firestone Library, Princeton University, Princeton, PA
SPE	Supremo Poder Ejecutivo
SPSP	Folder 8, Box 1, Samuel P. Savage Papers (Ms. N-885.4), Massachusetts Historical Society, Boston
TNA	The National Archives, Kew, UK

Introduction

1. "Plano Ideal," MPK 1/53, TNA.

2. "Plano Ideal—Proposed Communication between Pacific Ocean, Lake Nicaragua, Central America, by Canal," 169050696, RG 77 "Records of the Office of the Chief of Engineers, 1789–1999," Civil Works Map File, https://catalog.archives.gov/id/169050696. I learned of this copy from Christian Brannstrom, "Almost a Canal: Visions of Interoceanic Communication across Southern Nicaragua," *Ecumene* 2, no. 1 (Jan. 1995): 65–87.

3. For maps of the Spanish Empire as treasure maps for English buccaneers, see Matthew Restall, "Imperial Rivalries," *Mapping Latin America: A Cartographic Reader*, eds. Jordana Dym and Karl Offen (Chicago: University of Chicago Press, 2011), 79–83.

4. "Plano Ideal," MPK 1/53, TNA.

5. "Plano Ideal," NA2.

6. Originally coined by Thomas Paine, the term "Age of Revolution(s)" is often used to describe the late eighteenth and early nineteenth centuries, but its geographical, chronological, and thematic contours have been defined differently by different historians. Paine quoted in Nathan Perl-Rosenthal, *The Age of Revolutions: And the Generations Who Made It* (New York: Basic Books, 2024), 1. For a brief synthesis of the history of this concept, see David Armitage, foreword to *The Age of Democratic Revolution: A Political History of Europe and America, 1760–1800*, by R. R. Palmer (Princeton: Princeton University Press, 2014), xv–xxii.

7. Sophie Brockmann, *The Science of Useful Nature in Central America: Landscapes, Networks, and Practical Enlightenment, 1784–1838* (New York: Cambridge University Press, 2020), 150–51; Joaquim Rabella, *Aproximación a la historia de Rio San Juan, 1500–1995* (Managua, Nicaragua: Imprimátur Artes Graficas), 7–50; and Max Harrison Williams, "San Juan River—Lake Nicaragua Waterway, 1502–1921" (PhD diss., Louisiana State University, 1971), 14–90.

8. In the 1780s, British, Miskitú, and Rama soldiers seized the San Juan River's Spanish forts to secure the interoceanic route. Williams, "San Juan River," 72–82; Matthew P. Dziennik, "The Miskitu, Military Labour, and The San Juan Expedition of 1780," *The Historical Journal* 61, no. 1 (2018): 155–79; and Peter Linebaugh, *Red Round Globe Hot Burning: A Tale at the Crossroads of Commons and Closure, of Love and Terror, of Race and Class, and Kate and Ned Despard* (Berkeley: University of California Press, 2019), 154–64.

9. David S. Landes, *The Unbound Prometheus: Technological Change and Industrial Development in Western Europe from 1750 to the Present* (Cambridge: Cambridge University Press, 1969), 46–47; Charles Hadfield, *British Canals: An Illustrated History*, 4th ed. (New York: Augustus M. Kelley, 1969); and Carter Goodrich, introduction to *Canals and American Economic Development*, ed. Carter Goodrich (New York: Columbia University Press, 1961), 1–3. Opened in 1822, the Caledonian Canal connected the Atlantic Ocean and the North Sea through Scotland. Samuel Smiles, *The Life of Thomas Telford, Civil Engineer* (Cambridge: Cambridge University Press, 1867, 2014), 226–44.

10. On the Erie Canal inspiring other state-sponsored waterways, see John Lauritz Larson, *Internal Improvement: National Public Works and the Promise of Popular Government in the Early United States* (Chapel Hill: The University of North Carolina Press, 2001), 71–107, 195–224.

11. "Plano Ideal," NA2.

12. Brockmann, *Science of Useful Nature*, 26, 222.

13. "Plano Ideal," MPK 1/53, TNA. Miskitú erasure was not universal in colonial maps, but eastern Central America was typically depicted as devoid of detail relative to the cities and towns that formed the Pacific-oriented Audiencia of Guatemala. Labeled as the Province of Taguzgalpa in seventeenth-century maps, this Spanish name was replaced with "Mosquito Coast" in maps produced after the Miskitú asserted their regional authority in the early eighteenth century. Karl Offen, "Edge of Empire," *Mapping Latin America: A Cartographic Reader*, eds. Jordana Dym and Karl Offen (Chicago: University of Chicago Press, 2011), 88–92. Historians, anthropologists, and Miskitú people have spelled the name of this nation differently at different times. Nineteenth-century sources typically describe these people as "Mosquito." Twentieth-century scholars often spelled the name "Miskito." More recent scholars frequently use "Miskitu." I found the accented spelling "Miskitú" in online documents produced by this nation and in at least one archive. In accordance with the best practices encouraged by the Smithsonian National Museum of the American Indian, I have adopted the accented spelling as it appears to be "the terminology the members of the community use to describe themselves collectively." For best practices, see "The Impact of Words And Tips for Using Appropriate Terminology: Am I Using The Right Word?," National Museum of the American Indian, Smithsonian, https://americanindian.si.edu/nk360/informational/impact-words-tips. For examples of earlier spellings, see Thomas Strangeways, *Sketch of the Mosquito Shore, Including the Territory of Poyais, Descriptive of the Country; With Some Information as to Its Productions, the Best Mode of Culture, &c. Chiefly Intended for the Use of Settlers* (Edinburgh, 1822), 4; Michael D. Olien, "Miskito Kings and the Line of Succession," *Journal of Anthropological Research* 39, no. 2 (Summer 1983): 198–241; and Damien Clavel, "The Rise and Fall of George Frederic Augustus II: The Central American, Caribbean, and Atlantic Life of a Miskitu King, 1805–1824," *Business History Review* 96 (Autumn 2022): 525–58. For use of "Miskitú," see "Urgent Letter from The Indigenous Miskitu and Mayangnas People of Nicaragua to the OAS and Mr. Luis Almagro, its Secretary General," *Revista Abril*, 14 June 2021, https://revistaabril.org/urgent-letter-from-the-indigenous-miskitu-and-mayangnas-people-of-nicaragua-to-the-oas-and-mr-luis-almagro-its-secretary-general/; and "Archivo Mesoamericano," Center for Latin American and Caribbean Studies, Indiana University Bloomington, https://clacs.indiana.edu/research/archivo-meso.html.

14. While there is a growing literature on the Miskitú nation, whose centuries-long interaction with British subjects produced significant documentation, few scholarly works study the Rama nation. Exceptions include Gerald Riverstone, *Living in the Land of Our Ancestors: Rama Indian and Creole Territory in Caribbean Nicaragua* (Managua: ASDI, 2004); and *El Pueblo Rama: Luchando por Tierra y Cultura/The Rama People: Struggling for Land and Culture*, ed. Miguel Gonzales et al. (Managua: URACCAN, 2006).

15. "Plano Ideal," MPK 1/53, TNA.

16. For biological diversity, see Lynn Foster, *A Brief History of Central America*, 2nd ed. (New York: Facts On File, 2007), 3.

17. Juan Jose Quiñones and Demetrio del Castillo to Charles Burk, 29 Mar. 1824, EBFP.

18. Thomas Russell Lill, *National Debt of Mexico: History and Present Status* (New York, 1919), 12; Philip Frederick Flemion, "Manuel José Arce and the Formation of the Federal

Republic of Central America" (PhD diss., University of Florida, 1969), 88; and Jordana Dym, *From Sovereign Villages to Nation States: City, State, and Federation in Central America, 1759–1839* (Albuquerque: University of New Mexico Press, 2006), 193.

19. Manuel Antonio de la Cerda to Pedro Molina, 20 July 1823, in Franco Cerutti, "Documentos sobre el Proyecto del Canal por Nicaragua," *Revista del Pensamiento Centroamericano* 172-73 (July–Dec. 1981): 100-105, 101, translated for author by James Irving; Henry Dunn, *Guatimala* (New York: G. & C. Carvill, 1828), 180; and Flemion, "Manuel José Arce," 91. "Guatimala" was a common spelling of Guatemala in this era. As much as possible, I have preserved the orthography and punctuation of the original text.

20. "A.N.C, Secion del 7 de Nov.," in Cerutti, "Documentos," 102.

21. José del Valle probably borrowed the map, which featured in his anti-canal speeches; he may have shown it to the British agent who created the colorful copy. George Alexander Thompson, *Narrative of an Official Visit to Guatemala from Mexico* (London: John Murray, 1829), 202–4, 208–11; and José del Valle and Jorge del Valle Matheu, eds., *Obras de José Cecilio del Valle* (Guatemala City, 1929), 1:134, translated for author by James Irving.

22. "Plano Ideal," MPK 1/53, TNA.

23. In his published travel memoirs, the British diplomat included a regional map with a small, black and white inset of the western portion of the "Plano Ideal." Jordana Dym, "Initial Boundaries," *Mapping Latin America: A Cartographic Reader*, eds. Jordana Dym and Karl Offen (Chicago: University of Chicago Press, 2011), 144–47.

24. Juan Jose Quiñones and Demetrio del Castillo to Charles Burk, 29 Mar. 1824, EBFP.

25. "Plano Ideal," NA2.

26. Brockmann, *Science of Useful Nature*, 194–229.

27. Jon Lee Anderson, "The Comandante's Canal," *The New Yorker* (10 Mar. 2014): 50–69.

28. In *The Nicaragua Route*, David I. Folkman Jr. devotes two pages to Spanish interest in a canal and two paragraphs to 1820s proposals before jumping to the 1840s. David McCullough dismisses early nineteenth-century canal proposals as "hopelessly unrealistic if not preposterous" (32). His study quickly jumps to the 1840s and then the late nineteenth century. Similarly, Walter LaFeber pauses for only three sentences to consider US canal plans in 1825–26 before jumping to later eras. In the Spanish-language literature, Frances Kinloch Tijerino briefly discusses 1820s canal debates as part of a larger exploration of the significance of the potential waterway for Nicaraguan history. David I. Folkman Jr., *The Nicaragua Route* (Salt Lake City: University of Utah Press, 1972), xi–xii, 13; David McCullough, *The Paths Between the Seas: The Creation of the Panama Canal, 1870–1914* (New York: Simon and Schuster, 1977), 32; Walter LaFeber, *The Panama Canal: The Crisis in Historical Perspective*, rev. ed. (New York: Oxford University Press, 1989), 7–8; and Frances Kinloch Tijerino, *El Imaginario del Canal y la Nación Cosmpolita: Nicaragua, Siglo XIX* (Managua: IHNCA-UCS, 2015), 181–83. An article-length exception is Jose Maria Herrera, "The Rise and Fall of a Speculative Bubble: Geostrategic Concerns, Public Debate, and the Promotion of an American Trans-oceanic Canal in the 1820s," *American Nineteenth Century History* 19 (2018), no. 2: 131–58.

29. Writing about plans for a sea-level ship canal primarily in the twentieth century, Christine Keiner challenged historians to see the value in the history of "unbuilt mega-

projects." Christine Keiner, *Deep Cut: Science, Power, and the Unbuilt Interoceanic Canal* (Athens: University of Georgia Press, 2020), 3.

Chapter One

1. Norman H. Jensen, "Reproduction of the Bull Shark, *Carcharhinus leucas*, in the Lake Nicaragua-Rio San Juan System," *Investigations of the Icthyofauna of Nicaraguan Lakes* 40 (1976), https://digitalcommons.unl.edu/ichthynicar/40, 555.

2. Jensen, "Reproduction of the Bull Shark," 554–57; R. D. Pillans et al., "Environmental Influences on Long-Term Movement Patterns of a Euryhaline Elasmobranch (*Carcharhinus leucas*) within a Subtropical Estuary," *Estuaries and Coasts* 43 (2020): 2152–69, 2153. Brackish water may offer newborn bull sharks protection from non-euryhaline predators. Michelle R. Heupel et al., "Shark Nursery Areas: Concepts, Definition, Characterization and Assumptions," *Marine Ecology Progress Series* 337 (2007): 287–97, 293.

3. H. A. Lessios, "The Great American Schism: Divergence of Marine Organisms after the Rise of the Central American Isthmus," *Annual Review of Ecology, Evolution, and Systematics* 39 (2008): 63–91.

4. For dating the arrival of humans, see Lynn Foster, *A Brief History of Central America*, 2nd ed. (New York: Facts On File, 2007), 6–11.

5. Alexander von Humboldt, *Political Essay on the Kingdom of New Spain*, trans. John Black (London: Longman, Hurst, Rees, Orme, and Brown, 1811), 1:18.

6. Humboldt, *Political Essay* (1811), 1:24.

7. Humboldt, *Political Essay* (1811), 1:25.

8. Humboldt, *Political Essay* (1811), 1:24. Emphasis in original.

9. Damien Clavel, "The Rise and Fall of George Frederic Augustus II: The Central American, Caribbean, and Atlantic Life of a Miskitu King, 1805–1824," *Business History Review* 96 (Autumn 2022): 525–58, 535.

10. Frank Griffith Dawson, "The Evacuation of the Mosquito Shore and the English Who Stayed Behind, 1786–1800," *The Americas* 55, no. 1 (July 1998): 63–89, 64–65; Michael D. Olien, "Miskito Kings and the Line of Succession," *Journal of Anthropological Research* 39, no. 2 (Summer 1983): 198–241, 205; and Craig L. Dozier, *Nicaragua's Mosquito Shore: The Years of British and American Presence* (Tuscaloosa: University of Alabama Press, 1985), 13–15.

11. Dozier, *Nicaragua's Mosquito Shore*, 15; Olien, "Miskito Kings," 198–241; and Mary Helms, "Of Kings and Contexts: Ethnohistorical Interpretations of Miskito Political Structure and Function," *American Ethnologist* 13, no. 3 (1986): 506–23. The succession of Miskitú leadership did not depend on the British. Michael D. Olien, "Governor, General, and Admiral: Three Miskito Lines of Succession," *Ethnohistory* 45, no. 2 (Spring 1998): 277–318, 313.

12. Only authoritative at war, these men kept power by consulting Miskitú elders and distributing trade goods. Caroline A. Williams, "Living Between Empires: Diplomacy and Politics in the Late Eighteenth-Century Mosquitia," *The Americas* 70, no. 2 (2013): 237–68; Helms, "Of Kings," 506–23; and Olien, "Governor, General, and Admiral," 277–318.

13. Vincent Carretta, *Equiano, The African: Biography of a Self-Made Man* (New York: Penguin, 2005), 181.

14. Olien traces the "often stated view that the Miskito kings were nothing but puppets of the British" to US diplomat E. G. Squier, who diminished the sovereignty of the

Miskitú to support his canal negotiations with Nicaragua. The British referred to "Mosquitia" as an "independent political entity." Olien, "Miskito Kings," 220, 224, 228.

15. Olaudah Equiano, *The Interesting Narrative of the Life of Olaudah Equiano, or Gustavus Vassa, the African, Written by Himself*, ed. Werner Sollors (New York: W.W. Norton, 2001), 155; Olien, "Miskito Kings," 212; and Carretta, *Equiano*, 180.

16. Equiano, *Interesting Narrative*, 154–55; and Olien, "Miskito Kings," 211–12.

17. Olien, "General, Governor, and Admiral," 279.

18. Equiano, *Interesting Narrative*, 155.

19. Williams, "Living Between Empires," 238.

20. Equiano, *Interesting Narrative*, 157. Although unnamed by Equiano, the leader was Governor Colvill Briton, who was eventually hanged. Olien, "General, Governor, and Admiral," 300–301.

21. In the seventeenth century, English buccaneers ascended the river and raided Spanish cities on the lake's western shore. Before earthquakes reconfigured the river's rapids, pirates sailed up to Granada; afterward, the invaders ascended by canoe. In the eighteenth century, the British military and Miskitú allies mounted attacks that resulted in the on-and-off British occupation of the mouth of the river for decades. Williams, "San Juan River," 56–73.

22. Williams, "San Juan River," 74; and Dziennik, "The Miskitu," 155–79.

23. Dziennik, "The Miskitu," 169–71. One British leader sought a translator who spoke the Rama language. Linebaugh, *Red Round Globe*, 160.

24. Williams, "San Juan River," 76–79.

25. British officers used this pejorative term. Dziennik, "The Miskitu," 172–73.

26. Williams, "San Juan River," 79–80.

27. Dawson, "Evacuation," 66.

28. "Convention between His Britannick Majesty and the King of Spain. Signed at London, the 14th of July, 1786," quoted in Dawson, "Evacuation," 63.

29. Dawson, "Evacuation," 67–68.

30. Dawson, "Evacuation," 68–70, 87; and Williams, "Living Between Empires," 237–68.

31. George Henderson quoted in Dawson, "Evacuation," 88.

32. William Davis Robinson, *Memoirs of the Mexican Revolution: Including a Narrative of the Expedition of General Xavier Mina. With Some Observations on the Practicability of Opening a Commerce between the Pacific and Atlantic Oceans, Through the Mexican Isthmus in the Province of Oaxaca, and at the Lake of Nicaragua; and on the Future Importance of Such Commerce to the Civilized World, and More Especially to the United States* (Philadelphia, 1820), 339. Robinson's book appeared in a two-volume edition in London the next year. William Davis Robinson, *Memoirs of the Mexican Revolution: Including a Narrative of the Expedition of General Xavier Mina. With Some Observations on the Practicability of Opening a Commerce between the Pacific and Atlantic Oceans, Through the Mexican Isthmus in the Province of Oaxaca, and at the Lake of Nicaragua; and on the Future Importance of Such Commerce to the Civilized World, and More Especially to the United States*, 2 Vols. (London: Lackington, Hughes, Harding, Mavor, & Lepard, 1821), 2:264.

33. Robinson, *Memoirs* (1820), 340. Emphasis in original.

34. Robinson, *Memoirs* (1820), 346.

35. Robinson, *Memoirs* (1820), 347.

36. On the Rama, canoes, and sharks, see Riverstone, *Living in the Land*, 13.

37. Robinson, *Memoirs* (1820), 347.

38. Robinson, *Memoirs* (1820), 348. Emphasis in original.

39. Robinson, *Memoirs* (1820), 348–49. Emphasis in original.

40. Robinson, *Memoirs* (1820), 349. Emphasis in original.

41. Robinson, *Memoirs* (1820), 350.

42. Robinson, *Memoirs* (1820), 350–51.

43. Olien, "Miskito Kings," 214.

44. Lady Nugent quoted in Olien, "Miskito Kings," 216.

45. Olien, "Miskito Kings," 216.

46. Orlando W. Roberts, *Narrative of Voyages and Excursions on the East Coast and in the Interior of Central America* (Edinburgh, 1827), 133.

47. Olien, "General, Governor, and Admiral," 292, 301–2, 307–8; and Olien, "Miskito Kings," 218.

48. Damian Clavel, "What's in a Fraud? The Many Worlds of Gregor MacGregor, 1817–1824," *Enterprise and Society* 22, no. 4 (Dec. 2021): 997–1036, 1009–10.

49. Clavel similarly interprets King George Frederic as seeking to consolidate power at home and to achieve recognition of his sovereignty abroad. Clavel, "Rise and Fall" (2022), 525–58. See also the forthcoming translation of Damien Clavel, *Créer Un Pays, le Royaume de Poyais: Gregor MacGregor, Emprunts d'État et Fraude Financière 1820–1824* (Neuchâtel: Éditions Livreo-Alphil, 2022).

50. Robinson, *Memoirs* (1820), 351.

51. Robinson, *Memoirs* (1820), 351.

52. Jeremy Bentham, *The Works of Jeremy Bentham: Published Under the Supervision of His Executor John Bowring* (London: William Tait, 1843), 2:561. Suggesting the plan was written before June 1822, Miriam Williford notes the difficulty of determining "when Bentham began to develop his canal project." Miriam Williford, *Jeremy Bentham on Spanish America: An Account of His Letters and Proposals to the New World* (Baton Rouge: Louisiana State University Press, 1980), 94.

53. Bentham, *Works*, 2:561. Williford points out that Robinson favored a canal through the Isthmus of Tehuantepec, but Bentham presented him as promoting only the Nicaragua route. Williford, *Jeremy Bentham*, 94–95.

54. Jeremy Bentham to Bernardino Rivadavia, 13–15 June 1822, Catherine Fuller, ed., *The Correspondence of Jeremy Bentham* (Oxford: Clarendon Press, 2000), 11:112.

55. F. Rosen, "Jeremy Bentham (1748–1832)," *Oxford Dictionary of National Biography*, (Oxford: Oxford University Press, 2004), https://doi.org/10.1093/ref:odnb/2153. The Hermitage's location is now the headquarters of the Ministry of Justice. Tim Causer, "New Online Publication: 'A Visit (in 1831) to Jeremy Bentham', by George Wheatley" (18 Feb. 2015), https://blogs.ucl.ac.uk/bentham-project/2015/02/18/new-online-publication-a-visit-in-1831-to-jeremy-bentham-by-george-wheatley/.

56. Jeremy Bentham to Francis Hall, 17 May 1822, Fuller, 11: 75–81; Jeremy Bentham to Thomas Foley, 5 June 1822, Fuller, *Correspondence*, 11:91–93; and Williford, *Jeremy Bentham*, xiv.

57. Jeremy Bentham to José de San Martín, 31 May–6 June 1822, Fuller, *Correspondence*, 11:96. Emphasis in original.

58. Bentham to Rivadavia, 13–15 June 1822, Fuller, *Correspondence*, 11:112n6.

59. Bentham, *Works*, 2:569.

60. Bentham, *Works*, 2:568.

61. Bentham, *Works*, 2:568–69.

62. Bentham, *Works*, 2:567. Emphasis in original.

63. Bentham, *Works*, 2:565.

64. Bentham, *Works*, 2:562. Emphasis in original.

65. Jill Lepore, *The Name of War: King Philip's War and the Origins of American Identity* (New York: Alfred A. Knopf, 1998), 165.

66. Bentham, *Works*, 2:563. Emphasis in original.

67. Bentham, *Works*, 2:568.

68. Bentham, *Works*, 2:562.

69. Bentham, *Works*, 2:567.

70. Bentham, *Works*, 2:569, 2:563.

71. Bentham, *Works*, 2:567.

72. Bentham, *Works*, 2:563.

73. Bentham to Foley, 5 June 1822, Fuller, *Correspondence*, 11:92n8; and Bentham to Rivadavia, 13–15 June 1822, Fuller, *Correspondence*, 11:115–17.

74. "Grant of Land by George Frederic, King of the Mosquito Nation, Caribbean, to Sir Gregor MacGregor," 29 Apr. 1820, LBGA; and Clavel, "Rise and Fall" (2022), 525–58.

75. Clavel calculates the land as "more than thirty-three thousand square kilometers." Clavel, "What's in a Fraud?," 1006. For more on the network of mercenaries involved with George Frederic, see Vanessa Mongey, *Rogue Revolutionaries: The Fight for Legitimacy in the Greater Caribbean* (Philadelphia: University of Pennsylvania Press, 2020).

76. Robert A. Naylor, *Penny Ante Imperialism: The Mosquito Shore and the Bay of Honduras, 1600–1914, A Case Study in British Informal Empire* (Rutherford, NJ: Farleigh Dickinson University Press, 1989), 80.

77. Matthew Brown, "Inca, Sailor, Soldier, King: Gregor MacGregor and the Early Nineteenth-Century Caribbean," *Bulletin of Latin American Research* 24, no. 1 (2005): 44–70, 45–46; and Clavel, "What's in a Fraud?," 1004–5. For footloose Napoleonic veterans more broadly, see Rafe Blaufarb, *Bonapartists in the Borderlands: French Exiles and Refugees on the Gulf Coast, 1815–1835* (Tuscaloosa: University of Alabama Press, 2005); Mongey, *Rogue Revolutionaries*; and Moises Enrique Rodriguez, *Freedom's Mercenaries: British Volunteers in the Wars of Independence of Latin America*, 2 vols. (New York: Hamilton Books, 2006).

78. For Miskitú influences on the region's maps, see Karl H. Offen, "Creating Mosquitia: Mapping Amerindian Spatial Practices in Eastern Central America, 1629–1779," *Journal of Historical Geography* 33 (2007): 254–82.

79. Sophie Brockmann, *The Science of Useful Nature in Central America: Landscapes, Networks, and Practical Enlightenment, 1784–1838* (New York: Cambridge University Press, 2020), 123.

80. "Grant of Land by George Frederic, King of the Mosquito Nation, Caribbean, to Sir Gregor MacGregor," 29 Apr. 1820, LBGA.

81. Note, "Grant of Land by George Frederic, King of the Mosquito Nation, Caribbean, to Sir Gregor MacGregor," 29 Apr. 1820, LBGA. The note references Thomas Jefferys,

A Complete Pilot for the West-Indies, Including the British Channel, Bay of Biscay, and all the Atlantic Islands (London: Robert Laurie and James Whittle, 1795), chart 18.

82. Jefferys, *A Complete Pilot*, chart 8, 18. It was a large territory that appears even wider and larger when the coordinates are charted on a modern map. Clavel, "What's in a Fraud?," Figure 1, 1007.

83. Roberts, *Narrative*, 164.

84. Since at least the early eighteenth century, Miskitù leaders had been enslaving Poyais people—also described as Pech, Paya, or Poyer. Olien, "General, Governor, and Admiral," 285, 291, 293–94; and Karl Offen, "Mapping Amerindian Captivity in Colonial Mosquitia," *Journal of Latin American Geography* 14, no. 3 (Oct. 2015): 35–65, 44. For harvesting and uses of sarsaparilla, see Thomas Strangeways, *Sketch of the Mosquito Shore, Including the Territory of Poyais, Descriptive of the Country; With Some Information as to Its Productions, the Best Mode of Culture, &c. Chiefly Intended for the Use of Settlers* (Edinburgh, 1822), 131–33.

85. "Grant of Land by George Frederic, King of the Mosquito Nation, Caribbean, to Sir Gregor MacGregor," 29 Apr. 1820, LBGA.

86. "Grant of Land by George Frederic, King of the Mosquito Nation, Caribbean, to Sir Gregor MacGregor," 29 Apr. 1820, LBGA.

87. Quoted in David Sinclair, *The Land that Never Was: Sir Gregor MacGregor and the Most Audacious Fraud in History* (Cambridge, MA: Da Capo, 2004), 33.

88. Strangeways, *Sketch*, 3.

89. Strangeways, *Sketch*, vi.

90. Strangeways, *Sketch*, 4.

91. Strangeways, *Sketch*, 31.

92. Strangeways, *Sketch*, 38, 31.

93. Strangeways, *Sketch*, 32.

94. In 1824, the king issued a grant of land at Bluefields near the San Juan River to a pair of British adventurers. Naylor, *Penny Ante*, 80.

95. Strangeways, *Sketch*, 33.

96. Strangeways, *Sketch*, 353.

97. José María del Barrio to Jeremy Bentham, 19 Nov. 1823, Fuller, *Correspondence*, 11:317.

98. Barrio to Bentham, 18 Nov. 1823, Fuller, *Correspondence*, 11:315.

99. Barrio to Bentham, 18 Nov. 1823, Fuller, *Correspondence*, 11:316.

100. Barrio to Bentham, 19 Nov. 1823, Fuller, *Correspondence*, 11:317.

101. Jeremy Bentham to Richard Rush, 4 Dec. 1823, Fuller, *Correspondence*, 11:329.

102. Richard Rush to Jeremy Bentham, 16 Jan. 1824, Fuller, *Correspondence*, 11:337–38.

103. Rush to Bentham, 17 Jan. 1824, Fuller, *Correspondence*, 11:339.

104. Richard Rush to John Quincy Adams, 19 Jan. 1824, 6 Feb. 1824, 9 Feb. 1824, 10 Feb. 1824, R26, M30, Despatches from U.S. Ministers to Great Britain, 1791–1906, RG59, NA2, accessed online, https://catalog.archives.gov/id/188519055.

105. Sinclair, *Land that Never Was*, 65, 38–40.

106. "Poyais Loan," *Liverpool Mercury* (England), 1 Nov. 1822.

107. *Morning Chronicle* (London), 23 Aug. 1823; and "Poyais Loan," *Morning Chronicle* (London), 14 Nov. 1822.

108. "Poyais Loan," *Morning Chronicle* (London), 14 Nov. 1822.

109. "Poyais Settlement," *Caledonian Mercury* (Edinburgh), 4 Sept. 1823.

110. "Poyais Settlement," *Caledonian Mercury* (Edinburgh), 4 Sept. 1823.

111. Frank Griffith Dawson, *The First Latin American Debt Crisis: The City of London and the 1822–25 Loan Bubble* (New Haven: Yale University Press, 1990), 41; "The King of Con-Men," *Economist* (22 Dec. 2012); and Sinclair, *Land that Never Was*. For a debunking of this reputation, see Clavel, "What's in a Fraud?."

Chapter Two

1. "A List of the Officers of His Majesty's Royal Marine Forces, on Full and Half Pay; with an Index" (London, 1822), ADM 192/13, TNA, 27; "John Bailey," UK Naval Officer and Rating Service Records, ADM 29/19, 291, TNA, accessed online through Ancestry.com; Domingo Juarros, *A Statistical and Commercial History of the Kingdom of Guatemala, in Spanish America: Containing Important Particulars Relative to its Productions, Manufactures, Customs, &c. &c. &c., with an Account of Its Conquest by the Spaniards, and a Narrative of the Principal Events down to the Present Time: From Original Records in the Archives; Actual Observation; and Other Authentic Sources*, trans. J. Baily (London: John Hearne, 1823); and Domingo Juarros, *Compendio de la Historia de la Ciudad de Guatemala*, 2 vols. (Guatemala: Ignacio Beteta, 1808, 1810).

2. Juarros, *Statistical and Commercial History*, iii.

3. Leland Jenks, *The Migration of British Capital to 1875* (New York: Alfred A. Knopf, 1927), 47. In 2024, £17.5 million would be worth more than £1.3 billion. "Inflation Calculator," Bank of England, www.bankofengland.co.uk/monetary-policy/inflation/inflation-calculator.

4. Juarros, *Statistical and Commercial History*, iii.

5. Baily's dedication is dated "Kennington, January, 1823." Juarros, *Statistical and Commercial History*, iii.

6. Juarros, *Statistical and Commercial History*, v. A review of recent works that included Baily's translation lamented the scarcity of "authentic" publications on the region and reminded readers that Humboldt's "researches were concluded more than twenty years ago." "Mexico," *The Quarterly Review* 30 (Oct. 1823): 151–84.

7. Juarros, *Statistical and Commercial History*, iii.

8. Juarros, *Statistical and Commercial History*, i; and *The Times* (London), 15 Apr. 1823. According to the British National Archives' currency converter, an unskilled laborer in 1820 worked for about five days to earn sixteen shillings; www.nationalarchives.gov.uk/currency-converter/. "New Guatemala" was another name for Guatemala City, which had replaced an earlier colonial capital of the same name that suffered from destructive earthquakes.

9. Juarros, *Statistical and Commercial History*, 323; and Brockman, *Science of Useful Nature*, 150–51.

10. Juarros, *Statistical and Commercial History*, 51.

11. Juarros, *Statistical and Commercial History*, 62.

12. Juarros, *Statistical and Commercial History*, 346.

13. For the development of nationalism as tied to Spanish American independence, see Benedict Anderson, *Imagined Communities: Reflections on the Origin and Spread of Nationalism*, rev. ed. (New York: Verso, 2006, 1983), 47–65.

14. Ron Pattinson, "Barclay, Perkins & Co.," *The Oxford Companion to Beer*, ed. Garrett Oliver (New York: Oxford University Press, 2012), 84. David's father, Robert Barclay, was

from a branch of the family that had moved to Pennsylvania in the early eighteenth century; in 1763, as a boy of twelve, Robert arrived in London and entered the family banking businesses. Margaret Ackrill and Leslie Hannah, *Barclays: The Business of Banking, 1690–1996* (Cambridge: Cambridge University Press, 2001), 36–7.

15. "Mexican Loan," *The Morning Chronicle* (London), 16 Jan. 1824; Howard Spencer, "Barclay, David (1784–1861), of Gloucester Place, Portman Square, Mdx.," *The History of Parliament: The House of Commons, 1820–1832*, ed. D. R. Fisher (Cambridge: Cambridge University Press, 2009), accessed online, www.historyofparliamentonline.org/volume/1820-1832/member/barclay-david-1784-1861; and Richard Roberts and David Kynaston, eds., *The Bank of England: Money, Power and Influence, 1694–1994* (Oxford: Clarendon Press, 1995), Appendix 2, 265. David Barclay's eldest brother headed "Barclay, Tritton, and Co.," a forerunner of the current Barclays conglomerate.

16. Dawson, *First Latin American Debt Crisis*, 26–7.

17. Eliga H. Gould, *Among the Powers of the Earth: The American Revolution and the Making of a New World Empire* (Cambridge, MA: Harvard University Press, 2012), 2–3.

18. Dawson, *First Latin American Debt Crisis*, 20, 32; and Trevor Jackson, *Impunity and Capitalism: The Afterlives of European Financial Crises, 1690–1830* (Cambridge: Cambridge University Press, 2022), 219–59.

19. Dawson, *First Latin American Debt Crisis*, 28.

20. Dawson, *First Latin American Debt Crisis*, 30.

21. For wages, see "Currency Converter: 1270–2017," TNA, www.nationalarchives.gov.uk/currency-converter/. £100,000 in 1822 equates to roughly £10 million in 2024. "Inflation Calculator," Bank of England, www.bankofengland.co.uk/monetary-policy/inflation/inflation-calculator.

22. "Mexican Loan," *The Morning Chronicle* (London), 16 Jan. 1824.

23. For "Charles Herring the younger," Richard Jaffray, and John Potter's partnership in BHRC, see Thompson v. Barclay, c13/883/49, TNA. For the elder Herring and Jaffray's work together in support of Spanish American liberation, see Matthew Brown, "Impious Adventurers? Mercenaries, Honour, and Patriotism in the Wars of Independence in Gran Colombia" (PhD diss., University of London, 2004), 55. Christopher Richardson's father may have been William Richardson, who was an auditor of the Colombian Association for Agricultural and Other Purposes along with David Barclay and Richard Jaffray. This directorship also included Colombian loan contractors Charles Herring, William Graham, and J. D. Powels as well as B. A. Goldschmidt, BHRC's competitor for Mexican debt. Barclay's brother's house served as the organization's bankers. Brown, "Imperious Adventurers," 51; and "Mexican Loan," *The Morning Chronicle* (London), 16 Jan. 1824.

24. Francisco Borja de Migoni to Emperor Iturbide, quoted in Dawson, *First Latin American Debt Crisis*, 69.

25. "Law Intelligence," *Morning Chronicle* (London), 7 July 1823.

26. "Law Intelligence," *Morning Chronicle* (London), 22 Dec. 1823.

27. Jones v. Garcia del Rio, George Turner and James Russell, *Reports of Cases Argued and Determined in the High Court of Chancery During the Time of Lord Chancellor Eldon* (London: Saunders and Benning, 1832), 1:299.

28. "Law Intelligence," *Morning Chronicle* (London), 13 Feb. 1823.

29. Dawson, *First Latin American Debt Crisis*, 35.

30. "Appointment of Consuls to the Spanish American States," *Caledonian Mercury* (Edinburgh), 23 Oct. 1823.

31. Only four days after Emperor Iturbide's coronation, the Mexican Congress authorized a loan, but this deal fell through with significant financial consequences in Mexico but little effect in London. Richard J. Salvucci, *Politics, Markets, and Mexico's "London Debt," 1823–1887* (New York: Cambridge University Press, 2009), 29–31, 60–61.

32. For accounts of Mexico's loans of the 1820s, see Salvucci, *Politics*, 28–99; and Dawson, *First Latin American Debt Crisis*, 69–72. For colonial era Anglo Mexican financial relations, see Guadalupe Jiménez Codinach, *La Gran Bretaña y la Independencia de México, 1808–1821* (México: Fondo de Cultura Económica, 1991).

33. Matías Romero, "British Investors and the Real Del Monte Mine: Mexico, 1824–1848," *Foreign Investment in Latin America: Cases and Attitudes*, ed. Marvin D. Bernstein (New York: Alfred A. Knopt, 1966), 73; and "Correspondence 1820s," Folder 93, G. G. Manning and Mackintosh Collection, BLAC, translated for author by James Irving.

34. Freshfield, Kaye, and Freshfield to Marshall and Manning, 9 Apr. 1825, Folder 93, "Correspondence 1820s," Manning and Mackintosh Collection, BLAC.

35. "Friday and Saturday's Posts," *Manchester Mercury* (England), 3 Feb. 1824.

36. Larry Neal, "The Financial Crisis of 1825 and the Restructuring of the British Financial System," *Federal Reserve Bank of St. Louis Review* (May/June 1998): 53–76, 64. This translates to as much as two trillion pounds in 2024. "Purchasing Power of British Pounds from 1270 to Present," MeasuringWorth, www.measuringworth.com/calculators/ppoweruk/.

37. For the history of joint stock companies, see James Taylor, *Creating Capitalism: Joint-Stock Enterprise in British Politics and Culture, 1800–1870* (Woodbridge: Boydell Press, 2006); and Philip J. Stern, *Empire, Incorporated: The Corporations that Built British Colonialism* (Cambridge, MA: Harvard University Press, 2023).

38. Neil Johnson, "The History of the Parliamentary Franchise," Research Paper 13/14, House of Commons Library (1 Mar. 2013), https://commonslibrary.parliament.uk/research-briefings/rp13-14/.

39. "Imperial Parliament of Great Britain and Ireland," *Morning Chronicle* (London), 24 Feb. 1825.

40. "Imperial Parliament of Great Britain and Ireland," *Morning Chronicle* (London), 24 Feb. 1825.

41. "The Funds," *The Morning Chronicle* (London), 8 Mar. 1825.

42. "The Funds," *The Morning Chronicle* (London), 8 Mar. 1825. The Atlantic and Pacific Canal Company, Grand Junction Canal Company, and Junction Canal Company could all be found in lists of the era's joint-stock companies. Henry English, *A Complete View of the Joint Stock Companies Formed during the years 1824 and 1825* (London, 1827), 12, 20.

43. "Miscellanea," *Manchester Mercury* (England), 19 Apr. 1825.

44. The General Constituent Assembly announced the draft of its constitution on 22 Nov. 1824. Hector Perez-Brignoli, *A Brief History of Central America*, trans. Ricardo B. Sawrey A. and Susana Strettri de Sawrey (Berkeley: University of California Press, 1989), 67.

45. George Alexander Thompson, *Narrative of an Official Visit to Guatemala from Mexico* (London: John Murray, 1829), 197.

46. Freshfield, Kaye, and Freshfield to Marshall and Manning, 9 Apr. 1825, Folder 93, "Correspondence 1820s," G. G. Manning and Mackintosh Collection, BLAC.

47. Thompson, *Narrative*, 138.

48. "Puertos," *Gaceta del Gobierno Supremo de Guatemala* (Guatemala City), 9 Apr. 1825, 315.

49. Thompson, *Narrative*, 138.

50. *A Brief Memoir of the Life of James Wilson (Late of Edinburgh), with Extracts from his Journal and Correspondence, Written, Chiefly, during a Residence in Guatemala, the Capital of Central America* (London, 1829), 61.

51. Edwin Hodder, *George Fife Angas: Father and Founder of South Australia* (London: Hodder and Stoughton, 1891), 38, 40.

52. Frederick Crowe, *The Gospel in Central America* (London, 1850), 328–29, 448.

53. Hodder, *George Fife Angas*, 39–40.

54. Crowe, *Gospel in Central America*, 329.

55. *Brief Memoir of the Life of James Wilson*, 114.

56. Hodder, *George Fife Angas*, 40.

57. Hodder, *George Fife Angas*, 40.

58. For the list of "casas inglesas y norte-americanas," see Alejandro Marure, *Memoria Historica sobre el Canal de Nicaragua* (Guatemala, 1845), 13.

59. Thompson, *Narrative*, 193.

60. Thompson, *Narrative*, 266.

61. *Times* (London), 19 Aug. 1825; and Dawson, *First Latin American Debt Crisis*, 109.

62. Dawson, *First Latin American Debt Crisis*, 109.

63. "London, Saturday, April 9," *Salisbury and Winchester Journal* (England), 11 Apr. 1825.

64. *Bath Chronicle and Weekly Gazette* (England), 14 Apr. 1825.

65. "City, Saturday," *Morning Chronicle* (London), 11 Apr. 1825.

Chapter Three

1. JQADD, vol. 35, 24 Mar. 1824.

2. Daniel Walker Howe, *What Hath God Wrought: The Transformation of America, 1815–1848* (New York: Oxford University Press, 2007), 93.

3. JQADD, vol. 35, 7 May 1823. For Savage's genealogy, see Lawrence Park, *Major Thomas Savage of Boston and His Descendants* (Boston, 1914), 36.

4. Jessica M. Lepler, "Introduction: The Panic of 1819 by Any Other Name," *Journal of the Early Republic* 40, no. 4 (2020): 665–70.

5. W. H. Savage to Charles Savage, 25 June 1822, Folder 12, Box 4, Savage and Company Records, 1820–1822 (Ms. N-882), MHS; and W. H. Savage to Charles Savage, 28 June 1822, Folder 12, Box 4, Savage & Co., MHS. A Meskwaki delegate sought to protect the mines in the treaty negotiations of August 1824. Pee-mash-ka Speech, "Ratified treaty no. 121, documents relating to the negotiation of the treaty of August 4, 1824, with the Sauk and Fox Indians," Digital Collection, University of Wisconsin-Madison Libraries, http://digital.library.wisc.edu/1711.dl/History.IT1824no121. For the lead rush, see Lucy Eldersveld Murphy, "'Their Women Quite Industrious Miners:' Native American Lead Mining in the Upper Mississippi Valley, 1788–1832," *Enduring Nations: Native Americans in the Midwest*, ed. R. David Edmunds (Urbana: University of Illinois Press, 2008), 36–53; and Christina Snyder, *Great Crossings: Indians, Settlers, and Slaves in the Age of Jackson* (New York: Oxford University Press, 2017), 49–50.

6. JQADD, vol. 35, 8 May 1823.

7. JQADD, vol. 34, 26 June 1823.

8. Henry Ammon, "Monroe, James (28 April 1758–04 July 1831), Fifth President of the United States," *American National Biography* (2000), https://doi.org/10.1093/anb/9780198606697.article.0300338.

9. Jonathan Elliot, *Diplomatic Code of the United States of America* (Washington, DC, 1827), 537.

10. Elliot, *Diplomatic Code*, 537, 539, 550.

11. Individuals in need of consular assistance paid these fees. Elliot, *Diplomatic Code*, 537; and "In Senate of the United States, May 4, 1826," S. Rep. 88, 19th Cong., 1st Sess. (1826), 15–21.

12. Elliot, *Diplomatic Code*, 540.

13. Elliot, *Diplomatic Code*, 539, 549.

14. S. Rep. 88, 19th Cong., 1st Sess. (1826), 15–21; and Charles Stuart Kennedy, *The American Consul: A History of the United States Consular Service, 1776–1914* (New York: Greenwood Press, 1990), 1–4, 7, 51–70.

15. Nicole M. Phelps, "A Brief Introduction to the U.S. Consular Service," accessed 31 Oct. 2019, http://blog.uvm.edu/nphelps/a-brief-introduction-to-the-us-consular-service/.

16. Kennedy, *American Consul*, 58.

17. JQADD, vol. 35, 7 May 1823; vol. 34, 26 June 1823.

18. JQADD, vol. 35, 5 Mar. 1824.

19. JQADD, vol. 35, 19 Mar. 1824.

20. Charles Savage to John Quincy Adams, 25 Mar. 1824, R15, M439, RG59, NA2.

21. JQADD, vol. 35, 26 Mar. 1824; and Savage to Adams, 30 Mar. 2024, R15, M439, RG59, NA2.

22. JQADD, vol. 35, 30 Mar. 1824, 1 Apr. 1824.

23. JQADD, vol. 35, 1 Apr. 1824; and Savage to Adams, 30 Mar. 2024, R15, M439, RG59, NA2.

24. Savage to Adams, 30 Mar. 2024, R15, M439, RG59, NA2.

25. JQADD, vol. 35, 5 Apr. 1824.

26. JQADD, vol. 35, 6 Apr. 1824.

27. JQADD, vol. 35, 9 Apr. 1824.

28. JQADD, vol. 35, 10 Apr. 1824.

29. Park, *Major Thomas Savage*, 36.

30. JQADD, vol. 35, 12 Apr. 1824.

31. JQADD, vol. 35, 12 Apr. 1824.

32. JQADD, vol. 35, 13 Apr. 1824.

33. *Journal of the Executive Proceeding of the Senate of the United States of America* (Washington, DC, 1828), 3:370, 3:372.

34. Marcial Zebadúa to Charles Savage, 28 Feb. 1825, Vol. 87, RG84, NA2.

35. Adams to Savage, 25 June 1824, R2, M78, RG59, NA2.

36. Adams to Savage, 25 June 1824, R2, M78, RG59, NA2.

37. Savage to Adams, 15 July 1824, R1, T337, RG59, NA2.

38. For age, see Savage to Lemuel Shaw, 13 Apr. 1839, SPSP.

39. Despatch 1, 6 Mar. 1825, Vol. 5, RG84, NA2.

40. Passport dated 21 Jan. 1825, Vol. 87, RG84, NA2; and Marcial Zebadúa to Charles Savage, 21 Feb. 1825, Vol. 87, RG84, NA2.

41. Charles Savage to Hope Savage, 2 Apr. 1825, SPSP. For the relationship between Henry and Charles, see John Williams to Henry Clay, 15 June 1826, R2, M219, RG59, NA2.

42. Marcial Zebadúa to Charles Savage, 21 Feb. 1825, Vol. 87, RG84, NA2.

43. Zebadúa to Savage, 28 Feb. 1825, Vol. 87, RG84, NA2.

44. Elliot, *Diplomatic Code*, 540.

45. JQADD, vol. 35, 6 Apr. 1824. Mann previously had been recommended for a diplomatic post in Colombia. JQADD, vol. 35, 11 Mar. 1824; and "Thomas N. Mann," R11, M439, RG59, NA2.

46. "Thomas N. Mann," R11, M439, RG59, NA2.

47. Adams to Mann, 21 Apr. 1824, R2, M78, RG59, NA2.

48. William S. Powell, "Mann, Thomas Nicholson," NCpedia, www.ncpedia.org/biography/mann-thomas-nicholson.

49. JQADD, vol. 34, 11 May 1824.

50. JQADD, vol. 34, 11 May 1824.

51. "Paralelos y Biografias," *Estudios Historicos* (San Salvador: Imprenta Nacional, 1941), 50–53.

52. "Act of the Congress of St. Salvador de Guatemala," in William R. Manning, ed., *Diplomatic Correspondence of the United States Concerning the Independence of the Latin-American Nations* (New York: Oxford University Press, 1925), 2:875.

53. Thomas L. Karnes, *The Failure of Union: Central America, 1824–1960* (Chapel Hill: University of North Carolina Press, 1961), 27; and "The New State," *Providence Patriot*, 7 May 1823. Flemion calls it "a pathetic gesture." Flemion, "Arce," 75. Dym argues that the declaration was emblematic of problems of nation-building in Central America. Jordana Dym, "Actas de Independencia: de la Capitanía General de Guatemala a la República Federal de Centroamérica," *Independencias, Estados, y Política(s) en la Centroamérica del Siglo XIX: Las Huellas Históricas del Bicentenario*, eds. David Díaz Arias and Ronny Viales Hurtado (San José, C.R.: Centro de Investigaciones Históricas de América Central, 2012), 3–24, 18.

54. "Manifesto of José Matías Delgado," in Manning, *Diplomatic Correspondence*, 2:878–79.

55. Manuel José de Arce and Juan Manuel Rodríguez to John Quincy Adams, 9 Sept. 1823, reproduced in Manning, *Diplomatic Correspondence*, 2:871. Some have suggested that for Arce this was a desperate flight from execution. "Paralelos y Biografias," 51.

56. *Farmer's Cabinet* (Amherst, NH), 17 May 1823; *Rhode-Island American* (Providence), 27 June 1823; and Flemion, "Arce," 55.

57. "Philadelphia, June 26," *New-Hampshire Sentinel* (Keene), 4 July 1823.

58. JQADD, vol. 34, 11 Sept. 1823.

59. Arce and Rodríguez to Adams, 9 Sept. 1823, in Manning, *Diplomatic Correspondence*, 2:871.

60. Arce and Rodríguez to Adams, 11 Sept. 1823, in Manning, *Diplomatic Correspondence*, 2:872.

61. The literature on the Monroe Doctrine is abundant but, to my knowledge, does not discuss the Salvadorans' mission. For examples, see William Earl Weeks, *Dimensions of the*

Early American Empire, 1754–1865, vol. 1 of *The New Cambridge History of American Foreign Relations*, ed. Warren I. Cohen (New York: Cambridge University Press, 2013), 114–20; and Ernest R. May, *The Making of the Monroe Doctrine* (Cambridge, MA: Harvard University Press, 1975), 65–131. The term "Monroe Doctrine" appeared later in the mid-nineteenth century. Jay Sexton, *The Monroe Doctrine: Empire and Nation in Nineteenth-Century America* (New York: Hill and Wang, 2011). For Spanish American contributions to later interpretations of the Monroe Doctrine, see Juan Pablo Scarfi, "In the Name of the Americas: The Pan-American Redefinition of the Monroe Doctrine and the Emerging Language of American International Law in the Western Hemisphere, 1898–1933," *Diplomatic History* 40, no. 2 (Apr. 2016): 189–218; and "Forum: The Monroe Doctrine at 200," *Diplomatic History* 47, no. 5 (Nov. 2023): 731–870.

62. Flemion, "Arce," 93.

63. JQADD, vol. 34, 11 May 1824.

64. JQADD, vol. 34, 14 May 1824, 20 May 1824.

65. Mann to Adams, 15 May 1824, R2, M219, RG59, NA2.

66. JQADD, vol. 34, 21 May 1824.

67. "Zebadúa, Marcial. Laws and Decrees, 17 y 19 de abril de 1824" (Decree abolishing slavery within the country), Folder 4, Box 1, Miscellaneous Broadsides, BLAC.

68. JQADD, vol. 34, 21 May 1824.

69. Mann to Adams, 2 July 1824, R2, M219, RG59, NA2.

70. Mann to Adams, 4 July 1824, R2, M219, RG59, NA2.

71. Mann to Adams, 4 July 1824, R2, M219, RG59, NA2.

72. Adams to Mann, 17 July 1824, R5, M77, RG59, NA2.

73. Daniel Brent to Beaufort R. Watts, 21 July 1824, R5, M77, RG59, NA2.

74. Mann to Adams, 4 July 1824, R2, M219, RG59, NA2.

75. Brent to Watts, 21 July 1824, R5, M77, RG59, NA2.

76. Savage to Zebadúa, 21 Mar. 1825, Vol. 87, RG84, NA2. In a later letter, he explicitly stated that assessing "the practicability of having a ship canal" was one of the purposes of his proposed trip. Savage to Clay, 28 Nov. 1826, Vol. 5, RG 84, NA2.

77. Charles Savage to Hope Savage, 2 Apr. 1825, SPSP.

78. Zebadúa to Savage, 5 Apr. 1825, Vol. 87, RG84, NA2.

Chapter Four

1. Christopher G. Collier, *Hydrometeorology* (Chichester, UK: John Wiley & Sons, 2016), 1–40.

2. Carolyn Hall and Héctor Pérez Brignoli, *Historical Atlas of Central America* (Norman: University of Oklahoma Press, 2003), 18.

3. Hall and Pérez Brignoli, *Historical Atlas of Central America*, 18.

4. Max Harrison Williams, "San Juan River—Lake Nicaragua Waterway, 1502–1921" (PhD diss., Louisiana State University, 1971), 19, 26.

5. Salvador Montenegro-Guillén, "Lake Cocibolca/Nicaragua," Paper presented at Lake Basin Management Initiative Regional Workshop for Europe, Central Asia, and the Americas, Saint Michael's College, VT (18–21 June 2003), 4–5, 12, http://arks.princeton.edu/ark:/88435/dsp015m60qr95q.

6. Nearly twenty feet of rain falls annually near the river. Riverstone, *Living in the Land of Our Ancestors*, 17, 28.

7. 11 Apr. 1825, EBJ.

8. Williams, "San Juan River," 60.

9. E. Bradford Burns, *Patriarch and Folk: The Emergence of Nicaragua, 1798–1858* (Cambridge, MA: Harvard University Press, 1991), 5–35.

10. "Plano Ideal," MPK 1/53, TNA; "Plano Ideal," NA2; and Juan Jose Quiñones and Demetrio del Castillo to Charles Burk, 29 Mar. 1824, EBFP. Florencio del Castillo had been born in Cartago, Costa Rica, educated in León, Nicaragua, and settled in Oaxaca, Mexico. He sat for Nicaragua in 1822. Mario Vázquez Olivera, *El Imperio Mexicano y el Reino de Guatemala: Proyecto Político y Campaña Militar, 1821–1823* (Mexico City: Fondo de Cultura Económica Universidad Nacional Autónoma de México), 127n13; and Nettie Lee Benson and Charles R. Berry, "The Central American Delegation to the First Constituent Congress of Mexico, 1822–1823," *Hispanic American Historical Review* 49, no. 4 (1969): 679–702.

11. For the Nicaraguan Civil War of 1823–24, see Esteban Duque Estrada Sacasa, *Nicaragua: Historia y Familias, 1821–1853* (Managua, 2001), 65–117; and Sara L. Barquero, *Gobernantes de Nicaragua, 1825–1947*, 2nd ed. (Managua, 1945), 27–36.

12. Franco Cerutti, "Documentos sobre el Proyecto del Canal por Nicaragua," *Revista del Pensamiento Centroamericano* 172-73 (July–Dec. 1981): 100-105, 103, translated for author by James Irving.

13. Cerutti, "Documentos," 105.

14. Quiñones and Castillo to Burk, 29 Mar. 1824, EBFP; Benson and Berry, "Central American Delegation," 679–702; and Beatriz Pérez Sánchez, "Demetrio Castillo," Real Academia de la Historia, https://dbe.rah.es/biografias/51952/demetrio-castillo.

15. For the enduring irony of needing foreign investment to achieve independence, see Frances Kinloch Tijerino, *El imaginario del canal y la nación cosmopolita: Nicaragua, Siglo XIX* (Managua: IHNCA-UCA, 2015).

16. Quiñones and Castillo to Burk, 29 Mar. 1824, EBFP. They were accompanied by Mateo Llanos, a Mexican soldier and author. "Art. VII," *Quarterly Review* 30, no. 59 (Oct. 1823): 177; Mateo Llanos, *Nuevo Establecimiento Nacional de Educacion* (Mexico City, 1821); and *The Recognition, the Loan, and the Colonization of Colombia* (London: Baldwin, Cradock, and Joy, 1822), 11–13.

17. Lyman Coleman, *Genealogy of the Lyman Family in Great Britain and America* (Albany, NY: J. Munsell, 1872), 290; "Notice," *The Repertory* (Boston), 9 May 1816; and "Notice," *The Repertory* (Boston), 29 May 1817.

18. "Domestic Official Papers," 19 Sept. 1807, *Cobbett's Political Register* (London) 12, supplement to no. 12: 464; and *Buenos Ayres: The Trial of Lieut. Gen. Whitelocke* (Dublin: M. Keene, 1808). Bourke was also spelled Bork, Burk, and Burke.

19. Quiñones and Castillo to Burk, 29 Mar. 1824, EBFP.

20. Quiñones and Castillo to Burk, 29 Mar. 1824, EBFP.

21. "From Mexico," *City Gazette* (Charleston, SC), 16 June 1824; and 1824 Baltimore Passenger List, R1, M596, RG36, NARA, *Baltimore, Passenger Lists, 1820–1948 and 1954–1957* database, accessed online through ancestry.com (Provo, UT: Ancestry.com, 2006).

22. Charles Bork to J. R. Poinsett, 28 Dec. 1825, Box 2, R153, Letters and correspondence, 1807–30, Poinsett (Joel Roberts) Papers, 1807–31, Dolph Briscoe Center for American History, University of Texas, Austin.

23. Robert Bolton, *Genealogical and Biographical Account of the Family of Bolton* (New York: John A. Gray, 1862), 114–20.

24. William M. Emery, *The Howland Heirs: Being the Story of a Family and a Fortune and the Inheritance of a Trust Established for Mrs. Hetty H. R. Green* (New Bedford, MA: E. Anthony & Sons, 1919), 395–96; and Howard Pell, ed., *Extracts from the Journal of Sarah Howland* (New York City, 1890), 10–13.

25. "Marine Journal," *New-York American*, 1 June 1824.

26. "Translator," *New-York American*, 12 Apr. 1824.

27. John H. Howland & Co and J. & C. Bolton to Robert Clossey, 8 Sept. 1824, and John H. Howland & Co and J. & C. Bolton to Edmund Blunt, 4 Sept. 1824, EBFP.

28. George Ripley and Charles Dana Anderson, *The American Cyclopaedia: A Popular Dictionary of General Knowledge* (Appleton, 1873), 2:761; *Boston Commercial Gazette*, 5 Jan. 1824; and "Union of the Atlantic and Pacific," *Newburyport Herald* (MA), 1 Feb. 1825. The latter article erroneously suggests that the Mexican government sanctioned Blunt's canal mission.

29. John H. Howland & Co and J. & C. Bolton to Edmund Blunt, 4 Sept. 1824, EBFP.

30. 13 Oct. 1824, EBJ.

31. 30 Jan. 1825, EBJ.

32. 11 Oct. 1824, EBJ.

33. 12 Oct. 1824, EBJ.

34. 30 Jan. 1825, EBJ.

35. Howland and Bolton to Clossey, 8 Sept. 1824, EBFP; and 13 Oct. 1824, EBJ.

36. 13 Oct. 1824, EBJ.

37. 25 Oct. 1824, EBJ.

38. 26 Oct. 1824, EBJ; and Blunt to Howland and Bolton, 4 Nov. 1824 and 24 Dec. 1824, EBFP.

39. 10 Oct. 1824, EBJ.

40. 19 Oct. 1824, EBJ. For gender and expansionism, see Amy Greenberg, *Manifest Manhood and the Antebellum American Empire* (Cambridge: Cambridge University Press, 2005).

41. 23 Nov. 1824, EBJ.

42. 27 Nov. 1824, EBJ.

43. 21 Nov. 1824, EBJ.

44. Lyman to Blunt, 4 Dec. 1824, EBFP. For Blunt's lingering concerns, see Blunt to Howland and Bolton, 21 Feb. 1825, EBFP.

45. Blunt incorrectly believed that one of the politicians would join Bourke in Oaxaca, Mexico for the overland journey to Guatemala City. Blunt to Howland and Bolton, 24 Dec. 1824 and 21 Feb. 1825, EBFP.

46. Lyman to Blunt, 4 Dec. 1824, EBFP. Parker is described in John Williams to Henry Clay, 31 Nov. 1826, R2, M219, RG59, NA2.

47. Blunt to Howland and Bolton, 24 Dec. 1824, EBFP.

48. 27 Dec. 1824, EBJ.

49. 7 Jan. 1825, EBJ.

50. Report, EBFP.

51. 11 Jan. 1825, EBJ.

52. Lyman to Blunt, 4 Dec. 1824, EBFP.

53. Bolton's "very voluminous and valuable" correspondence appears to be lost. Bolton, *Genealogical and Biographical Account*, 119.

54. JQADD, vol. 33, 28 Jan. 1825.

55. JQADD, vol. 33, 1 Feb. 1825.

56. JQADD, vol. 33, 29 Jan. 1825, 1 Feb. 1825, 3 Feb. 1825, 8 Feb. 1825, 9 Feb. 1825, 12 Feb. 1825.

57. JQADD, vol. 33, 3 Feb. 1825.

58. *New Hampshire Patriot and State Gazette* (Concord), 21 Mar. 1825; and *City Gazette* (Charleston, SC), 23 Mar. 1825. Emphasis in original. Blunt reported that Bolton traveled on the "U.S. Brig Spark." 11 Apr. 1825, EBJ.

59. *Newport Mercury* (RI), 14 May 1825.

60. "By the Mails," *Columbian Centinel* (Boston, MA), 18 May 1825. Emphasis in original.

61. "The Grand Canal," *Haverhill Gazette* (MA), 2 July 1825.

62. *Newburyport Herald* (MA), 15 July 1825.

63. In 1838, Bolton argued that he had gone under the "countenance" of "my associates and the Government." Curtis Bolton to Samuel L. Southard, 20 May 1838, Box 61, Folder 4, SLSP. See also H. Rpt. 322, 25th Cong., 3rd Sess., 159; and Curtis Bolton to Daniel Webster, 24 July 1850, R8, M873, RG59, NA2. His family kept alive the lore that "he was appointed by the United States Government, in company with Blunt and other civil engineers, to survey a canal route through Guatemala, in Central America." Bolton, *Genealogical and Biographical Account*, 119.

64. 11 Apr. 1825, EBJ.

65. Edmund Blunt to J. H. H. & Co. and J. & C. Bolton, 21 Feb. 1825, EBFP. "Bongies" or "bongos" were common on Colombian rivers. Edward Posada Carbó, "Bongos, Champanes y Vapores en la Navegación Fluvial Colombiana del Siglo XIX," *Boletín Cultural y Bibliográfico* 26, no. 21 (1989): 2–13.

66. Blunt to Howland and Bolton, 21 Feb. 1825, EBFP.

67. Riverstone, *Living in the Land*, 15; and 15–16 Jan. 1825, EBJ.

68. 20 Jan. 1825, EBJ.

69. Kendra McSweeney, "The Dugout Canoe Trade in Central America's Mosquitia: Approaching Rural Livelihoods through Systems of Exchange," *Annals of the Association of American Geographers* 94, no. 3 (Sept. 2004): 638–61.

70. Burns, *Patriarchy and Folk*, 9. Dym describes the population of Granada and León as majority mixed race. Dym, "Appendix C.2," *From Sovereign Villages*, 271.

71. Baron L. Pineda, *Shipwrecked Identities: Navigating Race on Nicaragua's Mosquito Coast* (New Brunswick: Rutgers University Press, 2006), 23, 26, 34–36.

72. 20 Jan. 1825, EBJ.

73. 20 Jan. 1825, EBJ. Emphasis in original.

74. 22 Jan. 1825, EBJ.

75. Humboldt, *Political Essay*, 1:26; Cynthia S. Willett, Robert R. Leben, Miguel F. Lavin, "Eddies and Tropical Instability Waves in the Eastern Tropical Pacific: A Review," *Progress in Oceanography* 69, 2 (2006): 218–238; and Paul C. Fiedler, *"The Annual Cycle and Biological Effects of the Costa Rica Dome," Deep-Sea Research Part I* 49 (2002): 321–38.

76. Blunt to Howland and Bolton, 21 Feb. 1825, EBFP.

77. 24 Jan. 1825, EBJ.

78. 28 Jan. 1825, EBJ; and Blunt to Howland and Bolton, 21 Feb. 1825, EBFP.

79. Blunt to Howland and Bolton, 21 Feb. 1825, EBFP.
80. 30 Jan. 1825, EBJ.
81. 1 Feb. 1825, EBJ.
82. 2 Feb. 1825, EBJ.
83. 3 Feb. 1825, EBJ.
84. 4 Feb. 1825, EBJ.
85. 4 Feb. 1825, EBJ.
86. 5 Feb. 1825, EBJ.
87. 6–7 Feb. 1825, EBJ.
88. 11 Feb. 1825, EBJ. Emphasis in original.
89. 12 Feb. 1825, EBJ.
90. 13 Feb. 1825, EBJ.
91. 14 Feb. 1825, EBJ.
92. 16 Feb. 1825, EBJ.
93. Edmund Blunt to J. H. H. & Co. and J. & C. Bolton, 21 Feb. 1825, EBFP.
94. 25 Feb. 1825, EBJ.
95. 4 Mar. 1825 and 8 Mar. 1825, EBJ.
96. 16 Mar. 1825, EBJ.
97. 17 Mar. 1825, EBJ.
98. 18 Mar. 1825, EBJ
99. Blunt to John Bolton, 10 May 1825, EBFP.
100. Edmund Blunt to J. H. H. & Co. and J. & C. Bolton, 11 Mar. 1825, EBFP.
101. 11 Apr. 1825, EBJ.
102. Blunt to Bolton, 10 May 1825, EBFP.
103. 22 Apr. 1825, EBJ; and Blunt to Bolton, 10 May 1825, EBFP.
104. 24 Apr. 1825, EBJ.
105. 25 Apr. 1825, EBJ.
106. 26 Apr. 1825, EBJ.
107. 29 Apr. 1825, EBJ.
108. Bolton to Southard, 3 Apr. 1826, Folder 5, Box 21, SLSP.
109. Blunt to Bolton, 10 May 1825, EBFP.
110. Blunt to Howland and Bolton, 21 Feb. 1825, EBFP; and Bork to Poinsett, 28 Dec. 1825, Box 2R153 Letters and correspondence, 1807–30, Poinsett (Joel Roberts) Papers, 1807–31, Dolph Briscoe Center for American History, University of Texas, Austin.
111. Bolton to Southard, 3 Apr. 1826, Folder 5, Box 21, SLSP.
112. *Poulson's American Daily Advertiser* (Philadelphia), 4 July 1825; *North Star* (Danville, VT), 26 July 1825; and Robert H. Parker to Edmund Blunt, 27 Apr. 1825, EBFP.
113. "The Grand Canal," *Haverhill Gazette* (MA), 2 July 1825; and *Newburyport Herald* (MA), 15 July 1825.
114. Blunt to Howland and Bolton, 11 Mar. 1825, EBFP.
115. May 1825, EBJ. Emphasis in original.
116. *El Indicador* (Guatemala), 22 May 1825, No. 31, 126, Archivo General de Centroamérica.
117. Blunt to Bolton, 10 May 1825, EBFP.
118. Blunt to Howland and Bolton, 1 Sept. 1825, EBFP.

119. 13 May 1825, EBJ.
120. 14 May—1 June 1825, EBJ.
121. Blunt to Howland and Bolton, 1 Sept. 1825, EBFP.
122. 1–2 June 1825, EBJ.
123. Report, EBFP.
124. 1 June 1825, EBJ.
125. Blunt to Howland and Bolton, 1 Sept. 1825, EBFP.
126. Report, EBFP; and 19 Oct. 1825, EBJ.
127. Nov. 1825, EBJ.
128. "Finis," EBJ.
129. Account Sheet, EBFP.
130. Ripley and Dana, *American Cyclopedia*, 2:761.
131. Report, EBFP.
132. José D. Gámez, *Historia de Nicaragua: Desde Los Tiempos Prehistóricos Hasta 1860, en sus Relaciones con España, México y Centro-América* (Managua, 1889), 383–98.

Chapter Five

1. JQADD, vol. 35, 4 Aug. 1824; undated entry following 31 July 1824; undated entry following 31 Aug. 1824; and Judah Delano, *The Washington Directory* (1822), 13. For the location of Adams's swims, see Andrew H. Browning, *The Panic of 1819: The First Great Depression* (Columbia: University of Missouri Press, 2019), 307. According to Adams, August 4 was fair and sixty degrees Fahrenheit in the morning, seventy-two at noon, and sixty-three in the evening. John Quincy Adams, Weather Diary, Aug. 1824, MHS.

2. Central American recognition is mentioned in passing in some scholarship. William F. Slade, "The Federation of Central America," *The Journal of Race Development* 8, no. 1 (July 1917): 87; William Spence Robertson, "The Recognition of the Hispanic American Nations by the United States," *The Hispanic American Historical Review* 1, no. 3 (Aug. 1918): 262; and R. A. Humphreys, "Presidential Address: Anglo-American Rivalries in Central America," *Transactions of the Royal Historical Society*, 5th ser., vol. 18 (1968): 180. On 6 August 1824, the *Baltimore Patriot* covered Central American recognition in a two-sentence paragraph. As reprinted in the *Providence Patriot* of 14 August 1824, *The National Intelligencer* devoted only a single clause to Monroe's reception of the minister from "Guatemala." The records of the Central American legation have not been located.

3. JQADD, 4 Aug. 1824. For more on Cañas, see: Rafael Hellodoro Valle, "Antonio José Cañas, Procer Centroamericano," *Revista de Historia de América*, no. 41 (June 1956): 66–70; and Victor Jerez, "Antonio José Cañas," *Estudios Historicos* (San Salvador: Imprenta Nacional, 1941), 211–15.

4. "Envoys from Guatimala," *Newport Mercury* (RI), 12 June 1824; and "Envoy from Guatimala," *Rhode-Island American* (Providence), 15 June 1824.

5. Cañas to Adams, 6 July 1824, R1, T34, RG59, NA2.

6. Cañas to Adams, 6 July 1824, R1, T34, RG59, NA2.

7. For Cañas's stature, see "Paralelos y Biografias," 55.

8. "Paralelos y Biografias," 50–53.

9. "Paralelos y Biografias," 51.

10. The only trace of Cañas's diplomatic instructions are in the minutes of a private legislative session held on 30 March 1824, when he was authorized to discuss a hemispheric congress and request rifles. Expediente 2945, Legajo 112, Signatura B, Archivo General de Centroamérica.

11. Cañas to Adams, 6 July 1824, R1, T34, RG59, NA2.

12. Adams to Cañas, 10 July 1824, R3, M38, RG59, NA2.

13. Cañas to Adams, 4 Aug, 1824, R1, T34, RG59, NA2; Cañas to Adams, 26 July 1824, R1, T34, RG59, NA2; and JQADD, vol. 35, 4 Aug. 1824.

14. Joseph Durant de Mareuil, *Memoires du Baron Joseph Durant de Mareuil*, ed. Gérald Sim (Paris: L'Harmattan, 2020), 305.

15. Mareuil, *Memoires*, 305–6.

16. Gérard Sim, *Le Corps Diplomatique et Consulaire Français aux États-Unis, 1815–1904* (Paris: Les Indes Savantes, 2020), 577–9. Since 1822, Mareuil's brother had served as French consul in Washington. He would later become a baron like Mareuil and serve in the French diplomatic corps.

17. Mareuil, *Memoires*, 308. Other French diplomats described Washington as an exile. Sim, *Le Corps* (2020), 170.

18. Sim, *Le Corps* (2020), 198, 578.

19. Mareuil, *Memoires*, 308–9.

20. Gould, *Among the Powers*, 10–11.

21. J. P. T. Bury, *France, 1814–1940* (Taylor and Francis, 2003); and May, *Making of the Monroe Doctrine*, 85–108.

22. Count Charles Julius de Menou trained as a lawyer in Litchfield, Connecticut, and practiced law in Baltimore, Maryland. A bachelor, he found himself rotating in and out of French diplomatic service as he tried and failed at several speculations. "The Ledger," Litchfield Historical Society, www.litchfieldhistoricalsociety.org/ledger/students/813; and Sim, *Le Corps* (2020), 628–29.

23. *Baltimore Patriot*, 6 Aug. 1824.

24. JQADD, vol. 35, 4 Aug. 1824.

25. For correspondence regarding this issue, see Special Message of James Monroe, 23 Dec. 1824, www.presidency.ucsb.edu/documents/special-message-298. For the text of the Louisiana Purchase, see https://www.archives.gov/milestone-documents/louisiana-purchase-treaty. For an interpretation of the treaty, see Max Farrand, "The Commercial Privileges of the Treaty of 1803," *The American Historical Review* 7, no. 3 (1902): 494–99.

26. May, *Making of the Monroe Doctrine*, 15.

27. JQADD, vol. 35, 4 Aug. 1824. All four men spoke French. Mareuil could understand but not speak English. Sim, *Le Corps* (2020), 198.

28. Adams explained Monroe's desire succinctly. JQADD, vol. 34, 8 Jan. 1824. For the election of 1824, see Donald Ratcliffe, *The One-Party Presidential Contest: Adams, Jackson, and 1824's Five-Horse Race* (Topeka: University Press of Kansas, 2015).

29. For a summary of the scandal, see Browning, *Panic of 1819*, 305–9.

30. JQADD, vol. 35, 29 July 1824.

31. JQADD, vol. 34, 8 Jan. 1824.

32. For Adams's support of the Louisiana Purchase, see Charles N. Edel, *Nation Builder: John Quincy Adams and the Grand Strategy of the Republic* (Cambridge, MA: Harvard University Press, 2014), 90.

33. Ratcliffe, *One-Party Presidential Contest*, 144.

34. For Jefferson's sartorial politics, see David Waldstreicher, "Why Thomas Jefferson and African Americans Wore Their Politics on Their Sleeves: Dress and Mobilization between American Revolutions," *Beyond the Founders: New Approaches to the Political History of the Early American Republic*, ed. Jeffrey Pasley et al. (Chapel Hill: The University of North Carolina Press, 2004), 79–103.

35. Ratcliffe, *One-Party Presidential Contest*, 144.

36. By late August, Crawford's allies in the press launched a campaign against Adams. JQADD, vol. 35, 27 Aug. 1824.

37. JQADD, vol. 35, 4 Aug. 1824. For Loudon, see "Oak Hill," National Park Service, http://web.archive.org/web/20230927112118/https://www.nps.gov/nr/travel/presidents/monroe_oak_hill.html; and Christopher Fennell, "An Account of James Monroe's Land Holdings," www.histarch.illinois.edu/highland/ashlawn5.html.

38. JQADD, vol. 35, 3 Aug. 1824.

39. JQADD, vol. 35, 4 Aug. 1824.

40. In this era, fights for republicanism and the creation of new nations were occurring in Europe and the Americas. Recent scholarship links the Greek fight against the Ottoman Empire to Spanish American revolutions. Maureen Connors Santelli, *The Greek Fire: American-Ottoman Relations and Democratic Fervor in the Age of Revolutions* (New York: Cornell University Press, 2020).

41. Robertson, "Recognition," 251.

42. Edel ties Adams's goal of "continental expansion" to a "grand strategy" aimed at "vindicating republicanism"; before the ratification of the Adams-Onís Treaty, Adams saw involvement in foreign revolutions as "dangerous distractions." By 1822, he reversed this position. Scholars disagree about his motivation. Edel argues that Adams thought the benefits of recognizing the new Spanish American countries "had begun to outweigh the costs." Fitz explains the reversal as part of Adams's campaign strategy. Lewis argues that geopolitical "fears" moved Adams toward recognition. Edel, *Nation Builder*, 8–9, 132, 168; Fitz, *Our Sister Republics*, 188; and Lewis, *American Union*, 166.

43. Robertson, "Recognition," 257.

44. Robertson, "Recognition," 248.

45. In 1822, the United States recognized Peru, Chile, the United Provinces of the Río de la Plata, Colombia, and Mexico. In 1824, the United States recognized Brazil. Fitz, *Our Sister Republics*, 189. The Portuguese monarchy in what became Brazil recognized at least one Spanish American nation. Robertson, "Recognition," 257.

46. Frederick Waymouth Gibbs, *Recognition: A Chapter from the History of the North American & South American States* (London, 1863), 30–34.

47. France's July Revolution of 1830 ended the Bourbon Restoration and led to French official recognition of Spanish American independence. Iwan Morgan, "French Policy in Spanish America: 1830–48," *Journal of Latin American Studies* 10, no. 2 (1978): 309–28.

48. William Spence Robertson, "The Recognition of the Spanish Colonies by the Motherland," *The Hispanic American Historical Review* 1, no. 1 (1 Feb. 1918): 70–91.

49. Robertson, "Recognition," 259.

50. JQA to Cañas, 4 Aug 1824, R3, M38, RG59, NA2.

51. JQADD, vol. 35, 11 Aug. 1824. For Gadsby's, see Jonathan Elliot, *Historical Sketches of the Ten Miles Square Forming the District of Columbia* (1830), 314.

52. JQADD, vol. 35, 4 Aug. 1824.

53. JQADD, vol. 35, 4 Aug. 1824.

54. JQADD, vol. 35, 4 Aug. 1824; and Adams to Cañas, 4 Aug 1824, R3, M38, RG59, NA2.

55. Cañas to Monroe, 6 July 1824, Cañas to Adams, 24 July 1824, 4 Aug 1824, R1, T34, RG59, NA2.

56. Jordana Dym, *From Sovereign Villages to National States: City, State, and Federation in Central America, 1759–1839* (Albuquerque: University of New Mexico Press, 2006), 193.

57. Ricardo Gallardo, *Las Constituciones de la Republica Federal de Centro-America* (Madrid: Instituto de Estudios Politicos, 1958), 2:667–72, 2:669. Flemion describes debate over "the 'true' date of Central American independence." Philip Frederick Flemion, "Manuel José Arce and the Formation of the Federal Republic of Central America" (PhD diss., University of Florida, 1969), 117n8.

58. Gallardo, *Las Constituciones*, 2:670.

59. Ayuntamientos were historically more powerful than provinces. Dym, *From Sovereign Villages*, 196.

60. Flemion, "Arce," 93.

61. Flemion, "Arce," 98–99.

62. Dunn, *Guatimala*, 180; and Flemion, "Arce," 102–9.

63. Hubert Howe Bancroft, *West American History* (New York: Bancroft, 1902), 77; and Flemion, "Arce," 111.

64. "Peace, amity, commerce and navigation TS 39," Document 50, Hunter Miller, ed., *Treaties and Other International Acts of the United States of America* (Washington, DC: US Government Printing Office, 1933), 3:234.

65. Flemion, "Arce," 112; and Expediente 2945, Legajo 112, Signatura B, Archivo General de Centroamérica, Guatemala City.

66. Flemion, "Arce," 135.

67. Título I, Sección Primera, Artículo 1, Constitución de las Provincias Unidas del Centro de América de 1824, https://www.cervantesvirtual.com/nd/ark:/59851/bmcmdos1.

68. Título II, Sección Primera, Artículo 9, Constitución de las Provincias Unidas del Centro de América de 1824, https://www.cervantesvirtual.com/nd/ark:/59851/bmcmdos1.

69. Others have noted the inconsistencies in the Central American government's name. Miller, *Treaties*, 3:234–37.

70. JQADD, vol. 35, 4 Aug. 1824.

71. JQADD, vol. 35, 31 July 1824.

72. JQADD, vol. 35, 31 July 1824.

73. JQADD, vol. 35, 4 Aug. 1824.

74. The furnished clothing were probably officers' uniforms. William T. Hagan, *The Sac and Fox Indians* (Norman: University of Oklahoma Press, 1958), 95; and John Quincy Adams, Weather Diary, Aug. 1824, MHS.

75. By the 1820s, most white men could vote. Donald Ratcliffe, "The Right to Vote and the Rise of Democracy, 1787–1828," *Journal of the Early Republic* 33, no. 2 (2013): 219–54.

76. Ronald Angelo Johnson, *Diplomacy in Black and White: John Adams, Toussaint Louverture, and Their Atlantic World Alliance* (Athens: University of Georgia Press, 2014); Richard Newman, *Transformation of American Abolitionism: Fighting Slavery in the Early Republic* (Chapel Hill: The University of North Carolina Press, 2002), 11; and Ratcliffe, "Right to Vote," 247.

77. Matthew Costello, "The Enslaved Households of President James Monroe," White House Historical Association, 25 Feb. 2020, www.whitehousehistory.org/the-enslaved-households-of-president-james-monroe.

78. In the late 1820s, states began passing laws claiming sovereignty over Indigenous people even though their nations were recognized as foreign powers by the federal government. The federal government adopted this position in 1831 when the Supreme Court defined Indigenous nations as "domestic, dependent nations." Claudio Saunt, *Unworthy Republic: The Dispossession of Native Americans and the Road to Indian Territory* (New York: W.W. Norton, 2020), 37–41, 99, 162; and Christina Snyder, *Great Crossings: Indians, Settlers, & Slaves in the Age of Jackson* (New York: Oxford University Press, 2017), 135–36. According to Viola, "the fiction of regarding the tribes as independent nations"—dependent or not—ended after the Civil War. Herman J. Viola, *Diplomats in Buckskins: A History of Indian Delegations in Washington City* (Smithsonian Institution Press, 1981), 29.

79. Lepore, *The Name of War*, 165.

80. Richard Peters, ed., *The Public Statutes at Large of the United States of America* (Boston: Little, Brown, 1854), 7:229–32.

81. Robert Lee, "Federal Disbursements for Indian Title in the Louisiana Territory, 1804–2012" (Philadelphia: McNeil Center for Early American Studies, 2017), https://doi.org/10.48659/jkmn-j470, Table 1.

82. The Louisiana territory was not simply purchased in 1803. Robert Lee, "Accounting for Conquest: The Price of the Louisiana Purchase of Indian Country," *Journal of American History* 103, no. 4 (Mar. 2017): 921–42, 921; and Lee, "Federal Disbursements."

83. Thomas J. Lappas, "'A Perfect Apollo': Keokuk and Sac Leadership during the Removal Era," in *The Boundaries Between Us: Natives and Newcomers Along the Frontiers of the Old Northwest Territory, 1750–1850*, ed. Daniel Barr (Kent, OH: Kent State University Press, 2006), 226; Hagan, *Sac and Fox*, 95; Herman J. Viola, *The Indian Legacy of Charles Bird King* (Washington, DC: Smithsonian Institution and Doubleday, 1976), 44; and Viola, *Diplomats in Buckskins*, 9. For a list of the peoples' names and affiliations, see "Indians," *Niles Weekly Register* (Baltimore), 31 July 1824.

84. For the larger forces and conflicts, see Hagan, *Sac and Fox*, 84–96. For a discussion of Keokuk's lack of power over war parties, see Lappas, "'A Perfect Apollo,'" 219–35, 223–24. For mourning war, see Daniel Richter, *Facing East from Indian Country: A Native History of Early America* (Cambridge, MA: Harvard University Press, 2001), 64. Brooks shows how Anglo-American promotion of male Indigenous leaders over female leaders served the interest of land acquisition. Lisa Brooks, *Our Beloved Kin: A New History of King Philip's War* (New Haven, CT: Yale University Press, 2018).

85. For the Indian Removal Act, see Claudio Saunt, *Unworthy Republic.*

86. Lappas, "'A Perfect Apollo,'" 220–21. Seen as an accommodationist, Keokuk is often overshadowed in the history of the Sauk and Meskwaki peoples by Black Hawk, who fought against the United States and visited Washington as a prisoner of war. Kelderman argues that Keokuk was not a US "puppet." Frank Kelderman, "Rock Island Revisited: Black Hawk's Life, Keokuk's Oratory, and the Critique of U.S. Indian Policy," *J19: The Journal of Nineteenth-Century Americanists* 6, no. 1 (Spring 2018): 67–92, 67–69, 81.

87. Keokuk's first speech, "Ratified treaty no. 121, documents relating to the negotiation of the treaty of August 4, 1824, with the Sauk and Fox Indians," Digital Collection, University of Wisconsin-Madison Libraries, http://digital.library.wisc.edu/1711.dl/History.IT1824no121.

88. Peters, *Public Statutes,* 7:229.

89. Tai-mah's second speech, "Ratified treaty no. 121, documents relating to the negotiation of the treaty of August 4, 1824, with the Sauk and Fox Indians," Digital Collection, University of Wisconsin-Madison Libraries, http://digital.library.wisc.edu/1711.dl/History.IT1824no121. Demands for written documentation suggest, according to Kelderman, Indigenous leaders' embrace of "translation and transcription" as well as their "implicit criticism of Americans' disregard for treaties." Kelderman, "Rock Island Revisited," 82.

90. Peters, *Public Statutes,* 7:230; and Lappas, "'A Perfect Apollo,'" 227. Hagan argues that compelling arguments by the eloquent Keokuk convinced Secretary of War Calhoun to draw up the treaty. Hagan, *Sac and Fox,* 94–95. For the accusations against Keokuk's "personal aggrandizement," see Thomas Burnell Colbert, "'The Hinge on Which All Affairs of the Sauk and Fox Indians Turn': Keokuk and the United States Government," *Enduring Nations: Native Americans in the Midwest,* ed. R. David Edmunds (Urbana, IL: University of Illinois Press, 2008), 54–71, 67.

91. Peters, *Public Statutes,* 7:231–2.

92. Keokuk's second speech, "Ratified treaty no. 121, documents relating to the negotiation of the treaty of August 4, 1824, with the Sauk and Fox Indians," Digital Collection, University of Wisconsin-Madison Libraries, http://digital.library.wisc.edu/1711.dl/History.IT1824no121.

93. Bernstein emphasizes the Ioway's increasing need for protection from the Sioux. David Bernstein, "'We are not now as we once were': Iowa Indians' Political and Economic Adaptations during U.S. Incorporation," *Ethnohistory* 54:4 (Fall 2017): 605–37, 610.

94. Peters, *Public Statutes,* 7:231.

95. For more on the Ioway's diminished sovereignty, see Frank Kelderman, "Na'hjeNing'e's Rivers: Indigenous Maps, Diplomacy, and the Writing of Ioway Space," *Altre Modernità* 22 (2019): 43–54.

96. Flemion, "Arce," 151.

97. JQADD, vol. 35, 31 July 1824.

98. JQADD, vol. 35, 31 July 1824.

99. JQADD, vol. 35, 4 Aug. 1824.

100. Newspapers do not seem to have printed transcripts to these speeches; excerpts of some of Keokuk's other speeches appeared in newspapers. "The Indian Chiefs," *National Gazette and Literary Register* (Philadelphia), 17 Aug. 1824.

101. JQADD, vol. 35, 31 July 1824. "spectator (*n.*), Etymology," *Oxford English Dictionary* (June 2024), https://doi.org/10.1093/OED/8452467146.

102. JQADD, vol. 35, 5 Aug. 1824.

103. Viola, *Indian Legacy*, 50.

104. For the history of the lithographs, see Viola, *Indian Legacy*, 68–87; and James D. Horan, *The McKenney-Hall Portrait Gallery of American Indians* (New York: Crown, 1972).

105. For example, see "Mahaskah," reproduced in Horan, *McKenney-Hall*, 303. For the distribution of the medals, see JQADD, vol. 35, 4 Aug. 1824. For peace medals, see Viola, *Diplomats in Buckskins*, 104–5.

106. In the 1830s, Henry Inman copied King's 1824 portrait of Keokuk. Henry Inman after Charles Bird King, *Keokuk (Sauk and Fox)*, c. 1831–34, The High Museum, Atlanta, GA, https://high.org/sites/inman/index.html#keokuk. Alfred M. Hoffy after Charles Bird King, "Keokuk—Chief of the Sacs and Foxes" published in Thomas L. McKenney and James Hall, *The History of the Indian Tribes of North America*, 3 Vols. (Philadelphia: Frederick W. Greenough, 1838). A digitized version of the 1836 lithograph is available from the National Portrait Gallery, Smithsonian: https://npg.si.edu/object/npg_NPG.99.168.13.

107. For peace medals as reminders of federal promises, see John C. Winters, *'The Amazing Iroquois' and the Invention of the Empire State* (New York: Oxford University Press, 2023), 16.

108. Quoted in Viola, *Diplomats in Buckskins*, 104.

109. Thomas Easterly, *Keokuk c. 1790–1848*, Sixth-plate daguerreotype, 1847. The daguerreotype is included in Kelderman, "Rock Island," 76. It is also available online: https://npg.si.edu/exhibit/frontier/pop-ups/02-01.html.

110. For sailors trading in ports, see Brian Rouleau, *With Sails Whitening Every Sea: Mariners and the Making of an American Maritime Empire* (Ithaca, NY: Cornell University Press, 2014), 164–94. For relatively small trade with South America, see Douglas A. Irwin, "Exports, by country of destination: 1790–2001," Table Ee533–550, and "Imports, by country of origin: 1790–2001," Table Ee551–568 in *Historical Statistics of the United States, Earliest Times to the Present: Millennial Edition*, ed. Susan B. Carter et al. (New York: Cambridge University Press, 2006).

111. JQADD, vol. 35, 4 Aug. 1824.

112. In 1821, Talleyrand provided Laborie, "a young Frenchman," with a letter of introduction; he became a frequent guest at the Adams residence. JQADD, vol. 32, 13 Oct. 1821.

113. JQADD, vol. 35, 4 Aug. 1824, 27 Aug. 1824.

114. JQADD, vol. 35, 31 Mar. 1824.

115. JQADD, vol. 35, 27 Aug. 1824.

116. JQADD, vol. 34, 8 June 1824.

117. JQADD, vol. 35, 4 Aug. 1824.

Chapter Six

1. *A Brief Memoir of the Life of James Wilson (Late of Edinburgh), with Extracts from his Journal and Correspondence, Written, Chiefly, during a Residence in Guatemala, the Capital of Central America* (London, 1829), 77–78.

2. "John Bailey," UK Naval Officer and Rating Service Records, ADM 29/19, 291, TNA, accessed online through Ancestry.com.

3. Philip Frederick Flemion, "Manuel José Arce and the Formation of the Federal Republic of Central America" (PhD diss., University of Florida, 1969), 135, 139–41.

4. Flemion, "Arce," 125.

5. Flemion, "Arce," 125–28.

6. Flemion, "Arce," 137–41.

7. "Guatemala, Or Central America," *Times* (London), 23 Aug. 1825.

8. Charles Savage to Juan Francisco de Sosa, 2 May 1825, Vol. 87, RG84, NA2.

9. Charles Savage to Samuel P. Savage, 7 Apr. 1826, Folder 8, Box 1, SPSP.

10. Susan (Wood) Savage died on 10 May 1825. Lawrence Park, *Major Thomas Savage of Boston and His Descendants* (Boston, 1914), 36.

11. Charles Savage to Henry Clay, 15 Aug. 1825, Vol. 5, RG84, NA2.

12. Park, *Major Thomas Savage*, 36; and "Susan Savage, 1825," www.capecodgravestones.com/barnpixweb/sav25bcob.html.

13. JQADD, vol. 37, 12 Nov. 1825.

14. Savage to Lemuel Shaw et al., 7 Apr. 1826, Folder 8, Box 1, SPSP.

15. Savage to Clay, 28 Nov. 1826, Vol. 5, RG84, NA2.

16. Savage to Shaw et al., 7 Apr. 1826, Folder 8, Box 1, SPSP.

17. Savage to Clay, 28 Nov. 1826, Vol. 5, RG84, NA2.

18. Daniel Brent to Savage, 6 Dec. 1826, Roll 2, M78, RG59, NA2.

19. Savage to Shaw et al., 7 Apr. 1826, Folder 8, Box 1, SPSP.

20. Savage to Shaw, 13 Apr. 1839, Folder 8, Box 1, SPSP.

21. Savage to Shaw, Oct. 1839, Folder 8, Box 1, SPSP.

22. Savage to Sosa, 4 May 1825, Vol. 87, RG84, NA2. Emphasis in original.

23. Donald Ratcliffe, *The One-Party Presidential Contest: Adams, Jackson, and 1824's Five-Horse Race* (Topeka: University Press of Kansas, 2015), 128, 228–57.

24. Ratcliffe, *One-Party Presidential Contest*, 228–57.

25. Ratcliffe, *One-Party Presidential Contest*, 238–39.

26. JQADD, vol. 49, 1 Jan. 1825, 2 Jan. 1825.

27. JQADD, vol. 36, 9 Jan. 1825.

28. JQADD, vol. 36, 9 Jan. 1825.

29. Ratcliffe, *One-Party Presidential Contest*, 228–57, Jackson quoted on 255.

30. JQADD, vol. 36, 9 Jan. 1825.

31. Ratcliffe, *One-Party Presidential Contest*, 228–57.

32. JQADD, vol. 33, 9 Feb. 1825.

33. Sosa to Savage, 4 May 1825, Vol. 87, RG84, NA2.

34. Savage to Clay, 15 Aug. 1825, Vol. 5, RG 84, NA2.

35. *A Brief Memoir of the Life of James Wilson*, 114–15; and "8. de Sosa, Juan Francisco. Laws and Decrees, 16 de junio y 1 de agosto de 1825," "Impresos guatemaltecos, 1825," Folder 5, Box 1, Miscellaneous Broadsides, BLAC, translated for author by James Irving.

36. "8. de Sosa, Juan Francisco. Laws and Decrees, 16 de junio y 1 de agosto de 1825," "Impresos guatemaltecos, 1825" Folder 5, Box 1, Miscellaneous Broadsides, BLAC. The terms are also printed in Alejandro Marure, *Memoria Historica sobre el Canal de Nicaragua* (Guatemala City: Imprenta de la Paz, 1845), 13.

37. *A Brief Memoir of the Life of James Wilson*, 117–18.

38. *A Brief Memoir of the Life of James Wilson*, 95.

39. John Hynes, whom Thompson described as having "come out to propose a loan on the part of Messrs. Simmonds," structured his proposal, according to Savage, as "a loan."

This would not accord with the decree's terms. In Thompson's idiosyncratic orthography, Baily became "Bayley" and "Hynes" was "Hines." Thompson, *Narrative*, 208–9; and Charles Savage to Hope Savage, 2 Apr. 1825, Folder 8, Box 1, SPSP.

40. "8. de Sosa, Juan Francisco. Laws and Decrees, 16 de junio y 1 de agosto de 1825," "Impresos guatemaltecos, 1825" Folder 5, Box 1, Miscellaneous Broadsides, BLAC.

41. "Guatemala, or Central America," *Times* (London), 23 Aug. 1825. Baily is identifiable as the author of these excerpted letters because he describes himself as "engaged the whole of the morning" of 18 May with presenting Thompson to "the President &c." In his travel account, Thompson identified Baily as performing presentations on that day. Thompson, *Narrative*, 138.

42. *Times* (London), 19 Aug. 1825; and *Times* (London), 23 Aug. 1825.

43. This was an even more private spot than the tavern where BHRC accepted bids for its Mexican loan. "New Mexican Loan," *Times* (London), 7 Feb. 1825; and *Times* (London), 19 Aug. 1825.

44. For the weather, see www.pascalbonenfant.com/18c/geography/weather.html. For previous sales, see Dawson, *First Latin American Debt Crisis*, 37–38.

45. *Times* (London), 23 Aug. 1825.

46. *Times* (London), 23 Aug. 1825.

47. William Ward, mezzotint, "John Diston Powles" (c. 1820–26), NPG D40385, National Portrait Gallery (London), www.npg.org.uk/collections/search/portrait/mw203029/John-Diston-Powles.

48. Malcolm Deas, "Powles, John Diston (1787–1867)," *Oxford Dictionary of National Biography*, published online 23 Sept. 2004, version accessed 26 May 2016, https://doi.org/10.1093/ref:odnb/57749.

49. "Bankrupts," *Stamford Mercury* (England), 14 Jan. 1820.

50. Alfred William Powles is named as a defendant in "Thompson v. Powles," (1828) Nicholas Simons, *Reports of Cases Decided in the High Court of Chancery by The Right Hon. Sir Anthony Hart, and The Right Hon. Sir Launcelot Shadwell, Vice-Chancellors of England* (London: J. & W. T. Clarke, 1831), 2:194. Alfred is identified as John's brother in an exposé pamphlet written by former BHRC partner Christopher Richardson in opposition to Powles's later attempt to obtain political office. Christopher Richardson, *Mr. John Diston Powles: Or, The Antecedents, As a Promoter and Director of Foreign Mining Companies, of An Administrative Reformer* (London, 1855), 8.

51. "Lloyd's," *Morning Post* (London), 24 July 1824.

52. Deas, "Powles;" and Benjamin Disraeli, *Vivian Grey* (London, 1826).

53. Dawson, *First Latin American Debt Crisis*, 54.

54. In January 1825, shareholders had paid in only £10 per share, but the stock traded on the exchange for £158. Shares of the Real del Monte Company, a competing Mexican mining company, were trading in the secondary market at £1,350 per share when only £70 per share had been paid to the company. Dawson, *First Latin American Debt Crisis*, 102–3.

55. Historic Hansard, HC Deb., 16 Mar. 1825, Vol. 12, cc 1048, https://api.parliament.uk/historic-hansard/commons/1825/mar/16/peruvian-mining-company-bill.

56. Historic Hansard, HC Deb., 16 Mar. 1825, Vol. 12, cc 1063–65, https://api.parliament.uk/historic-hansard/commons/1825/mar/16/peruvian-mining-company-bill.

57. Dawson, *First Latin American Debt Crisis*, 107–8.

58. Thompson v. Powles, (1828) Simons, *Reports of Cases Decided*, 2:195.

59. William Thompson's full name is listed in the chancery rolls for his case against BHRC and Powles. "Thompson v. Barclay," c13/883/49, TNA. Thompson served as a director of three mining companies, several with connections to the partners of Barclay and Powles. Henry English, *A General Guide to the Companies Formed for Working Foreign Mines* (London: Boosey & Sons, 1825), 4, 20, 23.

60. Thompson v. Powles, (1828) Simons, *Reports of Cases Decided*, 2:196.

61. Thompson v. Powles, (1828) Simons, *Reports of Cases Decided*, 2:197.

62. Only a little more than 10 percent of the bonds found buyers willing to make the initial installment payments. Dawson, *First Latin American Debt Crisis*, 110.

63. *Times* (London), 30 Aug. 1825.

64. Dawson, *First Latin American Debt Crisis*, 116, 110–20; and Jackson, *Impunity and Capitalism*, 248–51.

65. "Death of Mr. Goldschmidt," *The Examiner* (London), 26 Feb. 1826, 132.

66. "Death of Mr. Goldschmidt," *The Examiner* (London), 26 Feb. 1826, 132; and "L. A. Goldschmidt, Esq.," *Times* (London), 20 Feb. 1826.

67. "L. A. Goldschmidt, Esq.," *Times* (London), 20 Feb. 1826.

68. *Hampshire Telegraph and Sussex Chronicle* (Portsmouth, England), 22 Feb. 1826.

69. Edwin Jaggard, "Small Boroughs and Political Modernization, 1832–1868: A Cornwall Case Study," *Albion: A Quarterly Journal Concerned with British Studies* 29, no. 4 (Winter 1997): 622–42, 626, 634, 637.

70. "General Election," *Times* (London), 19 June 1826.

71. "Anglo-Mexican Mining Company," *Times* (London), 29 Aug. 1826.

72. "From the *London Gazette*, Friday, Sept. 15," *Times* (London), 16 Sept. 1826. See also "Partnerships Dissolved," *Birmingham Gazette* (England), 18 Sept. 1826; and "Partnerships Dissolved," *Manchester Courier and Lancashire General Advertiser* (England), 30 Sept. 1826.

73. Thompson v. Powles, (1828) Simons, *Reports of Cases Decided*, 2:197, 2:199.

74. J. D. Powles, "To The Editor of the Times," *Times* (London), 11 Feb. 1828.

75. Taylor v. Barclay, (1828) Simons, *Reports of Cases Decided*, 2:215.

76. J. D. Powles, "To The Editor of the Times," *Times* (London), 11 Feb. 1828.

77. Robert S. Smith, "Financing the Central American Federation, 1821–1838," *The Hispanic American Historical Review* 43, no. 4 (1 Nov. 1963): 483–510, 486; and Marcial Zebadúa, *Manifestacion Publica del Ciudadano Marcial Zebadua Sobre Su Mision Diplomatica Cerca de Su Magestad Británica* (Guatemala, 1832), 9, translated for author by James Irving.

78. Zebadúa, *Manifestacion Publica*, 10–12.

79. Dawson, *First Latin American Debt Crisis*, 159.

80. Thompson v. Powles, (1828) Simons, *Reports of Cases Decided*, 2:202.

81. Thompson v. Powles, (1828) Simons, *Reports of Cases Decided*, 2:203.

82. Taylor v. Barclay, (1828) Simons, *Reports of Cases Decided*, 2:215. Emphasis in original.

83. Taylor v. Barclay, (1828) Simons, *Reports of Cases Decided*, 2:216–17. Emphasis in original.

84. Taylor v. Barclay, (1828) Simons, *Reports of Cases Decided*, 2:220. The Foreign Office verified the lack of Central American recognition. 105–108, FO 15/8, TNA.

85. Taylor v. Barclay, (1828) Simons, *Reports of Cases Decided*, 2:223.

86. Thompson, *Narrative*, 194.

87. English, *A Complete View*, 3, 12, 17.

88. Deas, "Powles"; and Jonathan Parry, "Disraeli, Benjamin, earl of Beaconsfield, 1804–1881," *Oxford Dictionary of National Biography*, published online 23 Sept. 2004, version accessed 19 May 2011, https://doi.org/10.1093/ref:odnb/7689.

Chapter Seven

1. JQADD, vol. 35, 21 July 1824; and Frank B. Woodford, *Mr. Jefferson's Disciple: A Life of Justice Woodward* (East Lansing: Michigan State College Press, 1953), 22.

2. JQADD, vol. 35, 31 Mar. 1824.

3. JQADD, vol. 35, 24 June 1824.

4. JQADD, vol. 35, 22 July 1824.

5. JQADD, vol. 35, 9 Aug. 1824.

6. JQADD, vol. 35, 20 Aug. 1824, 27 Aug. 1824.

7. JQADD, vol. 33, 4 May 1825.

8. JQADD, vol. 31, 17 Feb. 1820. Dr. Thornton would later seek the "Mission to Guatemala." JQADD, vol. 49, 9 Dec. 1824.

9. JQADD, vol. 35, 3 Aug. 1824; vol. 31, 14 Apr. 1819; vol. 37, 16 Nov. 1825.

10. JQADD, vol. 32, 6 Aug. 1822.

11. JQADD, vol. 31, 18 Aug. 1819; vol. 32, 6 Aug. 1822, 10 Nov. 1821; vol. 35, 14 Apr. 1824.

12. JQADD, vol. 31, 25 Mar. 1820.

13. JQADD, vol. 49, 11 Dec. 1824.

14. Jonathan Martin, "William Miller (1783–1825)," North Carolina History Project, https://northcarolinahistory.org/encyclopedia/william-miller-1783-1825/; and William Henry Hoyt, *The Papers of Archibald D. Murphey* (Raleigh: E. M. Uzzell, 1914), 2:19n1.

15. William Miller, R11, M439, RG59, NAMA.

16. JQADD, vol. 33, 26 Feb. 1825, 7 Feb. 1825.

17. JQADD, vol. 33, 1 Mar. 1825.

18. William Miller, R11, M439, RG59, NAMA.

19. Compare to today's average of less than two gallons per year. Daniel Walker Howe, *What Hath God Wrought: The Transformation of America, 1815–1848* (New York: Oxford University Press, 2007), 167.

20. William Miller, R11, M439, RG59, NAMA; and JQADD, vol. 33, 1 Mar. 1825.

21. JQADD, vol. 33, 5 Mar. 1825.

22. "Monday, March 7, 1825," *Journal of the Executive Proceedings of the Senate of the United States of America, 1815–1829*, 3:441, accessed online, www.congress.gov/browse/19th-congress.

23. Henry Clay to William Miller, 24 Mar. 1825, R5, M77, RG59, NA2.

24. Richard John, *Spreading the News: The American Postal System from Franklin to Morse* (Cambridge, MA: Harvard University Press, 1995).

25. "Grand Project," *Norwich Courier* (CT), 6 Nov. 1822.

26. "Grand Canal," *Boston Daily Advertiser*, 7 Dec. 1822. See also "Colombia," *Baltimore Patriot*, 1 Sept. 1823. A second British canal projector pursued a Colombian contract in 1824. "Darien," *Jamaica Journal* (Kingston), 19 June 1824.

27. "Canal of Darien," *City Gazette* (Charleston, SC), 29 Nov. 1822; "Inter-Oceanick Canal," *Rhode-Island American* (Providence), 14 Jan. 1823; and *Alexandria Herald* (VA), 13 Nov. 1822.

28. "Ship Canal through Central America," *Newport Mercury* (RI), 23 Apr. 1825.

29. Occasionally, Humboldt was referenced, see "Canal of Darien," *City Gazette* (Charleston, SC), 29 Nov. 1822; and "Inter-Oceanick Canal," *Rhode-Island American* (Providence), 14 Jan. 1823.

30. "Great American Canal," *Republican Star* (Easton, MD), 17 Dec. 1822.

31. "Great American Canal," *Republican Star* (Easton, MD), 17 Dec. 1822.

32. "Communication," *New-Bedford Mercury* (MA), 20 Dec. 1822.

33. "Inter-Oceanick Canal," *Rhode-Island American* (Providence), 14 Jan. 1823.

34. John Lauritz Larson, *Internal Improvement: National Public Works and the Promise of Popular Government in the Early United States* (Chapel Hill: The University of North Carolina Press, 2001).

35. "Meeting of the Waters," *Baltimore Patriot*, 13 Oct. 1823.

36. "The Atlantic and Pacific to be joined," *Columbian Centinel* (Boston), 6 Sept. 1823.

37. *Providence Patriot* (RI), 23 June 1824.

38. "Atlantic and Pacific Oceans," *Boston Commercial Gazette*, 22 July 1824; *Newburyport Herald* (MA), 31 Dec. 1824; and "Darien Canal," *Portsmouth Journal of Literature and Politics* (NH), 1 Jan. 1825.

39. "Pacific and Atlantic," *Rhode-Island Republican* (Providence), 18 Nov. 1824.

40. "Pacific and Atlantic," *Providence Gazette* (RI), 11 Dec. 1824.

41. Many newspapers circulated a short account of the mission; see "Union of the Atlantic and Pacific," *Newburyport Herald* (MA), 1 Feb. 1825.

42. Woodford, *Mr. Jefferson's Disciple*, 143–64.

43. For agricultural improvement as a scientific movement, see Emily Pawley, *The Nature of the Future: Agriculture, Science, and Capitalism in the Antebellum North* (Chicago: University of Chicago Press, 2020); and Ariel Ron, *Grassroots Leviathan: Northern Agricultural Reform in the Slaveholding Republic* (Baltimore: Johns Hopkins University Press, 2020). For the founding of the Agricultural Society of Middle Florida, see James Owen Knauss, "William Pope DuVal: Pioneer and State Builder," *Florida Historical Society Quarterly* 11, no. 3 (Jan. 1933): 95–139, 121.

44. "Mortuary Notice," *Eastern Argus* (Portland, ME), 4 June 1839.

45. "Hindostan," *Independent Chronicle & Boston Patriot*, 26 June 1819.

46. "Mortuary Notice," *Independent Chronicle & Boston Patriot*, 19 Oct. 1822.

47. "Atlantic and Pacific Canal," *National Aegis* (Worcester, MA), 18 May 1825.

48. JQADD, vol. 33, 6 May 1825; vol. 33, 28 May 1825; vol. 37, 10 Dec. 1827.

49. "Atlantic and Pacific Canal," *National Journal* (Washington, DC), 28 Apr. 1825.

50. *National Journal* (Washington, DC), 8 Apr. 1825.

51. *National Journal* (Washington, DC), 9 Apr. 1825.

52. "Province of Nicaragua," *National Journal* (Washington, DC), 11 Apr. 1825. M. G. Saravia's authorship is credited in a different article.

53. "Population, Towns, Agriculture, Mines, and Commerce of Nicaragua," *National Journal* (Washington, DC), 16 Apr. 1825; and "Central America: Abolishment of Slavery," *National Journal* (Washington, DC), 15 Apr. 1825.

54. "Another Canal," *National Journal* (Washington, DC), 12 Apr. 1825.

55. "Canals," *National Journal* (Washington, DC), 21 Apr. 1825.

56. Reports on the creation of British canal companies appeared earlier elsewhere. *New-Hampshire Republican* (Dover), 12 Apr. 1825; and "Foreign," *Richmond Enquirer* (VA), 15 Apr. 1825.

57. "British House of Commons: Peruvian Mining Company," *National Journal* (Washington, DC), 25 Apr. 1825.

58. "English Canal Company," *National Journal* (Washington, DC), 27 Apr. 1825.

59. "Atlantic and Pacific Canal," *National Journal* (Washington, DC), 28 Apr. 1825.

60. Humboldt, *Political Essay* (1811), 1:31. Wilko Graf von Hardenberg, "Measuring Zero at Sea: On the Delocalization and Abstraction of the Geodetic Framework," *Journal of Historical Geography* 68 (2020): 11–20.

61. Humboldt, *Political Essay*, 1:33–34.

62. "Atlantic and Pacific Canal," *National Journal* (Washington, DC), 28 Apr. 1825.

63. "Atlantic and Pacific Canal," *National Journal* (Washington, DC), 29 Apr. 1825.

64. "Atlantic and Pacific Canal," *Independent Chronicle and Boston Patriot*, 4 May 1825.

65. "Schiff-Canal Zwischen Dem Atlantischen Und Stillen Meer," *Readinger Adler* (Reading, PA), 17 May 1825.

66. "Union of Oceans," *Newburyport Herald* (MA), 10 May 1825. Emphasis in original.

67. For example, see "Union of Oceans," *New Hampshire Patriot and State Gazette* (Concord), 16 May 1825; and "Atlantic and Pacific Canal," *Boston Commercial Gazette*, 12 May 1825.

68. "Continental Internal Improvements," *Eastern Argus* (Portland, ME), 5 May 1825.

69. For the history of the Richmond Junto, which controlled the *Enquirer*, see Harry Ammon, "The Richmond Junto, 1800–1824," *The Virginia Magazine of History and Biography* 99, no. 1 (Jan. 1991): 63–80.

70. "Atlantic & Pacific," *Richmond Enquirer* (VA), 20 May 1825. Emphasis in original.

71. "Remarks on Doane and Woodward's Observations," *Essex Register* (Salem, MA), 23 May 1825. Another critic suggested that the descent of the water would be only "three inches to a mile," hardly a gush that could create a new Gibraltar. "Grand Project," *Connecticut Gazette* (New London), 8 June 1825.

72. "Remarks on Doane and Woodward's Observations," *Essex Register* (Salem, MA), 23 May 1825. The author was probably Theophilus Parsons Jr., who used the pseudonym S. X. in later articles. Guy R. Woodall, "The Record of a Friendship: The Letters of Convers Francis to Frederic Henry Hedge in Bangor and Providence, 1835–1850," *Studies in the American Renaissance* (1991): 1–57, 33.

73. "Grand Project," *Connecticut Gazette* (New London), 8 June 1825.

74. "Junction of the Atlantic and Pacific," *Hallowell Gazette* (ME), 25 May 1825.

75. For example, see "From the National Journal. Atlantic and Pacific Canal," *Edwardsville Spectator* (IL), 31 May 1825; and "From the Nashville Republican: Atlantic and Pacific," *Weekly Arkansas Gazette* (Little Rock), 5 July 1825.

76. Daniel Brent to William Miller, 21 Apr. 1825, R5, M77, RG59, NA2.

77. Henry Clay to William Miller, 22 Apr. 1825, R5, M77, RG59, NA2.

78. Clay to Miller, 23 Apr. 1825, R5, M77, RG59, NA2.

79. Clay to Miller, 23 Apr. 1825, R5, M77, RG59, NA2.

80. Brent to Miller, 21 Apr. 1825, R5, M77, RG59, NA2.

81. Miller to Adams, 28 Mar. 1825, R2, M219. RG59, NA2.

Chapter Eight

1. Antonio José Cañas to John Quincy Adams, 8 Feb. 1825, R1, T34, RG59, NA2. The penmanship probably belonged to Secretary of Legation Fernando Valero.

2. *Oxford English Dictionary*, s.v. "diplomat, n., Etymology," Sept. 2023, doi.org/10.1093/OED/6094770169, "diploma, n., sense 1.a", "diploma, n., Etymology," Sept. 2023, doi.org/10.1093/OED/3973269028.

3. Cañas to Adams, 8 Feb. 1825, R1, T34, RG59, NA2; and Cañas to Adams, 8 Feb. 1825, Manning, 2:881–2. The map is no longer archived with the letter.

4. JQADD, vol. 33, 28 Jan. 1825.

5. Curtis Bolton to Daniel Webster, 24 July 1850, R8, M873, RG59, NA2.

6. Cañas to Adams, 8 Feb. 1825, Manning, 2:881–2.

7. Clay to Cañas, 18 Apr. 1825, R3, M38, RG59, NA2.

8. Clay to Cañas, 18 Apr. 1825, R3, M38, RG59, NA2.

9. Clay to Cañas, 18 Apr. 1825, R3, M38, RG59, NA2.

10. John Lauritz Larson, *Internal Improvement: National Public Works and the Promise of Popular Government in the Early United States* (Chapel Hill: The University of North Carolina Press, 2001).

11. Clay to Cañas, 18 Apr. 1825, R3, M38, RG59, NA2.

12. Clay to Miller, 22 Apr. 1825, R5, M77, RG59, NA2.

13. JQADD, vol. 33, 28 Apr. 1825.

14. Miller to Clay, 15 June 1825, R2, M219, RG59, NA2.

15. J. A. Alvarado to William Miller, 2 June 1825, enclosed in Miller to Clay, 15 June 1825, R2, M219, RG59, NA2.

16. Brent to Miller, 17 June 1825, R5, M77, RG59, NA2; and "Decoy," *Dictionary of American Naval Fighting Ships*, Naval History and Heritage Command, www.history.navy.mil/research/histories/ship-histories/danfs/d/decoy.html.

17. Brent to Miller, 29 June 1825, R5, M77, RG59, NA2; and Miller to Brent, 24 June 1825, R2, M219, RG59, NA2. Adams described Miller's friend, Dr. Frederick Baker, as a son of J. M. Baker, who was, in Adams's words, "a perpetual solicitor of Office." JQADD, vol. 49, 29 June 1825; vol. 30, 18 May 1818; vol. 33, 21 Apr. 1825.

18. Frederick C. Baker to Brent, 3 July 1825, R2, M219, RG59, NA2; and "Norfolk, July 6," *Providence Patriot* (RI), 16 July 1825.

19. For histories of yellow fever, see J. R. McNeill, *Mosquito Empires: Ecology and War in The Greater Caribbean, 1620–1914* (Cambridge: Cambridge University Press, 2010); Kathryn Olivarius, *Necropolis: Disease, Power, and Capitalism in the Cotton Kingdom* (Cambridge, MA: Harvard University Press, 2022); Jan Golinski, "Debating the Atmospheric Constitution: Yellow Fever and the American Climate," *Eighteenth-Century Studies* 49, no. 2 (2016): 149–65; and Julia Mansfield, "Sickness and Stagnation: The Interplay of Disease and Markets in 1819," *Journal of the Early Republic* 40, no. 4 (Winter 2020): 703–8.

20. Baker to Clay, 21 Sept. 1825, R2, M219, RG59, NA2.

21. Clay to Cañas, 13 Sept. 1825, R3, M38, RG59, NA2.

22. On Eliza Clay's illness, see Clay to Adams, 21 July 1825 and 25 July 1825, in *The Papers of Henry Clay*, ed. James F. Hopkins (Lexington: University Press of Kentucky, 1972), 4:546,

4:550. On her death, see JQADD, vol. 49, 23 Aug. 1825; and "Eliza Hart Clay," Find a Grave, www.findagrave.com/memorial/57866158/eliza-hart-clay.

23. For Clay's illness, see JQADD, vol. 49, 22 Aug. 1825.

24. Cañas to Clay, 7 Sept. 1825, R1, T34, RG59, NA2.

25. Clay to Cañas, 13 Sept. 1825, R3, M38, RG59, NA2.

26. "Peace, amity, navigation and commerce," *Treaties and Other International Acts of the United States of America* (Miller) 3 (1824): 163–94.

27. JQADD, vol. 37, 29 Nov. 1825.

28. Cañas to Clay, 14 Nov. 1825, in Manning 2:883.

29. Clay to Cañas, 30 Nov. 1825, R3, M38, RG59, NA2.

30. Cañas to Clay, 14 Nov. 1825, in Manning 2:883.

31. Clay to Cañas, 30 Nov. 1825, R3, M38, RG59, NA2.

32. Caitlin Fitz, *Our Sister Republics: The United States in an Age of American Revolutions* (New York: Liveright, 2016), 194–239.

33. "Peace, amity, commerce and navigation," *Treaties and Other International Acts of the United States of America* (Miller) 3 (1825): 209–38, 209.

34. Miller, *Treaties*, 3:228.

35. Miller, *Treaties*, 3:211.

36. Miller, *Treaties*, 3:231.

37. Miller, *Treaties*, 3:232.

38. Miller, *Treaties*, 3:232–33.

39. No. 413, *American State Papers*, Senate, 19th Cong., 1st Sess., Foreign Relations 5:774.

40. JQADD, vol. 37, 16 Dec. 1825.

41. For the votes, see Senate Executive Journal, 29 Dec. 1825, www.congress.gov/browse/19th-congress. For the dates, see Miller, *Treaties*, 3:209.

42. Mann's supporters were Crawford men; Miller's detractors were Crawford men. Ratcliffe, *One-Party Presidential Contest*, 29–32; and Harold J. Counihan, "Branch, John" (1979), www.ncpedia.org/biography/branch-john.

43. Ratcliffe, *One-Party Presidential Contest*, 192–96.

44. Leota Driver Maiden, "Colonel John Williams," *The East Tennessee Historical Society's Publications* 30 (1958): 7–46, 10, 11, 30–31; and Robert V. Remini, "Jackson, Andrew," *American National Biography* (2000), https://doi.org/10.1093/anb/9780198606697.article.0300238.

45. Williams quoted in Maiden, "Colonel John Williams," 12.

46. Maiden, "Colonel John Williams," 11.

47. Charles Grier Sellers Jr., "Jackson Men with Feet of Clay," *The American Historical Review* 62, no. 3 (Apr. 1957): 537–51, 545.

48. Williams quoted in Maiden, "Colonel John Williams," 13.

49. Maiden, "Colonel John Williams," 16.

50. Maiden, "Colonel John Williams," 19.

51. Maiden, "Colonel John Williams," 25–27.

52. Maiden, "Colonel John Williams," 28.

53. JQADD, vol. 31, 19 Feb. 1821.

54. Maiden, "Colonel John Williams," 31.

55. Maiden, "Colonel John Williams," 32.
56. JQADD, vol. 32, 12 Apr. 1822.
57. Maiden, "Colonel John Williams," 29.
58. Sellers, "Jackson Men," 537–51.
59. Maiden, "Colonel John Williams," 37.
60. Clay to Williams, 10 Nov. 1825, R5, M77, RG59, NA2.
61. Williams to Clay, 25 Nov. 1825, R2, M219, RG59, NA2.
62. Senate Executive Journal, 26 Dec. 1825, 461.
63. JQADD, vol. 37, 28 Dec. 1825.
64. Senate Executive Journal, 14 Dec. 1825, 29 Dec. 1825, 468–69; and Miller, *Treaties*, 3:209.
65. JQADD, vol. 37, 26 Jan. 1826.
66. Clay to Williams, 10 Feb. 1826, R6, M77, RG59, NA2.
67. Clay to Williams, 11 Feb. 1826, R6, M77, RG59, NA2.
68. JQADD, vol. 37, 11 Feb. 1826.
69. *Richmond Enquirer* (VA), 14 Mar. 1826.
70. Fred Brown, "Williams Descendants Put Money, Sweat Into Restoring Piece Of History," 14 Sept. 2008, *Knoxville News Sentinel*, www.knoxnews.com/entertainment/life/williams-descendants-put-money-sweat-into-restoring-piece-of-history-ep-411055506-359778981.html, archived webpage in author's possession.
71. "From the Norfolk Beacon," *Baltimore Patriot*, 22 Mar. 1826.
72. Henry Clay to Gustavus H. Scott, 8 Mar. 1826, R6, M77, RG59, NA2.
73. Clay to Scott, 14 Mar. 1826, R6, M77, RG59, NA2.
74. Clay to Williams, 15 Mar. 1826, R6, M77, RG59, NA2.
75. Clay to Scott, 14 Mar. 1826, R6, M77, RG59, NA2.
76. "From the Norfolk Beacon," *Baltimore Patriot*, 22 Mar. 1826.
77. Williams to Clay, 10 Apr. 1826, R2, M219, RG59, NA2.
78. Scott to Clay, 10 Apr. 1826, Folder 1, Box 1, A1 Entry 53, NA2.
79. Scott to Clay, 25 Apr. 1826, Folder 1, Box 1, A1 Entry 53, NA2.
80. Williams to Clay, 10 Apr. 1826, R2, M219, RG59, NA2.
81. Scott to Clay, 25 Apr. 1826, Folder 1, Box 1, A1 Entry 53, NA2
82. Scott to Clay, 25 Apr. 1826, Folder 1, Box 1, A1 Entry 53, NA2.
83. Scott to Clay, 25 Apr. 1826, Folder 1, Box 1, A1 Entry 53, NA2. In the end, Scott's five-month, 132-day journey cost the government $968.32. Despite his experiences, Scott applied to serve again in 1827. Scott to Clay, 17 May 1826, J. M. Macpherson to Gustavus Scott, 12 May 1826, Folder 1, Box 1, Entry 53, A1, RG59, NA2; "Expenditures in the Department of State," H. Rpt. 226, 20th Cong., 1st Sess. (5 Apr. 1828), 1005; and JQADD, vol. 50, 25 Jan. 1827.
84. Williams to Clay, 10 Apr. 1826, R2, M219, RG59, NA2.
85. Williams to Clay, 3 Aug. 1826, R2, M219, RG59, NA2.

Chapter Nine

1. For Arce's appearance, see *A Brief Memoir of the Life of James Wilson (Late of Edinburgh), with Extracts from his Journal and Correspondence, Written, Chiefly, during a Residence in Guatemala, the Capital of Central America* (London, 1829), 77. For hog, see *Newburyport Herald* (MA), 12 July 1825.

2. "8. de Sosa, Juan Francisco. Laws and Decrees, 16 de junio y 1 de agosto de 1825," "Impresos guatemaltecos, 1825," Folder 5, Box 1, Miscellaneous Broadsides, BLAC, translated for author by James Irving.

3. George Alexander Thompson, *Narrative of an Official Visit to Guatemala from Mexico* (London: John Murray, 1829), 186.

4. Thompson, *Narrative*, iii–iv. Emphasis in original.

5. Thompson, *Narrative*, 136–37.

6. Thompson, *Narrative*, 189.

7. Thompson, *Narrative*, 138.

8. Thompson, *Narrative*, 163.

9. Thompson, *Narrative*, 138, 141–43.

10. Thompson, *Narrative*, 187.

11. Thompson, *Narrative*, 209.

12. José del Valle, "Un Proyecto de Don José Cecilio del Valle," *Gral. Don Manuel Jose Arce*, ed. Miguel Angel García (San Salvador: Imprenta Nacional, 1945), 2:22–26, 2:24, translated for author by James Irving. Valle's realization came when Thompson gave him a copy of what he called "my *American Dictionary*." Thompson, *Narrative*, 210.

13. Thompson, *Narrative*, 209. The version of the plan published in Arce's papers suggests that the original document in the Guatemalan National Archives is hand-dated 7 September 1825. This date is shortly after Thompson's departure from Central America, but Thompson referenced what must have been a draft in his narrative. Valle, "Un Proyecto," 2:22, 2:26; and Thompson, *Narrative*, 209.

14. Valle, "Un Proyecto," 2:22–26, 2:25.

15. Valle, "Un Proyecto," 2:22–26, 2:23.

16. Thompson, *Narrative*, 210.

17. Thompson, *Narrative*, 185, 208, 210, 319, 321.

18. For Thompson's copies of the maps, see MPK 1/53/3, TNA. For other documents, see FO 15/3, TNA.

19. George Alexander Thompson, Appendix 34, "Proposed Communication between the Seas by the Lake of Nicaragua," *Report on Guatemala*, FO 15/3, TNA.

20. Thompson, Appendix 34, FO 15/3, TNA.

21. Thompson, Appendix 34, FO 15/3, TNA. For Thompson's failure to visit the route, see Thompson, *Narrative*, 204.

22. Thompson, *Narrative*, 193–94.

23. Thompson, Appendix 34, FO 15/3, TNA.

24. Robert Arthur Naylor, "British Commercial Relations with Central America, 1821–1851" (PhD diss., Tulane University, 1958), 19; and Thompson, *Narrative*, 396–99.

25. Thompson, *Narrative*, 398.

26. Joseph Planta to G. A. Thompson, 21 Jan. 1826, Folder 4, Box 1, Selected Papers of George Alexander Thompson (C0963), PUL. According to MeasuringWorth, the British pound was worth $4.83 in 1825. This means that Thompson's total compensation of £1525 for 2.25 years of work was worth $7,365.75 or $3,273.67 per year. This salary was approximately three-quarters of US Chargé Williams's annual salary of $4,500. Lawrence H. Officer, "Dollar-Pound Exchange Rate from 1791," MeasuringWorth, accessed 11 Sept. 2021, www.measuringworth.com/datasets/exchangepound/result.php.

27. "Recepcion del Consul Ingles," *Gral. Don Manuel Jose Arce,* ed. Miguel Angel García (San Salvador: Imprenta Nacional, 1945), 2:28–30, translated for author by James Irving.

28. Naylor, "British Commercial Relations," 21; and Robert A. Naylor, "The British Role in Central America Prior to the Clayton-Bulwer Treaty of 1850," *The Hispanic American Historical Review* 40, 3 (Aug. 1960): 361–82, 366.

29. "Guatemala," *Times* (London), 27 July 1826.

30. Williams to Bolton, 13 June 1826, enclosed in Southard to Adams, 23 Aug. 1826, Reel 477, AFP.

31. Manuel José Arce, "Mensaje del Presidente de la República de Centro-América al Congreso Federal," *Gral. Don Manuel Jose Arce,* ed. Miguel Angel García (San Salvador: Imprenta Nacional, 1945), 2:75–87, 2:76, translated for author by James Irving.

32. Arce, "Mensaje," 2:75–87, 2:76.

33. Arce, "Mensaje," 2:78.

34. Arce, "Mensaje," 2:86–87.

35. Louis E. Bumgartner, *José del Valle of Central America* (Durham, NC: Duke University Press, 1963), 222–23, 229, 230, 233.

36. Arce, "Mensaje," 2:86–87.

37. Arce, "Mensaje," 2:87.

38. Juan Francisco de Sosa, "Esposicion: Presentada al Congreso Federal al Comenzar la Sesión Ordinaria del Año de 1826," *Gral. Don Manuel Jose Arce,* ed. Miguel Angel García (San Salvador: Imprenta Nacional, 1945), 2:88–116, translated for author by James Irving.

39. Sosa, "Esposicion," 2:93.

40. Sosa, "Esposicion," 2:93.

41. Sosa, "Esposicion," 2:110.

42. Sosa, "Esposicion," 2:111.

43. Bumgartner, *Valle,* 246–48, 253.

44. José Cecilio del Valle, "El Grandioso Proyecto del Canal de Nicaragua y la Ambición Extranjera," *Obras de José Cecilio del Valle,* ed. José del Valle and Jorge del Valle Matheu (Guatemala, 1929), 1:132, translated for author by James Irving.

45. Valle, "El Grandioso Proyecto," 1:132–33.

46. Valle, "El Grandioso Proyecto," 1:133–34.

47. Valle, "El Grandioso Proyecto," 1:134–35.

48. Valle, "El Grandioso Proyecto," 1:135–38.

49. Valle, "El Grandioso Proyecto," 1:135–38.

50. Valle, "El Grandioso Proyecto," 1:136–37.

51. Valle, "El Grandioso Proyecto," 1:135–38.

52. Valle, "El Grandioso Proyecto," 1:138–41.

53. For Valle's legal career, see Bumgartner, *Valle,* 25–53.

54. Valle, "El Grandioso Proyecto," 1:141–46.

55. Valle, "El Grandioso Proyecto," 1:141–46.

56. Valle, "El Grandioso Proyecto," 1:145.

57. HR 145, 30th Cong., 2nd Sess. (20 Feb. 1849), 365–66.

58. Valle, "El Grandioso Proyecto," 1:141–46.

59. Valle, "El Grandioso Proyecto," 1:148–49.

Chapter Ten

1. HR 145, 30th Cong., 2nd Sess. (20 Feb. 1849), 362, 367.

2. Rather than a "Secretario de hacienda," Gómez de Argüello is listed as having been appointed a "Gefe de S[ección] de [Hacienda]" in June 1826. Alejandro Marure, *Efemérides de los Hechos Notables Acaecidos en la República de Centro-América desde el Año de 1821 hasta el de 1841* (Guatemala, 1844), 60.

3. HR 145, 30th Cong., 2nd Sess. (20 Feb. 1849), 367.

4. Clay to Williams, 10 Feb. 1826, R6, M77, RG59, NA2.

5. Passenger List *Diomede*, 11 Apr. 1822, R2, M259, RG36, NARA, *New Orleans, Passenger Lists, 1813–1945* database, accessed online through Ancestry.com (Provo, UT: Ancestry.com Operations, 2006).

6. Passenger List *Diomede*, 11 Apr. 1822.

7. Passenger List *Diomede*, 11 Apr. 1822.

8. For Beneski's birth in 1797, see Witold Langrod, "The Ups and Downs of Charles Beneski: An Attempt to Reconstruct a Distant Life History," *The Polish Review* 26, no. 2 (1981): 64–75, 65, 71–72. Langrod's article is the only English-language biographical study of Beneski; it does not include citations. He wrote a monograph on Beneski in Polish with citations, but a Mexican effort to translate it into Spanish stalled. Witold L. Langrod, *O niespokojnym życiu i smutnej śmierci Karola Beneskiego* (Kraków: Wydawnictwo Literackie, 1981); and Gerardo de la Concha, "Carlos Beneski; el Coronel Polaco que Luchó por México," *La Razón de Mexico*, 11 Sept. 2010, www.razon.com.mx/spip.php?article46277, archived webpage in author's possession.

9. Blaufarb, *Bonapartists in the Borderlands*; and Mongey, *Rogue Revolutionaries.*

10. Langrod, "Ups and Downs," 65.

11. Langrod, "Ups and Downs," 73.

12. Langrod, "Ups and Downs," 73.

13. Timothy J. Henderson, *The Mexican Wars for Independence* (New York: Hill and Wang, 2009), 193–204.

14. Quoted in Langrod, "Ups and Downs," 66.

15. Henderson, *Mexican Wars*, 205–7.

16. Langrod, "Ups and Downs," 66. For the family's experience, see Augustin de Iturbide, "Don Agustin de Iturbide," *Records of the American Catholic Historical Society* 27, no. 1 (Mar. 1916): 16–44, 31.

17. Charles de Beneski, *A Narrative of the Last Moments of the Life of Don Augustine de Iturbide, Ex-Emperor of Mexico* (New York, 1825), 22.

18. Iturbide, "Don Agustin," 33.

19. Beneski, *Narrative*, 4–5.

20. Quoted in Iturbide, "Don Agustin," 37.

21. Beneski, *Narrative*, 16–19, 41.

22. Iturbide, "Don Agustin," 38–39.

23. "List of Passengers Entered in the District of Baltimore by Vessels from Foreign Ports from 1st of October to 31 December, 1824," R1, M596, RG36, NARA, "Baltimore, Passenger Lists, 1820–1948" database, accessed online through Ancestry.com.

24. Beneski, *Narrative*, 3.

25. HR 145, 30th Cong., 2nd Sess. (20 Feb. 1849), 367.

26. José del Valle, "Quién Es El Contrante?," *Obras de José Cecilio del Valle*, ed. José del Valle and Jorge del Valle Matheu (Guatemala, 1929), 1:146–48, translated for author by James Irving. Emphasis in original.

27. Louis E. Bumgartner, *José del Valle of Central America* (Durham, NC: Duke University Press, 1963), 179.

28. Bumgartner, *Valle*, 185. The Guatemalan city of Chiquimula also elected Valle to the Mexican Congress, but he accepted the appointment from Tegucigalpa, Honduras.

29. Valle quoted in Bumgartner, *Valle*, 200.

30. Bumgartner, *Valle*, 154, 204–5.

31. Bumgartner, *Valle*, 209.

32. Valle, *"Quién,"* 1:146–48.

33. Valle, *"Quién,"* 1:146–48. Emphasis in original.

34. Clay to Williams, 10 Feb. 1826, R6, M77, RG59, NA2.

35. Clay to Williams, 10 Feb. 1826, R6, M77, RG59, NA2.

36. Clay to Williams, 10 Feb. 1826, R6, M77, RG59, NA2.

37. Williams to Clay, 3 Aug. 1826, R2, M219, RG59, NA2.

38. "400 Pesos Para La Recepcion de Los Diplomaticos," *Gral. Don Manuel Jose Arce*, ed. Miguel Angel Garcia (San Salvador: Imprenta Nacional, 1945), 3:134–35; and Williams to Clay, 3 Aug. 1826, R2, M219, RG59, NA2.

39. The *New York American*'s translation was reprinted as "Central America," *Niles Weekly Register* (Baltimore), 19 Aug. 1826. The speech was also printed with a different translation as "Recognition of the Republic of Guatemala by the United States of America," *Supplement to the Honduras Gazette* (Belize), 12 Aug. 1826.

40. "Central America," *Niles Weekly Register* (Baltimore), 19 Aug. 1826.

41. "Recognition of the Republic of Guatemala by the United States of America," *Supplement to the Honduras Gazette* (Belize), 12 Aug. 1826.

42. Clay to Williams, 10 Feb. 1826, R6, M77, RG59, NA2.

43. "Central America," *Niles Weekly Register* (Baltimore), 19 Aug. 1826.

44. "Recognition of the Republic of Guatemala by the United States of America," *Supplement to the Honduras Gazette* (Belize), 12 Aug. 1826.

45. John Howland & Co and J. & C. Bolton to Edmund Blunt, 4 Sept. 1824, EBFP; and Robert H. Parker to Blunt, 27 Apr. 1825, Folder 1, Box 1, EBFP.

46. *New-Hampshire Patriot & State Gazette* (Concord), 18 July 1825; and "8. de Sosa, Juan Francisco. Laws and Decrees, 16 de junio y 1 de agosto de 1825," "Impresos guatemaltecos, 1825" Folder 5, Box 1, Miscellaneous Broadsides, BLAC.

47. Bolton to Southard, 17 Mar. 1826, Folder 5, Box 21, SLSP.

48. JQADD, vol. 34, 8 Nov. 1823.

49. Bolton to Southard, 17 Mar. 1826, Folder 5, Box 21, SLSP. Although Williams acknowledged receipt of this letter in Guatemala, its text has not survived. Williams to Bolton, 13 June 1826, enclosed in Southard to Adams, 23 Aug. 1826, Reel 477, AFP.

50. Bolton to Southard, 3 Apr. 1826, Folder 5, Box 21, SLSP.

51. Southard to Bolton, 7 Apr. 1826, Folder 5, Box 21, SLSP.

52. Southard to Bolton, 7 Apr. 1826, Folder 5, Box 21, SLSP.

53. Bolton to Southard, 13 Apr. 1826, Folder 5, Box 21, SLSP. For corrupt use of franking privileges, see Woody Holton, "Abigail Adams: Bond Speculator," *The William and Mary Quarterly* 64, no. 4 (Oct. 2007): 821–38, 832–33.

54. Bolton to Southard, 17 Mar. 1826, Folder 5, Box 21, SLSP. Emphasis added.

55. Valle, "*Quién,*" 1:146–48.

56. Williams to Bolton, 13 June 1826, enclosed in Southard to Adams, 23 Aug. 1826, Reel 477, AFP.

57. HR 145, 30th Cong., 2nd Sess. (20 Feb. 1849), 367. Emphasis added.

58. Williams to Bolton, 13 June 1826, enclosed in Southard to Adams, 23 Aug. 1826, Reel 477, AFP.

59. Williams to Clay, 15 June 1826, R2, M219, RG59, NA2. Emphasis in original. For the men's living arrangement, see John Williams to William B. Rochester, 30 Aug. 1827, MM-2006-001, C. M. McClung Historical Collection, East Tennessee History Center, Knoxville, TN.

60. William Phillips to Henry Clay, 8 Aug. 1827, R2, M219, RG59, NA2.

61. "Dispatch No. 1," Williams to Clay, 3 Aug. 1826, R2, M219, RG59, NA2.

62. Flemion, "Arce," 163; and Bumgartner, *Valle*, 252–53.

63. "Dispatch No. 1," Williams to Clay, 3 Aug. 1826, R2, M219, RG59, NA2.

64. "Dispatch No. 1," Williams to Clay, 3 Aug. 1826, R2, M219, RG59, NA2.

65. The dispute runs throughout much of the correspondence of John Williams and William Phillips with the State Department, see especially Williams to Clay, 29 Aug. 1826, and Phillips to Clay, 12 May 1827, R2, M219, RG59, NA2.

66. "Dispatch No. 1," Williams to Clay, 3 Aug. 1826, R2, M219, RG59, NA2.

67. Manuel José Arce, "Reservado," *Gral. Don Manuel Jose Arce*, ed. Miguel Angel Garcia (San Salvador: Imprenta Nacional, 1945), 3:123, translated for author by James Irving. For Cañas's illness, see Clay to Cañas, 24 June 1826, R3, M38, RG59, NA2. For his journey to Central America, see *Rhode-Island American* (Providence), 18 July 1826; *Daily National Journal* (Washington, DC), 17 July 1826; *Daily National Journal* (Washington, DC), 16 Sept. 1826. He traveled on the *Mary Livingston* to the mouth of the San Juan River.

68. Arce, "Reservado," 3:123. Whereas the full text of Cañas's instructions have been lost, González's instructions survive in a 1940s transcription. It refers to "Mr. Bobester" as "representative" of Palmer. Bobester was likely a bad transcription of Beneski, suggesting that a century after the dissolution of the Central American republic, the history of Beneski's negotiation for the canal contract had mostly been forgotten.

69. "Atlantic and Pacific Ocean Company," *The Honduras Gazette and Commercial Advertiser* (Belize), 8 July 1826; and "Shipping Information," *The Honduras Gazette and Commercial Advertiser* (Belize), 8 July 1826.

70. *Baltimore Patriot & Mercantile Advertiser*, 11 Aug. 1826.

71. "Providence, R.I., Aug. 5," *Ohio State Journal* (Columbus), 24 Aug. 1826.

Chapter Eleven

1. HR 145, 30th Cong., 2nd Sess. (20 Feb. 1849), 362.

2. HR 145, 30th Cong., 2nd Sess. (20 Feb. 1849), 365–67.

3. Nathaniel Bowditch, *The New American Practical Navigator*, 6th ed. (New-York: Edmund M. Blunt, 1826). For the book's purpose, see Tamara Plakins Thornton, *Nathaniel*

Bowditch and the Power of Numbers: How a Nineteenth-Century Man of Business, Science, and the Sea Changed American Life (Chapel Hill: The University of North Carolina Press, 2016).

4. The Palmer and Haight families' Quaker history can be found in the Nine Partners, Oblong, and New York Monthly Meeting records, which are held on microfilm at the Friends Historical Library, Swarthmore College.

5. "Boarding & Day School," *Hudson Gazette* (NY), 8 Jan. 1799; "Boarding School," *Weekly Museum* (New York), 6 July 1799; "Advertisement: Insolvency of Peter Palmer," *Daily Advertiser* (New York), 16 Sept. 1795; and "Advertisement: Insolvency Notice for Peter Palmer," *Daily Advertiser* (New York), 9 Dec. 1795.

6. *The Balance and Columbian Repository* (Hudson, NY), 20 Sept. 1803. Other papers described the illness as the "prevailing fever" or "malignant fever." *Mercantile Advertiser* (New York), 6 Sept. 1803; and *Columbian Centinel* (Boston), 10 Sept. 1803.

7. "Obituary: Professor Mariano Velazquez De La Cadena," *New York Herald*, 14 Mar. 1860; and *New-York Weekly Museum*, 29 July 1809.

8. *American Citizen* (New York), 15 Aug. 1810.

9. Mariano Velázquez de la Cadena, *Elementos De La Lengua Inglesa Para Uso De Los Españoles* (New York: Roberto McDermut, 1810), iv. Emphasis in original.

10. "Obituary: Professor Mariano Velazquez De La Cadena," *New York Herald*, 14 Mar. 1860. A revised edition of his bilingual dictionary is still in print. Cecilio Garriga Escribano and Raquel Gállego Paz, "Velázquez de la Cadena y la Lexicografía Bilingüe Inglés / Español," *Proceedings of the 13th Euralex International Congress* (2008): 1105–14.

11. "Advertisement," *New York Evening Post*, 12 Mar. 1807; and "Advertisement," *Public Advertiser* (New York), 10 Sept. 1807.

12. "An Extraordinary Talent for Acquiring Languages," *The Medical Repository of Original Essays and Intelligence, Relative to Physic, Surgery, Chemistry, and Natural History* (1800–1824), vol. 6 (Feb.–Apr. 1809).

13. Dael Norwood, "Mr. Jefferson's Mandarin, Or, a Controversial Promotion," *Readex Report* 8, no. 4 (Nov. 2013).

14. Samuel Latham Mitchill to Thomas Jefferson, 12 July 1808, https://founders.archives.gov/documents/Jefferson/99-01-02-8305.

15. "A List of the Members of the New York Manumission Society," Friends Historical Library of Swarthmore College, https://digitalcollections.tricolib.brynmawr.edu/object/sc275026.

16. Aaron H. Palmer to James Madison, Feb. 1809, James Madison Papers, Library of Congress, http://hdl.loc.gov/loc.mss/mjm.10_1109_1110. Palmer's missing 1810 letter to Dolley Madison is referenced in an enclosing letter to James Madison. Palmer to Madison, 25 June 1810, James Madison Papers, Library of Congress, http://hdl.loc.gov/loc.mss/mjm.12_0367_0368.

17. Aaron H. Palmer to Robert Smith, 10 Jan. 1811, R6, M438, RG59, NA2.

18. "Insolvents, Petitioning under the New Insolvent Law," *Balance and State Journal* (Albany, NY), 23 Apr. 1811; and 1 May 1811, NY MM 1805–1812, Friends Historical Library, Swarthmore College.

19. "Translations," *New-York Gazette*, 27 Aug. 1811.

20. 1812–1814 Return, Warren 17.85, Grand Lodge Archives Collection, Chancellor Robert R. Livingston Masonic Library, New York; and Aaron H. Palmer, Act of 55–120 W.T. 11976, War of 1812, Bounty Land File, NARA.

21. 14 Feb. 1815, M233, RG94, NARA, "U.S. Army, Register of Enlistments, 1798–1914" database, accessed online through Ancestry.com; 22 June 1815, Roll 1, "Registers and Indexes for Passport Applications, 1810–1906" database, accessed online through Ancestry .com; "Notice," *Commercial Advertiser* (New York), 2 Oct. 1815; Benjamin Waterhouse, *Journal of a Young Man of Massachusetts* (Boston, 1816), 201; and 8 Mar. 1816, R75, M124, RG45, NARA.

22. *Documents of the Assembly of the State of New York*, 141st Sess., 29, no. 62 (Albany, 1918), 144.

23. "Land for Sale," *National Advocate* (New York), 24 Aug. 1816; and "Mayor's Court," *Courier* (New York), 31 Aug. 1815.

24. "Appointments by the Council," *Columbian* (New York), 10 Apr. 1816.

25. For examples, see James Willett v. Leonard Lispenard (8 July 1817), CL 151, 759, CCNYC; and Richard Udall v. John T. Champlin et al., CL 159, 76–80, CCNYC. For list of duties of masters of chancery, see D. T. Blake, *An Historical Treatise on the Practice of the Court of Chancery of the State of New York* (New York, 1818), 11.

26. Authors continue to tell this story. For recent examples, see Oscar Handlin, "The Bill of Rights in Its Context," *The American Scholar* 69, no. 2 (Spring 1993): 177–86, 183; Benedicta Ada Susu, *Law of Torts* (Lagos, Nigeria: CJC Press, 1996), 240; John D. Gordan III, "The Price of Vanity, or The Lawyer with the Ears of an Ass," *The Historical Society of the Courts of the State of New York* 1, no. 2 (Spring/Summer 2004): 3–6; Eugene Volokh, "Symbolic Expression and the Original Meaning of the First Amendment," *Georgetown Law Journal* 97, no. 4 (Apr. 2009): 1057-84, 1065; and Katlijne Van der Stighelen, "A Self-Portrait by Francesco Mezzara (1774–1845), the Italian Painter Who Changed New York State Constitutional Law with a Pair of Ass's Ears," *Nineteenth-Century Art Worldwide* 13, no. 2 (Autumn 2014), www .19thc-artworldwide.org/autumn14/new-discovery-a-self-portrait-by-francesco-mezzara.

27. *Columbian* (New York), 25 Mar. 1818. Emphasis in original.

28. Juando v. Taylor, 2 Paine 652 (1818), 2 Paine 655, 3 Wheeler C.C. 382, 13 F.Cas. 1179, No. 7558, Westlaw, page 1. For the names of the other attorneys, see "Commodore Taylor's Cases," *New-York Judicial Repository* 1, no. 3 (Nov. 1818): 121.

29. John Wesley Jarvis, "Aaron Haight Palmer" (1819). This image appears in Van der Stighelen, "A Self-Portrait" (2014).

30. For legal work, see "In Chancery," *Evening Post* (New York), 21 June 1819; "In Chancery," *National Advocate* (New York), 6 Dec. 1819; *Columbian* (New York), 23 Dec. 1819; "In Chancery," *National Advocate* (New York), 4 Jan. 1820; *Commercial Advertiser* (New York), 22 Jan. 1820; "In Chancery," *National Advocate* (New York), 21 Nov. 1820; "A Very Valuable Estate for Sale," *Evening Post* (New York), 28 Apr. 1821; "In Chancery," *Evening Post* (New York), 28 Apr. 1821; *In the Court for the Trial of Impeachments and the Correction of Errors between Thomas Gibbons, Appellant, and Aaron Ogden, Respondent, Case on the Part of the Appellant* (New York: Clayton & Kingsland, 1819), 38–39; Bogert v. Commereau et al. (1819), CL225 and CL412, CCNYC; Dixey v. Cox (1819), BM 796-D, CCNYC; and Dixey v. Cox (1820), CL-266, CCNYC.

31. *National Advocate* (New York), 22 Nov. 1820.

32. "New-York Athenaeum," *National Advocate* (New York), 13 Jan. 1819; and "An account of monies collected on account of the New-York Historical Society from the Members for arrears up to the 1st January 1820 by S. B. Hutchings, Sub-Librarian," Folder 2, Box 7, John Pintard Papers, NYHS.

33. Edward T. Schultz, *History of Freemasonry in Maryland* (Baltimore: J. H. Medairy, 1888), 4:686, 4:690.

34. "Palmer, Aaron H. (1821)," R13, M439, RG59, NA2.

35. Aaron H. Palmer to James Madison, Feb. 1809, James Madison Papers, Library of Congress, http://hdl.loc.gov/loc.mss/mjm.10_1109_1110; and Palmer to Smith, 10 Jan. 1811, R6, M438, RG59, NA2.

36. Jacob Morton to James Monroe, 10 Mar. 1821, "Palmer, Aaron H. (1821)," R19, M439, RG59, NA2.

37. JQADD, vol. 31, 16 Mar. 1821.

38. JQADD, vol. 32, 3 Apr. 1821.

39. *Washington Gazette* (DC), 15 May 1821.

40. "From the National Intelligencer, May 16," *New-York Evening Post*, 18 May 1821.

41. JQADD, vol 23, vol. 48, May 1821. Full diary entries resume in August 1821.

42. JQADD, vol. 32, 5 Apr. 1821, 11 Apr. 1821, 15 Apr. 1821, 16 Apr. 1821, 20 Apr. 1821, 23 Apr. 1821, 26 Apr. 1821, 27 Apr. 1821, 7 May 1821, 9 May 1821.

43. James Hogg v. George Kenning (1824), BM 1741-H, CCNYC. See also "Spanish Claims," *Evening Post* (New York), 23 Apr. 1821. For evidence of his continued legal practice, see "In Chancery," *Evening Post* (New York), 28 Apr. 1821; "A Very Valuable Estate for Sale," *Evening Post* (New York), 3 May 1821; and John Wesley Jarvis's letter to the mayor of Savannah included in Harold E. Dickson, *John Wesley Jarvis: American Painter, 1780–1840* (New York: New-York Historical Society, 1949), 237.

44. *New-York Evening Post*, 21 May 1813; *National Advocate* (New York), 19 Oct. 1816; *New York Columbian*, 22 May 1817; and *New-York Daily Advertiser*, 2 Aug. 1820.

45. Patricia Cline Cohen, *The Murder of Helen Jewett: The Life and Death of a Prostitute in Nineteenth-Century New York* (New York: Alfred A. Knopf, 1998).

46. José M. Géigel to Mariano Velázquez de la Cadena, 10 Sept. 1825, Azoy Family Papers, Private Collection, translated for author by James Irving.

47. "Extract of a Letter," *Connecticut Mirror* (Hartford), 15 Sept. 1823.

48. Ramon R. Gonzalez to Mariano Velázquez de la Cadena, 21 Apr. 1826, Azoy Family Papers, Private Collection, translated for author by James Irving.

49. "Obituary: Professor Mariano Velazquez de la Cadena, of Mexico," *New York Herald*, 14 Mar. 1860.

50. *New York Evening Post*, 25 July 1825, *U.S. Newspaper Extractions from the Northeast, 1704–1930* database, accessed online through Ancestry.com. Ancestry's transcription suggests Mary was 53 years old. Given her marriage to Peter Palmer in 1780, she was likely a decade older.

51. *Journal of the Assembly of the State of New York at Their Forty-Eighth Session* (Albany, 1825), 41; and "In Assembly. An Act to Incorporate the President, Directors, and Company of the Interest Bank" (1825), Folder 1, Misc MSS Hendricks, NYHS. He had recently been admitted as a counselor before the US Supreme Court perhaps related to his work on the case of *Gibbons v. Ogden*. "Supreme Court," *Richmond Enquirer* (VA), 14 Feb. 1824.

52. "Stock, Exchange, and Loan Office," *Republican Advocate* (Batavia, NY), 5 Aug. 1825. Emphasis added. For examples in newspapers, see *Rochester Telegraph* (NY), 30 Aug. 1825; *Sentinel and Witness* (Middletown, CT), 21 Sept. 1825; "Stock, Exchange, and Loan Office," *Connecticut Courant* (Hartford), 1 Nov. 1826; and *Ohio State Journal* (Columbus), 3 Nov. 1825. A French language version emphasized claims related to St. Domingue. *Le Réveil* (New York) 1, no. 6 (19 Nov. 1825).

53. HR 145, 30th Cong., 2nd Sess. (20 Feb. 1849), 367.

54. JQADD, vol. 35, 4 July 1826.

55. JQADD, vol. 35, 6 July 1826.

56. JQADD, vol. 35, 8 July 1826.

57. JQADD, vol. 35, 9 July 1826.

58. JQADD, vol. 35, 9 July 1826, 10 July 1826.

59. JQADD, vol. 35, 11 July 1826.

60. JQADD, vol. 35, 4 July 1826.

61. JQADD, vol. 35, 12 July 1826.

62. JQADD, vol. 35, 13 July 1826.

63. JQADD, vol. 35, 5 July 1826.

64. JQADD, vol. 35, 14 July 1826.

65. JQADD, vol. 35, 12 Aug. 1826.

66. JQADD, vol. 35, 14 Aug. 1826.

67. JQADD, vol. 35, 27 July 1826, 5 Aug. 1826.

68. JQADD, vol. 35, 8 Aug. 1826. Adams continued to pursue the purchase of the house, hiring a surveyor and seeking a decree from the probate court "to sanction the proceeding."

69. JQADD, vol. 35, 17 Aug. 1826.

70. James E. Lewis Jr., *The American Union and the Problem of Neighborhood: The United States and the Collapse of the Spanish Empire, 1783–1829* (Chapel Hill: The University of North Carolina Press, 1998), 199–205. Lewis argues that both Jackson's supporters' opposition and the president's own choices should be blamed for the failures of his ambitious agenda.

71. Adams quoted in Lewis, *American Union*, 207.

72. Lewis, *American Union*, 207.

73. Cañas to Clay, 14 Nov. 1825, in Manning, *Diplomatic Correspondence*, 2:883. Bolívar's vice president and the Mexican government had also extended invitations to Washington. Charles R. Vaughan to H. G. Ward, 13 Feb. 1826, in "The Papers of Sir Charles Vaughan," *The American Historical Review* 7, no. 2 (Jan. 1902): 304–29, 316; and N. Andrew N. Cleven, "The First Panama Mission and the Congress of the United States," *The Journal of Negro History* 13, no. 3 (July 1928): 225–54, 226.

74. Clay to Cañas, 30 Nov. 1825, R3, M38, RG59, NA2.

75. Henry Clay to John Sargeant, 24 Nov. 1825, R5, M77, RG59, NA2; and Henry Clay to R. G. Anderson, 25 Nov. 1825, R5, M77, RG59, NA2.

76. Clay to Rochester, 30 Nov. 1825, R5, M77, RG59, NA2.

77. Clay to Anderson, 25 Nov. 1825, R5, M77, RG59, NA2.

78. Fitz, *Our Sister Republics*, 200; and Andrew Shankman, "Daniel Raymond, Mathew Carey, the Missouri Crisis, and the Global 1820s," *A Fire Bell in the Past: The Missouri Crisis*

at 200, ed. Jeffrey L. Pasley and John Craig Hammond (Columbia: University of Missouri Press, 2021), 373–99.

79. Lewis, *American Union*, 203–14; Fitz, *Our Sister Republics*, 194–239; Andrew R. L. Cayton, "The Debate over the Panama Congress and the Origins of the Second American Party System," *The Historian* 47, no. 2 (Feb. 1985): 219–38; Cleven, "The First Panama Mission," 225–54; and Jeffrey J. Malanson, "The Congressional Debate over U.S. Participation in the Congress of Panama, 1825–1826: Washington's Farewell Address, Monroe's Doctrine, and the Fundamental Principles of U.S. Foreign Policy," *Diplomatic History* 30, no. 5 (Nov. 2006): 813–38.

80. Clay to Anderson, 15 Mar. 1826, R6, M77, RG59, NA2; and Cayton, "Debate over the Panama Congress," 222.

81. Gustavus Scott to Henry Clay, 25 Apr. 1826, Folder 1, Box 1, A1 Entry 53, RG59, NA2; and Clay to Williams, 15 Mar. 1826, R6, M77, RG59, NA2.

82. Clay to Anderson, 15 Mar. 1826, R6, M77, RG59, NA2.

83. Clay to Rochester, 10 May 1826, R6, M77, RG59, NA2. The next day, Clay conveyed the choice to Sargeant; Sargeant threatened to resign rather than travel to the Isthmus of Panama during the summer. Clay to Sargeant, 11 May 1826, R6, M77, RG59, NA2.

84. Clifton Wharton to Henry Clay, 26 May 1826, 27 May 1826, Folder 1, Box 1, A1 Entry 53, RG59, NA2.

85. Clay to Rochester, 10 May 1826, R6, M77, RG59, NA2.

86. Clay to Wharton, 22 May 1826, R6, M77, RG59, NA2; and Wharton to Clay, 29 June 1826, Folder 1, Box 1, A1 Entry 53, RG59, NA2.

87. Wharton to Clay, 27 June 1826, Folder 1, Box 1, A1 Entry 53, RG59, NA2; and Jan Schoonhoven and Casper Tymen de Jong, "The Dutch Observer at the Congress of Panama in 1826," *The Hispanic American Historical Review* 36, no. 1 (Feb. 1956): 28–37, 30.

88. Wharton to Clay, 27 July 1826, Folder 1, Box 1, A1 Entry 53, RG59, NA2.

89. John Lynch, *Simón Bolívar: A Life* (New Haven: Yale University Press, 2006), 214; Graham H. Stuart, "Simón Bolívar's Project for a League of Nations," *The Southwestern Political and Social Science Quarterly* 7, no. 3 (Dec. 1926): 238–52, 247; and Schoonhoven and de Jong, "Dutch Observer," 28–37.

90. James F. Hopkins and Mary W. M. Hargreaves, eds., *The Papers of Henry Clay* (Lexington: University Press of Kentucky, 1973), 5:636. In the fall of 1826, Sargeant and Rochester were directed to travel to Tacubaya, Mexico, where the congress aimed to reconvene. When they arrived, they found few delegates and nothing diplomatic unfolding. Clay to Sargeant, 14 Nov. 1826, R6, M77, RG59, NA2; and Schoonhoven and de Jong, "Dutch Observer," 35. In early 1827, the Senate confirmed US Minister to Mexico Joel Poinsett as Anderson's replacement. Cayton, "Debate over the Panama Congress," 236.

91. Both the manuscript and print versions span more than thirty pages. Clay to Anderson and Sargeant, 8 May 1826, R6, M77, RG59, NA2; and Hopkins and Hargreaves, *Papers of Henry Clay*, 5:313–44.

92. Hopkins and Hargreaves, *Papers of Henry Clay*, 5:335–36.

93. JQADD, vol. 35, 17 Aug. 1826.

94. Hopkins and Hargreaves, *Papers of Henry Clay*, 5:335–36.

95. Hopkins and Hargreaves, *Papers of Henry Clay*, 5:335–36.

96. Hopkins and Hargreaves, *Papers of Henry Clay*, 5:343n61.

97. Hopkins and Hargreaves, *Papers of Henry Clay*, 5:336.

98. Hopkins and Hargreaves, *Papers of Henry Clay*, 5:336.

99. Hopkins and Hargreaves, *Papers of Henry Clay*, 5:336.

100. Simón Bolívar, "Reply of a South American to a Gentleman of this Island," *Selected Writings of Bolivar*, ed. Harold A. Bierck Jr. (New York: Colonial Press, 1951), 1:118.

101. Bolívar, "Reply," 1:119.

Chapter Twelve

1. HR 145, 30th Cong., 2nd Sess. (20 Feb. 1849), 362; and Thomas Longworth, *Longworth's American Almanac, New-York Register and City Directory* (New York, 1826), 26, 31, 368. New York City's street addresses have shifted over time. Henry B. Hoffmann, "Changed House Numbers and Lost Street Names in New York of the Early Nineteenth Century and Later," *The New-York Historical Society Quarterly Bulletin* 21 (1937): 67–92, 71. For a recreation of an 1822 map of Wall Street, see Henry Wysham Lanier, *A Century of Banking in New York, 1822–1922* (New York: George H. Doran, 1922).

2. Longworth, *Longworth's American Almanac* (1826), 90; and "The Guide through The City of New-York is Longworth's Explanatory Map and Plan," (New York, 1817). The Bolton estate would now be located at the corner of Eleventh and Bleeker Streets.

3. Bolton to Southard, 14 Aug. 1826, enclosed in Southard to Adams, 23 Aug. 1826, Reel 477, AFP.

4. David Longworth, *Longworth's American Almanac, New York Register, and City Directory* (New York, 1816), 129; and "Evening Post Marine List," *Evening Post* (New York), 13 Nov. 1815.

5. Robert Bolton, *Genealogical and Biographical Account of the Family of Bolton* (New York: John A. Gray, 1862), 112–41.

6. Bolton, *Genealogical and Biographical Account*, 129–37.

7. Bolton, *Genealogical and Biographical Account*, 118–19.

8. "Bank of the United States," *Poulson's American Daily Advertiser* (Philadelphia), 3 Jan. 1820.

9. "Institution for the Deaf and Dumb," *Patron of Industry* (New York), 30 May 1821; and John Summerfield, *A Sermon, Preached in the Reformed Dutch Church, in Nassau-Street, In Behalf of the New-York Institution for the Instruction of the Deaf and Dumb* (New-York, 1822), 15.

10. In the 1825 city directory, John Bolton is listed as living at the corner of Herring Street and Hammond Street. The brothers are listed as sharing a mercantile firm at 84 South Street (86). The next year, Curtis is described as a merchant at 63 Washington Street, and the home at Herring and Hammond is listed under Curtis's name (90). John is listed only by the Delaware and Hudson Canal Company's address at 13 Wall Street (90, 29). In the 1827 directory, Curtis's office has relocated to 129 Maiden Lane, but John's address and Curtis's association with the house remain unchanged (92).

11. "Curtis Bolton" and "John Bolton," New York Ward 1, New York, New York, page 24, M33, *1820 United States Federal Census* database, accessed online through Ancestry.com; Dawn Morin, "Out of the Archives: Bolton Family of Savannah Georgia," *The Samuel Harrison Society Newsletter* (Fall/Winter 2008–9): 6–7; and Bolton, *Genealogical and Biographical Account*, 129–37.

12. Leslie Harris, *In the Shadow of Slavery: African Americans in New York City, 1626–1863* (Chicago: University of Chicago Press, 2003), 94.

13. The brothers invested in ships, which transported cotton, tobacco, rice, hides, chocolate, tea, iron, sugar, wood, china, and more to places in the United States, Europe, the Caribbean, and South America. See for example, *Commercial Advertiser* (New York), 4 June 1816; *Commercial Advertiser* (New York), 11 July 1816; *New York Gazette*, 14 Mar. 1817; *Commercial Advertiser* (New York), 30 Apr. 1817; *New-York Daily Advertiser*, 15 July 1817; "For Savannah," *New-York Gazette*, 30 Oct. 1817; *New-York Daily Advertiser*, 26 July 1819; *Evening Post* (New York), 28 July 1819; and *Mercantile Advertiser* (New York), 10 Jan. 1826. Along with their third surviving brother, Edwin, they invested in a sawmill. *Washington Whig* (Bridgeton, NJ), 12 Apr. 1819. For real estate sales, see *Mercantile Advertiser* (New York), 15 Mar. 1819; "For Sale," *Evening Post* (New York), 15 Oct. 1819; and *Mercantile Advertiser* (New York), 8 Mar. 1820.

14. *New-York Evening Post*, 14 June 1826.

15. "Chapter LXI. Of the Laws of Pennsylvania, Passed in the Session of 1822–23. An Act to Improve the Navigation of the River Lackawaxen," *Charter of the Delaware and Hudson Canal Company, with the Several Acts Supplementary to the Same* (New York, 1859), 3–17; Sally M. Schultz and Joan Hollister, "The Delaware and Hudson Canal Company: Forming, Financing, and Reporting on an Early 19th Century Corporation," *The Accounting Historians Journal* 41, no. 2 (2014): 111–51; and Sean Patrick Adams, "Warming the Poor and Growing Consumers: Fuel Philanthropy in the Early Republic's Urban North," *The Journal of American History* 95, no. 1 (June 2008): 69–94.

16. "An Act to Incorporate the President, Managers and Company of the Delaware and Hudson Canal Company," *Charter of the Delaware and Hudson Canal Company, with the Several Acts Supplementary to the Same* (New York, 1859), 18–32, 18.

17. "An Act to Incorporate," *Charter of the DHCC*, 19.

18. "An Act to Incorporate," *Charter of the DHCC*, 21.

19. Schultz and Hollister, "Delaware and Hudson Canal Company," 119.

20. "An Act to Amend the Act Entitled 'An Act to Incorporate the President, Managers and Company of the Delaware and Hudson Canal Company,'" *Charter of the Delaware and Hudson Canal Company, with the Several Acts Supplementary to the Same* (New York, 1859), 33.

21. "An Act Further to Amend the Act Entitled 'An Act to Incorporate the President, Managers and Company of the Delaware and Hudson Canal Company,'" *Charter of the Delaware and Hudson Canal Company, with the Several Acts Supplementary to the Same* (New York, 1859), 34–37.

22. Schultz and Hollister, "The Delaware and Hudson Canal Company," 120.

23. Ironically, the DHCC gained a significant market for its coal by selling it to the city's institutions that supported the poor; Philip Hone played a role in convincing philanthropic institutions to adopt the DHCC's anthracite heat. Adams, "Warming the Poor," 69–94.

24. Schultz and Hollister, "The Delaware and Hudson Canal Company," 113.

25. Thomas Longworth, *Longworth's American Almanac, New-York Register and City Directory* (New York, 1825), 29.

26. Schultz and Hollister, "The Delaware and Hudson Canal Company," 120. Until his 1851 death, Hone continued to serve on the DHCC board.

27. Longworth, *Longworth's American Almanac* (1826), 29.

28. "To Let," *New-York Evening Post*, 19 Apr. 1826.

29. Williams to Bolton, 13 June 1826, enclosed in Southard to Adams, 23 Aug. 1826, Reel 477, AFP.

30. Bolton to Southard, 14 Aug. 1826, enclosed in Southard to Adams, 23 Aug. 1826, Reel 477, AFP.

31. HR 145, 30th Cong., 2nd Sess. (20 Feb. 1849), 362–66.

32. Bolton to Southard, 14 Aug. 1826, enclosed in Southard to Adams, 23 Aug. 1826, Reel 477, AFP.

33. "An Act to Incorporate," *Charter of the DHCC*, 16, 23, 36. Interestingly, the Pennsylvania Legislature repealed this provision in 1852. Meanwhile, New York added an option to buy back shares in the canal when in 1827, the DHCC needed even more capital to build its canal, and the state backed its additional stock issue. "Chapter LXI," *Charter of the DHCC*, 16–17; and "An Act to Loan the Credit of the People of the State of New York, to the President, Managers, and Company of the Delaware and Hudson Canal Company, and for Other Purposes," *Charter of the Delaware and Hudson Canal Company, with the Several Acts Supplementary to the Same* (New York, 1859), 49–50.

34. Bolton to Southard, 14 Aug. 1826, enclosed in Southard to Adams, 23 Aug. 1826, Reel 477, AFP.

35. "An Act to Incorporate," *Charter of the DHCC*, 23.

36. "An Act to Loan," *Charter of the DHCC*, 47.

37. Bolton to Southard, 14 Aug. 1826, enclosed in Southard to Adams, 23 Aug. 1826, Reel 477, AFP.

38. "Chapter LXI," *Charter of the DHCC*, 12. Protecting the lumber industry, the Pennsylvania charter entitled wood-based commodities to reduced rates or free passage if ramps that preserved the existing rafting course were not constructed by the company.

39. "Chap. LXXVIII. Of the Laws of Pennsylvania. A Supplement to the Act Entitled, 'An Act to Improve the Navigation of the River Lackawaxen,'" *Charter of the Delaware and Hudson Canal Company, with the Several Acts Supplementary to the Same* (New York, 1859), 40.

40. "An Act to Incorporate," *Charter of the DHCC*, 27.

41. "An Act to Loan," *Charter of the DHCC*, 50–51.

42. Bolton to Southard, 14 Aug. 1826, enclosed in Southard to Adams, 23 Aug. 1826, Reel 477, AFP.

43. Clay to Cañas, 24 June 1826, R3, M38, RG59, NA2.

44. *Daily National Journal* (Washington, DC), 17 July 1826.

45. *Rhode-Island American* (Providence), 18 July 1826.

46. Bolton to Southard, 14 Aug. 1826, enclosed in Southard to Adams, 23 Aug. 1826, Reel 477, AFP.

47. *Daily National Journal* (Washington, DC), 16 Sept. 1826.

48. Flemion, "Arce," 171.

49. Flemion, "Arce," 167.

50. Flemion, "Arce," 171.

51. Flemion, "Arce," 172–74.

52. Flemion, "Arce," 168–71.

53. Esteban Duque Estrada Sacasa, *Nicaragua Historia y Familias, 1821–1853* (Managua, 2001), 119–25.

54. Williams to Clay, 31 Nov. 1826, R2, M219, RG59, NA2.

55. Until his death in 1844, Cañas navigated the region's tumultuous politics, serving in high offices both in the Republic of Central America and in El Salvador. Víctor Jerez, "Dr. Antonio Jose Cañas," *Biografias de Vincentinos Ilustres* (San Salvador: Imprenta Nacional, 1935), 29–36; and Roberto Molina Y Morales, *Los Minestros de Hacienda, 1838–1871* (San Salvador: Ministerio de Hacienda, 1970), 25–36.

56. Bolton to Southard, 14 Aug. 1826, enclosed in Southard to Adams, 23 Aug. 1826, Reel 477, AFP.

57. Bolton to Southard, 14 Aug. 1826, enclosed in Southard to Adams, 23 Aug. 1826, Reel 477, AFP.

58. Williams to Bolton, 13 June 1826, enclosed in Southard to Adams, 23 Aug. 1826, Reel 477, AFP.

59. Southard to Adams, 23 Aug. 1826, Reel 477, AFP.

60. JQADD, vol. 35, 19 Oct. 1826.

61. Clay to Adams, 12 Aug. 1826, 20 Sept. 1826, Hopkins and Hargreaves, *The Papers of Henry Clay*, 5:610–11, 5:695.

62. Charles Vaughan to George Canning, 2 Oct. 1826, "The Papers of Sir Charles Vaughan," *American Historical Review* 7, no. 2 (Jan. 1902): 304–29, 311–12.

63. Vaughan to Canning, 2 Oct. 1826, "Papers of Sir Charles Vaughan," 311–12.

64. "Atlantic and Pacific Canal," *Salem Gazette* (MA), 10 Oct. 1826.

65. "Canal between the Atlantic and Pacific," *Essex Register* (Salem, MA), 24 Aug. 1826.

66. "A Great Enterprise," *New England Farmer* (Boston), 8 Sept. 1826.

67. 20 Jan. 1825, 16 Mar. 1825, 20 Mar. 1825, EBJ.

68. "A Great Enterprise," *New England Farmer* (Boston), 8 Sept. 1826.

69. "From the Savannah Georgian, Sept. 5. From Guatemala," *City Gazette* (Charleston, SC), 7 Sept. 1826.

70. HR 145, 30th Cong., 2nd Sess. (20 Feb. 1849), 365.

71. "From the Savannah Georgian, Sept. 5. From Guatemala," *City Gazette* (Charleston, SC), 7 Sept. 1826.

72. *Richmond Enquirer* (VA), 1 Sept. 1826.

73. "Atlantic and Pacific Canal," *New-Bedford Mercury* (MA), 8 Sept. 1826. It defended and expanded this view in several subsequent articles. "Atlantic and Pacific Canal," *Salem Gazette* (MA), 29 Sept. 1826; and "Atlantic and Pacific Canal," *Salem Gazette* (MA), 10 Oct. 1826.

74. "Atlantic and Pacific Canal," *Richmond Enquirer* (VA), 29 Sept. 1826. For Palmer's communication with the *National Intelligencer* and that newspaper's favorable interpretation, see "Canal of Nicaragua," *National Intelligencer*, 25 Sept. 1826 reprinted in HR 145, 30th Cong., 2nd Sess. (20 Feb. 1849), 375–77.

75. "Atlantic and Pacific Canal," *Richmond Enquirer* (VA), 29 Sept. 1826; "Atlantic and Pacific Canal," *Richmond Whig* (VA), 29 Sept. 1826; "Atlantic and Pacific Canal," *Niles Weekly Register* (Baltimore) 31 (20 Sept. 1826): 72–73; and "Atlantic and Pacific Canal," *Edwardsville Spectator* (IL), 20 Oct. 1826.

76. "Atlantic and Pacific Canal," *Richmond Enquirer* (VA), 29 Sept. 1826.

77. Vaughan to Canning, 2 Oct. 1826, "Papers of Sir Charles Vaughan," 311–12.

78. Vaughan to Canning, 2 Oct. 1826, "Papers of Sir Charles Vaughan," 312.

79. JQADD, vol. 35, 17 Aug. 1826.

80. "The Canal of the Isthmus," *Niles' Weekly Register* (Baltimore), 2 Sept. 1826.

Chapter Thirteen

1. 3 Sept. 1826, DWCD.

2. T. V. Cuyler, *T. V. Cuyler's Albany Directory, For The Year 1825: Containing an Alphabetical List of Residents within the City* (Albany, 1825), 27; and T. V. Cuyler, *T. V. Cuyler's Albany Directory, For The Year 1827: Containing an Alphabetical List of Residents within the City* (Albany, 1827), 27. For the chair, see Jeff Richman, "The Chair in which He Died," (6 Jan. 2014), www.green-wood.com/2014/the-chair-in-which-he-died/; and Celeste Brewer, "The *Other* DeWitt Clinton Chair," *News from Columbia's Rare Book & Manuscript Library* (31 Oct. 2019), https://blogs.cul.columbia.edu/rbml/2019/10/31/the-other-dewitt-clinton-chair/.

3. 13 Aug. 1826, 21 Aug. 1826, 22 Aug. 1826, 25 Aug. 1826, 31 Aug. 1826, DWCD. Compare to the lean, standing Clinton painted a decade earlier by John Wesley Jarvis, who painted Aaron H. Palmer around the same time. In the summer of 1826, Clinton also sat for sculptor William John Coffee. Only an earlier Clinton bust by Coffee survives. George Catlin, "De Witt Clinton (1790–1828)," c. 1825–27, NYHS, https://emuseum.nyhistory.org/objects/31602/de-witt-clinton-17091828; John Wesley Jarvis, "De Witt Clinton," c. 1816, NYHS, https://emuseum.nyhistory.org/objects/41061/de-witt-clinton-17691828; and William John Coffee, "DeWitt Clinton," c. 1817, NYHS, https://emuseum.nyhistory.org/objects/28704/dewitt-clinton-17691828. For Clinton's accident, see Evan Cornog, *The Birth of Empire: DeWitt Clinton and the American Experience, 1769–1828* (New York: Oxford University Press, 1998), 6, 138, 180.

4. DeWitt Clinton to Aaron H. Palmer, Letterbook vol. 22, p. 448, DWCP. Emphasis in original. For Clinton's career as a naturalist and his 1810 canal journal, see David I. Spanagel, *DeWitt Clinton & Amos Eaton: Geology & Power in Early New York* (Baltimore: Johns Hopkins University Press, 2014), 49–56, 87; and Cornog, *Birth of Empire*, 109–12. Clinton recorded his observations of Haudenosaunee life in this diary, which informed his famous 1811 speech at the New-York Historical Society. William W. Campbell, *The Life and Writings of De Witt Clinton* (New York: Baker and Scribner, 1849), 27–266.

5. For Clinton's cousin Simeon Dewitt, see Spanagel, *Clinton & Eaton*, 86–87; and Brian Phillips Murphy, *Building the Empire State: Political Economy in the Early Republic* (Philadelphia: University of Pennsylvania Press, 2015), 166–69. For the dispossession of the Haudenosaunee nations, see Laurence M. Hauptman, *Conspiracy of Interests: Iroquois Dispossession and the Rise of New York State* (Syracuse, NY: Syracuse University Press, 1999).

6. For Clinton's scientific career, see Spanagel, *Clinton & Eaton*, 44–62.

7. Edward A. Fitzpatrick, *The Educational Views and Influence of DeWitt Clinton* (New York: Arno Press, 1969, 1911), 131–35.

8. Samuel Rezneck, "A Traveling School of Science on the Erie Canal in 1826," *New York History* 40, no. 3 (July 1959): 255–69, 255, 259. For George's participation in the flotilla, see Spanagel, *Clinton & Eaton*, 236–37n43; and George W. Clinton, "Journal of a Tour from Albany to Lake Erie in 1826," *Buffalo Historical Society Publications* (Buffalo, 1910), 14:273–305.

9. Clinton to Palmer, 3 Sept. 1826, Letterbook vol. 22, p. 448, DWCP.

10. Schultz, *History of Freemasonry*, 4:686, 4:690.

11. 12 Oct. 1826, 13 Oct. 1826, DWCD.

12. "From the N. Y. Commercial Advertiser of the 19th Inst.," *Daily National Journal* (Washington, DC), 23 Sept. 1826; Matt Malette and Mike Allen, "Albany Archives: Masonic Lodge Home to Historic Sword," 8 July 2017, https://spectrumlocalnews.com/nys/capital-region/albany-archives/2017/09/7/albany-archives-masonic-lodge-home-to-historic-sword; and Steven C. Bullock, *Revolutionary Brotherhood: Freemasonry and the Transformation of the American Social Order, 1730–1840* (Chapel Hill: The University of North Carolina Press for the Omohundro Institute, 1996).

13. "Strange Transactions at Batavia," *Eastern Argus* (Portland, ME), 20 Oct. 1826.

14. In early 1827, a Virginian Mason wrote to Clinton about the local "excitement" surrounding "The Morgan affair." Office-holding Masons throughout the country saw their elections contested by Anti-Masonic Party candidates in the coming years. Jno Kern Jr. to DeWitt Clinton, 1 Feb. 1827, BV Clinton, MSS Collection, NYHS. Mark Schmeller is writing a history of the Morgan disappearance.

15. "Nominations," *Richmond Enquirer* (VA), 29 Sept. 1826; and "Republican Nomination: For Governor, De Witt Clinton" (1826), Broadsides, AAS.

16. "The Herkimer State Convention," *Watch-Tower* (Cooperstown, NY), 9 Oct. 1826.

17. Clinton's opponent Erasmus Root coined the moniker. Murphy, *Building the Empire State*, 181. For Clinton's trip, see 25 Sept. 1826, DWCD.

18. 5 Oct. 1826, DWCD.

19. Clay to Rochester, 30 Nov. 1825, R5, M77, RG59, NA2.

20. *A Directory for the Village of Rochester* (Rochester, 1827), 28; and "Map of Rochester" (1827), New York Public Library, New York, https://digitalcollections.nypl.org/items/d2954c80-160f-0134-9277-00505686a51c.

21. For the State Department's payment of Rochester's salary from the time of his appointment, see Clay to Rochester, 15 Nov. 1826, R6, M77, RG59, NA2.

22. "Herkimer State Convention," *Watch-Tower* (Cooperstown, NY), 9 Oct. 1826.

23. 5 Oct. 1826, DWCD.

24. 5 Oct. 1826, DWCD.

25. This description is based on his portrait by Thomas Sully in 1831 in the collection of Reynolda House Museum of American Art, Winston-Salem, NC, gift of Barbara B. Millhouse, https://reynoldahouse.emuseum.com/objects/88/jared-sparks.

26. "Sparks, Jared, 1789–1866. Papers of Jared Sparks: An Inventory," Finding Aid, UAI 15.886, Harvard University Archive, 4–5; and Lester J. Cappon, "Jared Sparks: The Preparation of an Editor," *Proceedings of the Massachusetts Historical Society*, 3rd ser., vol. 90 (1978): 3–21. For 1820s historical memory, see Michael D. Hattem, *Past and Prologue: Politics and Memory in the American Revolution* (New Haven: Yale University Press, 2020); Whitney Martinko, *Historic Real Estate: Market Morality and the Politics of Preservation in the Early United States* (Philadelphia: University of Pennsylvania Press, 2020); Margot Minardi, *Making Slavery History: Abolitionism and the Politics of Memory in Massachusetts* (New York: Oxford University Press, 2010); and Alfred F. Young, *The Shoemaker and the Tea Party: Memory and the American Revolution* (Boston: Beacon Press, 1999).

27. 18 Sept. 1826, "Journal of a Tour Commenced Sept. 18th, 1826," MS Sparks 141e, JSPP. (Hereafter "Journal.")

28. 3 Oct. 1826, "Journal," JSPP.

29. For the connections between the Erie Canal and the Hudson Valley School, see Spanagel, *Clinton & Eaton*, 185–95.

30. 5 Oct. 1826, "Journal," JSPP. The term "mammoth" likely referenced the mastodon skeleton exhibited in Philadelphia, where Sparks had recently traveled. Although mastodons were herbivores, the exhibit suggested it was a carnivorous American monster that ruled the continent. Sparks may have been implying that the interoceanic canal would also be a tyrant of the hemisphere. For the mastodon and monstrosity, see Paul Semolina, "Peale's Mastodon: The Skeleton in Our Closet," *Commonplace* 4, no. 2 (Jan. 2004), http://commonplace.online/article/peales-mastodon-the-skeleton-in-our-closet/. For Sparks's recent time in Philadelphia, see 12–13 June 1826, 18–20 June 1826, "Journal of a Southern Tour," MS Sparks 141e, JSPP.

31. 28 Sept. 1826, "Journal," JSPP.

32. 5 Oct. 1826, "Journal," JSPP.

33. Cornog interprets Clinton's financial troubles as evidence of his honesty as a politician. Cornog, *Birth of Empire*, 182. Colden confirmed that Clinton was not paid for his work on the canal. Cadwallader D. Colden, *Memoir Prepared at the Request of a Committee of the Common Council of the City of New York, and Presented to the Mayor of the City, at the Celebration of the Completion of the New York Canals* (New York, 1825), 57.

34. For Gallatin's "Report of the Secretary of the Treasury on the Subject of Public Roads and Canals," see John Lauritz Larson, *Internal Improvement: National Public Works and the Promise of Popular Government in the Early United States* (Chapel Hill: The University of North Carolina Press, 2001), 59–63.

35. Larson, *Internal Improvement*, 62, 73–4.

36. For the history of the "Bonus Bill," see Larson, *Internal Improvement*, 63–69.

37. Murphy, *Building the Empire State*, 159–206. The literature on the Erie Canal is vast; see especially Nathan Miller, *The Enterprise of a Free People: Aspects of Economic Development in New York State During the Canal Period, 1792–1838* (Ithaca, NY: Cornell University Press, 1962); Larson, *Internal Improvement*, 73–80; and Carol Sheriff, *The Artificial River: The Erie Canal and the Paradox of Progress, 1817–1862* (New York: Hill and Wang, 1996).

38. 5 Oct. 1826, "Journal," JSPP.

39. 5 Oct. 1826, DWCD.

40. Emily Pawley, *The Nature of the Future: Agriculture, Science, and Capitalism in the Antebellum North* (Chicago: University of Chicago Press, 2020), 23; and Spanagel, *Clinton & Eaton*, 63.

41. Spanagel, *Clinton & Eaton*, 63–66.

42. Cornog, *Birth of Empire*, 102.

43. Catherine Livingston Jones Clinton's mother (Margret Livingston) and Stephen Van Rensselaer's mother (Catherine Livingston Van Rensselaer) were sisters. https://en.wikipedia.org/wiki/Livingston_family.

44. "Copy of deed of trust between Aaron H. Palmer and De Witt Clinton," HR 145, 30th Cong., 2nd Sess. (20 Feb. 1849), 367–68. (Hereafter "Copy of deed.")

45. "Copy of deed," 367–68. Emphasis in original.

46. "Copy of deed," 368–70.

47. "Copy of deed," 370–71.

48. "Copy of deed," 367–68.

49. "Translation of Canal Contract," HR 145, 30th Cong., 2nd Sess. (20 Feb. 1849), 365.

50. "Copy of deed," 370–71.

51. "Copy of deed," 371.

52. "Copy of deed," 371. For corporate liability, see Hannah Farber, *Underwriters of the United States: How Insurance Shaped the American Founding* (Chapel Hill: The University of North Carolina Press for the Omohundro Institute, 2021), 92–93.

53. "Copy of deed," 367.

54. For Colden's appearance, see his 1819 portrait by Samuel Lovett Waldo in the City Hall Portrait Collection of New York City, https://www.nyc.gov/site/designcommission/archive/city-hall/portraits/portrait.page?portraitId=21.

55. Cornog, *Birth of Empire*, 4; *Proceeding of the Grand Lodge of Free and Accepted Masons of the State of New York, One Hundred and Tenth Annual Communication* (New York, 1891), 162–63, 256–57; *The One Hundred and Tenth Report of The Bank for Savings in the City of New York, Chartered 1819* (New York, 1928), 2; and Raymond A. Mohl, "Humanitarianism in the Preindustrial City: The New York Society for the Prevention of Pauperism, 1817–1823," *The Journal of American History* 57, no. 3 (Dec. 1970): 576–99, 590.

56. "Palmer, Aaron, Swartwout's N.Y. Militia," War of 1812 Bounty Land Files, 55-120-11976, 50-40-54811, NARA.

57. Cornog, *Birth of Empire*, 4.

58. Colden, *Memoir*, 6, 4, 8, 9.

59. The painter's grandfather and the banker's father were brothers. Walter E. Ziebarth Jr. and John W. Ziebarth, *Direct Connections: Ziebarth-Magill Ancestry* (New York, 1997), 13.

60. Philip G. Hubert Jr., *The Merchants' National Bank of the City of New York: A History of its First Century Compiled from Official Records at the Request of the Directors* (New York, 1903), 27–28. For Catlin's son, see "Lynde Catlin Genealogy," KMC_B03_F04_005, Kate Moody Collection, Webster Groves Historical Society, available online through Missouri Digital Heritage, https://mdh.contentdm.oclc.org/digital/collection/p16795coll28/id/1076.

61. *The One Hundred and Tenth Report of The Bank for Savings in the City of New York* (New York, 1928), 2, 11.

62. Edwin G. Burrows and Mike Wallace, *Gotham: A History of New York City to 1898* (New York: Oxford University Press, 1999), 444–45.

63. "Mr. Clinton's Removal," *Ithaca Journal* (NY), 12 May 1824.

64. "Aaron H. Palmer" (1821), R13, M439, RG59, NA2.

65. Miller, *Enterprise of a Free People*, 94.

66. "An Act to Incorporate the President, Managers and Company of the Delaware and Hudson Canal Company," *Charter of the Delaware and Hudson Canal Company, with the Several Acts Supplementary to the Same* (New York, 1859), 18.

67. Frank Walker Stevens, *The Beginnings of the New York Central Railroad: A History* (New York: G. P. Putnam's Sons, 1926), ix, 1–2, 8–10.

68. Rembrandt Peale, "Philip Hone (1780–1851)," c. 1823–26, NYHS, https://emuseum.nyhistory.org/objects/41322/philip-hone-17801851.

69. Michael R. Haines, "Table Aa832-1033. Population of Cities with at Least 100,000 Population in 1990: 1790–1990," *Historical Statistics of the United States*, Millennial Edition Online ed. Susan B. Carter et al. (New York: Cambridge University Press, 2006).

70. Significant property qualifications removed most Black men from the voter rolls, and women were forbidden from voting. Burrows and Wallace, *Gotham*, 284, 328–30, 512–14, 548–49, 548–54, 858.

71. *Salem Gazette* (MA), 10 Jan. 1826; *Norwich Courier* (CT), 11 Jan. 1826; and "The Mayor's Day," *Boston Commercial Gazette*, 12 Jan. 1826. Hone lost his seat on 26 Dec. 1825, when the new council members took their seats. The mayoral election ballots are also recorded. *Minutes of the Common Council of the City of New York, 1781–1831* (New York, 1917), 15:124, 15:146–47.

72. "The Mayor's Day," *Boston Commercial Gazette*, 12 Jan. 1826. According to the 1820 census four free people of color lived in Hone's household. "Philip Hone," New York Ward 3, New York, New York, *1820 US Federal Census* database, accessed online through Ancestry .com. For Tammanyites as Bucktails, see Burrows and Wallace, *Gotham*, 424.

73. "The Mayor's Day," *Boston Commercial Gazette*, 12 Jan. 1826.

74. Allan Nevins, "Introduction," *The Diary of Philip Hone, 1828–1851* (New York: Dodd, Mean, 1927), 1:viii–xi.

75. Schultz and Hollister, "The Delaware and Hudson Canal Company," 120.

76. Adams, "Warming the Poor," 69–94.

77. Alfred Mathews, *History of Wayne, Pike, and Monroe Counties, Pennsylvania* (Philadelphia: R. T. Peck, 1886), 340–41, 346–47, 371.

78. *The One Hundred and Tenth Report of The Bank for Savings in the City of New York* (New York, 1928), 2, 11–12.

79. The two men appeared together in the 1824 list of board members. *Fifth Annual Report of the Directors of the New-York Institution for the Instruction of the Deaf and Dumb, to the Legislature of the State of New-York* (New York, 1824), 2. Bolton was first elected to the board in 1821. "Institution for the Deaf and Dumb," *Patron of Industry* (New York), 30 May 1821.

80. "Masonic," *The Troy Sentinel* (NY), 4 July 1826.

81. For Van Rensselaer as Grand Master, see E. B. Wadsworth to DeWitt Clinton, 1 June 1825, BV Clinton, NYHS.

82. According to the 1821 Constitution, suffrage extended to all white men over the age of twenty-one "who had lived in their district for six months and had either paid taxes, served in the militia, or worked on the roads." Before the 1821 Constitution shifted the responsibility of selecting a mayor to the Common Council, mayors were appointed by the state Council of Appointment. Burrows and Wallace, *Gotham*, 513.

83. *Minutes of the Common Council of the City of New York, 1781–1831* (New York, 1917), 15:771.

84. Nevins, "Introduction," xi. After losing much of his fortune in the aftermath of the Panic of 1837, Hone held a federal appointment in New York City. Nevins, "Introduction," xii.

85. "Married," *Geneva Gazette* (NY), 16 May 1827; and "Charles A. Clinton," *South Dutch Church, Members, Records, 1812–1857*, (New Brunswick, NJ: The Archives of the Reformed Church in America), *U.S., Dutch Reformed Church Records in Selected States, 1639–1989* database, accessed online through Ancestry.com.

86. DeWitt Clinton to Stephen Van Rensselaer, C. D. Colden, Philip Hone, and Lynde Catlin (Draft), 6 Oct. 1826, Letterbook vol. 23, 12, DWCP; and 6 Oct. 1826, DWCD.

87. "No. 3," DeWitt Clinton to Stephen Van Rensselaer, C. D. Colden, Philip Hone, and Lynde Catlin, 6 Oct. 1826, HR 145, 30th Cong., 2nd Sess. (20 Feb. 1849), 371. (Hereafter "No. 3.")

88. *T. V. Cuyler's Albany Directory for the Year 1825* (Albany, 1825), 87.

89. *Longworth's New York Register for 1826* (New York, 1826), 23.

90. "No. 3," 371.

91. "Steam Navigation Company," and "X. October," *New York City Directory* (1826), Irma and Paul Milstein Division of United States History, Local History and Genealogy, New York Public Library, https://digitalcollections.nypl.org/items/0808a200-7702-0136-68eb-0b926e8a30b7.

92. 9 Oct. 1826, DWCD.

93. 7 Oct. 1826, "Journal," JSPP.

94. Noah Webster, "Visionary," *American Dictionary of the English Language* (1828), www.webstersdictionary1828.com/Dictionary/visionary.

95. Noah Webster, "Speculate," *American Dictionary of the English Language* (1828), www.webstersdictionary1828.com/Dictionary/speculate; and Webster, "Visionary" (1828).

96. Webster, "Speculate," (1828). Emphasis in original.

97. Webster, "Visionary," (1828).

98. 7 Oct. 1826, "Journal," JSPP.

99. For the canal diary, see Campbell, *Life and Writings*, 27–204.

100. 9 Oct. 1826, DWCD.

101. 9 Oct. 1826, DWCD; and 9 Oct. 1826, "Journal," JSPP.

102. 10 Oct. 1826, "Journal," JSPP.

103. 11 Oct. 1826, 13 Oct. 1826, "Journal," JSPP.

104. 21 Oct. 1826, "Journal," JSPP.

Chapter Fourteen

1. Philip Hone to DeWitt Clinton, 9 Oct. 1826, Letterbook vol. 14, DWCP. Emphasis in original.

2. Hone to Clinton, 9 Oct. 1826, Letterbook vol. 14, DWCP.

3. Eric Hilt, "Rogue Finance: The Life and Fire Insurance Company and the Panic of 1826," *Business History Review* 83, no. 1 (Spring 2009): 87–112; and Hannah Farber, *Underwriters of the United States: How Insurance Shaped the American Founding* (Chapel Hill: The University of North Carolina Press for the Omohundro Institute, 2021), 193–204.

4. Hone to Clinton, 9 Oct. 1826, Letterbook vol. 14, DWCP.

5. Hone to Clinton, 9 Oct. 1826, Letterbook vol. 14, DWCP; and *Longworth's New York Register for 1826* (New York, 1826), 23.

6. 11 Oct. 1826, DWCD.

7. Scott D. Heberling, *Canal in the Mountains: The Juniata Main Line Canal in the Lewiston Narrows* (Commonwealth of Pennsylvania, 2008), 3.

8. 11 Oct. 1826, "Journal," JSPP.

9. 11 Oct. 1826, DWCD.

10. 12 Oct. 1826, DWCD.

11. 13 Oct. 1826, DWCD.

12. 14 Oct. 1826, DWCD.

13. 19 Oct. 1826, DWCD.

14. Raymond Walters Jr., *Albert Gallatin: Jeffersonian Financier and Diplomat* (New York: Macmillan, 1957), 1, 11, 217.

15. For Gallatin's 1808 report, see John Lauritz Larson, *Internal Improvement: National Public Works and the Promise of Popular Government in the Early United States* (Chapel Hill: The University of North Carolina Press, 2001), 59–63.

16. Albert Gallatin to Hannah Gallatin, 6 June 1804, quoted in Walters, *Albert Gallatin*, 216. Walters inserted the term "Latin-American countries" here, but this concept did not exist in 1804. Michel Gobat, "The Invention of Latin America: A Transnational History of Anti-Imperialism, Democracy, and Race," *The American Historical Review* 118, no. 5 (Dec. 2013): 1345–75.

17. For his financing of the war, see Farber, *Underwriters*, 185; and Walters, *Albert Gallatin*, 254–58.

18. Walters, *Albert Gallatin*, 272–323.

19. Henry Clay to Albert Gallatin, 8 Nov. 1825, R5, M77, RG59, NA2.

20. James F. Hopkins, ed., *The Papers of Henry Clay* (Lexington: University Press of Kentucky, 1972), 4:813.

21. Clay to Gallatin, 11 Nov. 1825, Hopkins, *Papers of Henry Clay*, 4:814.

22. Gallatin to Clay, 14 Nov. 1825, Hopkins, *Papers of Henry Clay*, 4:826.

23. Clay to Gallatin, 2 May 1826, Hopkins, *Papers of Henry Clay*, 5:293–94.

24. Gallatin to Clay, 3 May 1826, Hopkins, *Papers of Henry Clay*, 5:296.

25. Gallatin wrote his fourteenth dispatch on 16 October 1826, and his fifteenth on 21 October 1826. Hopkins, *Papers of Henry Clay*, 5:705–6, 5:800, 5:812; and Walters, *Albert Gallatin*, 331, 333.

26. Burrows and Wallace, *Gotham*, 319. Gallatin's first marriage ended after one year with his wife's death. He would be married to his second wife, Hannah Nicholson, for more than half a century.

27. Dael Norwood, "Mr. Jefferson's Mandarin, Or, a Controversial Promotion," *Readex Report* 8, no. 4 (Nov. 2013); and Dael Norwood, *Trading Freedom: How Trade with China Defined Early America* (Chicago: University of Chicago Press, 2022), 47–49, 212n70.

28. De Witt Clinton to Albert Gallatin, 20 Oct. 1826, reel 36, Albert Gallatin Papers, NYHS.

29. 7 Oct. 1826, "Journal," JSPP.

30. 28 Oct. 1826, DWCD.

31. Clinton to Sparks, 28 Oct. 1826, Letterbook vol. 23, DWCP.

32. James Grant Wilson, *The Life and Letters of Fitz-Greene Halleck* (D. Appleton, 1869), 464–65.

33. Alexander von Humboldt, *Personal Narrative of Travels to the Equinoctial Regions of the New Continent, During the Years 1799–1804*, trans. Helen Maria Williams (London: Longman, Rees, Orme, Brown, and Green, 1826), vol. 6, part 1.

34. Clinton to Sparks, 28 Oct. 1826, Letterbook vol. 23, DWCP.

35. Clinton to Sparks, 28 Oct. 1826, Box 7, MS Sparks 153, JSPP.

36. 8 Oct. 1826, 9 Oct. 1826, DWCD.

37. Clinton to Sparks, 28 Oct. 1826, Box 7, MS Sparks 153, JSPP.

38. Sparks to Williams, 22 Nov. 1826, MS Sparks 147c, JSPP.

39. Sparks to Caesar A. Rodney, 28 June 1824, MS Sparks 147c, JSPP; Sparks to R. C. Anderson, 27 Oct. 1825, 13 Feb. 1826, MS Sparks 147c, JSPP; and Anderson to Sparks, 19 Apr. 1826, 19 May 1826, Box 1, MS Sparks 153, JSPP.

40. Sparks to Williams, 22 Nov. 1826, MS Sparks 147c, JSPP.

41. Sparks to Williams, 22 Nov. 1826, MS Sparks 147c, JSPP.

42. Jared Sparks to unidentified recipient, 23 Nov. 1826, reproduced in *The Collector* 14, no. 1 (Nov. 1900): 1–2.

43. Along with the Erie Canal, the regular schedule of transatlantic "packet" ships contributed to New York City's rise as a great metropolis. Robert Greenhalgh Albion, *Square-Riggers on Schedule: The New York Sailing Packets to England, France, and the Cotton Ports* (Princeton: Princeton University Press, 1938).

44. "To Aaron H. Palmer," *New-York Evening Post*, 22 Dec. 1826.

45. *Longworth's American Almanac, New-York Register, and City Directory for the Fifty-First Year of American Independence* (New-York: Thomas Longworth, 1826), 35, 37, 368.

46. *Longworth's* (1826), 296; and Chap. 297, *Laws of the State of New-York, Passed at the Forty-Ninth Session of the Legislature, Begun and Held at the City of Albany, The Third Day of January, 1826* (Albany, 1826), 348–50.

47. "To Aaron H. Palmer," *New-York Evening Post*, 4 Jan. 1827.

48. "Marine List," *New-York Evening Post*, 31 Oct. 1826; and *New-York Evening Post*, 2 Nov. 1826.

49. "Marine List," *New-York Evening Post*, 31 Oct. 1826.

50. Albion, *Square-Riggers*, 9, 199, 274.

51. "Prospectus issued by Aaron H. Palmer, in London, soliciting subscriptions to stock of the Atlantic and Pacific Canal Company," HR 145, 30th Cong., 2nd Sess. (20 Feb. 1849), 372, 375. (Hereafter "Prospectus.")

52. Walters, *Albert Gallatin*, 332.

53. "Prospectus," 372.

54. "Prospectus," 372–75.

55. "Catlett & Keith v. The Pacific Insurance Co. of New-York," John L. Wendell, *Reports of Cases Argued and Determined in the Supreme Court of Judicature, and in the Court for the Trial of Impeachments and the Corrections of Errors of the State of New York*, 2nd ed. (New York: Banks & Brothers, 1883), 1:562–79.

56. "Prospectus," 372–75. Catherine Livingston Jones Clinton was a distant cousin of Edward Livingston. https://en.wikipedia.org/wiki/Livingston_family.

57. For more on Livingston, see William B. Hatcher, *Edward Livingston: Jeffersonian Republican and Jacksonian Democrat* (Baton Rouge: Louisiana State University Press, 1940).

58. "Prospectus," 372–75.

59. "Prospectus," 372–75.

60. Gallatin to Clay, 12 Dec. 1826, *Papers of Henry Clay*, 5:996. The full text of this letter is in *American State Papers, Foreign Relations*, 6:658, www.loc.gov/item/97080286/.

61. Gallatin to Clay, 13 Dec. 1826, *Papers of Henry Clay*, 5:998.

62. "Canal from the Atlantic to the Pacific" enclosed in DeWitt Clinton to Albert Gallatin, 20 Oct. 1826, reel 36, Albert Gallatin Papers, NYHS.

Chapter Fifteen

1. William Phillips to Henry Clay, 8 Aug. 1827, R2, M219, RG59, NA2.

2. Williams to Clay, 23 Aug. 1826, 31 Nov. 1826, R2, M219, RG59, NA2.

3. Williams to Rochester, 30 Aug. 1827, MM-2006-001, C. M. McClung Historical Collection, Knox County Public Library, Knoxville, TN. For Phillips's background, see Williams to Clay, 15 June 1826, R2, M219, RG59, NA2.

4. Williams to Clay, 31 Nov. 1826, R2, M219, RG59, NA2; and Phillips to Clay, 8 Aug. 1827, R2, M219, RG59, NA2.

5. Phillips to Clay, 12 May 1827, R2, M219, RG59, NA2.

6. Williams to Clay, 31 Nov. 1826, R2, M219, RG59, NA2. He appointed Robert Parker, who had traveled the canal route with Blunt, to serve as temporary Salvadoran consul.

7. Sparks to Williams, 22 Nov. 1826, MS Sparks 147c, JSPP.

8. Phillips to Sparks, 30 Jan. 1827, Box 28, MS Sparks 153, JSPP. Phillips quoted Prospero in Act 4, Scene 1 of William Shakespeare's *The Tempest*.

9. Phillips to Sparks, 30 Jan. 1827, Box 28, MS Sparks 153, JSPP.

10. Phillips to Clay, 22 Mar. 1827, R2, M219, RG59, NA2.

11. Phillips to Sparks, 30 Jan. 1827, Box 28, MS Sparks 153, JSPP.

12. Arce and his eight-year-old son arrived in New Orleans on 9 January 1830; they would soon move to Mexico where Arce published his *Memoria*. "New Orleans, Passenger List Quarterly Abstracts, 1820–1875" database, accessed online through Ancestry.com; and Manuel José Arce, *Memoria del General Manuel Jose Arce*, 5th ed. (San Salvador: Dirección de Publicaciones e Impresos Consejo Nacional para la Cultura y el Arte CONCULTURA, 1997, 1830).

13. Alejandro Marure, *Memoria Historica Sobre El Canal De Nicaragua* (Guatemala: La Paz, 1845), 20, translated for author by James Irving. The irony of building independence on a canal constructed by foreigners is highlighted in Frances Kinloch Tijerino, *El Imaginario del Canal y la nación Cosmopolita: Nicaragua, Siglo XIX* (Managua: IHNCA-UCA, 2015).

14. Esteban Duque Estrada Sacasa, *Nicaragua Historia y Familias, 1821–1853* (Managua, 2001), 114.

15. Louis E. Bumgartner, *José del Valle of Central America* (Durham, NC: Duke University Press, 1963), 259–60, 268–69. For a concise overview of the shifting political structures of the region, see David Díaz Arias, "State-Making and Nation-Building," *The Oxford Handbook of Central American History*, ed. Robert H. Holden (New York: Oxford University Press, 2022), 285–308.

16. "A Guide to the United States' History of Recognition, Diplomatic, and Consular Relations, by Country, since 1776: Central American Federation," Office of the Historian, Department of State, https://history.state.gov/countries/central-american-federation.

17. Phillips to Clay, 3 Feb. 1827, R1, T337, RG59, NA2. Emphasis in original.

18. Phillips to Clay, 2 Mar. 1827 ("February 30, 1827"), R1, T337, RG59, NA2; Fernando Valero to Phillips, 9 Apr. 1827, R2, M219, RG59, NA2; Phillips to Clay, 4 July 1827, R2, M219, RG59, NA2; and Clay to Rochester, 15 Nov. 1827, R7, M77, RG59, NA2.

19. Phillips to Clay, 30 Feb. 1827, R1, T337, RG59, NA2; and Phillips to Clay, 8 Aug. 1827, R2, M219, RG59, NA2. Emphasis in original.

20. Phillips to Clay, 8 Aug. 1827, R2, M219, RG59, NA2. Emphasis in original.

21. Phillips to Clay, 6 Jan. 1828, R2, M219, RG59, NA2.

22. Phillips to Clay, 6 Jan. 1828, R2, M219, RG59, NA2.

23. Phillips to Clay, 15 May 1829, R2, M219, RG59, NA2; and Clay to Rochester, 11 Mar. 1827, R6, M77, RG59, NA2.

24. Phillips to Clay, 6 Jan. 1828, R2, M219, RG59, NA2. For an example of Williams's involvement in the raucous campaign, see JQADD, vol. 36, 14 July 1828.

25. Daniel Walker Howe, *What Hath God Wrought: The Transformation of America, 1815–1848* (New York: Oxford University Press, 2007), 210, 274–85, 328–66, 390.

26. From Ben Park, I learned that Theodore Parker popularized the idea that Adams accomplished more after his presidency than during his administration. Theodore Parker, *A Discourse Occasioned by the Death of John Quincy Adams* (Boston, 1848), 50.

27. *Congressional Globe*, 30th Cong., 1st Sess. (1848), 381.

28. Robert V. Remini, "Clay, Henry," *American National Biography* (Oxford: Oxford University Press, 2000).

29. Maiden, "Col. John Williams," 40–46.

30. Williams to Rochester, 30 Aug. 1827, MM-2006-001, C. M. McClung Historical Collection.

31. Rochester to Clay, 9 Oct. 1827, *Papers of Henry Clay*, 6:1128.

32. Phillips to Clay, 12 May 1827, 15 May 1829, R2, M219, RG59, NA2.

33. Savage to Clay, 20 Jan. 1828, R1, T337, RG59, NA2.

34. Savage to Clay, 10 Mar. 1828, R1, T337, RG59, NA2.

35. Lawrence Park, *Major Thomas Savage of Boston and His Descendants* (Boston, 1914), 36–37.

36. Clay to Rochester, 11 Mar. 1827, R6, M77, RG59, NA2.

37. For this debate, see Christina Snyder, *Great Crossings: Indians, Settlers, and Slaves in the Age of Jackson* (New York: Oxford University Press, 2017); and Claudio Saunt, *Unworthy Republic: The Dispossession of Native Americans and the Road to Indian Territory* (New York: W. W. Norton, 2020).

38. Clay to Rochester, 11 Mar. 1827, R6, M77, RG59, NA2.

39. The literature on continental colonization, the lust for land, and the era's imperialism is vast. For examples, see Michael J. Witgen, *Seeing Red: Indigenous Land, American Expansion, and the Political Economy of Plunder in North America* (Chapel Hill: The University of North Carolina Press for the Omohundro Institute, 2022); Michael Blaakman, *Speculation Nation: Land Mania in the Revolutionary American Republic* (Philadelphia: University of Pennsylvania Press, 2023); and Michael Blaakman et al., eds., *The Early Imperial Republic: From the American Revolution to the U.S. Mexican War* (Philadelphia: University of Pennsylvania Press, 2023).

40. Rochester to Clay, 16 May 1828, 11 June 1828, R2, M219, RG59, NA2.

41. Savage to Clay 20 June 1828, R1, T337, RG59, NA2.

42. Jeff Richman, "The Chair in which He Died," (6 Jan. 2014), www.green-wood.com/2014/the-chair-in-which-he-died/.

43. Evan Cornog, *The Birth of Empire: DeWitt Clinton and the American Experience, 1769–1828* (New York: Oxford University Press, 1998), 180–82.

44. Phillips to Clay, 3 Feb. 1827, R1, T337, RG59, NA2.

45. For the gory details of his execution, see Jerónimo Pérez, *Obras Históricas Completas del Licenciado Jerónimo Pérez* (Managua: Fondo de Promoción Cultural, Banco de América, 1975, 1928), 512.

46. Quoted in David Sinclair, *The Land that Never Was: Sir Gregor MacGregor and the Most Audacious Fraud in History* (Cambridge, MA: Da Capo, 2004), 308–9; and John Lynch, *Simón Bolívar: A Life* (New Haven: Yale University Press, 2006), 278–79.

47. Michael D. Olien, "Miskito Kings and the Line of Succession," *Journal of Anthropological Research* 39, no. 2 (Summer, 1983): 219–25.

48. R. A. Humphreys, "Anglo-American Rivalries in Central America," *Transactions of the Royal Historical Society* 18 (1968): 174–208.

49. Riverstone, *Living in the Land of our Ancestors*, 46. For turtle fishery, see Sharika Crawford, *The Last Turtlemen of the Caribbean: Waterscapes of Labor, Conservation, and Boundary Making* (Chapel Hill: The University of North Carolina Press, 2020).

50. Curtis Bolton to Daniel Webster, 24 July 1850, R8, M873, RG59, NA2.

51. Bolton to Webster, 15 Dec. 1850, R8, M873, RG59, NA2.

52. Bolton to Clayton, 26 Feb. 1850, R8, M873, RG59, NA2.

53. "Died," *Evening Post* (New York), 7 Feb. 1851.

54. "Religious Intelligence," *Evening Post* (New York), 12 Jan. 1850.

55. Robert Bolton, *Genealogical and Biographical Account of the Family of Bolton* (New York: John A. Gray, 1862), 120; W. Turrentine Jackson et al., "Introduction," *Engineers and Irrigation: Report of the Board of Commissioners on the Irrigation of the San Joaquin, Tulare, and Sacramento Valleys of the State of California, 1873*, Engineer Historical Studies 5 (Fort Belvoir, VA: Office of History, United States Corps of Engineers, 1990), 19–21; and Judge Alfred Stedman Hartwell, "Forty Years of Hawaii Nei," *Annual Report of the Hawaiian Historical Society* 54 (1945): 9–24, 18.

56. Bolton, *Genealogical and Biographical Account*, 120; "Correspondence of the Herald," *Commercial Advertiser* (New York), 27 Jan. 1849; and David I. Folkman Jr., *The Nicaragua Route* (Salt Lake City: University of Utah Press, 1972), 28–32, 50–52, 118.

57. Phillips to Clay, 3 Feb. 1827, R1, T337, RG59, NA2.

58. *A List of the Officers of Her Majesty's Royal Marine Forces, on Full and Half Pay* (London, 1846), 42, ADM 192/27, TNA.

59. John Baily, *Central America: Describing Each of the States of Guatemala, Honduras, Salvador, Nicaragua, and Costa Rica; Their Natural Features, Products, Population, and Remarkable Capacity for Colonization* (London: Trelawney Saunders, 1850). British subjects could not yet expatriate. Lucy E. Salyer, *Under the Starry Flag: How a Band of Irish Americans Joined the Fenian Revolt and Sparked a Crisis over Citizenship* (Cambridge, MA: Harvard University Press, 2018).

60. For British finance of US cotton production, see Leland Hamilton Jenks, *The Migration of British Capital to 1875* (New York: Alfred A. Knopf, 1927); and Jessica M. Lepler, *The Many Panics of 1837: People, Politics, and the Creation of a Transatlantic Financial Crisis* (New York: Cambridge University Press, 2013).

61. "Canal or Railroad Between the Atlantic and Pacific Oceans," HR 145, 30th Cong., 2nd Sess. (20 Feb. 1849), 207.

62. FO 925/1626, FO 925/1629, TNA. For more on Baily's survey, see Frances Kinloch Tijerino, *El Imaginario del Canal y la Nación Cosmpolita: Nicaragua, Siglo XIX* (Managua:

IHNCA-UCS, 2015); and Sophie Brockmann, *The Science of Useful Nature in Central America: Landscapes, Networks, and Practical Enlightenment, 1784–1838* (New York: Cambridge University Press, 2020), 213–16.

63. Phillips to Clay, 3 Feb. 1827, R1, T337, RG59, NA2.

64. Langrod, "Ups and Downs," 68–71.

65. Henry Savage to Martin Van Buren, 18 Nov. 1830, R1, T337, RG59, NA2; and Phillips to Clay, 15 May 1829, R2, M219, RG59, NA2.

66. Henry Savage to Van Buren, 3 Dec. 1830, R1, T337, RG59, NA2. For Phillips's widow, see Henry Savage to Edward Livingston, 3 Sept. 1831, R1, T337, RG59, NA2.

67. Aaron H. Palmer, "(Circular.) American and Foreign Agency for Claims" (New York, 1829), Folder 14, Portfolio 117, Printed Ephemera Collection, Library of Congress, Washington, DC, http://hdl.loc.gov/loc.rbc/rbpe.11701400.

68. Aaron H. Palmer, "Productions, Trade, and Commerce of the Oriental Nations," H. Doc. 96, 29th Cong., 2nd Sess. (Nov. 1847).

69. Tyler Dennett, *Americans in Eastern Asia: A Critical Study of the Policy of the United States with reference to China, Japan, and Korea in the 19th Century* (New York: Macmillan, 1922), 252; XI/38/199, II/10/1, II/10/2, II/10/3, II/10/4, II/10/5, II/10/6, II/10/7, Rothschild Archive, London; Aaron Haight Palmer, *Letter to the Hon. Charles J. Ingersoll* (New York, 1846); and Aaron H. Palmer to Mehemet Ali, Aaron H. Palmer to George Gliddon, Box 2, BANC MSS Z-Z 116, John Lloyd Stephens Papers, 1795–1882, Bancroft Library, University of California Berkeley.

70. *The New Mirror* (1844), 57; and Nathaniel P. Willis, *The Miscellaneous Works of N. P. Willis* (1847), 99.

71. Palmer, *Letter to the Hon. Charles J. Ingersoll*; Palmer, "Productions, Trade, and Commerce"; "Memorial of Aaron Haight Palmer, Praying Compensation for Services," S. Misc. Doc. 10, 33rd Cong., 2nd Sess. (18 Jan. 1855); Aaron Haight Palmer, *Letter to the Hon. John M. Clayton, Secretary of State* (Washington, DC: Gideon & Co., 1849); Aaron Haight Palmer, *Prospectus: The Unknown Countries of the East* (New York: Wiley & Putnam, 1847); Aaron Haight Palmer, *Memoir*, S. Misc. Doc. 80, 39th Cong., 1st Sess. (1848); Aaron Haight Palmer, *Peruvian Guano Trade: Statements and Documents in Relation to the Bill Reported by the Select Committee of the House of Representatives, on the 31st of July, 1854* (Washington, DC, 1854); and Aaron Haight Palmer, *Documents and Facts Illustrating the Origin of the Mission to Japan* (Washington, DC: H. Polkinhorn, 1857). By August 1850, he had written so much that his documents inspired a debate in Congress over the limits of government printing. For specific dates and documents, see Adelaide Rosalia Hasse, *Index to United States Documents Relating to Foreign Affairs, 1828–1861* (Washington, DC: Carnegie Institution, 1919), 2:1222.

72. "Charge of Granada," *Trenton State Gazette* (NJ), 13 June 1853; "American and Foreign Agency," *Sangamo Journal* (IL), 24 Oct. 1851; "Reply of Hon. George Road Riddle to the Letter of the Peruvian Vice Consul," *Delaware State Reporter* (Dover), 10 Nov. 1854; A1 Entry 767-A, Box 8, RG59, NA2; Francis L. Hawks, *Narrative of the Expedition of an American Squadron to the China Seas and Japan* (Washington, DC, 1856), 77; Palmer, *Letter to the Hon. Charles J. Ingersoll*, 13; Palmer "Memorial"; and Jessica Lepler, "'There is no need for anyone to go to America': Commercial Correspondence and Nineteenth-Century Globalisation," *The Rothschild Archive: Review of the Year April 2007—March 2008* (2008): 14–20.

73. Palmer, *Documents and Facts* (1857); and Hasse, *Index*, 2:1222–23.

74. "Aaron H. Palmer," Washington Ward 2, Washington, District of Columbia, 615, R102, M653, *1860 US Census* database, accessed online through Ancestry.com.

75. H.R. Rpt. 466, 36th Cong., 1st Sess. (20 Apr. 1860); S. Misc. Doc. 14, 46th Cong., 3rd Sess. (21 Dec. 1880), 275; and *Congressional Globe*, 36 Cong., 2nd Sess. (14 Feb. 1861), 897.

76. "The French Abolition Society," *New York Herald*, 27 Oct. 1860.

77. "Death," *Daily National Intelligencer* (Washington, DC), 11 Feb. 1863.

78. Sparks to Phillips, 10 July 1827, MS Sparks 147d, JSPP.

79. Sparks to Caleb Cushing, 5 July 1827, MS Sparks 147d, JSPP.

80. Phillips to Sparks, 30 Jan. 1827, Box 28, MS Sparks 153, JSPP; and Sparks to Cushing, 5 July 1827, MS Sparks 147d, JSPP.

81. "Art. V," *North American Review* 26, no. 58 (Jan. 1828): 127–28. Sparks deferred the article. Cushing to Sparks, 24 Oct. 1827, Box 9, MS Sparks 153, JSPP.

82. "Art. V," *North American Review* 26, no. 58 (Jan. 1828): 129.

83. "Art. V," *North American Review* 26, no. 58 (Jan. 1828): 140–43.

84. "The Darien Canal—Success of Mr. Caleb Cushing's Mission," *New York Times*, 16 Feb. 1869.

85. John M. Belohlavek, "A Philadelphian and the Canal: The Charles Biddle Mission to Panama, 1835–1836," *The Pennsylvania Magazine of History and Biography* 104, no. 4 (Oct. 1980): 450–61.

86. "Canal—Atlantic to Pacific," H.R. Rpt. 322, 25th Cong., 3rd Sess. (1839), 9.

87. H.R. Rpt. 322 (1839), 165.

88. H.R. Rpt. 322 (1839), 165; and George W. Cullum, *Biographical register of the officers and graduates of the U.S. military academy at West Point, N.Y., from its establishment, in 1802, to 1890* (Boston: Houghton Mifflin, 1891), 1:451.

89. William Radcliff was a New York merchant who had been appointed consul to Panamá and served in Lima. H.R. Rpt. 322, 160–62; and Ruth L. Woodward and Wesley Frank Craven, *Princetonians, 1784–1790: A Biographical Dictionary* (Princeton: Princeton University Press, 2014), 47–50.

90. H.R. Rpt. 322, 159.

91. Bolton to Southard, 20 May 1838, Folder 4, Box 61, SLSP.

92. H.R. Rpt. 322, 159.

93. H.R. Rpt. 322, 119.

94. "Canal across the Isthmus," *Centinel of Freedom* (Newark, NJ), 2 July 1839.

95. After brief mentions of earlier canal investigations, histories of the Nicaragua route often begin here. For example, see Lawrence A. Clayton, "The Nicaragua Canal in the Nineteenth Century: Prelude to American Empire in the Caribbean," *Journal of Latin American Studies* 19, no. 2 (Nov. 1987): 323–52. See also Introduction note 28.

96. H.R. Rpt. 145 (1849), 1.

97. H.R. Rpt. 145 (1849), 24, 26.

98. H.R. Rpt. 145 (1849), 3.

99. Michel Gobat, *Empire by Invitation: William Walker and Manifest Destiny in Central America* (Cambridge, MA: Harvard University Press, 2018); and Folkman, *Nicaragua Route*.

100. Folkman, *Nicaragua Route*, 108, 115–16. For disputes between Nicaragua and Costa Rica about sovereignty over the river, see Frances Kinloch Tijerino, "El Río San Juan: de Vía

Interoceánica a Ruta de migración Transfronteriza," *Revista de Historia*, no. 15–16 (2000): 49–58.

101. Folkman, *Nicaragua Route*, 72, 82.

102. Folkman, *Nicaragua Route*, 43–122.

103. Baily died in 1852. "Lists of Officers" (1852), 44, ADM 192/28, TNA, https://discovery.nationalarchives.gov.uk/details/r/C2154055.

104. Walter LaFeber, *The Panama Canal: The Crisis in Historical Perspective*, rev. ed. (New York: Oxford University Press, 1989), 13.

105. For a summary of recent scholarship on US involvement in Central America, see Michel Gobat, "Central American and the United States," *The Oxford Handbook of Central American History*, ed. Robert H. Holden (New York: Oxford University Press, 2022), 309–33. For the transcontinental railroad and westward expansion, see Elliott West, *Continental Reckoning: The American West in the Age of Expansion* (Lincoln: University of Nebraska Press, 2023); and Richard White, *Railroaded: The Transcontinentals and the Making of Modern America* (New York: W. W. Norton, 2011).

106. "Report of the Isthmian Canal Commission, 1899–1901," S. Doc. 54 (1904), 1, 10, 11.

107. S. Doc. 54 (1904), 14.

108. S. Doc. 54 (1904), 43.

109. S. Doc. 54 (1904), 43, 17.

110. S. Doc. 54 (1904), 29.

111. S. Doc. 54 (1904), 175.

112. The literature on this era is enormous. For a succinct summary, see LaFeber, *Panama Canal*, 21–45. For a summary of the historiography, see Alexander Missal, *Seaway to the Future: American Social Visions and the Construction of the Panama Canal* (Madison: University of Wisconsin Press, 2008), 3–20.

113. Christine Keiner, *Deep Cut: Science, Power, and the Unbuilt Interoceanic Canal* (Athens: University of Georgia, 2020); and Jordan T. Coulombe, "Mules, Fuels, and Fusion: Energy, Entropy, and the Crossing of the Panamanian Transit Zone, 1848–1990" (PhD diss., University of New Hampshire, 2019).

114. Marixa Lasso, *Erased: The Untold Story of the Panama Canal* (Cambridge, MA: Harvard University Press, 2019).

115. Julie Greene, *The Canal Builders: Making America's Empire at the Panama Canal* (New York: Penguin Press, 2009).

116. For examples of this large literature, see Ahsley Carse, "'Like a Work of Nature': Revisiting the Panama Canal's Environmental History at Gatun Lake," *Environmental History* 21 (Apr. 2016): 231–39; Pamela M. Henson, "A Baseline Environmental Survey: The 1910–12 Smithsonian Biological Survey of the Panama Canal Zone," *Environmental History* 21 (Apr. 2016): 222–30; Paul S. Sutter, "'The First Mountain to Be Removed': Yellow Fever Control and the Construction of the Panama Canal, *Environmental History* 21 (Apr. 2016): 250–59; and Paul S. Sutter, "Nature's Agents or Agents of Empire? Entomological Workers and Environmental Change during the Construction of the Panama Canal," *Isis* 98, no. 4 (Dec. 2007): 724–54.

117. Víctor Hugo Acuña Ortega describes canal plans as a form of Nicaraguan "manifest destiny" (*destino manifesto*). Acuña Ortega, Presentación to Frances Kinloch Tijerino, *El Imaginario del Canal y la Nación Cosmpolita: Nicaragua, Siglo XIX* (Managua: IHNCA-UCS, 2015),

15; and Roscoe R. Hill, "The Nicaraguan Canal Idea to 1913," *The Hispanic American Historical Review* 28, no. 2 (May 1948): 197–211.

118. Daniel Chávez, *Nicaragua and the Politics of Utopia: Development and Culture in the Modern State* (Nashville, TN: Vanderbilt University Press, 2015), 120, 320n12; and Michael J. Brodhead, "'A Wet, Nasty Job': Army Engineers and the Nicaragua Canal Survey of 1929–1931," *Federal History* (2013): 15–34.

119. Ernesto Cardenal, *The Doubtful Strait = El estrecho dudoso*, trans. John Lyons (Bloomington: Indiana University Press, 1995).

120. For example, see "Nicaragua en Sumo Imperio del Río San Juan: Documentos del Siglo XIX y XX, Catalogo" (2008), Instituto Nicaraguense de Cultural, Archivo General de la Nación, Managua, Nicaragua; "1994: Canal Interoceánico de Nicaragua—Executive Summary," Folder 17, Box 67, Sergio Ramírez Papers (C1123), PUL; and Moriz and Lester Bernstein Correspondence, 1897–1900, William L. Clements Library, University of Michigan.

121. "HKND Group Successfully Obtains Exclusive Right to Develop and Manage Nicaragua Grand Canal for 100 Years," *Wire Rope Exchange* (9 Aug. 2013), https://wireropeexchange.com/hknd-group-successfully-obtains-exclusive-right-to-develop-and-manage-nicaragua-grand-canal-for-100-years/. This document was originally published on the HKND website on 1 July 2013.

122. "Nicaragua and China Agree to Build Canal between Pacific and Caribbean, Similar to the One in Neighboring Panama," *International Business Times*, 11 June 2013.

123. Michael Weissenstein and Luis Manuel Galeano, "Nicaragua in Thrall of Ortega's Canal Dream," *AP Top News Package*, 13 Dec. 2013; and Greg Miller, "Why the Plan to Dig a Canal Across Nicaragua Could Be a Very Bad Idea," *Wired*, 26 Feb. 2014, www.wired.com/2014/02/nicaragua-canal/, accessed on 8 Mar. 2014.

124. Alek Boyd, "Who is Wang Jing? Man behind Nicaragua's Canal Project is as dodgy as They Come," blog post, 3 July 2013, http://alekboyd.blogspot.com/2013/07/wang-jing-hknd-nicaragua-canal-daniel-ortega.html, accessed on 19 May 2016; "AP Interview: Wang Coy on Past, Confident on Canal," *AP Top News Package*, 2 Sept. 2013; and Jon Lee Anderson, "The Comandante's Canal," *The New Yorker* (10 Mar. 2014): 50–61.

125. Weissenstein and Galeano, "Nicaragua in Thrall."

126. "Nicaragua And China Agree To Build Canal between Pacific And Caribbean, Similar to the One in Neighboring Panama," *International Business Times*, 11 June 2013.

127. The Associated Press Financial News, "Costa Rica Seeks Halt to Nicaraguan Canal Work," 14 Oct. 2013; The Associated Press, "UN Court Orders Nicaragua to Fill in Canal," *AP English Worldstream*, 22 Nov. 2013; and Andrew S. Hernández III, "Nexus of Rivalry: Nicaragua's Grand Canal and Inter-American Relations," *Caribbean Studies* 47, no 1 (2019): 37–65. The route is depicted and described in HKND group, "Nicaraguan Canal Project Description," Dec. 2014, https://web.archive.org/web/20160416235532/https://hknd-group.com/portal.php?mod=view&aid=148.

128. Associated Press, "Nicaragua's Top Court Rejects Challenges to Canal," *AP Financial News*, 19 Dec. 2013.

129. "The Great Interoceanic Canal Swindle," *CE Noticias Financieras*, English ed., 20 Aug. 2023.

130. Miller, "Why the Plan."

131. Jorge A. Huete-Perez et al., "Will Nicaragua's Interoceanic Canal Result in an Environmental Catastrophe for Central America?" *Environmental Science & Technology* 47, no. 23 (3 Dec. 2013): 13217–19.

132. "Nicaragua," *Caribbean Update* 29, no. 8 (Sept. 2013), 12–13; and "A Canal to Rival Panama's," *The Australian*, 8 June 2013, 10.

133. Associated Press, "Nicaragua: Canal Project Will Face 1 Year Delay," *AP English Worldstream*, 4 Jan. 2014.

134. Associated Press, "Nicaragua: Canal Construction to Begin This Year," *AP English Worldstream*, 7 Jan. 2014.

135. "Speech by Chairman Wang at Commencement Ceremonies," 25 Dec. 2014, http://web.archive.org/web/20160414125524/https://hknd-group.com/portal.php?mod=view&aid=151.

136. Michael D. McDonald, "China's Building a Huge Canal in Nicaragua, But We Couldn't Find It," *Bloomberg*, 19 Aug. 2015. Some suggested more subtle progress was being made on the canal. Sarah McCall and Matthew J. Taylor, "Nicaragua's 'Grand' Canal: Cuento Chino? Rhetoric and Field-Based Evidence on the Chinese Presence in Nicaragua," *Journal of Latin American Geography* 17, no. 2 (2018): 191–208.

137. "Preconstruction Archaeological Investigation in the Route of the Grand Canal in the Area of Brito, Rivas," 11 Mar. 2016, 31, https://web.archive.org/web/20160615100255/http://hknd-group.com/upload/pdf/20160311/EN/Report%20of%20Preconstruction%20Archaeological%20Investigation%20in%20Brito_HKND.pdf. Links with the dates of the project reports can be found here: https://web.archive.org/web/20161030233840/http://hknd-group.com/portal.php?mod=list&catid=54.

138. Richard Harris, "Scientists Fear Ecological Disaster in Nicaragua's Planned Canal," broadcast by NPR on *All Things Considered*, 20 Feb. 2014, https://www.npr.org/2014/02/20/279710270/scientists-fear-ecological-disaster-in-nicaraguas-planned-canal.

139. Tom Phillips, "Chinese Mogul behind Nicaragua Canal Lost 85% of His Fortune in Stock Market," *The Guardian*, 2 Oct. 2015; and "HKND Shelves Nicaragua Canal Construction," *World Maritime News*, 26 Nov. 2015, http://worldmaritimenews.com/archives/177457/hknd-shelves-nicaragua-canal-construction/, accessed 19 May 2016.

140. Blake Schmidt, "Ex-Billionaire Abandons Office in Prime Hong Kong Tower," *Bloomberg*, 26 Apr. 2018; and Blake Schmidt, "Chinese Ex-Billionaire Lauds Ortega after Nicaraguan Elections," *Bloomberg*, 12 Nov. 2021.

141. "The Nicaragua Canal Project Office, a Costly Ghost," *Real Estate Monitor Worldwide*, 5 July 2019.

142. HKND Group Website, 25 Oct. 2020, https://web.archive.org/web/20201025020310/https://hknd-group.com/.

143. "Ortega Insists on the Construction of an Interoceanic Canal through Nicaragua," *CE Noticias Financieras*, English ed., 15 Sept. 2022; and "Jorge Huete, el Destacado Científico que Fue Desterrado por la Dictadura de Nicaragua," *La Prensa*, 29 Sept. 2022.

144. Salvador Montenegro-Guillén, "Lake Cocibolca/Nicaragua," paper presented at Lake Basin Management Initiative Regional Workshop for Europe, Central Asia, and the Americas, Saint Michael's College, VT (18–21 June 2003), http://arks.princeton.edu/ark:/88435/dsp015m60qr95q.

145. Jennifer A. Leudtke et al., "Ongoing Declines for the World's Amphibians in the Face of Emerging Threats," *Nature* 622, no. 7982 (4 Oct. 2023): 308–14.

146. Thomas B. Thorson, "The Impact of Commercial Exploitation on Sawfish and Shark Populations in Lake Nicaragua," *Fisheries* 7, no. 2 (1982): 2–10.

Epilogue

1. Peter Gausmann, "Synopsis of Global Fresh and Brackish Water Occurrences of the Bull Shark *Carcharhinus leucas*," *Integrative Systematics: Stuttgart Contributions to Natural History* 4, no. 1 (2021): 55–213; Julia M. Constance et al., "A Review of the Life History and Ecology of Euryhaline and Estuarine Sharks and Rays," *Reviews in Fish Biology and Fisheries* 34, no. 1 (2024): 65–89; and Josh Davis, "Shark Evolution: A 450 Million Year Timeline," The Natural History Museum (UK), www.nhm.ac.uk/discover/shark-evolution-a-450-million-year-timeline.html.

2. Henry Bryant Bigelow to Robert Cummin, 17 May 1943, Folder C, Box 2, HBB.

3. Theodore Gill and J. F. Bransford, "Synopsis of the Fishes of Lake Nicaragua," *Proceedings of the Academy of Natural Sciences of Philadelphia* (1877): 175–91, 179–80.

4. Correspondence between Henry Bryant Bigelow and Francis B. Richardson, 30 Oct. 1941, 6 Nov. 1941, 13 Nov. 1941, 16 July 1943, and 29 July 1943, Folder R, Box 9, HBB; and Bigelow to Cummin, 17 May 1943, Folder C, Box 2, HBB. For 1940s Nicaraguan shark specimen collection, see Luis Marden, "A Land of Lakes and Volcanoes," *National Geographic Magazine* 86 (1944): 182–83.

5. Bigelow to Cummin, 17 May 1943, Folder C, Box 2, HBB; Lawrence Dame, "Harvard's New Guest," *Boston Herald* (9 May 1943); and MCZ Ichthyology 35896, "Ledger Entry," MCZ Ichthyology Fish 031601–037540, 174, https://mczbase.mcz.harvard.edu/guid/MCZ:Ich:35896.

6. Henry B. Bigelow and William C. Schroeder, "Sharks," *Fishes of the Western North Atlantic: Part One*, ed. John Tee-Van et al. (New Haven: Sears Foundation for Marine Research, Yale University, 1948), 378–82.

7. Henry B. Bigelow and William C. Schroeder, "*Carcharhinus nicaraguensis*, a Synonym of the Bull Shark," *Copeia* 3 (1961): 359.

8. T. B. Thorson, "Movement of Bull Sharks, *Carcharhinus leucas*, between Caribbean Sea and Lake Nicaragua Demonstrated by Tagging," *Copeia* 2 (1971): 336–38.

Index

Italic page numbers refer to illustrations.